Lily Monadjemi

A MATTER OF SURVIVAL

Hero, an imprint of Legend times group Ltd
51 Gower Street
London WC1E 6HJ
United Kingdom
www.hero-press.com

Copyright © Lily Monadjemi 2024

The right of Lily Monadjemi to be identified as the author of this work has been asserted in accordance with the Copyright, Designs and Patents Act 1988. British Library Cataloguing in Publication Data available.

All the pictures in this volume are reprinted with permission or presumed to be in the public domain. Every effort has been made to ascertain and acknowledge their copyright status, but any error or oversight will be rectified in subsequent printings.

All rights reserved. No part of this publication may be reproduced, stored in or introduced into a retrieval system, or transmitted, in any form or by any means (electronic, mechanical, photocopying, recording or otherwise), without the prior written permission of the publisher. This book is sold subject to the condition that it shall not be resold, lent, hired out or otherwise circulated without the express prior consent of the publisher.

Paperback ISBN: 9781835632093

Lily Izadi Monadjemi is an Iranian from a royal background. She was educated in the UK and United States and taught English and psychology at the National University of Iran.

After the Iranian Revolution, when loved ones were executed, properties confiscated and universities closed, together with her husband and two little daughters, she immigrated to Australia. Life was hard but with stamina, hope and hard work the most difficult bridges were crossed. That was when she realized, with her background, she had many stories to tell: tales of love, hate, loyalty, betrayal, acceptance, forgiveness and the history of her dynasty.

She has written several published books, including:

Blood and Carnations

Golestan: The Garden of Memories

The Mulberry Tree

Angels Can Hate Too

The Scent of Love

The latter was nominated by Sisters in Crime Australia for the best thriller written by an Australian female author.

I have no claim to be a historian. I am just a storyteller.

To my husband whose patience and understanding has brought the best out of me.

To my daughters who have made me a proud mother.

To my grandchildren, this book is for you to remember your roots.

Acknowledgements

I would like to thank the members of my extended family for allowing me to mention their names and touch upon their private lives. I am grateful to my late grandmother, Princess EZ-Saltaneh for giving me a series of pictures taken by her father Nasser Aldin Shah Qajar and my uncle Prince H. Amir-Aslani for allowing me to use his inherited Qajar Manuscripts and rare books. At Hero my thanks go to its founder Tom Chalmers for being the pillar of my strength. Finally, my greatest thanks go to my husband for allowing me the liberty to tell our story and my daughter Betty who is my harshest critic.

Author's Note

In Islam, there exists a tradition of intellectual interpretation and innovation known as IJTIHAD, practised by jurists and clerics to debate the meaning of Koranic teachings as well as their application to modern ideas and situations. Sunni Islam forgot about IJTIHAD centuries ago, but in Shia Islam, the process and spirit of IJTIHAD flourishes. IJTIHAD is central to Islamic Law, as sharia is only a set of principles and not a codified set of rules. A decision or opinion derived from the process of IJTIHAD means that a jurist evaluates a given matter, by applying reason and deduction and weighing the priorities of the concerns involved. For example soon after the revolution, Ayatollah Komeini ruled that state media could broadcast music despite the severe attitude of the senior clergy toward song. He judged that otherwise young people would be lured by Western radio and that ultimately this would be more harmful to the Islamic Republic. This was an act of IJTIHAD, in which an ancient convention was found obsolete.

On the one hand, IJTIHAD imposes flexibility on Islamic law and creates possibilities for adapting Islamic values and traditions to our modern lives. But this same flexibility makes IJTIHAD, and Islamic jurisprudence altogether, a difficult foundation on which to base indisputable, universal rights. IJTIHAD liberates us by doing away with definitiveness, allowing us to interpret and reinterpret Koranic teaching forever. It means it is possible for everyone, always to have a point. It means that chauvinist men and dictatorial regimes which repress in the name of Islam can exploit IJTIHAD to interpret Islam in the regressive, unforgiving manner that suits their whims and political agendas. Fighting for women's rights in the Islamic Republic is often not a battle of wits or reason, nor is it always a fair fight. This does not mean that Islam and equal rights for women are incompatible; it means that within a theocracy the interpretations can shift to serve the advantages of the most powerful party.

An interpretation of Islam that is in harmony with equality and democracy is an authentic expression of faith. It is not religion that binds women, but the selective dictates of those who wish them sheltered. In this story you will meet many women whose lives will hopefully shed light on your concept of a Moslem woman.

We shall exult, if they who rule the land
Be men who hold its many blessings dear
Wise, upright, valiant; not a servile band
Who are to judge of danger which they fear
And honor which they do not understand.

Wordsworth

Nineteenth century satirical map depicting Russian imperialistic designs on Persia. Reproduced by courtesy of the author.

Family Genealogical Tree of The Qajars

1726—Fath Ali Khan Qajar & Khatoon Qajar (the gift from Shah Sultan Hussain Safavi)

- Mohammed Hussain
  m. Jagman Qajar Quivadu
  - Agha Mohammed Shah (1748-1791)

- Mohammed Hussain
  m. A good actress

- Khadijeh Baygum
  m. Karim Khan Zand Shah of Iran

Hussain Gholi Jahansug Shah (c. 1771)
m. Mah Rakhsan Qajar

Fath Ali Shah (b. 1771-1834, r. 1797-1834)
m. Bado Jahan Khanum Qajar

- Bayyuan Jan Khanum   Mohammad Vali Mirza   Mohammad Ali Mirza   Ayad At-Dawla   Ali Mirza   Hussain Ali Mirza   Mohammad Gholi Mirza   Abass Mirza (1789-1834)   Fath Ali Mirza
  m. Amir Mohammad   m. Amir Sultaneh
  Ghassen Khan Qajar Quivadu

  - Sulayman Khan
  - Isa Khan
  - Amir Aslan Khan
    Amid At-Molk Majel Dawla
  - Jahan Khanum The Makel Olia   m. Mohammed Shah (1807-1848; r. 1834-1847)
    (1803-1873)

    - Farhad Mirza   Fargalon Mirza   Bahman Mirza   Jahangir Mirza   Khan Lar Mirza   Sultan Morad Mirza   Faruge Mirza

  - Haj Reza-Gholi Khan
    m. Amirzadeh Khanum
  - Nasser Gholi Khan (Governor of Khamseh) (1831-1896; r. 1847-1896)
    m. Princess Anwar Saltaneh
    - Nasser Al-Din Shah
      m. Makhouk Saltaneh
    - Malek Jadeh Khanum Izzat Dawleh
      m. Mirza Taghi Khan Amir Kabir

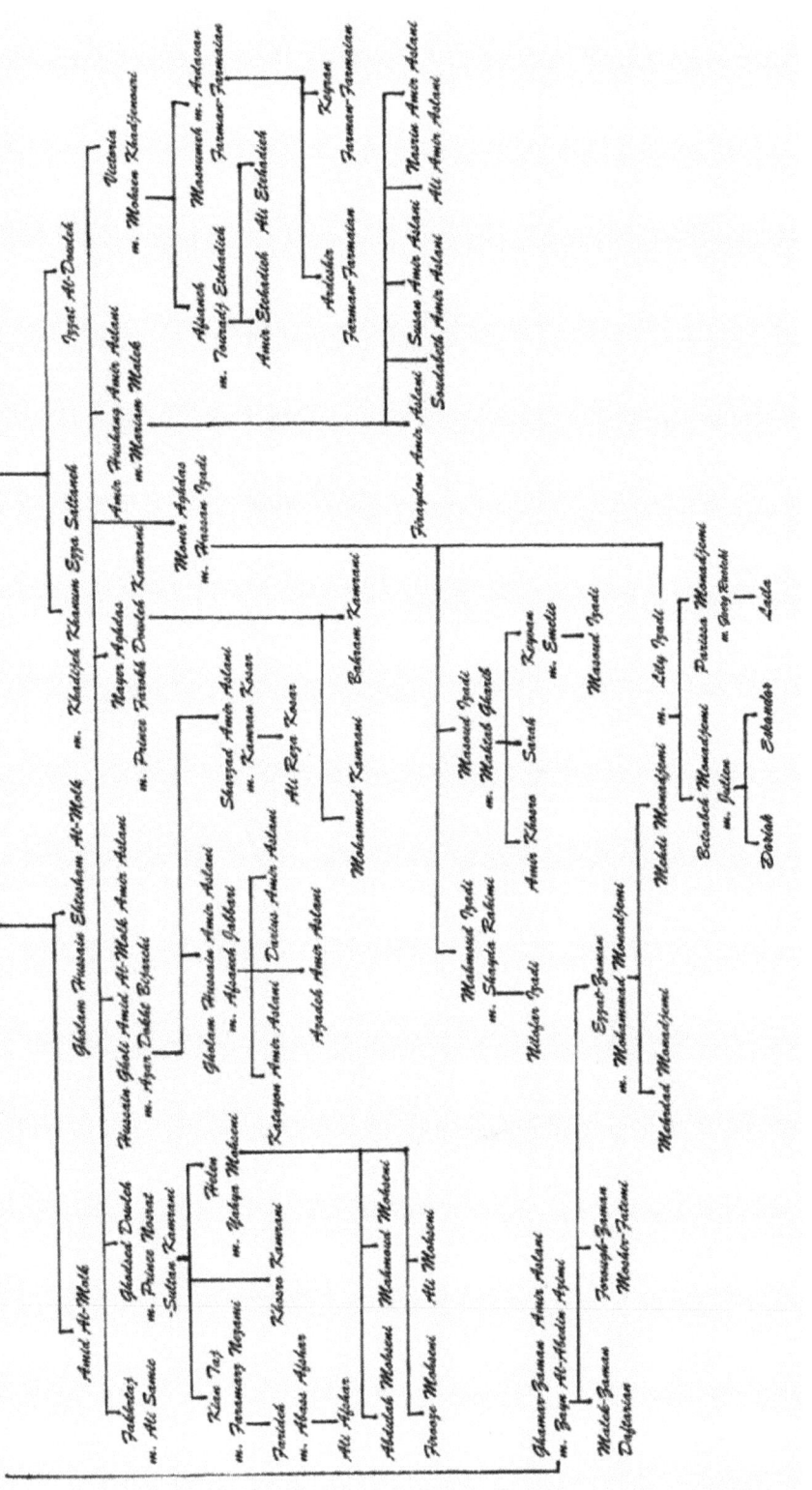

Prologue

In the name of God

It is alleged that the Gajars, a Turcoman tribe, were first seen in the Mughan Steppe around 897 AD. As their number grew the tribe divided into two sects and each sect, to more sub-sects. Thus each member not only bore the name of the tribe but also the name of the sect or the sub-sect to which he or she belonged.

Sometime during the 16th century, a brilliant young man by the name of Ismail who came from Ardabil in Azarbaijan founded the Safavid Dynasty. The mother of Ismail was the daughter of Uzon Hassan, the Gajar Shah of the Agha Guvanlu, who ruled Western Azarbaijan. This tie with the ruling dynasty gave the Gajars a great opportunity to acquire extensive political power particularly in the northern provinces of Iran. During the latter part of the Safavid reign the Gajars were centred in Garabagh.

The governance of Garabagh remained with the Gajar Khans until they were dispersed to the frontiers of the empire by Shah Abass Safavid. This dispersal was a deliberate policy that aimed on the one hand at reducing their power because they had become overwhelmingly influential and numerous in Garabagh, and on the other at protecting the empire against inroads made by the Uzbeks and Tatars. By the end of the 17th century the main concentration of the tribe was in Astarabad. There, by the river Atrak lived two sects: the Guvanlu, who were shepherds, and the Davalu, who were camel-herders. The Guvanlu had pastures below the Mubarakabad fortress of Astarabad and so were called Ashaghabash, [1] while the Davalu had pastures above the fortress and were therefore called Yukharibash [2]. In the 18th century the Ashaghabash

---

[1] Below the river

[2] Above the river (Both words are Turkish)

and the Yukharibash were split by internecine strife.

During the reign of Sultan Hussain Safavid, Mohammad Khan, a Turcoman from Gazvin, was appointed governor of Astarabad. He was induced by the Yukharibash to seize Fath Ali Khan, the leader of the Ashaghabash, who lived in the Mubarakabd fortress, and his brothers, Fazl Ali and Mohammad Ali Beg. Fath Ali subsequently escaped but his two brothers were killed. He took refuge with the Yamut of Sain-Khani and in due course recovered possession of Astarabad. The sources vary in their account of the activities of Fath Ali Khan during the last years of Safavid rule. According to most Gajar historians he went to help Shah Sultan Hussain during the Afghan invasion of Iran, though the precise circumstances in which he did this are not clear. As a token of his gratitude for the loyalty Shah Sultan Hussain gave Fath Ali Khan, from his royal harem a woman, daughter of Hussain Gholi Agha, a descendant of Yagub Sultan Gajar. Fath Ali Khan fell in love with this beautiful woman – who according to legend was already pregnant from Shah Sultan Hussain – and married her. [3] She gave him a son whom he named Mohammad Hassan. Powerful and brave, Fath Ali created many enemies who denounced him as dangerously ambitious. Disliking the life at the Court of the Shah, he left Isfehan and subsequently after an engagement with the Afghans, who had defeated Shah Sultan Hussain near Varamin, he joined Tahmaseb II of Safavids, who had escaped to Mazandaran. At this point in time the Iranian Empire had disintegrated and whoever felt strong enough to proclaim himself the Shah of his territory did so. Tahmasb II was fighting to regain the control for Safavids. He made Fath Ali Khan the governor of Astarabad and then the two set out for Khorasan. Nader Gholi, the chief of the Afshars, with whom Tahmaseb had entered into communication, joined them at Khabushan. Tahmaseb and his two generals reached Khaje Rabi outside Mashhad in the autumn of the same year. By this time acute rivalry had developed between Fath Ali Khan and Nader Gholi, who succeeded in poisoning Tahmaseb's mind against Fath Ali. Now secure in his position, on 14 Safar 1139, (11th

---

[3] Mohammad Hashim Rustam Al-Hukama,Rustam Al-Tawarikh, Ed. Mohammad Mushir.
Tehran 1969,pp,139,157,266
and Prince Ali Kadjar – Les Rois Oubliés. Edition Kian. Paris 1992 – pp17-18.

October 1726) Tahmaseb had Fath Ali put to death.

Fath Ali had two sons and a daughter: Mohammad Hassan, Mohammad Hussain and Khadije Beygum. Mohammad Hussain died in youth. After the death of his father, Mohammad Hassan Khan, because of the enmity of Nader and the intrigues of Mohammad Hussain Khan Davalu – who had been appointed the new governor of Astarabad – retired to the Turcoman Steppe. It was the son of Mohammad Hassan Khan who united Iran, under the banner of the Gajar dynasty, which ruled Iran from 1796 to 1925.

Shah Sultan Hussain's gift to Fath Ali I have christened Khatoon and reconstructed part of her legendary life.

Mah Rokhsar is also the name I have given to the mother of Fath Ali Shah. In history she is referred to as Mahd Olia.

Chapter 1

Isfehan-1129 Hejri (1710)

Iran is the land of brave warriors, renowned philosophers, passionate poets, ardent lovers and Shahs who built cities like Susa, Persapolice and Isfehan.

Isfehan is an oasis in the midst of a vast desert. It never snows there but winter is cold and today is very cold. The palace of Shah Sultan [4] Hussain Safavid is lively with gossip. Outside, the blue dome of the Shah Mosque is as majestic as ever and the small windows of Alighapo palace are opaque with fog. The bazaar is empty of bargain hunters and chatty vendors are warming their hands over their charcoal burning braziers while pondering over the consequences of the incident that has brought the palace out of its usual stupor. A group of audacious damsels had taken the capital's Chief Magistrate and the head of the Shah's security guard as hostage. The punishment for females who sinned in the Shia [5] society of the Safavids, subject to selective elucidations was to be enclosed in a sack and thrown into a well or down from the top of the citadel's wall. The place of a woman was inside the home and her duty to please her husband and bring up his children the best way possible. Not taking hostages!

"Had these pests no fear of chastisement?"

No one dared to speculate.

Yesterday the Sultan had received a letter from his daughter Masoumeh begging for mercy and inviting him to the Poplar Garden to hear her confession. The girl had explained that the audacious action had been in self-defence and only the Sultan's "pardon" could restore their honour in the eyes of society.

Amused by the novelty of the incident and curious to see these

---

[4] Sultan means Shah in Farsi the language of the Iranians.
[5] An Islamic sect made official in Iran by the Safavid dynasty to differentiate Persian Empire from that of Ottoman's

pests without any haya [6] the Shah decided to oblige the invitation. He had been to the famous garden several times before sending its owner to the gallows.

Early in the morning, cloaked in sable, Shah Sultan Hussain reluctantly left the warmth of his andaroon [7] and ahead of his guards rode through the wide, cobblestoned, tree lined streets of Isfehan. Muddy water rushed through the gutters that separated the pavements and the road. Farther behind the trees, high brick walls of private domains stretched beyond sight. Above, the sky was calm, not oppressive, an infinity of light and colours that stretched over the roofs of houses – red brick, marble and tiles. Brown minarets and the blue mosque domes dotted the horizon. Along his path, river Zayandeh roared with great anger. The Shah, short, plump and forever relaxed, followed by a few attendants, rode peacefully across the Thirty Three Bridge, then passed through the city gate where the guards collapsed on their knees in salutation, before entering the Poplar Garden in which the girls were anxiously awaiting him. This seemingly endless estate belonged to one named Hussain Gholi Agha, a prominent citizen whose ancestry was traced to Yaghub Sultan Gajar. Hussain Gholi Agha had been an emissary of the Safavid Shah to the French Court in Paris. There he had married Tresse, a French woman whom after converting to Islam he had named Sarah, and from whom he had a daughter named Khatoon [8]. Not long after his return to Iran poisonous tongues aroused the suspicion of the gullible Shah. The loyal servant fell out of favour and was executed.

Khatoon inherited her father's house but since her mother had remarried she lived at the andaroon of her stepfather and occasionally visited this garden into which the Shah was now riding.

The naked poplar trees on each side of the crowded path that was leading to the mansion hosted many crows. The sudden bustle of horse hooves disturbed the birds' tranquility and flapping their black wings, they flew away casting their ominous shadow over the intruders. The passageway led to an expansive lawn surrounded by pine trees. In the middle of the lawn stood a tall, gracious young eunuch and six girls in long, white tunics, wide pantaloons and white, wide linen scarves. The

---

[6] Virtue

[7] Andaroon is the private quarter where women live and no Namahram is allowed. In Islam fathers, brothers, and husbands are Mahram. Other men are Namahram.

[8] Khatoon is the name I have given this lady whom history only knows as the wife of Shah Sultan Hussain given to Fath Ali Gajar.

Shah instantly recognized the large black eyes of his daughter, Masoumeh, that were staring at him from the opening of her silk roobandeh [9]. The group gracefully prostrated. The Shah cautiously dismounted from his horse and gently commanded them to rise. Masoumeh stepped forward, took her father's soft, small hand, kissed it and then asked him to send the guards back to the gate. The Shah smiling at his daughter ordered his companions to leave and wait for him at the gate. As the guards turned towards the gate the tallest amongst the girls stepped forward and bowed again. Her air of confidence impressed upon the Shah that she, and not Shahzadeh [10] Masoumeh. was the leader. The girl, her posture erect, looking straight into the Shah's slanted black eyes, introduced herself as Khatoon, daughter of Hussain Gholi Agha.

Her black eyes were so beautiful and penetrating that they instantly melted the Shah's heart.

"What is the justification for your unbecoming action, daughter of Hussa Gholi Agha?"

"Your Majesty, it is to expose the dishonesty of men our Sultan trusts."

The Shah smiled thinking this girl, just a child, is not only beautiful but also courageous.

"Do you have a story to tell me, young girl?"

"If you allow me, sire, I have a confession to make."

The Shah glanced at his daughter and saw in her eyes expectation of sympathy.

"Go ahead, Khatoon Khanum [11]."

"Sire, my friends and I were bored with the monotony of our existence in the confines of the andaroon so I suggested that we should spend some time here where we could learn from my eunuch, Salim, riding, shooting and fighting like men – games more interesting than playing with toys at the andaroon. They saw no harm in my idea and we decided to come here twice a week. Because we had no permission from our parents we had to keep our activities a secret – only our nannies knew of our whereabouts. Your Majesty is aware that the names of those leaving or entering the city are registered at the city gates. Therefore, to remain incognito, I am ashamed to confess that through Salim, we

---

[9] Face cover
[10] This term refers to both male and female offspring of a king and follows through the paternal line
[11] Lady

offered the City Magistrate a brass coin a time, if he abstained from registering our names on his log book. Our offer was promptly accepted. Then three days ago he and five of his friends attacked this house, killed two of my guards and tried to force themselves upon us. With the help of Salim here, we defended our honour and took the Magistrate and the head of your Guard hostage – the other four escaped. Scared, we did not dare to return home through the city gate. The following day a messenger arrived threatening to expose our secret, blacken our names and shame our families if the hostages were not released. Shahzadeh Masoumeh confident, of Your Majesty's wisdom and boundless generosity, suggested we better subject our destinies to your mercy rather than become victims of blackmail."

Khatoon, finishing her report, looked straight into the Shah's amazed eyes imperiously expecting pardon for an action well justified.

The Shah could not but smile at the audacity of the lass. But to maintain his composure he forced a tight frown and asked:

"Where are these haramzadehs [12] now?"

"Your Majesty, I shall bring them to you," said Salim before disappearing behind a thick fence and a few minutes later reappearing ahead of the men, with pale faces, hands tied with rope and eyes cast down.

Khatoon drew a dagger out from under the frills of her long sleeve and cut off the rope from the wrists of the prisoners so that they could prostrate properly. Hastily the two dropped on their knees kissing the Shah's feet and weeping aloud.

The Shah withdrew his feet from their hold, kicked each of them on the face and automatically called for an executioner. Of course there were none present.

"Father have mercy upon them?" Masoumeh begged.

The Shah detested decision making and on the rare occasion that he did make one it proved calamitous. He pondered a little and then, frowning again shouted: "Leave and never come to my sight again."

Masoumeh took her father's hand and kissed it. Then he turned to the men and ordered them to rise and follow Salim to the gate where the Imperial guards were waiting.

The perpetrators grabbed the hem of the Shah's cloak, kissed it a hundred times and then rose and stepped backwards until within

---

[12] Bastards

a respectable distance where they turned and followed the eunuch to the gate.

Alone, in the company of the girls, the Shah asked them to show him their skills. Proud and agile they performed acrobatic acts on their white Arabian horses, threw daggers, and shot many flying birds; things the Shah had heard women in Frangastan [13] do. Their vitality excited him and their honesty pleased him so he granted them permission to return to their families without expecting any punishment.

The Shah left the garden with a sensation he had never felt before.

During those days, when women were locked in their quarters within andaroons and no namahram [14] could set eyes on their faces, marriage brokers fared well. Andaroons had their own social systems. With men having four wives and as many sigheh's [15] as they wished for, andaroons were centres of intrigue, excitement and murder. The royal andarnoons, in particular, were dangerous places especially for first-born sons with a claim to the throne. There, ambitious women, with their own staff, had no scruples about having the son of a rival poisoned or changing a new born son with an infant girl. Eunuchs, nannies and wet nurses played a prominent part in the intrigues. They also played the matchmaker when the girls grew beyond the age of puberty, which could be as low as ten.

The name of Khatoon was on the lips of all mothers with sons of marriage age, and one such mother was that of Mahmoud Gheljai, the son of Mervis who was from the city of Kandahar. Mervis was one of the richest men of his time and his son was only a few years older than Khatoon. Mervis was a friend of Khatoon's stepfather, Khosro Khan, also from Kandahar.

Mahmoud was a thin, ugly boy with dark skin, narrow eyes and manners of a barbarian. He was an excellent horseman and unrivalled shot with a heart that knew no mercy. He took pleasure in hurting all living things.

Mervis had heard about the beauty and virtues of Khatoon, whom

---

[13] Land of foreigners.

[14] Husbands, brothers and fathers are mahram and allowed in the andaroon. All other males are namahram.

[15] Sigheh means temporary marriage. The duration set for the marriage is accepted by the father of the bride and often it is indefinite. However the status of a Sigheh is inferior to that of a wife but their children are given the same status and rights of inheritance.

he thought would make a fine wife for his son. To this end he sent a message to his friend, Khosro Khan, promising the crown of Kandahar to his stepdaughter should she wed Mahmoud. The message was received with delight and taken to Khatoon by her mother. Khatoon had played with Mahmoud while they were under the age of nine; when boys and girls could mix. Her dislike for him was such that the thought of marrying him made her sick for two days. Her ceaseless tears compelled her mother to have her husband politely refuse the offer.

The news of the Khasegari [16] spread in the city's andaroons and reached the ears of the besotted Shah. Soon Mervis was posted back to Kandahar and Khatoon, only fourteen, found her way to the palace of Chelsotoon to become the Shah's wife. That was the year 1130 Hejri, (1711).

In Kandahar, within a few years of plotting, Mervis proclaimed himself the Shah of the Afghans and broke all ties with Iran. However he did not live long enough to enjoy his success and Afghanastan went to his brother. By this time, Mahmoud, hungry for power, could no longer wait to return to Isfehan and claim it for himself. He rose against his uncle, defeated him and headed for Iran – pillaging, raping and burning whatever was on his way. Only one battle he lost and that was to Fath Ali Khan; the chief of the Ashaghebash sect of the Gajar tribe, who dwelled in Astarabad by river Atrak. Blood was being shed on the soil of his land while Shah Sultan Hussain enjoyed the warmth of Khatoons' bed. He had two hundred wives but Khatoon was the apple of his eye. Not only because she was beautiful but because she was headstrong, intelligent and bright – totally different from the others. Khatoon knew exactly what she wanted from life. To be just the sogoli [17] was not enough for her. She had to be effective, and to be effective in the andaroon she had to have allies and no ally was as wise and powerful as the Shah's unmarried, strong-willed and wise aunt, Mariam Baygum. Soon Khatoon won her respect and the two became inseparable friends. Their alliance brought enlightenment to the andaroon. Neither of the women thought of themselves as just sex objects: there only to please their men. For some, it took time even to achieve this as the Shah's virility had its limits. Reciting poetry of Ferdowsi and Hafez, enjoying the music of the blind bands [18] and

---

[16] Khasegari means marriage proposal

[17] Sogoli: the favourite wife.

[18] Only blind male musicians were allowed to play in the andaroons.

applying the health suggestions of Avicenna to the care of royal children replaced malicious gossip, rivalry for royal favours and religious sofrehs [19] during which they listened to sad religious songs and cried for the days of their lives that were being wasted in futility. Yes, under Islamic law women had the right to property ownership. Yes, most of them managed to tame their husbands and got whatever they wanted. Yes, they were in charge of the children's education. But in matters of the heart applied to marriage, they had no choice whatsoever. It was just a matter of luck and Khatoon was very lucky.

At nights when she was not entertaining her husband she joined Mariam Baygum, and together, accompanied by her new eunuch, Sadegh Khan, they left the andaroon incognito for the bazaar where they gathered news and for the slums where they made donations to the needy. Recent news was frightening. There was unrest everywhere. The Baluchies, the Turcomans and the Arabs were in revolt against the central government and Mahmoud Afghan was on his way to Isfehan. Both women knew that the Shah was aware of everything but unlike his predecessors had no stomach for war. Safavid Shahs had brought much honour and greatness to the country. They had built dams, roads and caravanserai. They had distinguished their empire from that of the Sunni Ottoman by proclaiming Iran a Shia State [20]. Foreign envoys were received at their courts and commerce with foreign companies was encouraged. Iranians bore much respect for this dynasty. Yet Shah Sultan Hussain cared for nothing but the security of his harem and the bed of his wives. Instead of leading his army to defend Iran he went on his knees and prayed or asked the astrologers to create charts and the fortune-tellers to soothe his fears by their lies. Then one day as though his prayers had been answered the news arrived that Fath Ali Khan Ashaghabash Gajar, having defeated Mahmoud Afghan in a battle, was on his way to Isfehan. The brave Turcoman was coming to pledge his allegiance, and seek official command to get rid of the Afghan pestilence. This meant mobilization and a full-fledged war. War disturbed the tranquility of the Court life. So the wagging tongues of comfort-seekers spread enough malice to create fear of the Gajar in the delicate heart of the pious Shah.

---

[19] Are occasions dedicated to one of the twelve Immams in lieu of a wish granted through the interference of that Immam with Allah.

[20] Shia and Sunni are two different sects of Islam.

The Turcoman, on his way from Mashhad to Isfehan had observed the crumbling of the Sultan's Empire. Everywhere disobedient chieftains were minting coins under their own name or defecting to the Afghan. Confidence in the Shah's power to defend the country had faded and Fath Ali Khan hoped to open the royal eyes to the reality of the situation. For him, the grandeur of Isfehan – the city of great mosques, and squares, blue tiles and amazing architecture – had no fascination. Art and artistry, industry and trade were meaningless concepts to a nomad. Of importance to him were the cannons he needed to fight the Afghan with.

Standing beside his Shah, on the balcony of Ali-Ghapu palace, viewing the military manoeuvres in the expansive Shah Square, Fath Ali Khan prayed for the day he could bring peace to Iran. Sun and the wind had burnt his handsome face. His large black eyes, shaded by long up-turned eye lashes flickered with determination. A well-trimmed moustache covered the edge of his fine upper lip and hung down from the sides of his mouth to join his long, trimmed beard. His shapely head was covered by a sheepskin hat that was slightly tilted to the right. Groomed in the tribal white pantaloon and colourful, embroidered silk vest worn over a long sleeved, white silk shirt, he looked masculine and handsome to the few andaroon ladies watching him from behind the curtain that hid them from the eyes of namahrams [21].

The Shah, intimidated by the sheer confidence of the Khan, began doubting the wisdom of his decision to give him the sixty cannons that were gathering dust in the barracks. The thought of the nomad turning against him brought cold sweat to his narrow forehead and he began biting his thin, purple lips. The mullah standing by his left side noticed the Shah's anguish. He stepped closer and whispered into the royal ears: "What ails your Majesty?"

"A matter of great urgency. Go and summon our astrologer."

The mullah grabbed the end of his black aba [22], lifted its fold and hurriedly left the balcony, carefully descending the narrow wiggling steps that led to the ground floor and the outside.

After the ceremony the Shah found his pensive astrologer sitting cross-legged on the floor of the reception room with his instruments and charts spread out on the carpet. Gripping the edge of his aba the

---

[21] Men who are neither a kin nor a spouse.
[22] cloak

man attempted to rise but the Shah motioned him to remain seated and himself sat next to him facing the charts.

"Your Majesty, on what matter shall I consult the stars?"

"How can I send the nomad away, content, yet without giving him any cannons?"

The astrologer whose small shrewd eyes suddenly sparkled, busied himself with his apparatus for a considerable time before lifting his turbaned head up, looking into the expectant eyes of the sovereign, clearing his voice and saying:

"Your Majesty may not like the answer."

"Tell it or you will lose your tongue."

"Your Majesty, a gift from the harem is suggested."

"Who?"

"Your Sogoli, sire."

Instantly the Shah's pointed chin fell and a sharp pain stabbed his soft heart. He took his head between his hands and contemplated for a while. His fossilized brain couldn't function properly. It had already blocked out the existence of Mahmoud Afghan but it couldn't deny the existence of the Khan nor of Khatoon. He had seen the well-trained and disciplined Gajar army. A coward, he was scared of his own shadow let alone someone like Fath Ali Khan. And Khatoon! He would miss her soft body, rosy lips and vivaciousness. Yes he would miss her a lot. But under the circumstances she was the price he had to pay for his own security. Having decided he lifted his head up, looked into the eyes of the conniving man and said:

"So that shall be."

The Shah was too troubled to notice the slight smile that parted the narrow lips of the astrologer. He had hated Khatoon ever since she had tried to persuade the Shah to consult with his advisers rather than him.

That night the Shah visited Khatoon's quarters early, took his pleasure from her; shed a few royal tears and then left a bewildered Khatoon to face what was planned for her.

The next day the Court's mullah officially terminated the marriage.

Khatoon, before leaving the anderoon, went to bid farewell to Mariam Baygum [23]. The Shahzadeh, old and frail, was still beautiful. She was bedridden with a horrible sickness. Anxiety had settled into her stomach causing frequent nausea and bleeding. Her eunuch, with

---

[23] lady in Turkish

his hands folded across his broad chest stood by the entrance to her bedchamber. When he saw Khatoon, his face lit up with a genuine smile. He bowed, kissed her hand and told her not to stay long as visits tired his mistress. Khatoon shook her head in consent. She slowly opened the door, crept in and saw the Shahzadeh lying in her large European bed with her personal maid in attendance. She closed the door quietly and tiptoed towards the bed. Shahzadeh sensed her presence, brought her boney hands out from under the quilted cover and tried to rise whispering: "Khatoon, is that you?"

"Yes Baygum–e-aziz." [24]

"Come near, child."

Khatoon went to the bed and knelt by it. She took the skinny hand and kissed it several times.

"I have heard everything. It is for the best. Fath Ali Khan is an honourable man. You will be happy with him. Hussain has brought shame to us all."

She stopped, took a breath and then continued: "I pray for my end. I know what the barbaric Afghan will do to us all. I am glad that you will be leaving Isfehan."

Khatoon kept her hand in hers and squeezed it with affection but said nothing.

"Banoo, bring me my safe-box." Shahzadeh ordered.

The maid bowed, left the room and soon returned with a large silver coffer which she placed on the table near the bed. Then she slowly helped the Shahzadeh to sit reclining against her pillows. The maid gave a small silver key to her mistress.

Shahzadeh took the key, her hand shaking hard. She could not synchronize the key to its hole.

"Shahzadeh, allow me please."

Shahzadeh returned the key to the maid.

"Bring out the emerald-studded armband and the sealed envelope."

Banoo obeyed.

"The armband is your wedding gift and the documents in the envelope which have been under your name for a long time now are deeds to my properties in Isfehan. There are other pieces of jewellery in the coffer that I want you to give to your children from the Khan."

---

[24] Azis means dearest

Mariam Baygum began to pant. She found breathing too difficult so she stopped talking. The encounter was becoming too emotional.

The maid put the envelope and the armband back into the coffer, Locked it and gave the key to Khatoon.

"Had I a daughter, I couldn't have loved her more than I have loved you Khatoon. Take this box and go and face your destiny with courage."

Khatoon could not control her tears any longer. They began rolling down her rosy cheek staining it with the black of the sormeh [25] of her eyes. She embraced the Shahzadeh and the two remained locked in each other's hold for a long moment. Then Mariam Baygum let go, looked deeply into Khatoon's wet eyes and commanded: "Dearest, life is not to be wasted. Go now and let me rest in peace."

That night Shahzadeh Mariam peacefully fell into an everlasting sleep. Her good deeds had saved her from what awaited the royal andaroon.

In obedience of the Koranic law that requires a divorced woman to abstain from copulation in a re-marriage for one hundred days, so that if pregnant the child's rightful father is recognized, Fath Ali was to head for war (without the cannons) and his bride to Astarabad, the seat of his domain.

Khatoon left the palace without regrets and went to the house of her stepfather in which she was to meet her new husband.

Khosro Khan's house was almost as grand as Chelsetoon palace with its balcony facing a large rectangular pool fed by spring water that was dispersed through four canals that wiggled through the garden towards an invisible destination. The brick-paved courtyard was dotted by rectangular flower-beds in which aromatic annuals were in full bloom. Cherry and plum trees, dressed in white and pink blossoms, populated the orchard beyond. A deliciously scented breeze was teasing Khatoon's roobandeh. Seated on the floor facing her husband, her heart was filled with joy. Only a long, narrow, ivory-studded, low table, inundated with tantalizing dishes of sweets and fresh fruit separated the two. Eunuchs, in their long, flared, embroidered coats, arms crossed over their chests waited to serve. The balcony with its mirrored ceilings and frescoed walls had been tastefully prepared by Sarah for the bride and the groom's first face to face encounter.

---

[25] Kohl eye makeup

Fath Ali Khan, sat cross-legged with his back as straight as a pillar. The tail of his embroidered tunic spread on the red cushion on which he sat and his usually serious face was lit with delight as he longed for the moment he could lift the roobandeh and see the beauty hidden behind it. Yet etiquette demanded patience. The ivory studded door that connected the balcony to the inside crept open and Sadegh Khan entered with a silver tray on which sat two steaming tea glasses in silver frames. Slowly he put the tray on the table. First he served the Khan and then his mistress. He placed the silver cubed sugar holder in front of the Khan and then, stepping backward, disappeared behind the door where he remained to eavesdrop.

Khatoon took the Baghlava dish from the table and offered the Khan a sweet. He took one and with a shy smile bent over the table, lifted Khatoon's roobandeh and placed it into her half-open mouth, slightly touching her lips. The sensation raised in him such desire he had never felt for any of his other wives.

Khatoon blushed crimson. Slowly chewing the Baghlava she untied the roobandeh from behind her head and gently placed it on the floor beside her. Her large black eyes half hidden beneath her long curly lashes rose to the Khan. Devouring her with his eyes he noticed that the texture of her skin was silky; her lips, curved, pink and moist promising a taste of sweet plum and her nose, small and slightly tilted upwards made her look more beautiful than any flower he had ever seen.

Their eyes met. The world stood still and their hearts felt the fury of love.

They began conversing. His accent was Turkish, hers pure Farsi. He was naïve about almost everything except the art of war and animal husbandry. She was wise, quick-witted, intelligent, knowledgeable and worldly. His manners were tough and basic. Hers were sophisticated and refined. To him she appeared too glamorous to fit into the pattern of tribal life. Suddenly a wave of panic stabbed his besotted heart.

He took her hand, took it to his lips and kept it there for a long time – as if giving himself time to gather courage. Then holding the hand tight he looked into her questioning eyes and said:

"I am scared you might find life in the open not to your liking, Baygum." Flattered, a smiling Khatoon replied:

"No roof is higher than the sky, no pillow softer than the arm of my husband and God blesses those who live by the code of honour."

Her words evaporated his doubt. He again took her hand to his lips, inhaled its scent of rose and kissed the ends of her Hanna painted nails until the pain in his loins became too unbearable. He reluctantly released the hand, his entire body burning with desire.

Sadegh Khan saw the flickers of passion in his new master's eyes. He released a sigh of relief, sent a silent prayer and left his post knowing that he would remain loyal to this man forever.

To reach Astarabad Khatoon's caravan headed north, crossing dangerous paths that twisted around Mount Albourz, ascending and descending through thick forests where many gorges and rivers ran. After weeks of travel the caravan reached the road to Astarabad. Here, the Khan's cousin, young and handsome Mohammad Baik; the leader of the caravan, with a heavy heart left for the compound to prepare it for the reception of the bride. It was the end of their journey and being with Khatoon. He hated that.

The sun had not yet set when the bridal cavalcade reached the periphery of the settlement where hundreds of tribesmen, women and children, colourfully dressed, lined the path to welcome the bride by their cheers, whistles, burning of wild rue and the sound of tambourines. Women in their floating skirts, baskets filled with wild flowers hanging from their arms singing happy songs threw petals before the hooves of the horses. Khatoon, regal in a cream coloured embroidered silk coat and matching pantaloons, sat on her horse. Her long, white silk scarf matched her roobandeh. In front of her she saw yorts [26] – row after row, all the same but different in size. One stood out and that was white – erected for her to rest and change before being received by Fath Ali Khan's mother – the matriarch of the tribe.

Tribal life differed culturally from that of the city. Hard work necessitated equality of sexes. Here women rode side by side with their fellow men and worked as hard in the fields tending to their flocks and horses. They were as competent as their men in hunting and the art of warfare.

Khatoon knew this and loved it.

Mohammad Baik, who now was back by Khatoon's side stole a last quick glance from the subject of his adoration, and then walked ahead leading her to the tent, in the middle of which sat a huge tub

---

[26] Nomadic huts

of scented steaming water. Aided by her maid, Khatoon was washed, perfumed and dressed in the magnificent shirt, tunic and pants which her mother-in-law had ordered for her. The shirt and the pants were of pure white satin silk and the tunic was in blue embroidered fine cotton with a high collar and buttons of real gold, studded with pearls from the Persian Gulf. The ceremony that awaited her was to introduce her to the elders of the clan. The tall bride with her black eyes shining like two large black pearls, smiling and smelling of rose, stepped out of her tent and amidst a joyous singing and clapping crowd slowly walked to the yort of her Khan-Madar [27], whom she knew had been waiting for this moment since she had heard of the gift. Mohammad Baik, his head down, lifted the curtain to the yort for her. She bent her head and entered the yort. Straightening her back she stood erect, and smiling threw an appraising glance around the interior which was colourfully decorated with a large carpet from Tabriz. The same type of carpet covered the cushions that were set on the four corners of the sofreh [28] that was spread smooth on the floor and overwhelmed by large trays of saffron rice, kebabs of all kind, yogurts, dishes of fresh herbs and containers of goat's milk and fresh water. She noticed that all the guests had risen except Khan-Madar who sat cross-legged on the carpet, majestically reclining on her cushion, scrutinizing her from top to toe. Her white hair was hidden by a white scarf on which sat a green felt cap adorned with gold coins. No roobandeh covered her oval face that was deeply lined. Her tanned skin was thickened by climatic cruelty. Her large black eyes were the shape of almonds and they shone brilliantly without revealing her inner thoughts. The rest of her features, although deformed by age, told of a beauty lost. In stature she was diminutive yet her posture exuded authority. Expecting to find an arrogant woman unhappy with her fate, to her surprise she liked what she saw.

Smiling she gestured the "Gift" to come near. Khatoon, still smiling, nodded to the guests who bowed to her before resuming their seats and then walked to her mother-in-law and knelt by her. Khan-Madar cupped her beautiful face between her rough palms, looked deep into her eyes and beyond into her soul. Loving it she kissed her on both cheeks and then welcomed her in Turkish; the only

---

[27] Khan-Madar : Mother of the Khan

[28] The tablecloth that is laid on the carpet for meals. No tables existed amongst the tribes.

language she spoke. Khatoon thanked her in Turkish too. This surprised the old lady, it elevated 'the Gift' in her esteem and she decided to accept her as a daughter.

Khatoon with her household from Isfehan, settled into her new home at the fortress of Mubarakabad, the seat of the governor of Astarabad, and enthusiastically delved into her nomadic life as though she had never tasted the luxuries of the royal andaroon. Curious by nature, Khatoon had used the archives at the palace to learn about the origin of her ancestry. She had discovered that the Gajars were the oldest tribe in Iran. Of Turcoman origin, they had first been seen in the Mughan Steppe around 897 AD. Shah Abass the Great had used them as border guardians and when they grew too strong the central government deemed it necessary to disperse them by creating conflict between the sects. This was successfully achieved and now, instead of a united strong tribe, they were fragmented. So if the Gajars wanted to play a dominant role in the politics of Iran they had to set aside their long internecine strife and unite. To this end she decided to become the instrument of unity. One day, having procured the permission of Khan-Madar she took her maid, Sadegh Khan and a mule loaded with gifts to ride upstream and surprise the aunt of her husband, who was the wife of the chief of the Yukharibash sect of the Gajar tribe. The Yukharibash were Davalo Gajars living above the river Atrak and the Ashaghabash were Guvanlu Gajars living below the river. The two sects often fought for prominence in the northern territory.

The wife of the Davalo chief and the wife of the Guvanlu chief met for the first time in fifty years. At first the meeting was formal and cold but gradually Khatoon's genuine intentions and frankness broke the ice. Tea was sipped, mouths were sweetened and much appreciation was expressed for the unusual gifts from Isfehan. As the friendship grew in strength the old wounds healed, socializing began and weddings made ties stronger. Khatoon's accounts of her experiences at court and belief in her husband's patriotism and courage convinced the Davalos that united under her husband it was possible to save Iran from the Afghan menace.

Nomadic life is simple and nomads are self-sufficient. The Ashaghabash were flock-keepers. They had a summer and a winter location to which they migrated. During the Safavids the Gajars were given the governership of Astarabad and the Governor lived in the fortress of Mubarakabad. However the ordinary nomads lived in their yorts and their survival depended on the orderliness of nature. Natural phenomena affected their lives and they bore much respect for water and vegetation. It was by a sacred plane tree that Khatoon had a small room built in which both sects could join in prayer. There was not one single Gajar soul that did not love and respect the Khan's new bride and that included Fath Ali Khan's other wives.

One hundred days passed swiftly and on the first day of Ramadan Fath Ali – having won battles but not the war against the Afghan – returned to a blissful compound impatiently awaiting him. Sitting upright on his horse he waved at his people amongst whom were faces he had not seen for years. Puzzled he dismounted in front of his mother's yort outside which the elders and his mother were standing. Out of respect Khatoon stood behind Khan-Madar. The Khan's dusty face lit up when he saw his wife in a tribal dress looking even more beautiful than before. He gently kissed his mother and smiled at his wife. He longed to embrace her but any expression of love in public was taboo. The elders of both sects embraced the Khan and kissed him on both cheeks. Then they all entered the yort where the sofreh eftar, the breaking of the fast was spread on the carpet. The Khan sat between his mother and his wife and waited patiently. When the Azan [29] was heard, the fast was broken by sips of hot tea followed by a sumptuous meal. Then Mohammad Baik, the Khan's trusted second in command, enlightened him of all that had happened in his absence. Elated and proud, Fath Ali glanced at his wife with tenderness. She smiled and winked at him. Khatoon waited a little longer before whispering something into Khan Madar's ear. The old Baygum nodded and rose to her feet. Her gesture meant dismissal.

The lovers waited until the last individual left the yort and then they flew to their nest.

Their bedchamber at the fortress was large with high white walls. Plenty of lace dressed the windows. Their wooden bed was made to Khatoon's order. In a corner, on a wide mantlepiece, a long silver pitcher sat on its large silver bowl, used as a wash basin. Next to the basin lay two embroidered towels. Sadegh Khan stood in attention until he was dismissed. Earlier in the day he had made sure that all

---

[29] Recited verses that call the faithful to prayer and in Ramadan to the breaking of the fast.

hair was removed from his mistress's body, which was then rubbed with a coarse glove, oiled and perfumed to make it even more delicious for the hungry master. The Khan had a quick bath and then within the confines of their room they sat in anticipation. The Khan was not versed in the art of speech. The light breeze coming through the open window had its own melody. Fath Ali withdrew a folded white silk handkerchief from the large pocket of his aba, unfolded its pleats and placed it on the carpeted floor. On the silk fabric lay a small gold-rimmed mirror that was to bring luck and a diamond ring as large and round as the moon itself. He looked into the shining eyes of his wife and said: "You have made me a proud man. Khan-Madar has never spoken of anyone as highly as she spoke of you. You have elevated me in the eyes of my people. Khatoon, may God bless you and elevate you to your heart's desire."

"When you took me as your wife you elevated me to my heart's desire. You took me from my city and my mother. Instead you offered me freedom and another mother, kinder and wiser than my own."

The Khan took Khatoon's soft hand, kissed it and then fitted the ring on her long, slender finger. Their fingers entangled and they felt exalted. Suddenly Khatoon withdrew her hand, and in a tone as sweet as honey asked her husband to ride with her to the mouth of the Shah Diz Spring on the peak of a hill, not far from the fortress.

From there they could view the whole of the Gajar terrain dotted by yorts, sleeping flocks and horses. At that moment Fath Ali would have given Khatoon his life had she requested it. Minutes later the two, side by side, rode to the peak. There they tied their horses to a tree and holding hands stood by the bubbling spring gazing down at the expansiveness of their domain. The night was cool and the sky filled with stars. The only sound that could be heard was that of nature. Khatoon took the hand of her husband to her lips and kissed it several times and then looked into the large black eyes, which were fixed on her and said:

"I want you to take me here."

"Why, my love?"

"Because I know that your seed will grow in me tonight. It will be a boy and I want him to be as pure as nature, as brave as his father and as strong as our love for each other."

"The moment I set eyes on you I knew I would love you for ever.

But you – are you sorry for having left the palace?"

"Not at all! I liked the Sultan but I had no respect for him. Before being given to you not only had I heard about your chivalry but I had also seen you on the balcony of the Ali-Ghapu palace. I came to you because my heart had warmed to you. Had it not, I would have committed suicide before being given away as a gift."

The Khan's sigh of relief was lost in the wheeze of the wind.

He took off his aba, spread it on the grass and then took her hands and pulled her down to him. She sat on his knees and put her arms around his neck and her lips on his. They kissed and kissed and then they lay down with their hands untying and exploring and giving pleasure until the ultimate exhilaration of love rendered them wet and breathless. The stars kept shining, the moon smiled and the breeze cooled the lovers.

At dawn the chirping of the birds woke them up. They looked into each other's eyes, kissed and made love again. Then they bathed in the freezing water of the spring, mounted their horses and headed home.

Nine months later God granted a son to the Khan of the Gajars [30]. For three days and nights the fortress was filled with the sound of flutes and tambourines, clapping of hands and aroma of lamb kebabs. Khan-Madar named her grandson Mohammad Hassan.

As weeks and months passed Fath Ali Khan's sphere of influence expanded to include the prosperous province of Masandaran, that stretches along the shore of the Caspian Sea.

In the beautiful city of Isfehan, the merchants from all over the world continued to trade, the artisans created their crafts and poets composed their poetry as though nothing would ever touch the sanctity of their city. Citizens sincerely believed when the Shah decided to open his treasury, commission soldiers and utilize his cannons, the menace of the Afghan would evaporate into thin air. But instead of mobilizing the Shah was praying to a god who refused to listen to a king with no bravery. So Mahmoud Afghan arrived by the closed gates of the capital which he besieged and cut off all its water supply. Then he sent his master spy into the city through a secret passage to find Khatoon and bring her to him.

In Astarabad, Khatoon had already become mother to three children.

---

[30] There are historical rumors that Khatoon was already pregnant when given to Fath Ali.

Mohammad Hassan was five, Mohammad Hussain three and her daughter Khadijeh two.

Mahmoud's spy's account of Khatoon's marriage to the Gajar so infuriated him that he drew his dagger and pushed it into the stomach of the unlucky news bearer. Signs of madness had begun manifesting themselves in the heartless youth.

The besiege of Isfehan was in its ninth month. Famine, disease and murder turned the city into a vast morgue. The Shah did nothing but pray. The courtiers appealed to the astrologer for an ultimate solution. The charts demanded the Shah to smuggle out one of his sons to seek help from the chieftains. The Shah chose Tahmaseb, a spoilt eighteen year old youth who had never set foot outside the andaroon. At Ghazvin he settled into a comfortable life forgetting the reason for which he had been smuggled out.

In Isfehan, having eaten the dogs, cats and rats people had now resorted to cannibalism.

Outside Shaik Lotfollah mosque the heavy rain was washing away the stench of death. The downpour was so heavy that no procession, if there could have been any, could leave the mosque. No one had any energy for the usual self-flagellation performed to remember the martyrdom of Immam Hussain. It was the day of Ashora [31], the holiest day of the month of Moharam. People were mourning, this time not for the martyrs of Karbella but for themselves. Shah Sultan Hussain, avoiding the streets had walked to the mosque through the subterranean path that joined it to Ali-Ghapu. The mullah was singing his sad religious song. The audience was in tears. The Shah, his face pale and crinkled, his lips dry and cracked, his beard snow white and his large black eyes lacklustre, squatted in a corner and moaned like an orphan. Suddenly he rose, took off his green turban and in a voice that was lower than a whisper said:

"I swear by the soul of my ancestors that I cannot tolerate this horrible situation any longer. Tomorrow I shall go and put an end to your torments and my own anguish."

That night, to protect the honour of their families, many fathers killed their own daughters and wives and then committed suicide.
The next morning the only horse still alive was brought to the palace.

---

[31] Ashura or Ashora is the day during which Immam Hussain, the third Immam of the Shiat, the son of Ali and the grandson of Prophet Mohammad was beheaded by Yazid. It is a day of mourning and prayer.

The Shah gave his green turban, the crown of the Safavid Shahs to Etemad Douleh, his senior minister, to carry. Then he mounted his horse and with his entourage following him on foot, slowly passed through a city littered by corpses and vultures. No one had lined the streets to witness the death of a dynasty. The royal entourage crossed the Thirty Three Bridge, passed through the city's main gate, passed by the gate of Poplar Garden and reached the palace of Farahabad, that had been built for Shah Sultan Hussain, now inhabited by Mahmoud. At the gate of the palace an Afghan guard stepped forth and asked:

"What is your business here?"

The Shah himself answered: "We have come as guests of Mir Mahmoud Ibne Mervis."

The Afghan looked at the sovereign with expressionless eyes and asked:

"What is your name?"

"Mir Hussain of the house of Safavids."

"Wait here," the guard said before turning to go to the palace.

The Shah on his horse and the entourage on foot stood motionless waiting for a fate unknown. An hour skulked away in unbearable anxiety. In awe of what was about to happen, even nature stood still until an owl dared to come out of hiding and fly over the head of the monarch. Under ordinary circumstances, to remove the bad omen lambs would have been sacrificed.

Mahmoud, still diminitive in stature but more mature in his bearded face, dressed in white kaftans and riding boots, walked out of the gate and stood staring at the Shah with his narrow eyes that glazed with malice. The conqueror of the Persian Empire was only twenty years old. Uncouth, vain and barbaric even in the moment of his triumph he could not exercise magnanimity, nor courtesy. Shah Sultan Hussain climbed down from his horse, took a moment to regain his composure and then walked towards Mahmoud. He embraced the youth whispering into his ears:

"For peace I have come to appease you." The imperious Afghan withdrew from the Shah's hold and burst into thunderous laughter. He laughed and laughed until his face turned blue. "You are a liar, Mullah Hussain! You have come to save your own head."

The Shah remained silent. "Follow me to the grand hall you built for yourself," the Afghan commanded before turning towards the impressive building. Pale and pathetic, Hussain followed the conqueror to the grand hall that had lost its grandeur. Dirty, unruly soldiers had littered it with their spoils. It stank of perspiration and tobacco. Mahmoud, smiling, climbed the steps of the ornamental wooden throne of the Shah and ordered Hussain to sit on the ground by his feet. Dignity lost, the Shah felt nothing – in spirit he was already dead. To conclude the affair he told Etemad Douleh to place the crown of the Safavids on the head of the Afghan.

Mahmoud's frown changed his mind. Instead he rose himself, took the Green Turban from his minister, climbed the steps and crowned his foe.

The Sunni Afghan became the Shah of Shia Iran.

In the evening of the same day Etemad Douleh, together with Emanollah Khan, Mahmoud's minister, entered the city, went from palace to palace and to the Shah's treasury. Taking possession of the city, Emanollah Khan ordered it to be cleansed and the corpses to be taken away to be burnt. The next day Mahmoud unceremoniously entered Isfehan. People remained in their houses behind barricaded doors. The first Shia clergy who went to the minaret of Shah Mosque to sing the Azan was pushed down and killed.

Hussain was confined to his private quarters while Mahmoud took over his andaroon. The rapes and sodomies that followed drove many of the inhabitants to suicide.

A brutal religious cleansing followed. All Shia mullahs, Armenian priests and Jewish rabbis were beheaded.

In Gazvin loyal chieftains, including Fath Ali Khan, proclaimed Tahmaseb the Safavid Shah of Iran.

Mahmoud sent his cousin Ashraf to fight Tahmaseb only to discover that he had fled from Gazvin. Ashraf returned to Isfehan and the following day Mahmoud had fifteen hundred male members of the Safavid family rounded up and beheaded in the middle of Shah Square. It was not until Shah Sultan Hussain, now referred to by all as Mullah Hussain, went on his knees and begged Mahmoud that the killings stopped. Gradually the Afghan soldiers, unaccustomed to city duelling became restless and began leaving for home with their loot.

In spite of the prevalent anarchy there was no one in Isfehan to rise against Mahmoud and prevent the current political fragmentation. In Khorasan a man by the name of Nader was making fame for himself and also in Fars a Lor [32] by the name of Karim. In the North, Gajar bandits were robbing the Afghans of cargoes of war bounties that were going to Kandahar.

At nights Mahmoud could not sleep. The ghosts of his victims haunted him. To chase them away he would get out of bed, unleash the sword that never left his side and wander the corridors and the courtyards. In the morning mutilated bodies of eunuchs, chambermaids and guards were removed by tongue-tied soldiers. The more he killed the more ghosts he had to chase away at nights. And when he slaughtered Shah Sultan Hussain's remaining young family Amanollah Khan went to Ashraf and begged him to save the Afghans and the people of Isfehan from the mad man. Ashraf accepted the challenge, waited until nightfall then, sword drawn, went to Mahmoud's bedchamber. He was asleep. Swiftly the deed was done.

The following day Ashraf was proclaimed the Shah of Iran. The news travelled fast to the hostile neighbouring countries. Ottomans attacked Iran. The Russians who had no desire for a stronger Ottoman Empire announced their protection of the Safavid Shah. Immediately they sent their ambassador to ask Ashraf to step down in favour of Shah Sultan Hussain, and return to Kandahar. In retaliation Ashraf had the Shah beheaded and sent his head to the Ottoman Emperor with whom he was negotiating peace. In reprisal the Russian sovereign, aware of the Gajar's ambition, wrote to Fath Ali assuring him of the Russians' protection should he join forces with the Safavid to create a strong central government that could defeat the Afghans and stand against the Ottoman Turks. Fath Ali Khan, accompanied by Khatoon, took the letter to Shah Tahmaseb in Gazvin. The Shah, overjoyed, rewarded the Khan by inviting him to join forces with him and Nader Gholi Asfhar, who was coming to join the Shah in Khorassan. Fath Ali, delighted that finally a prohibitive force was about to be formed against the Afghans, promptly accepted the invitation.

Better than anyone else, Khatoon knew Tahmaseb so she asked him to swear on the holy book that he would not betray her husband. Tahmaseb saw no harm in doing so. He had already broken many vows that had not suited him.

Back at the compound Fath Ali informed the elders of his decision and the night before his departure he and Khatoon rode to the top of the hill by Shah Diz Spring. So much had changed since their first night there twelve

---

[32] Lors are a tribe that live in the Fars Province

springs back. Through facing the challenges of those turbulent years together their love had matured and they had become soul-mates – something quite unusual for the era of their existence. That night the breeze was cool, the moon bright and the sky clear. Lying on Fath Ali's aba and covered by Khatoon's cloak they made love and the sound of their love making intermingled with that of the waterfall and disappeared into the thickness of night.

In the morning the sound of drums echoed in the plain. Shaik Mofid stood in front of the Khan holding a volume of the Koran high for him to pass under. The holy book's power would safeguard him against all evils. Fath Ali kissed the edge of the Koran and bending his head, passed under it. Mothers and wives whirling their incense burners moved around so that the smoke of wild rue would burn evil eyes from the outgoing warriors.

Khatoon, silent and pensive, stood there holding the hands of Mohammad Hussain and Khadijeh. Mohammad Hassan, only eleven, was accompanying his father.

Fath Ali mounted his groomed horse and, without looking back, rode towards his destiny.

At Khabushan the Gajars joined the royal army and set up camp to wait for Nader. The Shah, who had brought his andaroon, settled into a life of indulgence. Fath Ali in his naivety believed Tahmaseb looked upon him as a father figure so he dared to criticize his unbecoming behavior. Tension began to mount between the two. Tahmaseb looked upon Fath Ali as a dispensable servant and Fath Ali thought of Tahmaseb as another Shah Sultan Hussain. Then Nader arrived at Khabushan. Tall, well built and handsome he was a ferocious warrior who commanded respect. Proud and ambitious he joined the Shah in his dislike of the Gajar Khan, whom he soon perceived to be a dangerous rival to be removed. He, unlike Fath Ali was cunning, loved women and enjoyed wine. As the Shah warmed to him his relationship with the Gajar cooled even more. Fath Ali his pride bruised, decided to ask the Shah's permission to return to Astarabad. Nader jumped at the chance and led the Shah to believe that the Turcoman had treason in his mind and should not be allowed to return to his domain. So when the Gajar asked the Shah for permission to leave, the monarch reminded him of their earlier oath and rejected his request.

That same night a shadow crept into Fath Ali Khan's tent and terminated him. Mohammad Hassan, sleeping at the feet of his father, saw the murder and shivering, remained silent until the murderer left the tent. Then quietly he tiptoed out of the tent, slithered into the adjoining tent of Mohammad Baik, hurriedly woke him up and weeping, whispered his news.

The next day the camp of Shah Tahmaseb was devoid of any Turcoman soldiers.

Chapter 2

Wrapped in white, on her knees, Khatoon was engrossed in her evening prayer. Her room was semi-lit. The candles in their elaborate stands were flickering and several flower pots were filled with pink roses – her favourite flower. The scent of roses together with her aura made the room's coziness hospitable. The sound of the door opening did not disturb her meditation. Mohammad Hassan slithered through and seeing his mother praying stood still, his throat tight, his limbs aching with pain and his heart burning with sorrow. The familiarity of the room broke his last reserve and tears began rolling down his handsome, dusty face. Not as tall as his parents, the boy was slender yet well built. He had inherited his father's large black eyes and his mother's small upturned nose. His skin was tanned and a shadow of a moustache was present above his fine upper lip that had cracked from dehydration. Non-stop they had ridden to the fortress. Usually he carried himself tall but at that moment, filled with shame, he felt as small as an ant.

Khatoon lifted her head from the Mohr [33], folded her prayer mat, untied the knot of her chador [34] that was holding the veil over her head and rose to her feet still facing Mecca and whispering the protection prayers for her family, which she habitually murmured after the end of each ritual.

"Mother!"

She turned with surprise. Her long chador slipped off her head and spread on her prayer mat. He ran to her. No words were necessary. She perceived it all. Her heart palpitating hard she opened her arms into which he lost himself. Intertwined they stood, shaking with emotion – their sorrow deep, their loss immense.

---

[33] A small baked mold of earth on which the forehead is placed during Moslem prayer, an indication of submission to the greatness of Allah.

[34] A long veil

"Mother, I am so ashamed."

"Hush, son," she said kissing the top of his head smudged with sweat and road dust.

"Mother, I was there. I saw everything and instead of defending my father I hid under the blanket. I am an unworthy coward. Please kill me and relieve me of my shame."

"You could have done nothing, son," she whispered, tightening her grip around his slender shoulders.

Mumbling between sobs Mohammad Hassan continued to deplore, "Please mother, kill me. I don't deserve to bear my father's name."

She kept him within her embrace until he ran out of words. Then holding his bony arm she led him to the two oak chairs by the window. Outside, the torch lights glowed over stationary carts and wagons. The town was in silent mourning. "Tell me what you saw," Khatoon asked, her voice quivering with emotion. Closing his eyes, Mohammad Hassan took a deep breath. He needed it to be able to deal with the ache of recollection. His throat was too tight. He took another breath before whispering:

"It was very dark. Father had just fallen sleep. I heard a movement. I thought it was the wind striking the pole of the tent. Then I saw the tip of a sword slither through the opening of the tent before a body sauntered through. I made a move to rise but as he did not notice me I remained still. He tiptoed towards father, sword in hand. I couldn't see his face but I noticed he was very tall, broad and swift with his sword."

"Nader Gholi! It must have been him. Who else would dare such an act?"

"How do you know, mother?"

"My spies brought me reports. I anticipated confrontation between the Khan and the Afshar but not murder. God's curse upon Tahmaseb for he has broken his vow." Khatoon fell silent, her eyes moistened and her voice became husky.

"We must leave the fortress. It is not safe for you here. I have lost two loved ones to Safavid paranoia. I am not going to lose you too. Promise me by the soul of your father that you will never forgive Tahmaseb and will avenge your father's blood."

"I made that vow when I saw my father's..." He stopped. He could not bring himself to finish his sentence. The incident was too horrific and the pain too deep.

"Enshallah, son, I will be still alive to see that day," Khatoon said raising her arms towards heaven.

The next day as the sun began to spread its golden wings across the cloudless sky, the elders of the tribe with their arms banded in black began to arrive at the fortress. They were coming to express their condolences and vow their allegiance to Mohammad Hassan. Fath Ali Khan had been a loved chieftain. Under his banner the tribe had enjoyed peace and prosperity.

The mourning ceremonies lasted seven days, during which the sound of prayer drifted out from every mosque and lines were long and thick with the needy holding their pots for the food served from the kitchen of the fortress.

The murder had astonished and angered the Ashaghabash elders and in consultation with Khatoon they were considering safety measures when a spy brought news that Nader and Tahmaseb had decided to terminate Gajar power by having Mohammad Hassan taken hostage. To this end Amir Ghasem Khan Afshar was on his way to Mubarrakabad. Khatoon understood the reason for the plot. A tribe without a leader, even one as young as Mohammad Hassan, had no choice but relinquish its hold on the Northern provinces and pursue nomadic life. The governance of Astarabad would be given to a Nader lackey making him the sole contestant for ultimate power. Sharing her thoughts with the elders, the decision was made to face the foe. Immediately a plan was formulated.

Amir Ghasem Khan had just trespassed into the Gajar domain when he suddenly found himself ambushed. Yonder on the outskirts of a small hill Khatoon, in black, sitting on her horse, her mind caressing the thought of revenge, in company of other Turcoman female warriors, was waiting for the right moment to strike. The sun was shining vengefully and the heat had created a mirage in which the images of the oncoming soldiers were distorted. Her sharp eyes were searching for the Afshar Amir and then she recognized him from the elaborate grooming of his horse. She raised her bow, aimed the arrow for the arm and released it. Whizzing through the air the arrow hit the target knocking the Amir off his horse. Khatoon galloped towards her victim. In rage, she circled around him over and over again. Then she flew off her horse and stood eyeing him. Amir Ghasem began to mumble the death prayer. The excited Gajars, hurrahing and waving their rifles in the air, surrounded the wounded, waiting to kill him. Khatoon, her eyes glowing with fury bent down and pulled the arrow out of the man's arm. He let out a scream, grabbed his arm and doubled on his stomach. Khatoon infused more hate in her glare and yelled:

"The wound in my heart is deeper than the one in your arm. Not only have you killed my husband but you have dared to come for my son!"

The Afshar was stunned for having been the target of a woman. The sting of shame was worse than that of the wound.

Khatoon, lifting her head up looked around and shouted:

"My people, witness that I am sparing this man's life, for Amir Ghasem Khan is also a Turcoman. Therefore as one of us he will deliver our request to Nader Gholi. He will tell his master that we are not a threat to him or to the Shah. We only demand that out of respect for our past loyalty, the head of our chief's murderer be delivered to us. I know Nader Gholi, a man of honour will not dismiss our right. An eye for an eye, it is written." Khatoon paused to catch her breath and then ordered: "Now we must see to the wound of our guest."

Baffled, the nomads could not comprehend the logic of their Baygum's decision. They jumped off their mounts and aimed their rifles to finish the aggressor. Hastily Shaikh Mofid stepped forward and with the spread of his arms gesticulated for calm.

"Baygum's words are our command. It is better to leave vengeance to God. Time has come for us to go on our knees and thank the Almighty for the blood we have not shed in lieu of this conquest." The Shaikh knelt and in obedience all followed.

The next day when the convoy was about to leave for Khorasan, Khatoon addressed Amir Ghasem Khan: "Tell that youth from Isfehan that only cowards kill their foes in sleep."

Amir Ghasem Khan, full of admiration and sympathy for this brave woman bowed to her, mounted his horse and led his men back to Mashhad. Isfeshan was still under Afghan occupation.

Khatoon and her family vacated the fortress of Mubarakabad and settled at their compound. One afternoon, in the privacy of their yort with a tray of tea and sugar candy in front of them, Mohammad Hassan broke his brooding, looked at his mother with questioning eyes and asked:

"Mother, why have you asked Nader Gholi for the head of my father's murderer, when you know he himself is the culprit?"

Khatoon, straightening her back, smiling, looked deep into her son's perplexed eyes and softly said: "I know that. But not all wars are fought on battle-fields. I want to buy time until you are old and wise enough to face a man such as Nader. Rest assured, my son, that should I live long enough, together we will see that all accounts are settled. For now we just have to be patient." She stopped to guage her son's grasp of her logic. His meek smile reassured her. Then she added: "Patience is a virtue, a virtue that if not innate should be cultivated."

Mohammad Hassan, regretting his earlier doubts, took his mother's hand and kissed it. Then light in heart, he left the yort to join the shepherds tending the flocks. The year had been good to them. The number of their sheep had tripled. That meant enough money to pay the annual government taxes that would be due soon.

Life went on. Nader Gholi grew stronger and Tahmaseb weaker.

The Ashaghebash continued their peaceful existence and the governance of Astarabad went to a Nader crony by the name of Sabez Ali Baik. He was cruel, shrewd and lascivious.

Five years passed. Nader defeated the Afghans and ousted them out of Iran. Tahmaseb, pomp and pompous, returned to Isfehan, occupied his father's throne and delved deeper into harem life until Nader had no further use for him. Then one morbid winter evening, when the Shah was in a drunken stupor, two ghosts entered his bedchamber, wrapped him in his bed sheets, and disappeared into the thickness of the night. The next morning he found himself shackled in a cold, smelly dungeon in Sabsevar. He shouted, banged and kicked on the thick wooden door to no avail. Then he sobbed and sobbed until he fell asleep only to be woken by the sound of a metal bowl banged on the stone floor. Completely disoriented he opened his puffy eyes, blinked a couple of times. Nothing was visible until his eyes, accustomed to the dark, discerned the outline of a toothless giant in rags towering over him. His odour was repulsive.

Pinching his large nose Tahmaseb whispered, "Where am I?"

"You are in Sabsevar, your Majesty, prisoner of Nader Gholi."

Throwing his hands up he shrieked, "That is not possible. There must be a mistake. Nader is my servant." The jailor threw him a contemptuous glance, shrugged his broad shoulders, raised a bushy eyebrow and said:

"It seems not any longer."

The Shah covered his face with his soft fat hands and burst into tears, his shoulders trembling hard. The jailor this time threw him a pitiful glance, let out a big fart that smelled foul, before leaving his Majesty to deal with his remorse. Memories returned. Mistakes revealed themselves and the dungeon became darker and more forebidding. Soon reality gave way to oblivion and Tahmaseb lost his mind.

Nader united all the provinces, becoming the sole chieftain of Iran. However, as his power grew his paranoia grew too. Tahmaseb, even in his madness became a threat to him. Thus one night, the door of the dungeon skulked open, a shadow crept in and terminated the sleeping Shah.

It was the year 1152 Hejri, 1740.

The news travelled fast – no one shed any tears.

At the compound the Gajars celebrated the prevalence of justice. For the first time since the death of her husband Khatoon felt light-hearted and a smile returned to her shapely lips. She was thirty-five and lonely amongst the crowd. Her sons had grown to become fine warriors, and her daughter, tall and beautiful, had inherited her courage and finesse.

Relieved from the burden of plotting vengeance, Khatoon turned her mind to finding a wife for her eldest son. He had to marry first before his younger brother. Within the family the order of marriage followed age hierarchy. To find a suitable bride was not easy. Matchmakers had to search hard amongst the eligible young damsels and once a choice was made then extensive research had to be made regarding the virtue of the girl herself and her entire family before Khasegari [35]. Virgins of families with tarnished reputations mostly died spinsters.

The choice for Mohammad Hassan's spouse fell on the daughter of Sulayman Khan Guvanlu, a Gajar virgin of noble blood by the name of Jayran. She was bright, beautiful and courageous. Mohammad Hassan had already stolen her heart but she had never dreamt of becoming his wife. Khatoon's emissary presented himself at the yort of Sulayman Khan carrying gifts for the parents and a huge emerald ring for the girl. Honoured by the proposal the consent was granted, charts were consulted and the most propitious day for the wedding fell on Prophet Mohammad's birthday.

It was a fine spring day in the year 1741 (1154 Hejri). The plain was covered with wild flowers of every colour and kind. The air was

---

[35] Formal proposal of marriage made by the parents of the man to the parents of the woman

sweet and Jayran happy – in fact ecstatic. Early in the morning she had been ceremoniously taken to the bath yort. There two ladies known for their happy marriages (those unhappily married were not even invited to any weddings for their unhappiness could be infectious!) had plucked her joint eyebrows, removed all unwanted hair from her body, bathed her in goat's milk, rubbed her soft skin with jasmine oil, combed and plaited her long, straight, jet black hair, and dressed her in white satin silk – and now at three in the afternoon, Sheik Mofid, in his white turban and brown aba was patiently waiting in front of the Khan's grand yort for her arrival. Singers were singing at every corner of the compound and nomads, in their colourful attire had gathered in the open floral expanse of the plain to watch the sacred tradition of grabbing the lamb.[36] When Jayran, dressed in an embroidered white gown, her face hidden behind white lace, seated in a camel mounted palanquin hugging a white lamb came into sight, cries of exultation reached heaven. Then from the opposite direction appeared Mohammad Hassan, in an elegant embroidered felt vest worn over a white linen round-collared shirt that was tied at the waist with a purple silk belt matching the colour of his pantaloons. Followed by eight of his peers and standing on his horse, he galloped to the palanquin and swiftly grabbed the white lamb from his bride and held it high. At that moment, Jayran smiled at her luck. The lamb cried and Mohammad Hassan's laughter was lost amongst the hurrah of the spectators. The palanquin slowly wobbled on and the nine riders now followed it. Musicians began playing the wedding song to the clapping of the guests. Near the yort the bride was helped off the seat by her father and led to where Shaik Mofid, Mohammad Hussain and the eldest member of the tribe, a man named Allahverdi waited to perform the ceremony. Mohammad Hassan dismounted his horse, gently let go of the lamb and joined the men. Allahverdi and Mohammad Hussain were witnesses for the groom, Jayran's father and brother for the bride. The young couple, showered with rose petals and sugar candies entered the ornately decorated yort where Khatoon and the elders had gathered around the sofreh aghad, which faced Mecca. The sofreh was adorned with a large gold framed mirror, on each side of which was a silver candelabrum holding elongated candles with flames that danced cheerfully and a volume of the Koran encased in green

---

[36] This tradition honoured fertility.

velvet, embroidered with pearls from the Persian Gulf. On the sofreh, inviting dishes of sweets, vases of flowers, trays of fresh herbs, loaves of bread, coloured eggs and wild rue seeds and a large fish bowl with two goldfish competed for attention.

These items represented happy aspects of married life. The couples each sat on a cushion facing Mecca and waited for the Sheik to read from the Koran. Jayran, her eyes hidden behind the lace, dared to glue her gaze on her betrothed's handsome profile. She loved his tanned skin, groomed beard and upturned moustache. She noticed he had very long upturned lashes and his nose was straight and a bit on the large side. A strange new feeling began to stir inside her and she longed to touch him. At that moment four women spread a wide piece of white lace over their head, each holding an end and another lady stepped forward and began rubbing two sugar cones against one another, the dust of which went through the lace and settled on the heads and shoulders of the couple.

His recital finished, the Shaikh first asked the groom and then the bride for their consent. That given, Mohammad Hassan, his black eyes shining with happiness, turned to Jayran and gently lifted the lace from her face. She smiled at him and he at her. Their eyes met, their hearts melted and they knew they would be soul-mates forever.

That night a seed was sown that would become a boy, who would become a king.

The merry-making went on for seven days and seven nights. The entire compound participated in feasting on lamb kebabs marinated in lemon juice and saffron, rice of all kinds, yogurt mixed with cucumber and mint. For drinks they consumed goat's milk mélange with honey, or pomegranate juice and the elders sipped hot tea laced with cardamom.

Far away Nader Shah conquered India, brought all its treasures to Iran [37] and hid them at Kalan Fortress. War became his hobby and for his endless campaigns he taxed the people. His tax collector's motto was "Tax or head". Each tribal chief, each Amir, each farmer had to pay tax to the governor of their province. And the governors, after deducting the cost of running the affairs of their province sent the remaining revenue together with the collected heads to Nader. As the conqueror became richer the nation became poorer. Sons of all the

---

[37] Nader brought one of the largest diamonds in the world, the Mountain of Light and the Peacock Throne to Iran from India.

chieftains were at his service including Mohammad Hussain. In reality they were his hostages so that their fathers would not dare to rise against him.

In Mashhad, Mohammad Hussain, by nature gentle and sociable, made friends with two of Nader's sons; Reza Gholi and Nasrollah Mirza. The latter was the son of Razieh Beygum – Khatoon's friend from the days of Poplar Garden. After getting to know Mohammad Hussain the Baygum became taken by the boy, regretted not having a daughter herself, and decided to find him a suitable wife. Her choice fell on the daughter of a Zand chieftain whose wife she knew well. Then a message was sent to Khatoon to come for the Khasegari.

A month later Khatoon's caravan, long and heavy with mules and horses struggling under their heavy loads set out for Mashhad. Spring was at its prime. Wild flowers covered the hills and the plains and the sky was pure blue and cloudless. Khatoon, riding side by side with her daughter Khadijeh and Sadegh Khan, felt as young as the days she accompanied her Fath Ali for hunts. Her face was still stunningly beautiful, though sun tanned – only a few lines had appeared on her forehead and around her large eyes, which in fact made her more attractive. Many men had asked for her hand only to receive an amicable smile and a whisper of "No". No one could replace Fath Ali in her heart.

On that fine spring day she was content. Zands were well known for their bravery and one of their Khans by the name of Karim was making a name for himself.

The caravan moved fast and suddenly from a distance the golden dome of Immam Reza's shrine twinkled like a huge moon. Seeing the Dome Sadegh Khan turned to his beloved mistress and said: "Shall I leave you now?"

"Yes, hurry Sadegh," she said bowing towards the shrine. [38]

Sadegh also made his bow to the shrine before galloping towards the city gate.

An hour later, the caravan was received by three well-groomed, handsome men standing by their horses next to Sadegh Khan. Khatoon's howdah (which she used for formal occasions) was carefully lowered to the ground. She turned her long legs that were hidden beneath the length of her black chador and stepped down. Her son kissed her hand that

---

[38] When on a pilgrimage as soon as the dome of the shrine becomes visible the pilgrim bows to the Immam.

protruded out from the fold of her chador. The two young men approached and bent their shapely heads in curtsy. Mohammad Hussain introduced them as Shahzadeh Reza Gholi and Nasrollah Mirza, sons of the Shahanshah [39] of Iran. Flattered, Khatoon smiled at the Shahzadehs happy for having had the foresight to bring two Arabian horses in case the need for Pishkesh [40] arose.

Nasrollah Mirza had come to take Khatoon to his mother's andaroon.

Nader's palace was nothing like Chehlsetoon. It was just a huge house with a beautiful garden. Nader had no taste for luxury living. He just loved to amass wealth. Not only did he not live in his palace for long, he changed camp frequently. Very few knew of his whereabouts. Now he had become suspicious of his own shadow.

At the Shah's andaroon Khatoon and Razieh Baygum met, embraced, shed tears of happiness and laughed at life's ups and downs. Out of respect for Reza Gholi who was Nader's heir, she invited the men to take tea with them. Khadijeh, to whom the two Afshars were namahram, was sent to the quarter designated for her mother. Two of the three men were namahram to Khatoon but she had her own interpretation of Islamic law. The boys seemed to be the same age as her son so she saw no harm in taking off her roobandeh in their presence. The young men exchanged meaningful glances and kept their gaze away from the stunning face that was smiling at them. Khatoon, forever alert, noticed their glances and smiled at their comradeship – not many royal step-brothers were friends.

Seated on the floor, reclining on comfortable cushions and enjoying the intimacy of camaraderie, the boys now feeling comfortable in the presence of the "Gift" (the name by which Tahmaseb had always referred to Khatoon behind her back) delved into a conversation that was far too complex for ordinary inhabitants of an andaroon. Reza Gholi had a keen interest in everything that concerned Iran. He knew Khatoon was in contact with the Russians and he wanted to hear her news.

In front of them, a short table inlaid with ivory was packed with trays of fresh almonds, still in their green skin and green sour plums – popular delicacies during spring. A servant arrived with a tray of tea

---

[39] King of kings
[40] Present

in gold-rimmed glasses. Minutes passed in small talk until Reza Gholi, oozing with pride, straightened his broad shoulders, turned his large black eyes to Khatoon and asked: "Baygum, are you aware that Daghestan has been added to our list of tributaries that now include India, Afghanestan, Bahrain and Mesopotamia?"

"Yes Shahzadeh. Your father is indeed a great conqueror," Khatoon replied with a smile. She had taken a liking to this tall and seemingly kind Shahzadeh and had he not been Nader's son, she would have wished to have him as a son in law.

The heir smiled back, arched his eyebrow and said: "Unfortunately, Russia stands in our way of expansion. We hear that their sovereign is a woman. We intend to increase our territory by crossing their borders. Do you know of the woman who reigns in Russia?"

"Yes Shahzadeh, I have heard of her. Our land is near their domain. We have to know what goes on there. I have learned that Russia has many factories making cannons, various artilleries and ships. Apparently their late Sultan Peter built a new city called St. Petersburg that has become the envy of Farangestan. [41] Russia has become very strong and Nader Shah would be wise to remain a friend rather than a foe of this ambitious neighbour."

Reza Gholi absorbed every word he heard, admired the knowledgeable lady (not the "Gift" any more) and said: "Thank you, Baygum, for your advice. I shall repeat all this to my father when he returns from his campaign. Mohammed Hussain also tells me you have dealings with foreigners in Iran."

"Yes, Shahzadeh, my involvement is with the Dutch East India Company. We trade with them. The revenue helps with the taxes the tribe pay. My contacts provide me with much foreign news. That pleases me more than the gains."

"Do you think as a preventive measure against any Russian aggression we should have a fleet on the Caspian?"

"That would be very wise, Shahzadeh. Their ships travel through our waters, mostly for trade purposes. But I am sure they are also armed."

Reza Gholi respected Khatoon's astuteness and made a mental note to use her advice once in power.

Khatoon never saw Reza Gholi again.

---

[41] Europe

Khadijeh, cheerful and vivacious, fell in love with the sophistication and security of city life. Her hostess took her to many luncheons during which she met interesting ladies, heard blind musicians play and saw dancers perform their art. Deep in her heart she wished she would never return to nomadic life again. Fortune was on her side. Well bred, soft spoken, and dignified she became a prize to win. Mothers with eligible sons could find no more suitable virgin than the Gajar beauty with bewitching, brown, almond-shaped eyes and interesting stories of "life in the wild". Marriage proposals were presented daily and ignored until the arrival of one which Khatoon could not refuse – that was from Karim Khan Zand, the youth she had heard so much about and who was now a senior commander in Nader's army.

Not much is known about the weddings of Mohammad Hussain and Khadijeh. Let it suffice that Khatoon left Mashhad a happy mother. Her daughter married a man who would become a king and her son married a woman who made him feel like a king.

Seasons changed, Iran grew larger and the people poorer. The nation mourned its youth and farmers went to bed hungry.

After a failed assassination attempt Nader's paranoia became incessant. His first victim was his innocent heir, Shahzadeh Reza Gholi whom he believed was involved with the assassination attempt. An executioner burnt those beautiful black eyes that had shone with intelligence and hope. Then the courtiers began to lose their tongues for the wrong word, their hands for the wrong gesture and their heads for possible contemplation of treason.

Chapter 3

On the night of the year 1742 (12th of Rabi Al Sani in the year 1155 Hejri) the people of Ashaghebash stood motionless under the starlit sky of the Turcoman Steppe, glaring intently at the star with two peeking eyes and a long divided tail. Terror glowed from their black slanted eyes. It seemed as though all things alive were in awe of the heavenly creature that maliciously blinked at them from above. The night was still. Even the insects seemed awestruck. Only the silver grey river roared. Suddenly an aged man turned his face from the star towards the yorts and shouted: "Allahverdi." Then remembering Allahverdi was almost deaf he ran to his yort, pushed the slit of the canvas away, burst in and shouted the name. An old man sitting cross-legged in front of a flickering lantern, was bent over the open Koran that lay on his lap. The intrusion disturbed his concentration. He calmly lifted up his white head and serenely looked at the panting caller.

"Allahverdi, there is a monster in the sky. Come and see if you recognize it."

The old man took the dry rose that lay on the carpet by his feet, put it between the pages of his Koran, courteously closed the holy book, kissed it, took it to his forehead, kissed it again and graciously placed it on its wooden stand. Then slowly he moved his unsteady hand to take his thick walking stick. The man gave him a helping hand. He rose with difficulty, grabbed the stick and leaning on it, limped out of his humble abode, into the expanse of the open where he was hit by the glare of the vile familiar star. His weak heart began to thump hard. Emotion gripped his chest. He stood still and took several deep breaths. His companion noticed the unease and asked:

"Allahverdi, is this the same tailed star you saw in your youth?"

"Yes son. It is Esrael [42] himself," replied the old man commencing his slow walk towards the crowd. Handfuls who saw

---

[42] Esrael is the angel of death.

them, rushed to make the same enquiry. Before the question was asked, the old man nodding, volunteered:

"Yes this is the Esrael I saw when I had gone through twenty springs. [43]"

"Allahverdi how many springs have you been through?" a man asked.

"God has granted me eight cycles. I have passed through 96 springs."

(The Gajars acknowledged the twelve animals of the Zodiac and thus calculated their age on the basis of twelve-year cycles. So when Allahverdi said he had gone through eight cycles and he had seen the star when he had gone through twenty springs, everybody understood that the tailed star had appeared 76 springs back. [44])

Allahverdi leaned on his stick and closed his eyes. Memories rushed back. Tears began rolling down his wrinkled face wetting his white beard. The past became vividly alive. He saw his children swept away by the flood, his wife dying of hunger and disease taking away his brothers. He wiped his tears with the edge of his wide sleeve and praying for the disappearance of the shining monster, limped back to his tent to resume the reading of his Koran.

From afar, the sound of galloping hooves stopped the whispers. Heads turned towards the sound. Under the moonlight they saw a thin black line approaching fast. Then figures emerged and a little boy sitting on the shoulder of his father shouted:

"It is the Khan."

The name was the magic needed to evaporate the panic. For them Mohammad Hassan had the key to all mysteries – worldly or heavenly. Wise and kind he had proved a leader to die for.

The nomads whose life is governed by the idiosyncrasies of nature know its dynamics intimately well. Their instinct is as acute as that of their animals and they can read and understand the patterns of nature as clearly as a literate can read and appreciate the verses of Omar Khayam. The sky was too clear and the star too bright for the liking of Mohammad Hassan. Apprehensive, he and his companions joined the crowd who were now chanting prayers; the power of which they hoped would dissolve the entity and save them from the disaster

---

[43] 21st of March is the first of spring, the new year of Iranian. In the absence of an official calender, the numbers of springs were calculated for recording purposes.

[44] The tailed star refers to Halley's comet.

foretold by Allahverdi.

That night Jayran and Khatoon were the only two individuals who had not set eyes on the star. Jayran, pale and perspiring, was in bed. Khatoon sat next to her, holding her hand and occasionally with a soft cloth wiped off the beads of sweat from her narrow forehead. The labour pains were intermittent but deep and painful. Then they became frequent. Biting her lips and digging her fingers into her palms Jayran began rolling from one side to the other. Khatoon calmly ordered the maid to bring a basin of hot water. A few minutes later two girls arrived carrying a large steaming basin with a strong smell of clove and placed it near Jayran's mattress. Khatoon told them to kneel down and lock Jayran's arms to the floor, and then she herself rolled her long sleeves up, knelt on the floor and expertly delivered her first grandchild. The girls washed the baby in the basin and swaddled him in the fine cotton cloth that had been prepared for him.

Finally dawn broke, the heavenly monster disappeared and the brooding nomads retired to their yorts to pray for safety. Perplexed and exhausted Mohammad Hassan stepped inside his yort. There his mother presented to him the greatest gift from God – a healthy son with a head full of black hair smelling of cloves. His panic faded, his exhaustion vanished and he was overwhelmed by joy. Proudly he gently took his son, looked at his face lovingly, held him tight and whispered into his ears the name of the Profit Mohammad.

The sun rose, the news spread and the cooks set to create their best. Celebration for life momentarily overcast the sense of omen that pervaded the compound. The birthday feast went past midnight when pregnant clouds gathered and hid the heavenly monster that had obstinately kept its stares on the pastures. Thunder broke out and lighting cut through the trees and crazed the beasts. Cries of fear joined the howl of the thunder. People ran to their yorts. A heavy rain began to fall. It poured for three days and nights. The river swelled, overflowed and turned into a cannibal. Panic broke out. People holding their children, or lambs, ran towards the hills. The old remained to die. Allahverdi kept reading his Koran until the water crushed his yort and swept him to eternity. The elders urged Mohammad Hassan to send his wife and baby to the house of Shaikh Mofid in Astarabad. Hastily a howdah was assembled on a horse, two mules were loaded with the rudimentary requirements and two strong men were chosen to lead the caravan that included Jayran's maid.

Jayran hugged and kissed Khatoon and then with the help of her maid tied Mohammad to her chest and sat on the howdah. Mohammad Hassan took her hand, squeezed it tightly and said:

"You take care of yourself and my son for me. In Astarabad keep a low profile and don't venture out of the andaroon unless necessary. Keep in mind that the governor of Astarabad is appointed by Nader. If you take one wrong step he might think you are there plotting against the Shah. And you know what Nader does with his enemies." He remembered his father's head on the floor and shivered. The wind became more violent and the rain too heavy. Jayran could not take her eyes away from her husband. He was her life. Keeping her voice from cracking she said:

"Rest assured that I shall not be an embarrassment or danger to you – my Khan!"

The assurance momentarily soothed his agitated mind. They were living in dangerous times. For power, sons were plotting against their fathers and fathers were blinding their sons. The phrase "tax or head" was a reality that petrified those who could not pay and now Mohammad Hassan had become one of them.

He looked deep into his wife's wet eyes, felt her sadness, kissed her hand and rushed back to help the evacuation. Khatoon came closer to the howdah, gently stroked the swaddled baby and said:

"Jayran, take good care of my grandchild. Do not trust anyone except Shaik Mofid. Use common sense in all endeavours and remember we all love you dearly."

Jayran swallowed the lump in her throat and nodded her small head in compliance. The two women gazed at each other with tenderness – both miserable, both courageous and both unconditionally devoted to their family.

The thunder roared, the rain lashed hard and the caravan swayed away in mud.

At Astarabad the entrance of a female on a howdah accompanied by two rifled Turcomen and a maid caused the precise excitement Mohammad Hassan Khan wished to avoid. Only the wealthy could travel thus. So who was this woman? And what was she doing in Astarabad? This was the question on everyone's lips including that of Sabez Ali Baik – the Governor of Astarabad. To satisfy his curiosity, he sent a messenger to Shaikh Mofid saying that he wished his sogoli to pay a visit to his andaroon's new entrant.

The baffled Shaikh had no choice but to offer an invitation.

Two days later Sabez Ali Baik's wife met Jayran and was so taken by her warmth, sense of humour and beauty that upon her return she had nothing but praise for her. Sabez Ali Baik became inquisitive. He ordered his wife to send her eunuch to invite the lady to tea.

Early in the afternoon of the visit the Governor, unseen, sauntered into an unobtrusive corner and waited. A few of his daughters appeared and disappeared, a hurrying eunuch carried a jar of pomegranate juice to the reception hall and then the head eunuch, escorting Jayran rustling in her full length tribal skirt without a roobandeh, passed him leaving behind a trail of jasmine fragrance. Suddenly Sabez Ali Baik's forever icy heart melted. He had never set eyes on such beauty and so much grace. Her shapely head was covered by a white muslin scarf over which she wore a green felt hat bordered with gold coins that trembled over her forehead. Her cheekbones were high, her nose small and straight, her lips cherry red and her eyes so black and so large that one could not look into them without trembling with desire. Bedazzled, he could not leave the andaroon while she was still there. So tiptoeing through a maze of halls and openings, he found another corner from where he could watch her. He gazed at her heaving breast and long ivory neck. He listened to her soft voice and deep sighs. He learnt of their affliction and smiled at destiny for putting the Khan under his mercy.

As soon as Jayran rose to leave, he ran to his office, called the tax collector and commanded him to go to Astarabad and demand the annual tax.

"Sire, it is not the time yet."

"Obey my order or your head will be sent to the Shah."

Then Sabez Ali Baik wrote a letter to his powerful friend, Mirza Mehdi Astarabadi, Nader's personal secretary, asking him to deny the Khan of the Gajars an audience with the Shah should he come to ask for one.

That night, in his dream Sabez Ali Baik took Jayran with the passion of the gods. In the morning his bed sheets were stained by love juice. That day the first thing Sabez Ali Baik did was to call for his pimp; an old woman by the name of Zobaydeh.

In the same afternoon, unexpected, Zobaydeh, chadored in her usual black arrived at the andaroon of Shaikh Mofid carrying a large silver dish of Baghlava for Jayran Baygum from the Governor's wife. She was guided to the reception room of the andaroon where Jayran was feeding her baby. Zobaydeh bowed, put the dish down and sat next to the Khan's wife. An eunuch brought tea and the two exchanged customary social trivialities until Zobaydeh, knitting her thick brows said:

"Baygum, you are a beautiful woman. I wonder why your husband has sent you here." She paused for a reaction. None came, only Jayran's shoulders stiffened.

"Baygum, men are awful creatures."

Blood rushed into Jayran's face. She handed Mohammad to her maid to take him to bed and then looked the pimp straight in the eyes daring her to come out with whatever was in her mind.

Now Zobaydeh frowned, brought her scarfed head towards Jayran's ear and murmured:

"Perhaps he wants to take another wife."

Jayran could no longer maintain her composure. She straightened her back, lifted her head high, brought a tight frown to her forehead and said:

"Khanum [45], I forbid you to talk to me in this manner. For your knowledge we have been sent here because my son is less than a week old and could have died had we remained at our compound. Flood has destroyed almost everything we have and my people are distraught. With us here the Khan can manage the situation with one less worry. Finally if my husband ever decides to take another wife it will be with my consent. We are not only man and wife we are also partners for life."

Aghast the pimp gathered her wits, raised a brow and said:

"Baygum, I am going to be frank with you. I am here on behalf of the Governor himself and not his wife. He is enamoured by you. Will you make him a happy man, even if it is for just one night?"

Jayran's face went purple, her heart filled with disgust and her fury beyond control. Had she had her dagger nearby it would have been already in the chest of the insolent bitch. Trembling hard she turned to the two eunuchs standing by the door and ordered them to usher the woman out of her sight. As the two stocky men walked towards Zobaydeh she started screaming. At that moment Shaik Mofid walked into the andaroon and saw his youngest wife pushing open the door

---

[45] Lady

to the reception room. Agitated he followed her into the room where they found Jayran and a struggling old woman held by two eunuchs. Out of respect for the Shaik the eunuchs stopped struggling with the old woman who suddenly fell silent. Jayran still trembling recounted the discourse. Colour vanished from the Shaik's face and his jaw dropped. He had been like a father to Mohammad Hassan. Biting his lower lip he pondered for a second then ordered the eunuchs to release the old woman. He withdrew two gold Naderi coins from his pocket, took her hand and put them on her sticky palm. The feel of the gold gave her eternal joy. She closed her fingers, withdrew her hand and plunged it into the wide pocket of her vest. She cast a venomous glance at Jayran, pulled down her roobandeh, bent and took her chador from the floor, put it on her head, held two edges of the chador between her crooked teeth and ran out of the andaroon.

The Sheikh sighed heavily, turned to Jayran who was pale in the face and said:

"Sabez Ali Baik is a shameless, notorious fox. He will not give up easily."

"He does not know me."

"Obviously not and he must have used this pimp often enough to have confidence in her craft."

"I am not afraid of this man. My fear is for you. I will write to my husband to send men to protect your house from him."

"No. That would be disastrous. If any of your men enter Astarabad he will make Nader believe that a conspiracy is contemplated and the Shah will turn his wrath upon me and your husband."

"Nader has already turned against us. Otherwise he would not have demanded 5000 gold Naderi."

"He has demanded that from all the chieftains. Nader has gone mad. If his suspicion is aroused, which will be by Sabez Ali Baik, he will have the tribe massacred without a moment of hesitation."

"Well. What do you suggest then?"

"You should leave immediately."

"If I go the Governor will punish you."

"No. I will tell him that I had no power to stop the wife of Mohammad Hassan Khan from returning to her husband. This is the truth and he will have to accept it."

"All right then, could you please send for packers. [46]

The governor was at his office when news arrived that packers were heading for the Shiekh's residence. He realized his prey was about to flee. To stop her he had to kidnap her.

At dawn Jayran put on her riding gear and sheepskin vest and quietly walked to the courtyard where the packers and the loaded mules were waiting. She had her maid securely fasten her swaddled infant to her back. Then she adjusted her long rifle and two pistol cases that were fixed firmly on her leather belt beneath the folds of her vest, before climbing on her hired horse and leading her small caravan towards home.

They had just crossed into the Turcoman zone when the leader of the packers saw moving black spots on the horizon. Shading his eyes with his hand he stared at the shapes that grew larger and larger. Pale with fear he yelled: "Turcoman bandits." Immediately the two men jumped off their horses, took out their knives and began to cut the ropes that bounded the loads to their mules. Now they could clearly see the bandits. Time was running out; it was either their life or their mules. Cursing their luck they left the mules with their loads hanging from the ropes, jumped on their horses, galloped away and then within a safe distance halted to watch.

The sight of five approaching Turcomen did not frighten Jayran or her maid for they knew no Turcoman would harm them. Once the riders came within hearing distance Jayran shouted: "Hey, Hey, Hey, Doghan (Chief) I am the wife of Mohammad Hassan Khan Gajar. Please turn back so that my packers will lose their fear and return to me."

Her words were lost in the sound of approaching hooves. She repeated herself to no avail. Then she noticed the men's faces were covered. Turcomen never disguised their faces. Instinctively she pulled out her pistol, aimed at the face of the closest and pulled the trigger. The bullet hit the man's forehead throwing him off his horse. Calmly she placed the empty pistol in its colt and pulled the other one out, aimed at the heart of the next man and sent him to hell.

---

[46] Those days packing luggage to be assembled on horse or mule back was a specialized job. The packers, skilled in their profession knew exactly how much weight they could wrap around the animals. The night before the journey the rope was tied around the bundles and then on the day of departure the bundles were secured in perfect balance on the back of the animals. The packers accompanied the traveller to his or her destination and then returned home with their mules.

Quickly she fitted the pistol in its case and drew out her rifle, turned to her right; aimed, pulled the trigger and killed the group leader. As he fell the other two pulled their horses' reins, swung round and fled. Jayran waited until they became spots on the horizon. Then she sent a silent prayer, relaxed her frown, turned her hand to her back and gently patted the tiny head of her crying son. The maid jumped off her horse and ran towards the mules. Jayran secured the rifle in its case before joining her.

The packers returned, dismounted and stood tongue-tied. Jayran threw them an icy glance, spat towards them and ordered her servant to uncover the faces of the dead men. To regain favour the two rushed to the corpses, pushed the maid aside and removed what was left of any covers. One man's face was completely blown out but the other two were recognized to be employees of the Governor.

Jayran's quick mind perceived Sabez Ali Baik's plot. She had to hurry home. So she left her maid in charge of the packers and rode home as fast as she could.

At the fortress of Mubarakabad an anticipating Sabez Ali Baik waited with a great bulge hidden within the pleats of his pantaloons. The knock on the door of his office produced a delicious feeling in his loins. He smiled. The bulge grew harder.

"Enter," He said softly.

The door burst open and the two servants rushed in, fell on their knees and began to sob.

The bulge faded. Excitement turned into rage. He stood up, took a couple of steps, lifted his right foot and began kicking the two wretched souls who quickly grabbed their heads with both hands. He kicked and kicked until exhausted. Breathless he collapsed on the cushion on the floor. A morbid silence encompassed the room. Sabez Ali Baik took some deep breaths and then made each of the bleeding men recount the story of their failure to catch one single woman. His anger reignited, he called for his guard and ordered him to take the men to the torture room to be falaked [47]. Fuming he went to his bedchamber, banged the door and remained there for two days. Plot after plot crossed his crooked mind. Eventually he convinced himself of his own invincibility. He returned to work and soon received news that the

---

[47] Falak was a widely used punishment. The punished was laid on the floor with his legs set between the falak instrument and then the soles of the feet were beaten by a thin stick that sometimes cut through the skin.

Gajar was on his way to Mashhad. He roared with laughter.

The compound of the Ashagehbash was in a sorrowful state. The river had retreated leaving behind broken tree trunks, collapsed yorts and corpses half buried in the mud. Only a few lambs, a handful of goats and some horses were grazing at the foothills where water had not ruined the grass. Erect yorts were few and their occupants in black. The only activity was digging graves. Khatoon was sitting on a large stone with many orphans at her feet trying hard to understand what she was reading to them. Jayran, unwilling to disturb the lesson quietly stood behind her waiting for the end of the session. A little girl saw her and called out her name.

Khatoon turned her head and saw Jayran with Mohammed tied to her back. Surprised she rose, dismissed the children and opened her arms to which Jayran ran. They kissed and Jayran asked for her husband and was told he had gone to Mashhad to ask Nader for time as the tax man had come asking for their dues earlier this year than previous years. Jayran asked Khatoon to untie Mohammad from her back. Once Mohammad was settled in his grandmorther's arms, Jayran stretched her back a couple of times and then following Khatoon to her make-shift yort, hurriedly recounted all that had happened. The two concluded that Sabez Ali Baik's connivance was involved with the early tax demand. To warn her husband she immediately wrote him a letter and gave it to their fastest courier to deliver.

Mohammad Hassan Khan had arrived at a capital devoid of its sovereign and his secretary. In the Shah's absence the affairs were handled by the capital's unpopular Governor; Ali Gholi Mirza, Nader's young nephew. Mohammad Hassan was told all applicants for a royal audience had to meet with the Governor or else wait indefinitely. Mohammad Hassan had not as yet decided what to do when Jayran's letter arrived. That made his mind up.

At the compound he found Sabez Ali Baik's second emissary waiting for him. As a precautionary step against bribes or murder, tax collectors moved in small groups. But this time only Lotfali Ghezelvag, a stocky, bearded man, known to Mohammad Hassan had come alone. Exhausted, dusty and hungry the Khan met and received him in his yort. Lotfali usually looked confident and haughty but today he was pale and listless. He kept fidgeting with his long calloused fingers and biting his lips. This surprised Mohammad Hassan and made him apprehensive. Calmly he asked the cause of the man's return.

Twice in one year was highly unusual. Lotfali bent his head fixed his gaze on the patterns of the Turcoman Kilm and said:

"Khan, I am a good Moslem, and I know you are one too. I cannot deceive you so I am going to tell you the truth. You have to save your tribe from retribution and there is only one way to do that."

"Enlighten me good man?"

"You have something the Governor wants badly."

"What may that be?"

"Your wife, Khan."

Mohammad Hassan's face crimsoned. His long moustache quivered. The veins in his temple began to throb. He wished for the earth to open and swallow him alive.

Outside the wind stopped blowing, the pole of the tent stopped rattling and a deadly silence befell the yort. The Khan lifted his proud head up, looked into the pitying eyes of the tax collector and said:

"Go in peace and tell your master, when the time comes, he can have my head but he will never have my wife."

Jayran, who had been listening to the conversation from behind the yort waited until the messenger left and then entered, took her husband's hand and kissed it several times. The man, his pride bruised, fatigued by travel, bent under the heavy burden of responsibility, remained frozen for a while and then took his hand away, put it around the slender waist of his wife, drew her close and hugged her tight. He plunged his head into her long wavy hair and burst into tears. She remained still, her heart bleeding, her mind racing for a solution. Then she cupped her husband's face between her palms and kissed his quivering lips. They remained locked in love and desperation. She withdrew, looked into his black eyes and said:

"Sabez Ali Baik is a man devoid of conscience and decency. He will stop at nothing. He will flame Nader's anger against us. He will make Nader believe that you have become rebellious and you know what becomes of Nader's enemies."

"I will fight until I am killed."

"That won't solve any problems. With you killed, they will slaughter all our men and send the women and the children to the slave market."

"You talk as if there is a way out?"

"Yes. We must go to the North and stay with the Yamuts [48]. They

---

[48] Yamuts were a Turcoman tribe friendly to the Ashaghebash. Their mountainous

will help us."

"I have nothing to offer them. We shall have no means of sustenance."

"We will take the horses and the sheep and ask them for a loan of livestock. They trust you and know that you will repay them. We must go before winter starts and Sabez Ali Baik has time to organize an army."

That afternoon Mohammad Hassan Khan met with Khatoon and the counsel of the elders. Dawn had not yet broken when the yorts were dismantled, mules were loaded and a long moving line wriggled through the pastures towards the north. Khatoon and Sadegh Khan took the opposite direction. She had decided to go to Semnan and lodge at an old fortress she had inherited from her father.

River Atrak roared in solitude, the wind blew away the debris and the only sign of life that remained were the pole marks of the yorts that would fill in shortly and the manure of the animals that would be washed away by autumn rains.

The Yamuts were already at their winter compound when the Ashaghebash joined them. The elders of the two tribes met, shook hands and agreed to lend Mohammad Hassan the number of horses and sheep he asked for. Akbar Khan, with five unmarried daughters, saw great opportunity in helping the young and handsome Gajar Khan and in time made sure the Khan and his wife knew what was expected of him. Mohammad Hassan loved Jayran and did not want to hurt her. Jayran knew this so one fine day when the two had returned from a successful deer hunt and were resting under a wild fig tree, she took his hand, kissed it, put it on her heart, looked deep into his eyes and said:

"My love, this beats only for you." Then she put her own hand on his heart and shyly asked: "Does this beat for me or the Khan's eldest daughter?"

Mohammad Hassan, took her hand that was still on his heart, took it to his parted lips, kissed it, licked it and kissed it again and then looked into Jayran's expectant eyes and said: "You are the love of my life, the light of my sight and the mother of my son. My heart will always beat for you."

"Then take the Yamut girl as a second wife."

---

domain was hard to access.

"I was scared you would not like that."

"I like what helps you and our people."

Mohammad Hassan, his heart lightened by the proposition, stretched his arms and Jayran crept into them. They kissed and kissed and made love to their hearts' desire. One week later a grand wedding cemented the union. Jayran dignified it with a smile that hid her inner turmoil, participated as 'the most important wife', and when the couple retired for zafaf[49] she took out a folded handkerchief from her pocket, and from its midst took a tiny opium pill, popped it in her mouth, sipped at her tea and then rose and walked to her yort hoping for a dreamless sleep.

In spite of having to share her husband with a younger woman, the years spent among the Yamuts were the happiest, most tranquil period of Jayran's life. Their first spring saw their sheep and horses multiply. This they took as a good omen. During their first summer they learnt how to farm corn and wheat.

They worked all day long till their eyes could see no more and then under the light of a lantern Jayran taught Mohammad how to read, write and calculate; how to use his power of rationality; how to keep his counsel and never put himself at the mercy of others. On Fridays she taught him how to ride, shoot and hunt. By setting an example she trained him to become disciplined, precise and frugal, all qualities required by the mobility and precariousness of their nomadic life. She also taught him how to listen to nature, read its signs, enjoy its beauty and be grateful for its bounty. To her delight Mohammad proved to be a worthy student. She admired his quick mind, agility and particularly his charisma. There was something awesome about her boy that at times startled her. He talked little but listened hard. He was inquisitive and keen to learn. He hardly ever lost a game and when he did he applied himself till he mastered the skill. He was hard on himself but kind to others. His peers obeyed and followed him without question. He was a born leader and that frightened Jayran. Rulers of the time took tall puppies as hostage and castrated them so that they would not be fit to contest their power. Jayran had a great sense of premonition about Mohammad. She never forgot the night he was born and she tried to protect him, the way she protected everyone else. People of Yamut loved her and cared for her with tenderness while she was

---

[49] Copulation

pregnant with her second son, to be named Hussain Gholi. Sometimes Mohammad Hassan had to leave the Yamuts and in his absence motherhood did not prevent Jayran from running the affairs of the tribe with an iron fist. Gradually they became prosperous enough to clear their debt and remain proud owners of hundreds of horses and sheep.

Four years passed peacefully until Khatoon's messenger brought news of Nader's demise. At first no one believed the messenger because not even God dared to oppose Nader. Such creature could never die. But he had – after all he was just a man like other men with a beginning and an end.

On a Sunday night, in the spring of the year 1160, 1747 four men, three Afshar and Mohammad Baik Gajar had, under cover of darkness, crept into Nader's tent at Fathabad in Ghochan, cut his head off and killed his young wife Setareh who was sharing his bed. The hatred for Nader was so deep that his death was celebrated. His head on the top of a spear was put on exhibit until its stench became too offensive. The soldiers joined the collaborators. The master mind of the plot, Ali Gholi Mirza, replaced his uncle and chose to call himself Adel Shah (the Just King). His first act was to break into the Kalan fortress and ransack its treasures. Then he had Nader's sons and grandchildren with the exception of Shahrokh Mirza killed.

To buy himself popularity he announced a two year tax exemption. This delighted the nation.

It was past midnight when the guards at Khatoon's fortress heard rapid knocks. Khatoon heard the knocks too. She got out of bed and tiptoed to the window of her chamber. Down below, the open gate was lit by the lantern of her guard. Amongst the riders she recognized Mohammad Baik. "Bad news!" she thought.

Quickly she put on her cloak and ran down the stairs into her reception hall. Her personal maid was already there. The sound of approaching footsteps increased her premonition. Suddenly the heavy door opened and Sadegh Khan entered, bowed and said: "Baygum, it is Mohammad Baik come to deliver good news,"

"Good news! What a surprise, usher him in Sadegh," she said smiling.

The eunuch left and returned accompanied by Mohammad Baik, grey with dust, and another dusty man carrying a large leather bag that smelled foul. The men bowed and the one with the bag put the trophy on the ground in front of Khatoon, and stepping backward left the room. Khatoon covered her nose with her hand. The stench was stomach-churning. Mohammad Baik, his sun-tanned face beaming came forward and said:

"Baygum, justice has prevailed again. It was done to him what he did to my cousin."

Completely disoriented Khatoon asked, "What do you mean Khan Aziz?"

Mohammad Baik crouched and untied the neck of the leather bag. The stench exploded making every face purple with revulsion.

"Look inside, Baygum."

"Khatoon, now covering her nose with the edge of her long sleeve stooped her long neck over the sack and what she saw brought bile to her mouth. She hurried to the open window, put her head out and threw up. Sadegh Khan ran to his lady, took a handkerchief out of his pocket and with both hands offered it to her. She took the cloth, wiped her mouth, muttered her thanks and turned to her guest.

Moments passed in silence. Memories raced in Khatoon's head. So much had happened since she wished for vengeance. Now finally her husband's spirit would rest in peace. But she thought the head was so grotesque and so telling of human cruelty that it made her ashamed for ever having wished for it. Time had mellowed her and now all she wanted was peace.

A triumphal smile tilted on the handsome face of Mohammad Baik who was eagerly waiting for his reward. Expectation blazed from his slanted narrow eyes. All his life he had loved this woman – patiently waiting for the time she would be ready to accept his offer of marriage. The sole reason for his participation in Nader's murder was to win her gratitude.

Khatoon knew he loved her. She loved him too – but as a brother. Forever perceptive she saw in his shining eyes that he was waiting for the only reward she could never be able to give him – herself. So she turned to Sadegh and said,

"Bury the head where no one can ever find it."

Then she turned her sad eyes to Mohammad Baik and with a gesture of her hand invited him to join her in sitting on the cushions that were laid on the floor against the white-washed wall of the room. The gloom in her eyes hurt the hopeful man. His heart tightened, and a lump began to swell in his throat. Yet he endeavored to control his emotions – albeit with difficulty.

"Now cousin, tell me what happened," she said, gently stroking his knee and looking at him with eyes that gleamed with gratitude. He made himself comfortable, crossed his legs and meticulously divulged all that had happened. She listened intently, the expression on her face changing from surprise, to anger, to revulsion and then to calm. The calm momentarily encompassed the room until Khatoon bent towards Mohammad Baik, took his right hand and kissed it. He shivered.

"God made you an instrument of justice. I am indebted to you to my dying day. In fact now I don't mind dying."

"Baygum, don't talk of death. Now with all scores settled you must start living again. I have my share of Kalan loot. That will be yours should you honour me with your hand in marriage." Khatoon expecting and dreading this request avoided his gaze. Mohammad Baik was like a father to her children. He had buried Mohammad Hussain when he had died in the first battle with India. He had always been there for her. She owed him much gratitude but she could never love him or any other man.

She lifted her head up, looked into his eyes and said:

"You have honoured me cousin by your offer. I have always admired and respected you but I cannot marry you for my heart will always belong to Fath Ali."

Mohammad Baik felt a rush of blood to his face, a throb of pain in his wrinkled forehead and a burning sensation in his brave heart. He bent his dusty head, with his gaze tracing the patterns of the Tabriz carpet. A sad silence encompassed the room. Khatoon saw that he was crying. She crept close to him, put her hands around his shaking shoulders, pulled him to herself and kissed his smudged graying head. He hugged her, put his head on her thin chest and for a moment felt her warmth. She let him be. Then he collected himself, freed her from his hold, looked deep into her tearful eyes and said.

"Azizam, my life is at your disposal. I will remain your servant forever."

"You remain the brother I never had, Mohammad Baik Aziz."

At the compound of the Yamuts, the council of the elders decided to return to their own compound by the river. However, before taking such an important step they had to find out if Sabez Ali Baik had managed to win the new Shah's favour and maintained his post or he had been ousted. To this end Allahverdi Oghlo volunteered to go to Astarabad. The trip caused much excitement amongst the women who wanted tokens from the town. They pleaded with Allahverdi Oghlo, who succumbed to their demands as he could not bear to see female tears. To make sure he would not forget anyone's request he had asked Jayran to make a list which he intended to hand to someone who could read in the bazaar.

The dew had turned into mist when Allahverdi Oghlo and his young son, in their sheepskin coats and hats set out for Astarabad. They rode non-stop, careful at mountain curves and careless across the pastures. The path was so familiar that they could traverse it asleep on horseback. But this time nostalgia kept them wide awake. When the sun left its domain to the light of the moon they camped by a creek, washed their faces, relinquished their thirst by handfuls of the fresh water and munched at their feta wraps. They found the direction to Ghebleh [50] through navigating the stars and stood to pray. The air was cold, the wind cutting and the howl of the wolves loud. Allah thanked, they spread their horse covers on the grass, put their heads on their saddles and slept a sleep full of enchanting dreams. The chill of the dawn woke them. They washed in the creek, prayed, ate their yogurt mixed with honey and set off. At sunset they arrived at their old empty compound and set up camp by the river. Khatoon's prayer room, a humble monument of love for Allah, stood empty. Its open door creaked every time a breeze fondled it. Father and son, tears running down their manly weather-beaten cheeks, took off their heavy shoes and woollen socks and using water from the river performed their ablution. Then they went inside the prayer room, faced the Ghebleh and prayed to Allah for keeping their pastures empty of usurpers.

Early morning the following day they went to Astarabad where they found out that Sabez Ali Baik was indeed very secure in his position. Disheartened they walked to the busy bazaar that was loaded by provisions of all kinds in open sacks, rolls of raw cotton and colourful silks, trays of gold bangles, earrings, necklaces and coins. Awestruck by the excitement surrounding them they hurriedly found a literate man willing to help for a brass coin and commenced their bargaining with stall owners. From a short distance a dignified man in his fifties wearing an expensive sheepskin hat which indicated his social

---

[50] The house of God in Mecca towards which Muslems stand to pray.

prominence, heard their Turkish accent and from their slanting eyes and sun burnt skins recognized their ethnic background. A cunning smile lit his bearded tranquil face and an idea immediately formulated in his active mind. Heaven had provided him with the opportunity he had been waiting for – to retrieve his state that Sabez Ali Baik had confiscated for himself – without his personal involvement. So with calculated steps he approached the Gajars and addressed the older of the two.

"Are you from Ashaghebash?"

Allahverdi Oghlo politely answered: "Yes we are, sire."

"Do you know Mohammad Hassan Khan?"

"Which Mohammad Hassan Khan?"

"I mean the chief of your tribe."

Suddenly Allahverdi Oghlo's antenna detected danger. He hesitated to gauge the identity of the stranger. Suspicion flickered out of his black eyes. Cautiously he assessed the stranger from top to toe, and then glanced across his shoulder at the two servants standing behind him. He noticed one of them was holding a hookah and the other an enamelled box. This meant the stranger was a man of substance. So politely he replied,

"Yes I do know Mohammad Hassan Khan. Sire, since you are inquiring about my Khan may I know your name so that I can tell him who asked after his health?"

"I am Mirza Mehdi Astarabadi the personal secretary of Nader and now Adel Shah. Good man, your chief would have heard of me."

Short of an answer Allahverdi Oghlo began to play with his long white beard, turned his gaze to the ground and cursed his luck.

Mirza Mehdi smiled at the nomad's prudence and continued:

"I know you have left your compound and I think it is time for you to return to it."

"Not while Sabez Ali Baik is still the Governor. He is our enemy, sire."

"I know that but at the moment he does not enjoy the Shah's favour and would not dare to take a step without His Majesty's consent."

"He is a conniving man. He will find a way."

"Not while I have the Shah's ears, good man. And I have no love for your Governor."

The words lightened the nomad's heart and brought a large grin to his narrow dry mouth.

He raised his hands to the sky and said: "Sire, it is the God's will that I have met you. I shall tell my chief, that you have said not to have any fear of the Governor and that God willing we can return to our land and till it now that we know how."

"Have you acquired new skills, good man?"

"Yes sire, now we know how to cultivate and not just rely on our flock."

"Good so prosperity awaits you. You hurry back and tell your chief that I am his friend and will help him against his enemy when need be. I leave for Mashhad tomorrow. I live at the palace where my offices are and your chief can reach me there without any appointment or wait."

Allahverdi Oghlo knelt by the perceived saviour and kissed his foot. Mirza Mehdi unaccustomed to such obeisance, slightly bent, took hold of the nomad's hand and gently helped him to rise.

Upon arrival at home Allahverdi Oghlo went straight to his chief and delivered his news. As they listened the people of Ashagehbash felt their hearts fill with joy and their bright glimmering eyes moisten with tears of happiness. Only one person felt uneasy and that was Jayran. Something in the recess of her vigilant mind was warning that there would be a price to pay for the assistance of a man who was neither kin nor a friend.

Mohammad Hassan Khan valued his wife's nuance and in the meeting that followed he asked her opinion on the matter. Jayran contemplated for a while and then said:

"Mirza Mehdi is a clever courtier. He would never offer to help anyone unless there was something in it for him. At the moment it suits us to follow his advice. In time we will learn of his intentions. If they are honourable we have gained a friend. If they are self-serving we will take preventative measures. However to protect ourselves against Sabez Ali Baik's plots, to show our respect for Adel Shah and to test Mirza Mehdi's loyalty we should ask him to obtain for us a royal decree reconfirming our ancestral right to our pastures." Jayran's proposal was so sound that immediately a letter was written to Mirza Mehdi and the scroll was given to Allahverdi Oghlo to deliver. That evening, men, women and children of Ashaghebash celebrated the opportunity to return to their ancestral land where their root was, from where their identity sprang out and where they wanted to be buried.

In Mashhad Mirza Mehdi received Allahverdi Oghlo without any delay and gave him what he had come for. As the Shah's personal secretary he wrote all his letters but he gave the Ashaghebash letter to his assistant to write. The official procedure was to write two documents – one to be sent to the governor of the province and the other to be given to the recipient of the decree. Needless to say that the decree infuriated Sabez Ali Baik and because the hand-writing was not Mirza Mehdi's he wondered how Mohammad Hassan Khan had been able to access the Shah. Jayran was still under his skin. It was good that she was going to come out of hiding and be within his realm. Now he had to find a way to get rid of her husband for good. A Royal decree absolutely forbade any act of aggression against the Gajars. However, if Mohammad Hassan Khan participated in any form of violence the same decree that had given him freedom to return to his land would condemn him to death. He could not accuse the Ashaghebash of being bandits. They were too respectable and the accusation unbelievable. Since the taxes were banned for two years he could not accuse him of tax evasion either – what then? Immediately a plan came to his crooked mind.

Up in the north, Ashaghebash decided to go through winter with their Yamut brethren and migrate to their land in early spring. That winter passed swiftly and nature's rejuvenation promised prosperity. The pregnant sheep confined their lambs and the jubilant tribe packed their seeds, dismantled their yorts, organized their flock and horses, carefully dropped the lambs into special fluffy sacks and tied the sacks to their mules. The hustle and bustle of the migration was both happy and sad. Deep friendships had been formed and mixed marriages had united the Yamuts and the Ashaghebash. All knew the interest of the tribe superseded that of the individual and returning to Astarabad was of crucial importance for the perpetuity of the Gajars. Eventually happy for some and unhappy for others, the caravan commenced its slow move waggling through the hazardous mountain paths towards the plains and their beloved river.

Patiently days turned into night and nights to days until they arrived by the shores of their river. This time they erected their yorts on the foothills and left the exposed fertile shore land for cultivation. The area became alive once more. Women and men worked side by side. Khans and ordinary folks shared the same rights to comfort, happiness and peaceful existence.

Mohammad Hassan, to expand his power and influence took more wives from amongst neighbouring tribes. But Jayran remained the apple of his eye. The expansion of his influence made the

Yokharibash Davalu chief envious. In spite of the fact that they had always coveted the more fertile land of down river they could not annex it while the Ashaghebash were in hiding. The annexation would have been counted as an appropriation, and an ignoble act amongst tribes. Now that Mohammad Hassan was back and yet not as powerful as before, with a good deal of encouragement from Sabez Ali Baik, they decided to fight him for his land. So they moved down river and began settling their women, children and animals in a camp away from the scene of confrontation. An Ashaghebash shepherd spotted them. He ran to inform his chief.

Bewildered, Mohammad Hassan ordered his men to mobilize. Swiftly farming tools were stored away and rifles taken up. Horses were saddled; animals and children were gathered and placed under supervision of the elderly. Commanders met and defence plans were formulated. Before joining the others Mohammad Hassan led Jayran to the edge of the river, their favourite spot, stole a quick kiss from her narrow forehead, looked into her questioning eyes with everlasting tenderness and said,

"Tonight I might not return. I want you to accept the responsibilities of the chieftain of the Ashaghebash until my son Mohammad becomes of age. People of our tribe love, respect and trust you. If I die there will be no one else but you to lead them."

Jayran trusted her sense of premonition and today she felt no fear.

"My love you will return and lead the tribe through better times."

Mohammad Hassan Khan took a few steps closer to her. He wanted to inhale her sweet smell and lock it in his nostrils as the elixir that would give him the will to survive. Jayran's perception was so acute that she often guessed what was going on in his mind. Unconsciously she gravitated towards him, took his face between her palms and kissed his lips. The warm energy exuded by their passion intertwined and evaporated all Mohammad Hassan's bad thoughts. She smiled and withdrew her hands. He fixed his dark eyes on her and softly ordered:

"For the sake of the tribe and our children I forbid you to engage in any physical confrontation."

Jayran straightened her back, raised a black arched brow and with a voice tinged with defiance objected,

"Are you telling me that if the enemy attack our yorts and want to take our sheep and horses I must surrender?"

"If I am killed the enemy will not attack the yorts. My death will give them what they want."

Jayran took her husband's rough hands, took them to her mouth and kissed them several times before saying:

"You are a good man. But others are not like you. I hope this will never happen. But if you are killed the enemy will come for our livestock so that our people are left with nothing and hunger will force them to disperse. That would mean the end of Ashaghebash. That I am sure is not what you want. Therefore I will fight them until I am killed too."

Mohammad Hassan had never lost his temper with his wife before, but now tension and insecurity had eroded his self-control. For the first time in his life he raised his voice and asked,

"What will happen to my children if you are killed?"

"Mohammad Baik will take our children to your mother. Khatoon will look after them better than I can. And your other sons will have their own mothers."

Mohammad Hassan Khan could not argue against logic. He abated his annoyance, gave her one last look of reprimand mixed with affection, took her into his arms, kissed her forehead and in pensive silence they walked back to their sons. The boys smiled at their father and Mohammad said: "God keep you safe for us, Baba." Mohammad Hassan crouched to his son's height, gazed at him with eyes that glowed with pride and said,

"God is on the side of the righteous, my son. We are defending our land and God willing we will be alive to see the moon shine again."

The boy, only ten, standing erect looked so imperious that his father could not stop himself from hugging him. Mohammad, embarrassed by this sign of affection, pulled himself off his hold, looked into his surprised eyes and said,

"Baba, rest assured I will look after mother and my brothers in your stead."

The Khan rose, patted his son on the shoulder and said: "I am sure you will, azizam. God save you for us all."

"Thank you father – I am glad you have confidence in me." Jayran admiring her son's sense of responsibility, looked at her husband and smiled with pride.

The confrontation did not last long and the Khan managed to defeat the enemy and secure peace and prestige for his tribe.

The news made Khatoon happy, Sabez Ali Baik furious and Mirza Mehdi expectant. The Shah's secretary, calculating and perceptive, immediately hurled dispatches to neighbouring Turcoman tribes with the message that should Mohammad Hassan Khan become involved in another conflict it was their blood duty to support him. One of his messengers crossed paths with that of Sabez Ali Baik, who was on his way to deliver to the Shah his master's report, which accused Mohammad Hassan Khan of having attacked the Yokharibash compound and looted their livestock.

Adel Shah found the report of the incident to his liking as it gave him the opportunity to order the capture of the Ashaghebash chieftain. Powerful leaders intimidated his sense of security. So the fewer they were the easier his hold on absolute power would be.

The dust of campaign had not settled yet when a small troop led by an emissary of Sabez Ali Baik carrying the Shah's Command arrived to take Mohammad Hassan away. Allahverdi Oghlo, the first watchman to see them was given the Command which he duly gave to Jayran to deliver to the Khan. Thinking it was a Royal Summons she unrolled the skin and began to read it. Her eyes filled with tears and her hand began to shake. Holding the scroll she ran to her husband's yort where he was taking his afternoon tea. Throwing the Command at his feet she collapsed on her knees, took hold of his muscular shoulders, and shaking them hard begged, "For the love of God kill me now. If I am no more, this depraved fox will let you be. This is another of his vile deeds. He doesn't know that even if you were dead I'd shoot myself before surrendering to him. Please for the sake of our children kill me, kill me now." Then frantic, she began to look for his dagger. It was on the floor near his tea tray. She grabbed it and was pointing it to her heart when Mohammad Hassan snatched her arm in the air shaking it so hard that the dagger fell on his tea tray breaking the tea glass. He had never seen his wife so hysterical. Letting go of her hand he drew her to him. She rested her head on his wide chest and began weeping hard. He stroked her tiny head and kissed her shoulder until she calmed down. He picked up the scroll and began to read it. As he read colour vanished from his face and a few veins began to thump on his temple. He read the content twice before letting the Command drop on the floor. He refocused on his wife with eyes that glowed with revenge fever. He cupped Jayran's red and wet face between his hands, kissed her trembling lips and said,

"You are my honour, the mother of my children and the captor of my heart; without you life will lose its meaning for us all." She gazed into his determined eyes; through them reached his soul and touched it with her gratitude. He felt the touch, took her arm and together they rose. She grabbed his hand and put it on her heart.

"This beats only for you."

"I know that, my love. I will not surrender to Sabez Ali Baik. I will write to the Shah and explain the whole situation and ask him to send his investigators. In the meanwhile Mirza Mehdi will help to change his opinion of us by finding a way to prove our innocence." Jayran reflected for a moment and then said:

"Even if the Shah sends an investigator to this area do you think for a moment that Sabez Ali Baik will allow him to report the truth?"

"No, but this will buy us time."

Mohammad Hassan presented himself to the group, cordially saluted them, thanked them for doing their duty and said that he would not surrender himself to them. They had to take him by force. The commander of the small group, aware that he was outnumbered, decided to abstain from armed conflict and return to Astarabad. The defiance of the royal decree was just what Sabez Ali Baik had expected. Punishment for defiance was being walled in. [51]

News of the Shah's intentions to send an army reached the Ashaghebash in time. They sought help from other Gajar sects. Those in receipt of Mirza Mehdi's request hastened to the compound by the river. Women and children together with their livestock and guards migrated to safer grounds. War broke out. The Gajars were defeated and Mohammad Hassan Khan became an outlaw.

---

[51] The victim was sandwiched between two walls erected to bury him alive.

Chapter 4

Once again security evaporated. Away from his capital in Teheran, Adel Shah was dethroned and blinded by his brother Ibrahim Khan. Sabez Ali Baik fled Astarabad and Mirza Mehdi regained his estate there. In Mashhad Shahrokh, the only surviving Afshar Shahzadeh was released from Adel Shah's prison and proclaimed the legitimate Shah of Iran. Betrayed by his father-in-law a mullah, he was dethroned and blinded. Mohammad Hassan came to his rescue and restored his sovereignty.

During this period of political turmoil the Ashaghebash continued to live by the river. Khatoon joined Jayran at the compound and the two tireless women concentrated their abundant energy on refining Mohammad's skills. At thirteen he was already a master shot, fencer and the fastest rider amongst his peers. He knew the Koran by heart. Books never left his side. Captured by his charisma and talents the elders bestowed upon him the title of Agha (the respected). Handsome, slender and of medium height he carried himself high. In Iran people with long foreheads are believed to have extraordinary destinies and Agha Mohammad Khan had a very long forehead.

One cold winter day when there was not much to do outdoors Jayran invited him to her yort. They took their sheepskin coats off, hung them on a pole and cross-legged sat on opposite sides of a sizzling brazier, warming their freezing hands and smiling at each other.

Agha Mohammad Khan who, from his mother's serious tone had guessed he was in for a long lecture, made himself comfortable and lovingly staring into her tired eyes waited for her to start. Jayran gently shook her head and in a tone laced with admiration said:

"As usual I see you have read my mind!"

"Yes, Bibi – it is advice time isn't it?"

Jayran gave him an affirmative nod, cleared her throat and commenced.

"Azizam, you were born on a special night – the night of the tailed star which caused the calamities that first upset our lives then led to the present greatness of your father, the master of Northern Iran. He is feared and respected. I believe the appearance of the ominous star on the night of your birth played a significant role in shaping our destiny. I am sure that during the course of your life you will face many trials and tribulations which will prepare you for eminence. I feel it in my heart that one day you will become a great man. A great man aims for excellence in all endeavours. You already have mastered many skills. But these skills by themselves do not make a man great. You must pursue the expansion of your knowledge. Knowledge is the wealth of the mind and the sharpest sword in any contest. A great man must not expect respect. He must earn it. A great man must not expect love. He must win it through the merits of his character and conduct. Exercise patience in all endeavours. Decide with your mind but act with your heart. Learn from the past; learn from the mistakes of others. Nader was brave and powerful but lacked compassion and wisdom. Wisdom and compassion solidify a ruler's base while hate and fear erode it. Nader's empire was built on sand. God has granted us intelligence – put it in good use. Self-discipline controls impulsive behavior – use it. God has given us a birth day and a death day – what we do with this time entirely depends on us. Use your time in such a way that your name will be carved with pride."

She paused to breathe. Lately she had become short of breath. The warmth that glowed from the black eyes of her son re-energized her.

The coals in the brazier were losing their glow. Mohammad picked up the tongs that lay on the under lay tray and manoeuvered the pieces until they began to blaze again. Then he moved back and reclined on his thick bolster.

Jayran thanked him with her smile and resumed her lecture:

"Azizam, you know that I love you dearly and the last thing I want to do is to separate you from myself but the time has come for you to leave us and join your father. He has sent a message for you to join him and fight by his side."

The news delighted Mohammad.

Jayran stopped, looked deep into the eyes that were fixed on her with the intensity of a blazing flame.

He gave her a bright smile and said:

"I am glad that father has at last asked for me and I promise you, Bibi joon, I will make you and him proud of me."

"I believe you will, my son. I hope I'll be still alive to see it."

"Enshallah, Bibi joon."

Jayran opened her arms and Mohammad crept into her embrace. He felt the thumping of her heart and, fully aware of her anguish he kissed her head and her face and then gently untangled himself from her loving grip, kissed her frown, rose, tidied his bolster and left the yort letting in a gush of icy air. Jayran, shivering, released a deep, sad sigh and let her tears roll down her sunken cheeks.

Mohammad was very special for her. Where Hussain Gholi was wild and uncaring, he was wise, perceptive and attentive. He understood her. He knew how she missed his father on his long absences and at times how desperately lonely she felt. So by giving her love, attention and respect he tried to compensate for the absence of his father. Now he was going too. His only consolation in leaving her alone was that Khatoon was there and the two loved each other and could cry on each other's shoulders.

The next day Agha Mohammad Khan, having passed under the Koran, and immersed in the smoke of burning wild rue seeds was sent to his father's camp.

The year was 1168, 1755, and Mohammad Hassan Khan was preparing to fight yet another battle, this time with his son-in-law, Karim Khan Zand, for the city of Isfehan.

On and off he had been separated from his family for almost five years. Constant fighting had turned him hard and wild but it had not wiped away the fine memories of his family – nor his love for them. His eldest son's arrival elated him and soon he observed that the boy knew no fear and when he set his mind on doing something he did it better than anyone else. And what delighted him most was his comradely behaviour towards ordinary commissioned soldiers with whom he took his meals and in whose tents he preferred to sleep. A proud father, he made him the commander of his forefront regiment.

During the years that followed the Gajar and the Zand fought many battles extending or shrinking the boundaries of their domains and Agha Mohammad Khan learnt from each and every experience that touched his life. With his books, rifles, swords and sharp intelligence he used every moment of his waking hours to make himself ready to face the challenges that lay on his path. He had inherited his mother's and grandmother's curiosity. Wherever he went he paid special attention to the way people lived, and what they produced. Nothing escaped his sharp eyes. He was an animal lover. So he learnt all about the fish that swam in the Caspian and the Caspian horses that differed from those they bred in Gorgan. The legend has it that no man ever knew more about the habits of the fox than Agha Mohammad Khan. It was said of him that he could even fool a fox! Because he was so perceptive he often knew who would be a friend and who a foe. He had never met his uncle Karim Khan but something in his heart warned him against him. He was soon to find out why.

A tall, powerfully built man with highly expressive features, Karim Khan had an air of casualness that was unusual in a man of high rank. He loved simplicity and unlike other chieftains shunned pomposity. A sportive man, he excelled in wrestling. Within the realm of his influence he encouraged exercise of justice. All in all he exuded a fatherly air that had gained him much support. Yet within the secret recesses of his heart lay an immense craving for power.

Long ago, the Zands had been friends of the Safavids and enemies of Nader, but because they were so afraid of the Afshar Shah they did not dare revolt against him. When Nader was killed, Karim Khan took advantage of the instability that followed and succeeded in expanding his zone of influence. Since Shahrokh was blind and confined to Mashhad he did not present any threat to him. His real foe was his brother-in-law and when he heard he was in Khorasan with Shahrokh he decided to attack Astarabad. Jayran was promptly informed by her spies. She mobilized and at the same time sent a message to her husband to return. The two armies met in Shahrood. Karim Khan was defeated badly but he managed to escape.

By a brook, under the shade of a poplar tree, exhausted and hopeless, he sat on a solitary rock, deep in thought. His back was hunched and his long arms dangled between his spread knees. What should be his next move? He did not know. His mind was too tired. Suddenly the sound of horses' hooves broke the thread of his thought. He looked up and saw a man attired in the grand style of the nobles, riding a magnificent Arabian horse with its tail painted red to show the purity of its stock, followed by two servants. As he watched they rode past him and then the nobleman pulled the strap of his horse, stopped the animal, turned his head back, and with his sharp curious eyes scrutinized the pale, dusty face that was staring at him. Their eyes met. Scared of being recognized, Karim Khan turned his head back and fixed his gaze on the rocky ground. The nobleman peacefully dismounted from his horse and calmly walked to the seated stranger. The sound of his footsteps made Karim turn again. The traveller saluted with his hand and politely asked:

"Pensive man, are you one of the soldiers of Karim Khan?"

Karim Khan looked at the curious man trying to read his mind.

The passenger detected caution in the hardened features of the pensive man and became even more inquisitive.

"I can tell you are a man of rank. May I know your name?"

"What is my name to you?" Karim responded with a voice that was tainted with glumness.

"Nobleman, I mean no disrespect. I am searching for someone and you might help me to find him."

Karim became impatient with the man's persistence. "I cannot give you my name unless I know who you are."

"I am Sabez Ali Baik."

The name was familiar. A tiny ray of hope passed through Karim's heart. The tension in his shoulders vanished and he became aware of his backache. Still cautious he asked:

"Are you the same Sabez Ali Baik who used to be the Governor of Astarabad?"

"Yes Agha. If I am permitted to know who you are, I will tell you who I am searching for."

"Assume I am one of Karim Khan's soldiers."

"May I sit on the stone by your side, sire?"

"That stone belongs as much to you as to me."

Sabez Ali Baik took a handkerchief out of his vest pocket and spread it over the wide stone, sitting facing Karim Khan and smiling, he said:

"I heard from the deserters of his army that God be praised, Karim Khan is alive."

"If he is alive what would you do with him?"

"I will join him and work for him."

Karim Khan frowned, fidgeted with his dusty long beard and asked: "Why would you want to join a defeated Khan?"

"I have my reasons, sire."

"What can they be, sire?" Karim asked in an amicable tone.

"Respect for Karim Khan and hatred for Mohammad Hassan Gajar."

A shadow of smile appeared on Karim Khan's thick purple lips and Sabez Ali Baik saw it.

Karim, totally at ease now, became more friendly and asked, "What did you do after Nader's assassination, Agha?"

"I worked for Adel Shah and now I am unemployed and am in search of Karim Khan. For I know I can help him."

"You have chosen a bad time to join Karim Khan."

"Why, sire."

"He has nothing to offer you."

"But you are wrong, Agha. People of Fars see in him a deliverer from injustice. Unlike other chieftains he is a man of the people. It will not take him long to gather strength again. He might have lost this battle but I am certain he will win the war. I think highly of him and that is why I am searching for him and hope I will find and offer him my services."

The words pacified the desperate man's spirit. He let out a heavy sigh and said:

"You are very optimistic, good man."

"Where is he now, Sire?"

"He is sitting on this rock in front of you."

Sabez Ali Baik, delighted with his luck, immediately went on his knees and kissed the earth by Karim Khan's feet:

"Please forgive me, your Excellency, for not recognizing you."

"This Excellency does not even have a horse."

"Khan, you have a nation waiting for you. It will be easy to gather another army. At the moment it is not wise to stay here. Mohammad Hassan might return to capture you."

"Yes, you are right."

"Sire, where do you wish to go from here?"

"I have to go to Teheran and from there to Isfehan."

"Sire, you ride my horse and I will ride my servant's and they will share the third horse. And if you give me the honour to be your servant I will accompany you to the end of the earth."

Karim Khan took the encounter as a good omen and offered his hand in friendship. Sabez Ali Baik took it greedily.

Gradually many men of wisdom joined Karim Khan's camp. His popularity grew fast and then he found himself asked to be the Shah of Iran. He accepted but instead of declaring himself the Shah chose to be called the Vakil, (the Protector of the People). In Karim Khan the nation found a wise and fair sovereign who had been able to unite most of the country and thus bring about certain security. However

Shahrokh kept his hold of Khorasan and Mohammad Hassan the northern territories.

Chapter 5

In time through truce and incentives Karim Khan tamed all the shrews except Mohammad Hassan Khan who was too strong.

Khatoon lived at Semnan. Khadijeh was Karim Khan's sogoli, hence prudent enough not to interfere in any political affairs. Nevertheless through her trusted friends she kept her mother and brother well informed. With her children seemingly prosperous Khatoon decided to look for something exciting to do. During her time at Chelsetoon she had met some of the wives of important Europeans who had visited the Safavid court on their way to India or China. Their tales and customs had fascinated her. She knew there was another world out there and now that she was not needed by anyone she could dare to venture into that world and to France – her mother's country. She could do that from Tajikistan where she had to go shortly. Her quick mind set up a plan. Communication would not be a problem. She had learnt French from her mother and Russian from her tailor in Semnan, the Armenian Jannet. She needed a man to protect her and no one was better than Sadegh Khan. So she let her family know of her decision. Their letters of objection arrived when she had already left.

The path to Europe from Iran was through Russia. A man by the name of Ali Ismailovsky looked after Khatoon's interests in the Dutch East India Company. Ali's wife, Nadia, was a friend of Empress Elizabeth, daughter of Peter the Great. Ali's daughter Anna had married Alexis, a Romanov prince. Thus the family was well connected to the Romanov Court. Ismailovsky was a Moslem from Georgia where Sarah Khatoon's mother now lived. Through Khatoon's intercession the Dutch East India Company had appointed Ali as their representative in the Russian Caspian regions. The company's head office at the time was in Tajikistan where to collect her dues Khatoon met Ali every Norooz [52]. Ali was a talkative man and from him Khatoon learnt much about Russian current affairs and technological advances in war

---

[52] Iranian New Year which always falls on spring's equinox.

machinery. She realized with her income she could buy modern guns for her son. To make the purchase she had to have the permission of the Russian Empress. She communicated her desire to Nadia and through her mediation the Empress invited Khatoon to Russia. Alexis and Anna were chosen to host her and arrange for her travel.

Twenty armed horsemen accompanied the gold crested, six-horse-carriage that drove Khatoon to St. Petersburg. Two smaller carriages, heavy with trunks filled with presents, Persian herbs and spices and Khatoon's maid and cook followed the cavalcade. Sadegh Khan, on an Arabian horse, rode next to the window through which he could spy on his mistress. She was sitting beside a namahram and that he did not like. This place that they had entered seemed to him strange and its women behaya [53]. They dared to go out without chador and expose their colourless, hairless arms for all to see. Did not their men have any sharaf [54]? Many such questions raced through the eunuch's mind, and when he failed to find satisfying answers he decided to dislike the farangies, their customs and particularly their food which was najest [55] anyway.

Sadegh Khan was a tall, fit and square shouldered man with black eyes that shone like two large black pearls and a head full of silver-gray hair that was always covered under his gray sheepskin hat. With an erect posture and serious composure he made an awesome figure no one dared to reckon with. Some said he was different from other eunuchs because he was in love with his mistress. Devotion to her had kept his masculine spirit alive. Always keen to please his mistress he had even tried to learn how to eat with spoon and fork instead of his hand. However he had found the chore too cumbersome, given up trying and decided never to eat within the sight of the farangies. At the age of eleven Sadegh had been bought at a slave auction and in order to be able to serve in Shah Sultan Hussain's andaroon he was castrated. Years later, loyal, brave and witty he became Khatoon's eunuch. Taken by his intelligence and devotion she asked her husband to relieve him from his bondage. A liberated Sadegh vowed to dedicate his entire life to the service of his Baygum.

In the carriage, Alexis, tall, blond with a shapely moustache that gave an air of distinction to his otherwise ordinary face sat content just

---

[53] Without virtue

[54] honour

[55] Unclean in a religious sense.

to hear the musical voice of his young wife. Anna, attired in pink silk, her round attractive face powdered white, was busy informing Khatoon of the events that had brought Elizabeth to power.

"Baygum, from Peter to Elizabeth sovereignty changed four times, all because Peter had not left an heir."

"That is the greatest mistake a Shah can make – not appointing an heir. This is exactly what happened with Nader."

"I entirely agree with you, Baygum. Elizabeth is a childless thirty year old widow and as shrewd as a fox. She has nominated her fourteen year old nephew and given him the title of Peter the Third of Russia."

"That is wise of Elizabeth. Women can think more clearly than the men and it is a pity that in Iran we cannot be sovereigns."

Anna smiled, nodded in agreement and said:

"In the old Iran, before the Arabs brought Islam we had two Queens."

"Yes I know that."

"This boy Elizabeth has chosen is a bit dumb but his wife, a German by the name of Sophie Fredericke, Princess of Anholt Zerbst, seems very alert and intelligent. She is addressed as Catherine."

"Am I to meet her, too?"

"Of course you will meet her."

In St. Petersburg Anna's tailors hastily created for Khatoon a complete European wardrobe within Islamic decorum. At forty she still looked stunning.

Khatoon fell in love with St. Petersburg. It was so different from all the cities she had visited in Iran. The wide, cobblestoned streets, the huge squares crowded by gilded carriages, the women in their extravagant outfits holding dainty parasols and men with robes that had tails all opened her eyes to a new world.

At Anna's mansion she met many ladies and from their conversations she learnt much about their lives. What surprised her most was that within the liberties these women enjoyed was an absence of the right to ownership of wealth and many other things. She was told that as soon as a woman marries, the spouse becomes in control of her wealth. She was told that people married for expediency and love was to be found outside of marriage and that children were brought up by governesses and mothers had no influence over their education. In fact, busy with their social lives, they hardly saw their children. Men here took mistresses instead of properly marrying the women or taking a Sigheh [56]. In divorce their situation was even worse than, Iranian women. In Iran brides had a bride-price, which in reality was their security if divorced. Here a woman could be divorced without being given anything at all – not even her own dowry. Having observed all these differences Khatoon decided that God had been kind to have made her a native of Iran.

During her first lunch with the sombre Empress; a woman of no beauty but lots of character, the two talked about Khatoon's social activities and the purpose of her trip to Paris. Elizabeth was surprised to find that Khatoon's mother was French and her purpose to visit France was to touch base with her French roots. The quest was so unusual, particularly from a Moslem woman, that the Empress offered to give Khatoon a letter of introduction to the Russian ambassador in Paris. The Empress took much joy in talking with this unusual woman from the orient, particularly that she, like herself was an expert hunter. Taken by Khatoon's simplicity, honesty and practical mind Elizabeth decided to trust her. As their friendship acquired momentum their talks became more personal.

Elizabeth told Khatoon about her hunting expeditions, picnics and parties – about her fears, hopes and aspirations – and about her daughter-in-law. Reading between the lines Khatoon surmised Elizabeth neither liked nor trusted Catherine.

It was on a sunny day when Khatoon, following Nadia, stepped onto the verandah of the German Princess's palace and found her sitting on a comfortable chair reading a book. Their presence was announced and the young princess, dressed in pink lace with her long blond, wavy hair spreading over her round shoulders languidly picked up a colourful feather, laid it between the pages she was reading, closed her book, put it on the table in front of her and lifted her head, acknowledging the presence of her guests. Then, smiling she stretched her plump, perfumed hand to be kissed. Nadia curtsied, took the hand and kissed it. Then she introduced Khatoon, who ignored the stretched hand and greeted the princess with a salam [57]. Catherine took the insolence as ignorance; withdrew her hand and took no offence. They sat around the round table that had been laid for tea.

---

[56] Sigheh - Temporary wife whose child will not be considered a bastard.
[57] Iranian greeting.

At first the conversation was formal; gradually the ice was broken, mutual interests, were discovered and time went by pleasantly. Catherine was inquisitive about Persia, the country so strategically important to Russia's expansionary aspirations. Khatoon enlightened her about the land of poets and warriors, where the air was pearl-white and soft, the sun expansive and bright, the sky forever paved with stars, and the earth fertile with the blood of those who had come to conquer it. She told her about her husbands and children and the apple of her eyes, Mohammad. Catherine in turn spoke about her love of learning, of her dreams for Russia and of a world in which justice could prevail. At times it seemed the two women, one from the West and the other from the East shared the same visions for humanity. But they each belonged to a different world, so their visions and judgments were coloured by the idiosyncrasies of that world. At the same time they were human beings. In that they were the same. In their sameness they knew they had to contribute to the betterment of the universe in which they were so privileged. Unlike most women of their time these two were intelligent, daring and willing. So in their willingness they found a way to connect, and to understand and to accept, and in this acceptance find friendship.

The afternoon lingered on in the excitement of new knowledge. Khatoon found Catherine very different from Elizabeth. She had charisma, curiosity and a fiery soul – and Khatoon identified with that soul. Catherine was beautiful. She glowed in the sunlight like a vision, her hair a stream of gold, her skin the colour of warm milk, her body round and voluptuous. She was also charming and had a great sense of humour. There was such positive energy between the tall woman and the plump German princess that they found parting difficult. But the horizon had turned crimson and etiquette forbade further stay.

On Catherine's invitation Khatoon visited her every Wednesday afternoon. During their subsequent encounters Khatoon realized that within the thick layers of Catherine's serenity not only was hidden immense vitality but also a maturity that defied age. In her she saw the qualities she had seen in her own grandson.

In turn Catherine was deeply impressed by the authority and the grace of this Persian woman who had bravely defied the strictures of her culture, could speak many languages and be her own mistress in a male-dominated world.

Once Khatoon felt secure with her royal connection she put forward her request to purchase the needed artillery. The Empress not only obliged her request but invited her to go to Moscow with her. It was there that Khatoon met with Sir Charles Williams, the English Ambassador; a close friend of the Grand Duchess. The Ambassador startled Khatoon by his extensive knowledge of Iran and his request to establish contact with Mohammad Hassan Khan. An intuitive person, Khatoon felt an instant dislike for the clever English diplomat with impeccable manners. Court gossip had it that Catherine would not blink without consulting with Sir Charles. Apparently he had urged her to get pregnant. The birth of a baby, he had advised, would give her status permanency. Now Catherine was pregnant. However there was much dispute over the paternity of this baby.

Time passed quickly and Khatoon's servants were preparing for departure when Nadia arrived with a command to take Khatoon to the Empress. The unexpected summons worried Khatoon. She thought perhaps the Empress had changed her mind and was not going to allow the shipment of the guns to Bandar Anzali [58]. Praying that she was wrong she hurried to her bedroom, changed into proper clothes and rode to the palace in Nadia's carriage. At the palace they were taken to the Empress's library where she was seated behind her huge mahogany desk, busy signing documents. The Empress immediately dismissed Nadia, drew open the drawer of her desk, took out a velvet pouch and put it on a piece of folded document. Then she rose from her chair, left her desk, took the document and the pouch and offered them to Khatoon.

"There is a ruby ring in the pouch for you and this document is my order bestowing upon you the title of a Russian Countess. I know it doesn't mean much to you but it is important to me that you should be revered as a Russian aristocrat while in my land."

Out of respect, when the Empress stood up, Khatoon rose too and facing Elizabeth she said:

"Your Majesty, I am besotted by your generosity."

The Empress opened her arms and the two embraced. Then gently Elizabeth withdrew, took hold of Khatoon's hand and led her towards the two armchairs that were near a French window, showcasing the manicured garden beyond. They sat facing each other. Outside a mild

---

[58] Bandar means Port. Bandar Anzali is Anzali port

breeze was fanning the leaves that were dancing on the flawless lawn.

"I have a favour to ask you, my friend."

"I am at your service, your Majesty."

"First I must swear you to secrecy."

"Your secret will go to the grave with me."

"There is a little girl I want you to take with you to Prussia. She is like a daughter to me." Elizabeth stopped to guage the reaction of the Persian woman to her request. She looked deep into the widely opened, unblinking eyes and tried to see through them. She saw nothing.

Khatoon's mind was racing fast and then suddenly everything dawned on her and she smiled – a knowing smile.

The Empress smiled back and continued.

"I want to entrust upon you her guardianship. I want you to take her and her governess to Prussia. There I want you to place her in the care of a family whose address will be given to you by my contacts in Potsdam. For her safety while on my soil you will have to introduce her as your daughter. The identification documents are on my desk. I shall give you fifty thousand roubles for the travelling expenses and as soon as your guns are ready they will be shipped to the port of Anzali in Iran."

Khatoon immediately realized she was being used and cursed her naivety.

Elizabeth, an eyebrow raised, fixed her gaze on Khatoon.

In the gaze Khatoon saw challenge.

She pondered a little and then said:

"I am honoured by your trust and I promise to look after this young girl like my own daughter while she is in my charge and I hope you will be kind enough to expedite the delivery of the guns."

"Then we have a deal."

"Yes, your Majesty."

Elizabeth stretched her hand to Khatoon for a shake. But since Khatoon had never shaken hands with anyone kept looking at it – not knowing what to do.

"In the West we shake hands as a sign of trust and friendship."

Khatoon forced an smile and stretched her hand which Elizabeth took and shook hard.

"Now you know what shaking a hand is?" she said with her eyes twinkling with tease.

"Baygum, I will give you letters to my close friends in Prussia who will open their doors to you, of course, as a Russian countess!"

"Your Majesty, God willing, my charge will be delivered safely."

That same afternoon, arrangements were made for Khatoon to meet the girl and her governess. The girl with her yellow skin, narrow eyes and black hair looked more oriental than farangi. Suddenly it dawned on Khatoon why she was chosen for the mission.

From the palace of Elizabeth, Nadia took Khatoon to bid Catherine farewell. The Grand Duchess, pale and plump, was behind her desk writing. She lifted her head up, smiled at her guests, did not offer her hand to Khatoon to kiss and said:

"Baygum, you are leaving us now."

"Yes, Your Highness. I have come to bid my farewell and tell you how much I enjoyed our conversations."

"You are a fascinating lady, Baygum. I, too, enjoyed your company."

Catherine did not ask the ladies to sit. Instead she rose. Khatoon, now aware of the farangi's custom of shaking hands stretched out hers with a smile.

Catherine took and pressed it with affection and looking into her shining eyes said: "Baygum not many ladies from your country have travelled so far. You should keep a journal of your European adventures. It will make a fantastic souvenir for your children and grandchildren."

That same night Khatoon began her journal that was handed down from generation to generation until it was lost. But the tale remained alive and reached me almost 300 years later.

The next evening, when St. Petersburg was asleep, two carriages from two different directions left the city.

In Potsdam, through the message sent by Elizabeth to Frederick the Great, Khatoon and her entourage were lodged in a grand house. In due course the Emperor received the Russian countess and her daughter at court. He was privy to Elizabeth's secret. Promptly the necessary arrangements were made and the girl and her governess were delivered to the chosen family.

Frederick was an enlightened monarch. He patronized artists, poets, philosophers and musicians. The library of his palace was one of the richest in Europe and soon it became Khatoon's paradise. There she spent hours reading. She read Montesquieu's *Les Lettres Persanes* and fell in love with Voltaire's vision of an enlightened society. She felt as though God had given her new sight. At times she compared Iran with Europe and felt miserable. Here, art and knowledge were valued, the artists and philosophers were supported by the kings and their courtiers. She had never seen so many portraits of men and women – taboo in the Islamic world as illustration of objects and people could allude to idolatry. Here the monarchs built bridges, museums, even whole cities. The Shahs Khatoon had known loved nothing but plundering and destroying – "tax or head"! That was the motto still ringing in her ears. And then when she could tolerate her regrets no more she would dream of the day her grandson would rise, unite Iran and become one such Frederick. Sitting on her armchair, close by the sizzling fire in the hearth that warmed her bones, she often thought and thought until she dozed off.

In Potsdam she stayed until she felt her charge was settled happily in her new home. She sent a comforting letter to Elizabeth and ordered Sadegh to pack for France.

At court she had heard disturbing news. From what she understood, it seemed the political situation in Farangestan was becoming tense over a far away land called America which she had never heard of and India where Nader had conquered several times and plundered mercilessly. All India's jewels were in Iran now and her limited knowledge could not reach a satisfying conclusion as to why a country from one end of the world would want to conquer an already looted country in another end. However, she knew these small countries made war machines no one on her side of the world, not even in Russia, had seen. She had also noticed that there were men like Sir Charles who had eyes and ears everywhere. These men were extremely informed; they had travelled to far-off lands and made unusual friends in important places. Things Iranian courtiers would never do. But recently whispers had replaced discussions and many visitors had disappeared from the society in which she circulated. It seemed there was some sort of friction that had caused polarization. Iran, through Afghanistan, bordered India and the English appetite for colonization she had learned was insatiable. It seemed that they had their fingers everywhere. Suddenly Sir Charles Williams's interest in establishing contact with her son came to her mind and frightened her.

Sadegh Khan was running here and there ordering the Persian servants to be more diligent when a courier from Georgia brought a letter for Khatoon. It was from Ali Ismailovsky informing her of

Sarah's illness.

A concerned Khatoon forgot about France and told Sadegh they would be going to Georgia instead of France. This made Sadegh very happy – Georgia was on the way back home.

Khosro Khan – Khatoon's stepfather, had owned a palatial residence in Tblisi at the Moslem side of the city. By a stroke of luck he, Sarah and their three children had managed to flee Isfehan just before Mahmoud's capture of the city. Had they remained they would have been amongst the first to be killed. Georgia was a Persian tutelage and Khosro Khan was a friend of its king. Upon arrival the family had been received at the Georgian Court with respect and they were able to establish themselves with ease and enjoy a peaceful existence. Khosro Khan's death a few months earlier had broken Sarah's will to live. She had fallen ill soon after. No doctor, even those from the Christian side, could diagnose her illness. Once tall and sturdy she was hunchbacked and bony. What was left of her blond hair was silver and her once soft skin was ravaged by age. There was pain in her and to reduce it she was given tiny opium pills which made her sleepy. Twice while dozing, her faithful eunuch had heard her call Khatoon's name. That is when he had realized she was waiting to see her once more before joining her creator in heaven. So he had written to Ismailovsky.

And now Khatoon had arrived to find her mother asleep. She crept into her bedchamber, knelt by her bed and stole a quick kiss from her grey hair. A familiar odour teased the sleeping woman's nostrils. She breathed again. A shadow of a smile passed over her dry, wrinkled lips. She opened her eyes and saw her Khatoon. To make sure it was not just a vision she blinked several times.

"Khatoon!" she whispered trying to rise. Khatoon smiled and hugged her tight. Knotted thus the clock stopped ticking for them and in that stillness the two became one and in their oneness felt abundant joy. Then Sarah pulled out from Khatoon's grip and with her shaky hands cupped her tearful face between her palms and said: "Azizam [59] let me look at you!"
Khatoon fixed her wet eyes on her and smiled, loving her more than ever.

One blissful week flew away. Khatoon sat by Sarah's bedside, told her the untold stories of her life, told her about her children and

---

[59] Darling

grandchildren, the wars, the deaths and the miracles. They reminisced, laughed and thanked the almighty for their shared moments and from behind door slits and curtain pleats Sarah's invisible eunuch watched them with satisfaction.

Most of the time Sarah hung to Khatoon's hand as though if she let go of it she would disappear again and there would be no more time to wait for her return. The grief lay in the reality of the fear and both women knew it. Then one morning a strange thing happened. Sarah let go of Khatoon's hand, filled her sick lung with air, brought her mouth to her ear and whispered: "Azizam, go home. They need you there."

Shocked Khatoon asked: "Why do you say, this Bibi joon?"

"I feel it in my guts." Aware of her mother's extraordinary intuitive sense, a rush of panic assailed Khatoon. She kissed Sarah's hand and cheek and told her not to worry about anything but getting well.

That night Khatoon could not sleep for a long time and then when she eventually did she dreamt of Mohammad, floating on white clouds that gradually turned red. Suddenly a thunder broke out and Mohammad somersaulting in the air crushed on Tbilisi soil headless. She was woken by her own scream. The gruesomeness of the dream had such a profound effect on her that two days later she left for Iran.

The morning after Khatoon's departure Sarah died in bed with a smile on her face.

In Iran, to get rid of the Gajar menace, Karim Khan gathered an army of thirty thousand men under the command of Shaikh Ali Khan Zand. He ordered Sabez Ali Baik to join the force, certain that his thirst for revenge would single out Mohammad Hassan Khan and hopefully kill him.

The day was Thursday 15th of Jamadi Sani of the lunar Hejri year of 1172 or 1758 AD. On that day, the sun hid behind dense clouds so that it could not witness the slaughter taking place outside the town of Ashraf. Mohammad Hassan Khan, his sons, Jayran and eighteen thousand Gajars battled hard, aware of being outnumbered. They fought with all that was in them. But that was not enough. Eventually Mohammad Hassan relinquished hope and together with his few remaining men retreated towards Astarabad. Sabez Ali Baik who had been monitoring the Khan's movements throughout the campaign found his opportune moment – the moment that he had been awaiting for years.

Ahead of a regiment of 300 he pursued his rival and somewhere near Astarabad besieged him. Jayran and her two sons managed to break the siege and escape. A fierce battle took place. Swords click-clacked, men fell, souls went to hell or heaven and wounded men and horses moaned in pain. Nature roared. Thunder broke out, a heavy rain began to fall and four men surrounded the Khan. They fought without result. Then a clever combatant pushed his sword into the side of Mohammad Hassan's horse. The beast and its rider toppled. Mohammad Hassan's head hit a stone and blood gushed out. Sabez Ali Baid jumped off his horse, knelt by the Khan and put the tip of his sword on his throat.

Mohammad Hassan collected what was left of life in him and spat it on the ugly face that was even uglier in his distorted, dying vision.

Sabez Ali Baik let out an excruciating cry, raised his sword and pushed it into the stomach of the dead man. Blood sprang up. Quickly he withdrew his sword, and with its tip slit the front of Mohammad Hassan's pantaloons, took hold of his shrunken genital, cut it off and threw it away, laughing hysterically. The rain kept falling and the madman kept roaring with laugher. The soldiers, mortified by what they saw, turned away and left the man to his madness. Sabez Ali Baik collected himself, cursed the departing soldiers, took out his sharp dagger and cut off Mohammad Hassan's head. Holding it by its long blood-smudged hair he rose, dropped the head into one of the wide pouches that was attached to his horse cover and smiling triumphantly, galloped to Shaikh Ali Khan's camp. Presenting the trophy to his commander he asked to be the messenger who takes the Fathnameh [60] and the head to Karim Khan. He knew the bearer of the news would be rewarded handsomely. His request granted, Sabez Ali Baik quickly found a leather bag, dropped the head in it, fastened the bag to his own back and galloped towards Teheran. It was past midnight when he arrived at the citadel where Karim Khan was lodging. After much negotiation and a few coins Sabez Ali Baik persuaded the Shah's chamber guards to let him waken the sovereign. They accompanied him to the chamber's closed door and stood behind it. Sabez Ali Baik coughed several times before Karim Khan asked: "Who is it?"

"It is Sabez Ali Baik with great news for your Majesty."

"Cannot your news wait till morning?"

---

[60] The letter bearing the news of a conquest.

"No sire. Only bad news can wait till the morning."

"Come out with your information?"

"As your great luck would have it your enemy is in hell and his army disintegrated. May I enter to deliver the Fathnameh and my trophy?"

"Enter."

The Shah, smiling now, sat in his bed and pulled his eiderdown over his hairy bare chest.

Sabez Ali Baik gently turned the brass handle, slowly opened the heavy oak door and stepped inside the dark, stuffy chamber lit by the flickering flame of a candle that stood in a red painted glass jar on a marble stand by the Shah's bed. He put his leather bag down, bowed very low, pulled the Fathnameh out of his coat pocket and holding it with both hands presented it to his sovereign.

Karim Khan, his large black eyes shining with pride took the scroll, unrolled it, slowly turned towards the light of the candle and read the report. Then he placed the scroll on his bed, stretched his long muscular arms towards heaven and thanked Allah. A few minutes passed in respectful silence before Karim Khan demanded to see the head.

Sabez Ali Baik untied the neck of the sack and pulled out the head. The stink of death permeated the room. The face had not deformed as yet and Mohammed Hassan Khan's eyes were open. Pinkish moisture dripped from the end of his shapely moustache and his black hair was smudged to his skull. Even in death the face was composed and dignified. Karim Khan shivered, turned his head away and asked forgiveness for the crime he had committed.

Outside the first rays of the sun were making the snowcapped mountains sparkle.

"Who decapitated him?" Karim Khan asked harshly.

"Your servant Sire."

"My order had not included decapitation. He was my brother-in-law. However the deed is done now. Tomorrow you shall receive your reward. Shaik Ali Khan informs me that he is going to Astarabad to finish off the rest of the Ashaghebash clan. No one of consequence is left except Mohammad Hassan Khan's eldest son, whom I have heard is an exceptional youth. He must be taken hostage, so that he would never rise against us. You know the district well and have influence there. You must help Shaikh Ali Khan in his mission. I will have a letter ready for him tomorrow. Now take the head, have it washed and give it a proper burial by the grave of Immam Abdul Azim in Ray. That would please my wife Khadijeh Baygum.'

Khadijeh never forgave her husband for having her brother murdered.

No sooner had Jayran and her sons arrived at their compound when they received news of Mohammad Hassan's decapitation by Sabez Ali Baik. The three went to Khatoon's prayer room and dealt with their sorrows in their own individual ways. The following day Jayran and her sons left their camp for the safety of the Yamut's compound.

It is during this period that the signs of Mohammad's castration began to manifest themselves. There are three rumours. One is that he was castrated by the order of Ibrahim Shah. That is a possibility because there were many confrontations between Mohammad Hassan Khan and Ibrahim Shah. The second is that a Zand chieftain, whose daughter he had deflowered is responsible for the act; and the last is that he was kidnapped and castrated by the order of Karim Khan. My cousin, Prince Ali Gajar (the present chief of the Gajar clan) guesses that it was Ibrahim Shah's act. However, the only three who knew the truth took it to their graves.

Sabez Ali Baik, confident that he would finally have Jayran, arrived at Astarabad only to be told she and her sons had already left the compound for an unknown destination. Infuriated he accused his informer of lying and had his tongue cut off. Then he sent a messenger to Karim Khan to inform him of the escape.

Karim Khan, to win the loyalty of the Yokharibash, appointed Mohammad Khan Davalu as the new Governor of Astarabad with Sabez Ali Baik acting as his advisor.

Sabez Ali Baik's first advice to the new Governor was to find and kill the family of Mohammad Hassan for as long as they lived the Governor would not be allowed peace in his domain. He was right. Agha Mohammad Khan was too ambitious to remain passive for long. He had already come to terms with his predicament and had vowed to overcome all the concomitant obstacles that might stand in his way to success. Against his mother's advice, incognito, he returned to the compound, chose one hundred of his clan's best shots, trained them in the art of partisan warfare and commenced his attacks and looting of the areas around Astarabad. His subsequent successes made him more daring. He had spies everywhere and when the trees began to lose their golden leaves he planned his most audacious assault. Autumn was the time for tax collection. The largest parcel of tax that filled the coffer of the government came from the Northern provinces where the land was most fertile and provided vast pastures for animal husbandry. The caravan carrying quantities of sacks containing silver and gold coins, started for the capital from Astarabad. Agha Mohammad Khan knew this and knew the exact time it left Astarabad and the route it took. So with his men on their fastest horses they lay in ambush until the caravan arrived within easy reach. Suddenly they appeared as though out of nowhere, killed the guards and took the sacks. The success of the assault angered Karim Khan enough to threaten the Governor of Astarabad to catch the bandit or lose his position. Mohammad Khan Davalu, in consultation with Sabez Ali Baik organized a large army which besieged the territory within which Agha Mohammad Khan operated. As days passed they tightened their circle. Sabez Ali Baik anticipated that Agha Mohammad Khan, to escape had to choose the route to the west and head for Gilan where its Governor was his friend. Therefore he stationed four thousand men in that vicinity. The noose was tightening and Agha Mohammad Khan had no choice but to attack and break the blockade. So in the early hours of a cold winter's day he and his five hundred men attempted the impossible. After a fierce fight only ten Ashaghebash managed to escape. Agha Mohammad was severely wounded yet they rode for four days, until exhaustion forced them to halt somewhere near Ashraf. Their presence in that vicinity raised the curiosity of the town's folk and news reached Mohammad Khan Savad Kohi, the Governor of Mazandaran. He immediately sent his men to capture the fugitives at the caravansary where they were resting.

Mohammad, handcuffed, was taken to Karim Khan at Kan. The Shah was surprised at how handsome his nephew was. Bleeding had taken the colour out of his sunburnt face but his eyes were alive, piercing and proud. The Protector of the People sitting comfortably on a divan smiled at the youth and said:

"You are a daring fellow, just like your father. I am sure you know that punishment for rebellion is death. But I know you have been castrated. A eunuch is fit for nothing of consequence. So I will spare your life. I have heard you are an exceptional youth with an active mind. Therefore to maintain your sanity I suggest you turn to the service of God and hope to acquire a better station in the next life."

Jayran's advice rushed through Mohammad's mind. Captivity had not broken his spirit. The experiences of the last years had turned his heart into stone and his will into steel. Nothing could ever shake the determination of this castrated youth. Straightening his boney shoulders and lifting an arched black brow he looked straight into the amused eyes of his captor and calmly said,

'My Shah, I thank you for sparing my life. In relation to serving God, I am sure Your Majesty knows that man can serve God better through his deeds than his prayer. Your Majesty, I shall obey your order and hope the path you have chosen for me will coincide with the one determined by Allah."

Karim Khan, astonished by the audacity of the youth and at the same time enchanted by his impeccable manner of speech, smiled and in a teasing voice said:

"Young man, you will never return to your people."

"Who will look after the affairs of my tribe then?"

"Your mother will. She is a capable woman. You will remain here as my hostage. You will go where I go. Your life depends on your behaviour. If I hear you are plotting against me you will be killed. But if you behave you will live in comfort. You must never ever dream of becoming a king. You are a eunuch – no one has any respect for eunuchs. Gradually you will lose your masculinity and become fat like others. People will look at you with disgust. Hence you are best to devote your life to God."

"My Shah, my life is already devoted to God. Since I never fail in my prayers and know the Koran by heart may I be allowed to read other books and perhaps do a bit of hunting?"

"You address me as your sovereign. If you were not my captive would you have done so?"

"Sire, each situation has its own merits."

Karim Khan began to be amused by this new addition to his host of hostages: "From now on you will live in the citadel with two soldiers watching you with orders to shoot you should you attempt escape. Every day you have to report to me. As I said your good behaviour will buy you advantages that would make your captivity more tolerable.'

"Sire, I have one request?"

"You are not in a position to make a request. But for the sake of Khadijeh Baygum speak up."

"Sire, without me, my accomplices will be of no threat to you. Please give them their freedom. That would please God immensely,

Your Majesty."

Karim Khan thought for a little while and began to like the youth. He looked him in the eyes, admired his sense of loyalty and promised him to free the nine Gajars in his jail.

For three days Agha Mohammad remained within the confines of his dingy quarters contemplating. Then resolute to defy defeat, on the forth day with two soldiers tailing him, he set out to explore the city. During his wanderings he found and entered the city's school at which the renowned scholar Shaikh Ali Tajrishi was lecturing. Deeply impressed by the knowledge of the Shaikh, he asked Karim Khan's permission to enrol at the school.

The eunuch's intellectual prowess amazed and enchanted both his teacher and his sovereign. The former found in his student an unquenchable thirst for learning and the latter a passion that might kill political ambition.

As his studies became more absorbing Agha Mohammad Khan found his room, facing a busy courtyard, noisy. So he asked the Shah to allow him to remove himself from the boundaries of the citadel and rent a quiet place in town. With his guards as his shadow, Karim Khan knew that he would never be able to escape. So he was given three tooman extra for his rent and allowed to leave the citadel. Mohammad was prohibited from receiving any funds from his family. He was a hostage and had to do with the meager handout from the Shah's coffer. However Mohammad's severe self-discipline, learnt from his mother, overcame all hardship. Happy with the little freedom gained he rented a small house with enough room to lodge his guards and managed to live on bread, cheese and onion soup which he shared with them.

With the passage of time Mohammad's skin lost its colour, his eyes their lustre, his beard and moustache disappeared, his face elongated and his voice lost its music and became so feminine that he never uttered a word unless it was absolutely necessary – even then he only whispered. One morning, combing his black hair in front of a small mirror that sat on his windowsill he saw the ugliness that would have broken any spirit other than his. He closed his eyes for a moment, subjugated the ache in his heart and then picked up the mirror and threw it out of his small, open window. It landed on the paved ground and shattered into a thousand sparkling pieces. He turned from the window and scrutinized his figure that was tall, lean and toned. He smiled at his fitness and decided to preserve it forever. From then on he began to measure his food – an action which, misunderstood, coined him as a scrooge for the rest of his life – and in history.

In Shiraz, to avoid falling into lethargy Mohammad set an active program for himself. Deeply religious, every dawn he performed his morning prayer followed by physical exercise. A breakfast of bread and cheese took him through the morning that was spent at school. As he could not afford lunch during his study time that stretched to late afternoon he satisfied his hunger by drinking hot water infused with a touch of cardamom powder that he carried in his robe pocket. Riding and hunting took him to sunset when he returned home for his onion soup and if lucky in his hunt some sort of game kebab that he would share with his two guards.

Gradually through prudence, diplomacy, intellectual superiority and the expansive repertoire of his knowledge he found a prominent place among the intellectuals of Shiraz, who frequently sought his counsel upon matters of importance. Karim Khan believed there was not a single book in Iran that the eunuch had not read. It pleased him. At court there were nights that the nobles gathered to debate, recite poetry and interpret the verses of the Koran or Hafez. Karim Khan would not attend the sessions unless the eunuch was present. As the Shah became more dependent on his hostage's intellectual contribution the hostage found more freedom.

He daily visited his aunt – being a eunuch he could visit the andaroon at all times. From her he learnt all the news that helped with his plans. She loved him very much – like the son she did not have. Through her he was constantly in touch with the elders of the tribe, his mother and grandmother.

They were all waiting and praying for the demise of the Vakil – apparently he was not well.

Chapter 6

The port of Anzaly was crowded with mostly merchants who had come to collect their merchandise or load it on the returning boats for export to Russia or Georgia. Men, carts, carriages, loaded donkeys and a few women mingled with haste and intent. At different corners pedlars, fortune tellers, pick pockets and packers were busy earning a living. Whereever there was a gathering there was push, pull, disputes and some sort of quarrel. Amidst such hustle and bustle Sadegh found two squatting Turcomen selling rugs. With a broad smile he saluted them first and then asked if they had any news of their Khan. The two looked at each other in wonder and then one of them asked Sadegh who did not look like a Turcoman, why he wanted to know. Sadegh gave himself an air of importance, cleared his voice like a gentleman and introduced himself.

The two hastily rose, each embraced the eunuch and then with moist eyes gave him the bad news. Colour vanished from Sadegh's face, tears gathered in his eyes and his knees began to shake. One of the Turcomen took hold of his arm and the other offered him his lit chopogh (pipe) to smoke and ease his nerves. Sadegh refused the chopogh. Khatoon, who was watching them from a distance became curious. She hurried towards them. The men bowed and with low, sad voices offered her their condolences. Her heart sank, her chin fell and softly she demanded to know everything. They told her what they had heard. Composed, she listened and at the end, calmly ordered Sadegh to give each man a gold coin for their tears of loyalty. Then she turned and walked to where her luggage was. There she almost collapsed on one of her trunks, pulled her chador over her face and began to cry. Her maid sent Sadegh an inquisitive glance. He motioned her to stay put and then he ran to find packers with adequate number of donkeys and horses willing to take them to Astarabad – a fair distance from Anzali.

At the compound Khatoon found Jayran sitting under her favourite tree by the river, staring at the ripples of the muddy water, pale, thin and aged beyond her years. She was so deeply in thought that Khatoon had to call her name a couple of times before she looked up at her with eyes that had no lustre. Then she rose and the two hugged, kissed and arm in arm, in tormenting silence walked to the prayer room, closed the door and gave in to the sorrow that had been suffocating them. Khatoon believed that death is the shadow of all warriors and one day it catches up with them. She had never expected her son to die in his bed. But what had happened to Mohammad she could not accept with grace. For many days aimlessly she rode in the wild. She became tongue tied and forlorn. Sadly Jayran, herself dry in spirit and feeble in stature could offer no consolation. The will to survive had died in her. She had become as fragile as a porcelain doll. Folks thought she would break if touched. When hungry she would faint, after heavy meals she would go blue in the face – none of the medicine men knew what physically ailed her. They believed it was melancholy that was eating her up. She spent her days either on her knees praying for death or by the river reminiscing. Khatoon couldn't stand living at the compound without her loved ones nor could she let Jayran wither away in loneliness. So she decided to take her to Semnan where her own Georgian alchemist could treat her. It was at Semnan they heard Sabez Ali Baik had been poisoned by one of his wives. Jayran did not smile nor did she cry with joy – instead she spread her prayer rug and prayed until she fainted. The medicine man came; he brought ice water and washed her face with it. He took a small bottle from his pocket, took the top off – a strong peppery smell seeped out. He put the mouth of the bottle under her nostrils. Signs of life returned. She moved, opened her eyes and with help sat down. The medicine man left. A tray of tea, bread and cheese arrived. She ate and felt better. Khatoon massaged her legs. She smiled. Then the two women began to laugh. Khatoon ordered ten lambs to be sacrificed and the meat given to the poor.

    Gradually time healed the wound in Khatoon's heart. Hope replaced despair and one milky dawn, when the air was laced with the aroma of spring and the sky was clear blue and full of promise she sat behind her huge oak desk, which she had brought from Russia, looked out of the open window at the blooming foliage, took a deep breath, put her hope in God and wrote a long letter to her son-in-law. The courier who delivered the letter to the Shah returned with an invitation from him for the two ladies.

Excited, Khatoon showed Jayran the summons.

"Jayran Aziz, do you feel strong enough to come with me? I am hoping he will allow us to see our sons." Karim Khan was the one man on earth Jayran could not set eyes on. If she could she would strangle him with her own hands – such was her hatred for him.

"I am too feeble to accompany you, Bibi joon. Besides I cannot face the man who has taken my sons away from me and killed my husband."

"I hate him, too, Azizam. But he is holding our sons hostage and it is for their sake that I am going to ingratiate myself with him. Khadijeh has sent words that he is sick. If he dies while our sons are in Shiraz they will both be killed by Karim's successor. I have to find a way to help Mohammad and obtain the release of Hussain Gholi."

"Khatoon Azizam, I do not know anyone as wise and strong as you. God bless you and keep you for us all." Jayran stopped and looked into Khatoon's eyes which were glimmering with determination and continued,

"I think I am dying. I hope it will be soon. I don't want to become a burden for you." Khatoon took her long index finger to her shapely nose and hushed her. Nodding her small head Jayran went on:

"I wish to return to our compound and die there."

"I will arrange that for you, Azizam, and for all our sakes stop this ridiculous talk about dying and death. We will all die one day. Do not go looking for it."

Jayran swallowed the growing lump in her throat, ignored what she had heard and asked:

"When I am dead, will you make sure I am buried on my spot by the river, the one under the weeping willow?" Then she looked up into Khatoon's kind eyes, wiped her tears with the edge of her sleeve, smiled a shy smile and said: "Did you know that Mohammad Hassan once made love to me there?" Khatoon giggled like a teenager and then said:

"And did you know that Fath Ali made love to me on the hill by Shah Diz Spring?"

Momentarily Jayran came out of her dire mood and they both laughed and laughed till tears began to run down their faces.

That was to be their last happy moment together.

The following day Jayran headed for the compound and Khatoon for Shiraz.

At Shiraz Khatoon was received at the royal andaroon where Khadijeh reigned supreme. She was the Shah's primary wife. Sixteen years ago Khatoon had left a young girl in her teens and now she found a graceful, sophisticated and confident lady in her prime. Khadijeh's black eyes were lined with kohl and her arched eyebrows were shapely plucked; her lips were round and pinkish and her skin smooth and silky. She had lost her Turkish accent and spoke fluent Farsi with a tinge of Shirazi accent. Her smile was soft and her glance tender. It pleased Khatoon to see at least one member of her family seemingly content with her fate.

Khadijeh lodged her mother at the palace of Rashke Behesht, a paradise on earth. The reunion with her daughter in the city of roses, nightingales, poets and wine energized Khatoon further and made her more focused on her plans.

A few days later, as custom dictated the nobles of Gajar, now in service of Karim Khan, came to offer their respect to the matriarch of Ashaghebash. Amongst them Khatoon recognized Ali Khan, an old faithful friend who had served both her husband and her son. He had the air of a man with a mission. She noticed his long bony fingers were curved around a small, embroidered pouch. White of hair and beard, bony and furrowed Ali Khan walked slowly but with purpose. When near Khatoon, she detected the sparkle of tears in his loyal eyes. Her own eyes moistened. She swallowed the nostalgia that had suddenly flared up inside her and said:

"What great luck to find you here, Ali Khan."

"Luck is your servant's, my Baygum."

The old gentleman bowed, offered Khatoon the pouch and said: "I thank Allah a thousand times for granting me the opportunity to fulfil the wishes of my friend, late Mohammad Baik. He asked me to deliver this to you."

"You say late Mohammad Baik. Is our cousin dead?"

"Yes, Baygum, he was killed in the war with the Ottomans."

Her face fell; lament surged inside her, her heart tightened, and in her mind's eyes she saw the brave, tall Mohammad Baik who till the moment of his death had loved her – so unselfishly. Filled with remorse, she nodded her regrets, took the pouch, pressed it with love, dropped it in the large pocket of her long robe, thanked the man and turned her attention to the next well-wisher.

Later, when she untied the band fastened around the neck of the pouch and emptied its content on her bed; she saw two huge pieces of glass that, under the light of the candle chandelier made a thousand rainbows on the ceiling – the Sea of Light and Taj Moon twinkled at her. The gems were brought to Iran by Nader and kept at Kalat fortress, looted after his murder by the four who killed him – one among them we know was Mohammad Baik.

She called Sadegh Khan. The eunuch, in the habit of sitting cross-legged behind her door instantly rose, came in and bowed. She showed him the stones. At first he could not believe they were real until he noticed the rainbows they made when held under the light. A broad smile deepened the lines on his face. Khatoon dropped the gems in the pouch and entrusted the pouch to his care. The eunuch pressed the small bag in his palm, and whispered: "My Baygum, take this as a good omen." Her eyes brightened and she threw him a happy glance which squeezed his heart.

Karim Khan, tall and muscular, with his gray curved beard reaching his chest; dressed simply in a white satin shirt under a camel hair robe, with a tight waist, and flared skirt that hung over his white pantaloons; was pacing up and down the path that led to a huge pillared verandah with mirror mosaic walls and ceiling, ivory inlaid doors and marble floor. Unlike other Shahs Karim Khan did not always bejewel his gowns – only his wide belt was studded with rubies and emeralds and a huge emerald glittered on his wedding finger. The air was cool and the nightingales were singing when Khatoon and Khadijeh entered the garden from the Andaroon. The Shah saw them and stood by the turquoise pool fed by a bubbling spring, his elongated shadow waving on the currents that rushed out into two canals that stretched beyond sight.

Khatoon, holding herself tall, bowed. Karim Khan acknowledged her presence with a friendly nod of his large turbaned head.

"Welcome to our home Baygum."

"Sire, I thank you for your invitation. I also thank you for the stability you have brought to our land."

"I hear you have been to Farangestan. Tell us about your experiences when we are seated."

The women, keeping a step behind the Shah, walked to the verandah and sat on the carpeted floor, around a square, low-legged marble table adorned with dishes of fruit and sweets. Eunuchs rushed in with their trays of tea and hookah which they circulated and then swiftly disappeared behind closed doors. Karim Khan was fond of his hookah. It relaxed his nerves. In an amicable atmosphere they drank their tea, indulged in small talk, puffed at their hookahs until Karim Khan put his aside, turned to Khatoon and said:

"Baygum, I admire your fearlessness. I do not know of any woman who has dared to venture beyond our shores, and that without a husband!"

"Thank you, Your Majesty. When one is amongst friends one needs have no fears. Ismailovskis are like family to me and Sadegh is my guardian angel. With him I can travel to the end of the world without fear."

He threw a loving glance at his wife, smiled and said:

"Now I know where my wife gets her courage from."

"You are too kind, Your Majesty," said Khatoon and then to win over his trust gave him a long, precise account of her journey (omitting the information about the purchase of the guns which never arrived) and providing him with some valuable information that would have never reached him otherwise.

Enthralled by the information, Karim Khan inundated his mother-in-law with various questions about Europe. He was interested in the relationship of the French, Prussians and the English with the Russians and the belligerent Ottomans who often attacked his borders. His curiosity satiated, Karim Khan turned to the subject for which Khatoon had requested the audience.

"We are very fond of your grandsons and Mohammad has won our respect by his sensible behaviour. I have granted them permission to meet with you tomorrow."

"Your Majesty's kindness is boundless. Enshallah God will grant you a long healthy life."

"Enshallah," Khadijeh said with a smile.

Karim moved to rise. Haydar Baik, forever hiding behind a door, rushed in to help Khatoon and his mistress to rise.

The next morning the spring sun was bright and kind, the perfumed air cool and the sound of the fountain in the blue pond soothing. All the windows were open wide. Khatoon and Khadijeh were taking paloodeh [61] when the thumping of heavy footsteps on the marble floor raised Khatoon's heart beats. The door to the sitting room

---

[61] An Iranian sorbet, the most delicious of which is made in Shiraz.

opened, Mohammad, followed by his brother, emerged and bowed. Khatoon rose, opened her arms and they ran into them, as when they were children. She held them tight. For a moment all the joys of the world were hers. Then she took her arm away and dared to scan Mohammad from top to toe. She noticed that his eyes had become deeply slanted giving the impression of pulling down with them the end of his brows. There was a deep wrinkle on his long forehead and one between his eyebrows that gave the impression of a permanent frown. The corners of his mouth were pleated, and his jaw had dropped down and become pointed. His face was hairless and his voice effeminate. Mohammad stood motionless, letting her evaluate the new him to see if she could still love him. Khatoon intentionally prolonged her tender stare. She knew he expected that of her. Then she cupped his face between her soft hands and kissed each and every deformed feature. The lump in Mohammad's throat vanished. He smiled. Now she kissed his long forehead. He took both her hands and kissed them several times. She exchanged one last loving look with him. He realized he was still the apple of her eye. It made all the difference in the world. His muscles lost their tension and he breathed easily. Besides his mother, she was the one single person in the entire world whose opinion mattered to him. Not only did he love her deeply but he also respected her profoundly. She was his mentor in every aspect of life. Khatoon saw what she wanted to see in his eyes. She smiled at him and then turned to Hussain Gholi. In him she recognized the resemblance to both her son and husband. He was very handsome. His features were refined and his eyes large and black but too wild. No she did not like his eyes at all. Nor did she like his aura – it made her shrivel inside.

They all sat on cushions around a sofreh laid with fruit, pastries and a large vase of roses. Khadijeh clapped her hands. Her eunuch, Haydar Baik entered with his tea tray. He placed the tray on the sofreh and disappeared. The boys enquired about their mother and Khatoon fibbed about her health. Then to change the subject she presented Hussain Gholi and Mohammad each with a gold watch that hung on a thick gold chain and taught them how to read time the European way. Then she handed Mohammad her journal, asked him to read it and pass it on to Hussain Gholi to read and pass on to his future wife and daughters. She was very proud of her adventures and wanted it to be remembered by her descendants. To make the occasion happier she revealed that Karim

Khan had promised to grant her one request. Mohammad immediately said:

"Bibi, please ask him to allow us to take the head of our father and bury it in Teheran."

The request surprised Khatoon. Mohammad Hassan Khan's head was already buried and to open a grave was sacrilegious in Islam.

"Such a request is preposterous – and anyway why Teheran, son?" Khatoon asked with a raised brow.

"Because Teheran will become the capital of the Gajar dynasty and therefore my father should be buried there."

So castration had not killed inspiration in her grandson! Khatoon thought with delight and smiling said, "Son, let the dead rest in peace. In Teheran you build a metropolis and let people remember you for that."

Mohammad pondered; saw the wisdom and nodding his submission fell silent. Then the door opened and Haydar Baik protruded his head in and announced that the boys had to leave.

Their parting was sad as all partings are.

Karim Khan pleased Khatoon by releasing Hussain Gholi to her care. She took him to Semnan where she could keep an eye over his activities for he was shrewd, rough and impulsive. He had to be controlled otherwise his actions could jeopardize his brother's safety. To smooth the grounds for Mohammad Khatoon set to work. Through her generosity she enticed the wives and children of Mohammad Hassan Khan, who after his death had left the compound to come and live in Semnan. The brothers had to be united. Mohammad Hassan's line had to perpetuate through Hussain Gholi. So she put her matchmakers to work. Not before long Mah Rokhsar [62], healthy, tall, olive-skinned and with a pair of large black eyes shaded by long turned lashes and voluptuous lips was chosen. Hours before the wedding the official bathers set to prepare her body for the special night of Zafaf when hopefully a seed of life would be sown into her. Her skin was scrubbed with crushed apricot kernels softened by rose oil, unnecessary hairs were removed by a wax made of condensed honey, vinegar and rose essence and then her skin was soothed in a bath of camel milk and massaged with rose oil.

Nine months later, she gave birth to a fine, robust boy whom

---

[62] This lady is mentioned in history only as the Mahd Olia (the title given to the mother of the Shah.) Mah Rokhsar is the name I have given her.

Khatoon named Khan Baba and whispered into his ears 'Fath Ali' the name by which history was to remember him. Two astrologers drew their charts and both foretold a great future with so many offspring he could not remember their names.

Fath Ali Shah fathered three hundred children.

(In 1968, at my biology class at university in the United States of America) I heard my professor of Biology who was lecturing on reproduction remark: "Fath Ali Shah Gajar of Iran is called the father of mankind for the number of children he fathered!" I smiled and wondered if he could ever believe that one of this Shah's descendants was present at his lecture!

As springs turned into summers and autumn leaves floated in the air and snow covered the mountains and the flowers bloomed again and again Mohammad remained in captivity and Hussain Gholi became more audacious. Jayran, dead in spirit but still alive, sat by the river waiting for Mohammad – and Karim Khan ruled uncontested.

In Russia, Peter succeeded his dead aunt, Elizabeth, and was promptly murdered. The crown of Russia went to his wife, Catherine. The year was 1762.

Catherine, clever and conniving, discovered the connection between the Ismailovskys and the hidden "bastard". She banished Nadia from her court and had all their properties in Russia confiscated. Ismailovskys returned to a Georgia whose king was now paying homage to Catherine. Wise and enlightened Catherine became great in power and prowess. Then there was a rebellion against her. Her generals, enamoured by their queen, fought hard, crushed the uprising and the leader, chained and caged, was paraded on the way to jail.

During the interrogations that followed the rebel confessed to his connection with Feodovora, the "legitimate" sovereign of Russia. The rebel was hanged.

Khatoon never found out what happened to Feodovora. Nor did she care. The Russian experience had become a dream and the Russian expansionist ambitions a great threat to Iran's sovereignty, which frightened Khatoon. However under the present circumstances she could do nothing but focus on infant Khan Baba. The boy was blessed with robust health, mesmerizing eyes, a sweet temper and a smile that stole the hardest heart.

In Shiraz, all was calm until news arrived that Hussain Gholi was plotting against Mohammad Khan Davalu, the Governor of Astarabad.

An angry Karim Khan ordered Agha Mohammad Khan to go to Astarabad and put some sense in his brother's head. He also thought it was about time for the Ashaghebash to see the new face of their captive chief.

Agha Mohammad Khan, contrary to what the Shah thought, saw the command as a valuable opportunity to return to Astarabad, where his people could see him, accept his ugliness and realize he was still a capable human being. So he asked Karim Khan to order the Governor of Astarabad to announce the day of his arrival and publicize his castration and ugly look. Karim Khan liked the idea and thought Mohammad was doing this to please him!

In Astarabad folks lined up on each side of the path leading to the Mubarakabad fortress, curious to see what had happened to the handsome boy they remembered.

The convoy from Shiraz arrived. One slender, beardless man in an embroidered vest coat rode between two rows of soldiers. He sat on his horse upright, proud and smiling. He was recognized immediately. It was him, the eunuch, riding ahead of the others, composed, confident and regal. No one cheered. Lips were beaten, tears were wiped and curses were sent to the devil responsible for the inhuman deed; and then one kind man shouted: "Long live Agha Mohammad Khan." An earthquake erupted. Cheers went up and reached the soul of Jayran who had been waiting for this moment, which arrived too late.

At the gate of the fortress the Governor met the eunuch, welcomed him to the city and expressed his condolences on the death of his mother. Jayran had withered away and her body lay in Khatoon's prayer room waiting for her son to bury her in her spot by the river. Face expressionless, head high, Mohammad thanked the Governor, pulled the reins of his horse and rode towards the room he knew so well. Before dismounting he asked his retinue to wait for him and then he walked into the room. Shrouded in white, Jayran lay on the carpeted floor facing Mecca. A long candle in a glass candelabrum lit the room. Above her corpse sat Shaikh Mofid, his long, white hair spread over his hunched shoulders and his long white beard touching his knees. In a melodious voice he was reciting verses from a Koran that rested on his lap. The room smelled of rosewater and reeked of death. As Agha Mohammad Khan entered the Shiekh looked up, then with both hands he lifted the Koran, kissed it and took it to his forehead for a sacrosanct contact before returning it still open, to its stand. He slowly rose, embraced his Khan, expressed his condolences, dried his wet eyes with the edge of his robe's sleeve and limped out of the room. Mohammad knelt down by his mother's corpse. Even in death her face looked serene and beautiful. On it was frozen an expression of peace, a tranquility she had not felt in life. As Mohammad sobbed, his tears dropped on the cheek that once had been rosy and rolled down her long neck still smooth. There were no wrinkles on her pale face for springs of her life had been only forty-four.

Mohammad rested his forehead on her leg, closed his eyes and let his mind travel through time. Vividly he saw her on her horse racing his father and purposely letting him win, then laughing at his arrogant boastings. He saw her gently attend to the needs of their flock as though they were her children and he saw her shiver when he told her what they had done to him. That day she had hugged and kissed him and then told him, for her and himself, he was the same person as before and that he should never ever allow the disability to affect his will to succeed. It had been that the coward had aimed to cripple by cutting it off. It was her love and belief in him that had given him the courage and strength to face the ordeals of his life. He let out a deep sigh and opened his eyes and saw her dead face. He kissed it and then whispered,

"Mother, I have not forgotten my promise to you. No Zand shall live when I am in power and Enshallah it won't be long now." He stopped, took another deep breath, rested his head on her bony chest and let the agony that had been locked inside him for so long become uncontrollable tears. He cried loud and hard and when his tears dried he kissed her cold forehead, stroked her gray hair, with his long fingers traced her forehead to her chin, and kissed her closed eyes. Murmuring the death prayer he rose, stretched himself high and with purposeful strides stepped out – one more reason to succeed.

Mohammad buried Jayran on her favourite spot near the weeping willow, by the river, facing Mecca. Later a poplar grew on the site and forever it was remembered as Jayran's tree.

Hussain Gholi, to avoid his brother, had left Astarabad for Semnan. So failed in mission, Mohammad silent and pensive, returned to his captivity.

Three years passed and Mohammad Khan Davalu Gajar, the Governor of Astarabad stopped paying his tax and proclaimed his independence.

Karim Khan sought the eunuch's advice. Agha Mohammad Khan suggested the Shah should appoint a strong, trustworthy leader for the Ashaghebash so that he could curb the ambitions of the rebellious Governor. Karim Khan volunteered to forgive and nominate Hussain Gholi as the new Governor of Astarabad. Mohammad, who had seen himself as the best candidate hid his disappointment and said: "Sire, it would be better to make my brother the Governor of Damghan for Davalu Gajar would never relinquish Astarabad without a fight. This will prevent war."

Karim Khan summoned Hussain Gholi to Shiraz and made him the governor of Damghan. Before his departure for Damghan, Mohammad took his brother for a walk in the garden of the palace where no ears could eavesdrop.

"To regain our power there are four steps you must take. As soon as you arrive at your post you must re-unite the Ashagehbash and the Yokharibash. As long as we are divided we remain vulnerable. You must order our stepbrothers to leave Semnan and join you. With Bibi they are not safe. Should things go wrong they can be taken as hostages by Karim Khan. At the moment I am his only hostage.

Later you must take Astarabad and keep it for us. It is the seat of our ancestors and must remain so. Karim Khan may threaten you with my life or kill me. That must not deter you. I am a castrated man. My life has no value for the tribe because my line will die with me. The perpetuation of the family line is your responsibility. Keep Khan Baba safe and train him well. Let him remain with Bibi and be educated by her. Only think of the survival and independence of the Gajars."

"You have always been wise, my brother. Rest assured that I shall follow your orders to the moment of my death," Hussain Gholi replied knowing well that he would not keep his promise.

Mohammad embraced his brother, kissed both his cheeks and sent him off to fulfil his mission.

That was their last meeting.

In Damghan, Hussain Gholi proved his capabilities and with Karim Khan's financial help managed to build an army that fought its way to Astarabad and proclaimed the city for the Shah. The rebellious Governor was killed. Hussain Gholi diplomatically appointed a Yokharibash as the Governor of Astarabad and returned to Damghan. This sign of goodwill cemented the two sects' unity again. Seasons went through their cycles, Karim Khan's physical vigour began to falter fast and Hussain Gholi's sphere of influence spread beyond the Shah's tolerance. Karim Khan dispatched a number of spies to the province. They were caught and killed. Consumed by vanity Hussain Gholi forgot his promise to his brother, proclaimed his independence from the central government and called himself Jahansouz [63] Shah Gajar.

In the summer of 1771, the Shah's army commanded by Mohammad Khan Davalu Gajar, was humiliatingly defeated by Jahansouz Shah.

Karim Khan ordered his hostage to write a letter to his brother, demanding his surrender. The letter was written and sent. Hussain Gholi, doped by success again defied his brother's orders. Now in amicable terms with his grandmother he followed her advice and created his own navy in the Caspian Sea. His rule of Mazandaran and Gilan entitled him to their taxes. Money poured in. Rice, fish, citrus fruit and silk were exported to Russia and Russian woollen fabrics and fur were imported to Iran. Business flourished, the Gajar coffer filled and power increased.

Karim Khan, unable to defeat Jahansouz in battle, planned his murder. Ali Khan Davalu, the son of the late Mohammad Khan Davalu, was chosen to implement the task. Ali Khan headed for Astarabad in search of a man who hated Hussain Gholi enough to kill him. Incognito he entered the city as a silk merchant and found his man. He was a Turcoman carpet merchant by the name of Ortog. Ali Khan bought a couple of carpets and asked him to deliver them to his lodgings. When Ortog arrived Ali Khan invited him in for dinner. The naïve nomad accepted the invitation and during the course of their dinner revealed his hatred for Jahansouz who had killed his son and brother. Between his sighs he added that had he had enough money to procure security for his family he would kill Jahansouz with his own hands.

Ali Khan clapped his hands and a servant appeared with a large steel coffer which he put in front of his master. Ali Khan lifted the lid, pushed the box towards Ortog and said: "500 gold coins: yours for the death of Jahansouz."

The man could not believe his eyes. He blinked several times before coming to terms with the reality of the fortune that could serve his family for generations. Awestricken he shook his head, pondered for a little and then asked:

"Why do you want him killed, my lord?"

---

[63] The one that burns the world.

"Like you I have an account to settle with him."

That night a vow of secrecy was made between the two avengers. Then Ortog left, carefully guiding his mule that carried the coffer wrapped in an old blanket.

It was a fine day and Sorkh Dasht dazzled under the summer sun. A cool breeze was fanning the leaves and the camp buzzed with life. Jahansouz had already left his tent to hunt. Deer hunting was a passion he had inherited from his late mother and the deer of Sorkh Dasht were a superior breed. The Shah's camp was crowded with merchants offering different merchandize. No one paid any attention to the Turcoman who manoeuvered his mule loaded with carpets around the Shah's tent, eventually settling at a vantage point from where he could observe the Shah's movements. Days passed and Ortog became familiar with the Shah's daily routine.

The dusk had spread its wing over the camp giving it the aura of remorse that follows all ends. Ortog stood on his usual spot but this time without his carpets. The Moez [64] had not as yet begun his Allah Akbar [65] when Hussain Gholi, ahead of his retinue arrived, riding slowly towards his tent. Ortog rushed towards the Shah, stood in his path and shouted:

"Instead of hunting deer why don't you hunt the thieves who have stolen my carpets?"

Hussain Gholi recognized his face but couldn't hear him. So he commanded:

"Come closer and tell me of your grievance."

Ortog moved forward and then suddenly with the speed of lightening jumped on the back of Hussain Gholi's horse and with one hand grabbed his neck and with the other drew out his dagger and slit open his throat. Blood sprang out, a pistol sounded and Ortog, dragging Hussain Gholi with him fell off the horse. The impact with the ground untied Ortog's hold. The horse went wild, towing the Shah whose foot was locked in the strap until the leather band gave in and the load with a dangling head smashed on to the earth splashing it with blood.

It was the year 1189 Hejri 1775 AD. Jahansouz had gone through twenty-six springs.

---

[64] The man who calls the Moslems to prayer.
[65] God is Great

Ali Khan Davalu was rewarded with the governorship of Astarabad. The unity between the two sects broke again and in the compound of the Ashaghebash a man by the name of Abass Gholi Baik was elected as the chief. He was one of the nine who was released from Karim Khan's prison through Mohammad's appeal. Still a friend he kept regular contact with Khatoon in Semnan and through her with Mohammad.

In the summer of 1192 Hejri, 1778, Karim Khan became seriously ill and Agha Mohammad Khan visited Khadijeh daily. News travelled to Semnan and brought Sadegh Khan, panting and heaving, white with dust and wet with perspiration to the andaroon with a message from Khatoon that if everything went according to plan, she wanted Mohammad to head for Semnan and not the compound. Khadijeh immediately sent for Mohammad.

Sadegh was near the end of his road but he was determined to linger on until his mistress's dream was realized. Then he could die a happy man. Mohammad hugged and kissed the old man, listened to his message and then told him to ride back and tell his Bibi that God willing, her anguish would be over soon.

Khadijeh gave Sadegh a handful of gold coins and sent him to Haydar Baik's quarters to refresh and rest. Mohammad rushed back home and put pen to paper instructing the chief of Ashaghebash to prepare the tribe for an impending confrontation. He advised him to select his bravest men and send them to Varamin which was near Teheran with strict orders to behave unobtrusively until he arrived there. Mohammad gave the letter to Torgol, one of his two guards; now his trusted servants, to deliver to Abass Gholi Baik.

Two weeks later, on the morning of 10th of Safar 1192 (1778) Khadijeh sent a message that Karim Khan was dying and as soon as he was dead she would light a lantern and hang it by the window of her bedroom which was on the top floor of the andaroon building. The moment Mohammad had been waiting for, for sixteen years was approaching and with it he knew the wind of his fortune would change. He summoned Torgol, who was just back from Astarabad, to his chamber and ordered him to pack his collection of books and guns and at noon when people were at prayer and the streets empty, to leave for Semnan. Then he withdrew his money from its hidding place, put on his hunting gear, took his guns and together with his other servant Zafar, left the city to hunt. He knew as soon as the Shah was announced dead, the gates of the city would be locked until the new Shah was proclaimed. With Karim Khan gone no Zand would want to spare his life.

Four days later, on the 14th Safar 1192, 1778, just when the last rays of the sun had melted away Mohammad saw the flickering of the light that burnt his bondage and freed him to pursue his ambition. The distance between Shiraz and Semnan is approximately 904 kilometres. He rode this distance in five days changing horse three times. [66]

It was summer when he fled Shiraz. Had it not been for his physical fitness and extraordinary self-discipline, he would have never been able to ride through the vast salt desert and reach his destination alive.

Dusty, hungry, thirsty and exhausted he arrived at the fortress of his grandmother who had been waiting for such a moment for so many years. Their joy was bondless and their actions fast yet cautious. Both knew time could not be wasted in sentimentality. Mohammad hurried to the bath house, undressed and dipped into the turquoise pond that bubbled with inflowing spring water. The water was cold and refreshing. The servant assigned to the duties of bathing, washed and scrubbed him with olive soap and a bristle sponge, then left him to relax in a second pond with warm water. Mohammad closed his eyes and let his lean body float for a while – only a short while. Thoughts raced through his head and deprived him of the peace of mind he so needed. Hurriedly he took a deep breath, slid under the water, massaged the soap residue out of his hair, emerged, shook the water out of his long hair and stood erect, in front of the servant holding his towel. The man quickly diverted his eyes pretending not to have seen the scar of deprivation. Mohammad cared not. He had come to terms with his loss.

Dressed in fresh clothes that Torgol had laid down for him on the tiled stand and perfumed with rosewater he went to dine with Khatoon. She was sitting on the cushioned floor, leaning on a mound of colourful, silk bolsters embroidered with tiny freshwater pearls and gold threads. Her smile was happy and her eyes twinkled with hope. She was in an excellent mood – and so was her talkative great-grandson, now thirteen. The boy was tall, slender, with long shiny black hair and a pair of large black eyes so beautiful that one could not but praise. His posture was regal and his behaviour immaculate. As soon as he

---

[66] He bought a new horse when the one he was riding became exhausted.

saw his uncle, he rose, prostrated deep and then stood to attention.

"I see you have grown into a handsome man."

"I thank you, great uncle. Praise to Allah for returning you to us. I am ready to die for you."

"I hear you are good with the sword?"

"My sword will kill for you, my great uncle."

"Your sword must kill for Iran."

The boy took the hand of his uncle and kissed it.

They sat to dine. Mohammad who had not eaten for five days forgot to measure his food – only this once. Feasting finished Khatoon sent Khan Baba out and turned to Mohammad and said:

"You must marry Mah Rokhsar."

The order surprised Mohammad.

"You know I cannot marry anyone, Bibi joon. Yet you ask me to do so. You must have a good reason for your request. What is it?"

"What reason better than she is the mother of Khan Baba. As her husband you will become responsible for him. You will train him to become your heir. A great king must have an heir. I don't want the Gajars to go through what the Afshars in Iran and Romanovs in Russia have done."

"Does Mah Rokhsar know what it means to marry a eunuch?"

"Yes. I have already discussed the matter with her. She knows what it means for her and her son, to be your wife."

"I don't have much time."

"You don't need time – she and Mullah Ali Gholi are waiting in the great hall. Let us join them."

Sadegh helped Khatoon rise. Then he picked her gold-handled cane from the ground and gave it to her, at the same time offering her his arm. Seventy-one springs of upheavals had exhausted Khatoon and slowed her movements. But age had not crippled her mind. Slowly the two descended the stone steps that led to the great hall where Mah Rokhsar, dressed in embroidered pink silk, sat talking with the honourable Mullah. Her hair, but not her face, was covered with a white and gold thread cotton mantle adorned with real pearls. Seeing Khatoon they both rose and prostrated. Sadegh left his Mistress and after a few minutes returned carrying a gold tray on which were piled a number of documents written on sheepskin, a small, white silk cushion on which two rings with blinding sparkles rested and a pouch filled with gold coins. He stood by a pillar, motionless, waiting his turn. Mah

Rokhsar stole a quick look at her future husband and shivered. Her tremble did not escape the sharp eyes of the eunuch who was admiring her beauty. Everyone knew what was expected of them. Sunlight poured in through the huge windows that were open and gave the room a celestial atmosphere. Mah Rokhsar made a short bow to her future husband and sat next to him on the carved wooden stool that was covered with white lace. The Mullah quickly opened his Koran and recited the verses that bonded the two in marriage. When he finished Sadegh Khan stepped forward and presented his tray to his Mistress. Khatoon took the huge emerald mounted on a simple gold band and gave it to Mohammad: "This was given to me by Shah Sultan Hussain and now it is yours to give to your bride." Mohammad looked at his grandmother with eyes that expressed tender love and then took the ring and fitted it onto his bride's slender finger. Khatoon took the second ring and offered it to her daughter-in-law saying: "This belonged to my father, now it is yours to give to Mohammad. Mah Rokhsar smiled at the woman she loved so dearly. She took the diamond ring and fitted it onto the long, bony finger that was presented to her by the eunuch. Then Khatoon took out from the wide pocket of her Turcoman robe, a white lace pouch. She untied the gold band around its neck, emptied its content of gold coins mixed with white sugar candy onto the palm of her hand and threw it over the head of the married couple, thus showering the union with luck. Mohammad took a candy that had settled on his lap and put it in the mouth of his bride. Their eyes met for the first time and instantly each saw a friend in the other.

Sadegh stepped forward again with his tray. This time Khatoon took the pouch of gold coins and handed it to the Mullah who took it with respect and stepped backward towards the door and then turned and disappeared. Now the room was devoid of strangers. Khatoon took a long laborious breath and picked a rolled skin from the tray and said:

"This is my will and I want you to read it when I reach the end of my road. The documents on the tray are deeds to my properties all over Iran and my shares of the Dutch East India Company. They are yours now. The documents will remain with Mah Rokhsar. When you become the Shah you honour your wife with the title of Mahd Olia (cradle of the sovereign) and from thence on, the mother of each Shah of Gajar shall bear the same title and should be considered the most honoured lady in the country."

Then she pushed up her wide sleeve until a large leather band wrapped around her arm appeared. She unfastened the armband, untied the thin leather bands that were fastening the mouth of the armband together and emptied the contents on the empty cushion on the tray. Two large, brilliant stones, cream of Nader's treasures, rolled over and settled in the middle of the cushion.

"These are in your custody now. Treasure them with respect for they belong to the people of Iran."

Mohammad was aghast by the enormity of the wealth at his disposal. Here lay the fortune that would finance his battles against the Zands.

"Bibi, I shall finish the job my father, and before him my grandfather left unfinished. I promise you I will realize your dream during your lifetime and bring unity to this ancient land of ours. Iranian blood was shed for these stones. As you said they belong to the Iranian people. I shall be their custodian."

Khatoon nodding his approval smiled and called Sadegh Khan. "Come, my friend, and take me to my bedchamber."

Sadegh Khan became Khatoon's crutch and the two in harmony limped away.

Man and wife, friends forever, held hands. He kissed hers and she his. That was the only kind of physical contact they were going to have. It pleased them both.

"I shall leave for Teheran at the crack of dawn."

Mah Rokhsar smiled at her husband, went to the Koran stand, picked up the holy book, took it to him and said:

"My sovereign, may the power of the Koran safeguard you and bring you back to us safely." She held the book high for Mohammad to kiss and pass under.

That night, as though a heavy burden had been lifted from her shoulders, Khatoon slept soundly and for the first time in her life missed her morning prayer. Mohammad also missed his. Dawn had not yet spread its milky wings when, commanding his grandmother's forces he galloped towards the town of Varamin where Abass Gholi Baik, his uncle Amir Sulayman Khan and his men were waiting for him. The two groups faced one another. Mohammad raised his hand in salutation, cleared his throat and said:

"Thanks be to Allah, our greatest enemy is dead. I left Shiraz with such speed that I am sure I have beaten any messenger to the Governor of Teheran."

A hurrah of joy went up to heaven and reached the spirits of Jayran, Mohammad Hassan and Fath Ali Khan.

Abass Gholi Baik waited until the excitement subsided and then asked:

"Sire, what is the situation like in Shiraz and who actually is Karim Khan's heir?"

"I imagine the situation would be chaotic because Karim Khan did not name his successor. Soon they will be at each other's throats, making our task easy."

Agha Mohammad Khan's prediction was accurate. The Zands became so entangled with themselves that they even forgot to bury the dead Shah. Karim Khan's corpse lay unattended for three sweltering days until its stench brought guilt to the conscience of those fighting for his kingdom. As soon as the city gates were opened a large caravan belonging to Khadijeh and her retinue left the capital for Semnan. She died soon afterwards.

Traditionally each new Shah appointed his own provincial governors from whom he received payment for their position. Upon hearing of Karim Khan's death the Governor of Teheran left his post for Shiraz. Thus when Agha Mohammad Khan's troops reached Teheran the city was defenseless. From Teheran Mohammad left for the Northern Provinces which he took with ease. The Zands' internecine activities provided enough time for Mohammad to organize and train his tribal forces and regain their respect and loyalty. At his camp, undisciplined conduct was harshly punished and excellence highly rewarded. The soldiers were fed well and paid on time – something unusual in the life of mercenaries. His fame and power grew daily yet it took the Zands a long time to admit that the eunuch had become a serious threat. Hence a large battalion was sent to end his menace once and for all. Agha Mohammed Khan whose spy network was expansive, got wind of the move and sent his stepbrother Jafar Gholi Mirza to intercept the enemy in the vicinity of Abassabad Strait where the terrain was hilly and the forest thick. Jafar Gholi Mirza was familiar with the terrain. He chose a hideout on an elevated position with a splendid view of the surroundings. The battle that ensued was short and effective. Triumphant, Jafar Gholi returned to Teheran and took his news to the simple house his brother had chosen for himself on the foothills of the snowcapped Elbors range, north of the city, in a village called Shemiran.

To unite Iran, Mohammad had to get rid of the Afshars in Khorasan, the Zands in Shiraz and the numerous chiefs who ruled independently from the central government. The task was enormous and required an equipped and organized army. Mohammad's nomadic upbringing had ingrained in his mind two major principles: democracy and fairness. He never made a decision without consulting with the elders and taking a vote. He knew loyalty was not to be expected but earned. So he set about creating a force that was disciplined, equipped and above all content. He personally undertook the training of his soldiers. Although he measured his own food, he fed them with three regular meals. After each conquest he shared his booty with his men. To protect Teheran's water canals [67] from being cut off during possible sieges, he ordered private citizens with means to dig wells in their gardens and he had many public wells excavated in the poorer areas.

Mohammad believed in family solidarity. He had seven surviving stepbrothers and he hoped his power and generosity would bond them together against the numerous enemies thirsty for their blood. Besides Jafar Gholi Mirza there were Mostafa Gholi, Morteza Gholi, Reza Gholi, Ali Gholi, Mehdi Gholi and Abass Gholi who died in infancy.

Before leaving for Mazandaran again Mohammad appointed Jafar Gholi Mirza the Governor of Teheran.

The Northern provinces, due to their proximity to the Caspian Sea, the heavy rain falls and fertile land, are immensely prosperous. Land there, at the time of the Gajars, belonged to wealthy landlords who abused their peasants pitilessly. Although free they were treated worse than slaves. Very little of the fruit of their labour went to them while their landlords became richer and greedier. Some of the landowners were so rich they could employ enough mercenaries to wage war against their governors. Their immense wealth was also the most lucrative source of income for the central government for they were heavily taxed. During peace they enjoyed a lifestyle often more luxurious than the Shahs' but they hated times of instability for the law of conquest automatically deprived them from their land in favor of the subjugator. However, as time passed and the landlords became more conniving they subscribed to the principles of Vaghf – donating the land to Islam with the oldest son in charge of its function. The income of such enterprise had to be shared in certain proportion with

---

[67] Most areas in Iran depend on snow water for irrigation. Canals are constructed to direct the water.

the clerical body in charge of Moghofeh [68]. In principle the entire income should go to the office of Moghofeh to fund charitable organizations like orphanages, schools and mosques. But in reality a pittance was donated to the Moghofeh and the rest went to the coffers of the mullahs in charge and the landlords. Thus the land was saved from being confiscated by any conqueror. These entities could never be sold so they remained in the ownership of the eldest sons of the same families forever.

In Mazandaran, Agha Mohammad Khan no sooner settled in the prosperous town of Barforoush when he faced the uprising led by the landlords of Larijan who were afraid of losing their land to the eunuch who was on very good terms with the clergy. Agha Mohammad Khan sent his brother Reza Gholi to subdue the rebellion. The landlords saw their only chance in turning brother against brother. So in the name of peace they arranged for a meeting. During this meeting they went on their knees, offered Reza Gholi their allegiance and begged him to lead them in their fight against his undeserving castrated brother. Flattered, the boy joined the enemy and besieged Barforoush. A messenger was sent to Agha Mohammad Khan demanding his surrender. Alone with only a few soldiers he had no choice but to capitulate. Handcuffed and spat on he was dragged out and put under house arrest until a proper safehouse could be found for him.

The next day Reza Gholi and his allies gathered to choose. One of the participants was a highly respected Turcoman by the name of Haji Khan, the Halal Khor (Haji Khan the honest). He was brave, kind, wise and gentle. Two long knife scars on his left cheek had not only spoilt his looks – but had added a kind of allure to it. Rumour had it that once he had been a prisoner of Karim Khan. That had been a long time ago and no one really cared to know why.

The debate over the possible choices was becoming too heated to be productive and Haji, who had been silent so far, seemed to be losing patience. His sighs and puffs were becoming frequent and it seemed he would soon break the string of the prayer beads that was going round and round in his right hand. Rolling his shrewd eyes around and around and then fixing them on a yawning Reza Gholi, he raised his hand for permission to speak (others were shouting and yelling in a

---

[68] The entity under vaghf. The concept of vaghf applys to property given to a religious body which will benefit from the income. These properties can never be sold, so they remain within the family property portfolio for ever.

disorderly manner). Reza Gholi ended his yawn, forced a placid smile and nodded his permission. Haji sat upright, cleared his throat and addressed the crowd:

"Brothers, I see that you cannot reach a satisfactory conclusion to the day's problem. My offer may help. I have an isolated cottage in the woods that might be suitable for our purpose? Guarded by my riflemen it will make a good safe. I will also send one of my servants to manage the house chores for the prisoner."

A sigh of relief broke the momentary silence.

Reza Gholi's sunburnt face now lit up with a happy smile. Nodding immediately he accepted the offer and thanked Haji a thousand times.

The next day Haji Khan had his riflemen surround the cottage and he, himself sat waiting for the prisoner. Around noon, blindfolded and handcuffed a skinny, tall man in torn clothes was delivered to his care. Once alone, Haji facing the prisoner, gently put his arms around his neck and untied the eye band from the back of his head, dropped it on the floor, and smiling stared into his eyes. Agha Mohammad Khan blinked several times and once his eyes got used to light he recognized his friend of yester years. A huge smile increased the lines on his forehead. The two embraced and kissed and then Haji went on his knees and offered him his allegiance.

Elsewhere at Barforoush, the landlords planned to first get rid of the eunuch and then his brother. Ebdal Khan the Kurd, a friend of Haji was chosen to go and persuade him to join their plot for five thousand tooman, half of which was to be paid in advance. Ebdal Khan invited himself to tea with Haji Khan. The friends talked and Haji told him he needed time to think things over and asked him to return at the same time the next day. As soon as Ebdal Khan left he hurried to his friend, informed him of the price on his head and together they conceived their own plan. The next afternoon when Ebdal Khan returned for his answer Haji told him he would cooperate only if the advance was paid that same evening. Ebdal's thick, graying, eyebrows knitted tight and, throwing an objecting glance at him, he said:

"Haji, you are making me run like an errand boy."

Haji Khan winked at his friend and in a pleasant voice replied: "Running will make you fit, my dear friend."

Evening and Ebdal Khan arrived together. Once the sack of gold was delivered Haji emptied it on the carpet, picked half of the coins and dropped them back into the sack. Then he looked deep into

Ebdal's eyes, stretched his hand and offered the bag to him.

"This is yours if you do as I ask you."

"Will that include killing a man?"

"No. It will include saving the life of a man."

"Then I am at your service, Haji Khan."

Two days later Reza Gholi Khan was informed that his brother was very sick. Immediately the Shah's doctor was sent to the patient. Haji's ten gold coins produced a report that the prisoner needed to be moved away from the humid air of Barforoush to somewhere with a dry climate. The young leader discussed the situation with Haji Khan, who reluctantly offered another house of his in Bandpay, a location with a suitable climate for the ailing prisoner.

That same afternoon the prisoner together with Haji Khan, his servant, Ebdal Khan and his riflemen set out for Bandpay. They had not moved far when Agha Mohammad Khan tried to escape and Ebdal Khan shot him in the back. He fell off his horse and sprawled on the ground bleeding. Ebdal shouted: "God be thanked. He is dead." Then he spat on the dead man, drew the rein of his horse and followed by his men returned to Barforoush to deliver his news.

By his masters he was rewarded handsomely.

One week later together with his family and his sacks of gold he left Barforoush for Bandpay.

Reza Gholi, too vain, too young and too unseasoned managed to make foes out of every friend he had. Soon the news arrived that Agha Mohammad Khan was alive and secure at Bandpay. Landlords searched for Ebdal Khan and Haji Khan without success. Then they discovered both were amongst those who had joined the eunuch.

Deposed and friendless, Reza Gholi asked for pardon. Agha Mohammad Khan spared his life but publicly disowned and banished him from his sight.

Five years passed and the eunuch never lost a battle. He reclaimed Teheran and on Sunday 11th Jamadi Al Aval of year 1200 (1785 AD) which had fallen on the first day of spring that coincides with the Iranian New Year's day, the Grand Immam of Teheran, in unison with the dignitaries of the areas under his control, proclaimed Mohammad the Shah of Iran. Coins were minted under his name. His first act as the Shah of a divided Iran was to appoint his adopted son his regent – together they would fight for total sovereignty and that would come only when Iran was united under one banner. Only then could he think of himself as a real sovereign.

Chapter 7

To win respect proved more difficult than the conquest of the realm for the eunuch Shah. Society was unkind, unforgiving and cruel. Eyes were closed to his finer qualities. They only saw a sexually defunct man fit for nothing but slander. For a long time no one could believe that his hold would last. So they kept plotting and re-plotting. Alas, to no avail! They accused him of being miserly because he weighed his food. They accused him of being cruel when he exercised prudence and justice. They whispered about his sexual behaviour and laughed at a eunuch with an andaroon! Conjectures were juicy and perverse as to how he pleased his women. On the other hand tittle-tattle about Mah Rokhsar was taboo. No one had the heart to belittle her – some even admired her. She was careful beyond measure. Her immaculate behaviour and generous heart defied malign. Her loyalty to a eunuch husband at the prime of her youth had set her aside and won her respect and sympathy of friends and foes. But there were other women, one in particular who the Shah took with him on his unifying campaigns. She was Georgian, tall, white skinned, soft spoken and seemingly happy with her eunuch. "What did she see in him?" people wondered. She saw behind the ugly mask the real man who like everyone else had a heart and a soul.

    Often their malicious objections manifested themselves in deception and betrayal. They had not as yet understood that the eunuch was resolute, ferocious and ruthless beyond their imagination. At first, in dealing with his enemies the eunuch chose leniency. That failed. So he resorted to customary punishment. One of the first to test his resilience was Ali Khan Afshar; a kin of Nader. Ali Khan revolted against the eunuch, was captured, pardoned and elevated in rank. Instead of being grateful, unable to bear the stigma of serving a eunuch, he spied for his foes. The Shah had eyes and ears everywhere. Ali Khan's conspiratorial correspondences were discovered and according to the rules of reprisal he was blinded. Many such incidences occurred, none of which shook the determination of the man with an iron will. Slandered or not, envied or not, betrayed or not Mohammad was going to create an empire that could neither be swallowed by the English, who were masters in India with eyes on Kandehar, nor the Russians, who wanted to reach the warm waters of the Mediterranean through Iran. Iran had to be saved from the tentacles of colonialism that were spreading wide and fast in the East. His spies were everywhere – even in neighbouring lands. He was continuously in contact with important foreigners who passed through Iran. He knew to maintain independence – he had to have a solid base and that base was to be created through tribal unity. This was on his mind when a fast dispatch arrived from the compound requesting his urgent presence there.

Mohammad lost no time. He knew Khatoon was ill. She had left the loneliness of her fortress and was now living by the river. Turned to Sufism she had a beautiful Khaneghah [69] built on the foothills of her beloved Shah Diz spring where she spent most of her time in the company of the dervishes who lived under her tutelage in the Khaneghah. Near there she had two graves constructed, one for herself and one for her faithful shadow. She was well into the autumn of her long blessed life with nothing else to look forward to except joining her Fath Ali.

At the Khaneghah life was simple, pure and holy. They took humble meals, recited poems of mystics, sang songs for Allah and Ali [70]. Some of the dervishes took hashish and danced and danced until they lost themselves in ecstasy. Khatoon loved resting on her cushioned sedan by her bubbling spring, the sprays of which wet her wrap and oozed out the stale smell of her lover. Often there was a gentle breeze that teased the long folds of her white cotton scarf. Totally lost in memory she would doze off. In her dreams she was young, active and with Fath Ali. Once she saw him standing on the peak of the hill calling her. She had run up and just as she was falling into his arms she had woken up. Immediately she had ordered Sadegh to send for her grandson and great-grandson.

They arrived in time.

Wrapped in the long white outfit of the Sufis she was playing with

---

[69] A Sufi temple.

[70] Immam Ali is the forth Khaliph of Islam, the son-in-law of prophet Mohammad and according to Shia belief his successor.

her agate prayer beads, when she heard the sound of trotting hooves. Her calm face lit up with a brilliant smile and joy encapsulated her shrinking body. She sent a big thanks to Allah and stretched out her arms. Mohammad and his adopted son jumped off their horses and ran to the light of their lives. In her fragile embrace they melted, unaware that the sky was cast with dark clouds, the autumn breeze was cold and the hill was yellow with dead leaves.

Khan Baba was closer to Khatoon than his own mother. He grabbed her bony hands and buried his head on the old wrap that covered Khatoon's long legs and let loose his sorrow. Mohammad still kneeling kept his head down preventing his tears from running. Khatoon untangled her long fingers from those of Khan Baba and placed them under Mohammad's quivering pointed chin and lifted his drawn face up. She looked into his wet eyes and whispered: "You have settled all accounts and carved the Gajar name with pride. I don't think any woman can ever be as privileged as I have been. I am proud of you my son. God bless you for all you have done for the blood line."

The Eunuch kept his stare at the black eyes that still mesmerized and said: "I love you, Bibi." He could say no more for his throat was tight and his tears impatient to run. He surrendered to despair and they began rolling down his hairless face dropping over the collar of his white shirt.

"I love you too, azizam."

Then Khatoon stopped, took a long breath, looked at young Fath Ali, summoned up all her zest and said:

"Son, your uncle is a remarkable man. Never fail him. Be worthy of being his heir. He is the founder of a dynasty which you and your descendants must preserve. In a dream I saw you father hundreds of children. I saw five Shahs of your seed who bore crowns. Be a good father. Teach your children that love, respect and loyalty must be won. Teach them it is better to build than to destroy. It is better to be respected than feared and never forget that regardless of our colour or creed we are all children of the same God. Those more privileged are responsible for the less privileged. In order to get you must give. The more you give, the more you will receive. Be deserving of the privileges God has granted you. And act in such a way that history will remember you with respect."

Khatoon ran out of breath again, so she stopped, moved her long skinny legs and closed her eyes.

Sadgeh Khan, who was standing by her feet, bent and straightened the wrap that had slipped from over her knees. She opened her eyes and looked at him. In her eyes he saw the shine of love and everlasting gratitude. He blushed like a novice lover. Inside the Khanegha dervishes were chanting. The clouds had cleared and the sun was shining again.

In a haze Khatoon smiled and said:

"Come now and let me kiss you goodbye."

Mohammad, red with emotions, hugged her and let her take a long kiss from his long forehead. Then he put his head on her soft chest, inhaled her scent of rose and tried to capture what he could of her warmth in him and cherish it for the rest of his short life. Fath Ali gently separated his uncle from Khatoon and himself rested his head on her chest. Sadegh saw the anguish in the old woman's face. He cleared his throat twice before Fath Ali realized he was being commanded to free the woman who was impatient to depart. He loosened his grip. She kissed him and then heard a voice calling her.

"Come, my love, you have kept me waiting long enough!" Wide-eyed she sharpened her hearing. She heard the same request again – this time a bit louder. She recognized the voice. She closed her eyes and saw him smiling at her. She smiled back. He opened his arms, and laughing like a teenager she ran into them. They kissed with the same passion as that first night when they had made love under the moonlit sky of Astarabad hearing the soothing sound of Shah Diz Spring. Then holding her hand he led her away – to eternity.

Khatoon left this world having passed through eighty three springs.

Shah Diz Spring bubbled, the autumn breeze turned into wind, the black clouds reappeared, thunder broke out and it began to pour.

Nevertheless life went on.

Sadegh Khan washed, shrouded and buried his lady himself. Then one night he bathed in the river, put his shroud on and went into his own grave that was beside hers, lay there and willed himself to die. The dervishes prayed and dancing, whirled and whirled until they lost themselves in God – in heaven they saw Sadegh still shadowing his lady.

I am you – you are me – there is no difference between you and me

– for we are one and the same Yahoo [71].

The Gajars mourned the death of their matriarch for forty days and forty nights. The poor were fed from the royal kitchen and prayers were sung in every mosque of the capital.

In Shiraz the Zands butchered one another until only one young noble was left to keep Fars from the folds of the eunuch.

Lotf Ali Khan, a nephew of Karim Khan was brave, handsome, generous and restless. He equalled the eunuch in every quality except in patience and foresight. The nobles of Fars took great pride in their young leader, whom they thought would wipe off the shame of having a eunuch for a Shah. The Shah knew of their desire. He was in Shemiran and that particular night he could hardly touch his meagre meal. Envy had filled him up and he was in no mood to listen to Shaikh Jafar Tonekaboni; his book reader's voice. His heart was heavy and his mind preoccupied with riddles he could not solve. People were whispering about the Zand and his plans to build roads connecting the large cities of Fars to his capital and a dam that would irrigate the land around Shiraz. That was admirable. But he had already created a metropolis out of a village. Yet eyes remained blind to his contributions. That was unfair. "What difference could sexual ability make in the man's ability to be a deserving human being?" To this riddle he found no answer.

Mohammad politely dismissed his book-reader and stepped out on to the wide veranda before his bedchamber. The air was cool; the sky wedged with twinkling stars and a moon that smiled. Damavand was capped with snow. Stillness prevailed – even the wolves, frightened to disturb the Shah had remained quiet. Shemiran, far from the centre of the city was as isolated as its Shah. Agha Mohammad Khan, the utterly friendless soul that he was, leaned against one of the pillars of the porch, and closed his eyes. The events of the past thirty years raced in his mind. Suddenly his nostrils filled with the sweet smell of jasmine and in the striking light of the moon Jayran appeared in his vision erect and proud. He heard her voice.

"Have you forgotten who you are?"

"No mother, I have not," he heard himself whisper.

"Have you forgotten your promise to me?"

"No mother, I have not."

---

[71] Oh God

"My son, the day will come when your enemies will bend to kiss your feet. Be patient and don't let remorse poison your mind."

"Okay, Bibi joon."

An envious cloud covered the moon. Jayran vanished from his vision and Mohammad opened his eyes to the stillness of the night.

A wolf howled. The cool breeze turned into cold wind. He shivered. To keep warm he crossed his long, lanky arms over his broad chest and slowly walked back into his bedroom where a hard, single, wooden bed awaited him.

The wolves kept howling till dawn spread its milky wings and a pleasant breeze made waking up a pleasure.

It was the year 1204, 1789. The Shah had finished his morning prayer when a dispatch from Mah Rokhsar arrived bringing news that God had granted Fath Ali four sons and one daughter from five different wives. All these wives were of Gajar blood. By the Shah's order the Gajar princes had to marry Gajar women so the sects would become blood-bound and remain united. Filled with joy, he immediately chose names for the infants and sent the list by the same dispatch to Mah Rokhar.

(I, the story teller, can proudly claim blood line with three of these infants: Abass Mirza, his younger brother by a few days Mahmoud Mirza and his sister Baygum Jan Khanum. Abass Mirza died before his father so his son Mohammad succeeded Fath Ali Shah. Princess Baygum Jan Khanum was ordered by Agha Mohammad Shah to marry Amir Mahmoud Ghasem Khan Gajar, the son of his faithful uncle Amir Sulayman Khan Quvanlu. One of their sons was Amir Aslan Khan Amid-Molk Majdouleh [72] and one of their daughters was Malek Jahan Khanum (1805-1875). Malek Jahan married Mohammad Shah, Abass Mirza's son and gave him a son, Nasser Al-Din Shah – my great-grandfather. Amir Aslan Khan's eldest son: Nasser Gholi Khan Amjad Douleh [73] married Princess Anvarsaltaneh, the daughter of his great uncle Prince Mahmoud Mirza, son of Fath Ali Shah. Their eldest son was Gholam Hussain Khan Ehtesham Almolk [74]. Ehtesham Almolk

---

[72] Amid Almolk Majdouleh is a title given by the Shah meaning the "the trusted by the Shah who also brings honour to the realm."
The Gajar titles were all abolished by the Pahlavi Shah.

[73] Amjad Dowleh: The one that brings conquest to the realm.

[74] The one that brings respect to the realm

married Princess Khadijeh Ezze Saltaneh [75] the daughter of Nasser Al-Din Shah – my grandmother.)

The struggle between the Zand and the eunuch continued. As the Gajar's might grew Lotf Ali's hold weakened. Governors and chieftains hurried to Teheran with their offerings of gifts, sons and daughters. Their respect healed the Shah's injured pride and brightened his outlook. He even found time to relax in his ever-expanding andaroon that was packed with beautiful women given to him as gifts. Yet Mah Rokhsar was his only confidante and soul mate. She was not as strong willed as Khatoon or Jayran but she was a good companion to a very complex man and a powerful and wise matriarch of a very unusual andaroon. The royal andaroon accommodated both the wives of the Shah and those of his adopted son.

Fath Ali was a brave warrior, but a spoilt man too keen to compensate for the sexual inability of his illustrious uncle. He was extremely handsome and extremely vain. He paid much attention to his outfits. Tall, slender, broad shouldered, with a tiny waist (which always was tightened by a bejewelled wide leather belt) looked immaculate in his royal silk robe of paisley design that touched his ankles and showcased his jewel studded shoes. His beard, jet black, flawlessly trimmed and oiled reached his waist. No one could look into his large, black sparkling eyes and not fall in love with them. His wives worshipped his shadow and tirelessly competed for his attention that was divided between so many! And his companions did nothing but flatter him.

It was to accommodate Fath Ali's large family that the Shah had ordered the building of the Golestan Palace, (Palace of Roses) with expansive rooms and endless corridors that stretched like a treacherous maze, leading to impressive halls with mirror mosaic ceilings and walls that multiplied a single image into a thousand, and where chandeliers with infinite tears of cut crystal illuminated the reflections of the elegant Shah. The apartments of the andaroon were constructed around a huge courtyard designed with dancing fountains and beds of roses that perfumed the dry dusty air of Teheran. In spring the brick walls, tiled with the images of the sovereign, were embraced by climber roses of all variety and colour smelling of heaven.

---

[75] The pride of the Shah

Encircling the palace were the ministerial buildings and the bazaar of Teheran. The city itself was surrounded by a high mud wall that was pierced by arched gates decorated with colourful tiles. Tekkyeh was the city's main square and here four thoroughfares crossed. Horse-drawn trolleys provided public transport and private folks rode in their carriages. The city overflowed with vendors, pedlars, mullahs, and soldiers. Mules, camels and donkeys, flocks of hens and turkeys muddled through the crowd of pedestrians. Entertainers carried their monkeys in colourful cages or on their shoulders. Veiled women rode alone, mullahs sat on padded saddles and beggars asked for alms. Amongst all this hustle and bustle buildings were going up fast. Gradually Teheran grew in importance mostly because of its proximity to the Caspian Sea which was the northern commercial vein of Iran connected to Russia, the great octopus of the epoch. Catherine the Great had her eyes on the domain of Khatoon's grandson unaware that the eunuch matched her in wisdom if not in artillery! With all her might she failed to defeat him and cross Iran.

It was winter and the Shah was in Shemiran. Mount Alborz and its foothills were dazzling white. The air was icy cold. A huge charcoal brazier was heating the Shah's sombre bedchamber and Shaik Jafar Tonekaboni was sitting cross-legged, in front of his elaborately carved book stand awaiting permission to start. The lantern beside his book was bright and the flickering shadows on the facing wall long and ominous. The Shah was sitting in bed staring at the shadows without seeing them. A colourful duvet covered his long legs. The Shaik, his eyes fixed on the Shah, sat mouth tight. He was very close to the Shah and was one of the very few people with whom Mohammad shared his private thoughts. That cold night, Agha Mohammad Khan's mind was on his rival again. It was getting late and the old man's crossed legs were in pain. So he fidgeted. The Shah sensed his discomfort.

"Stretch your legs, my friend."

The Shaik moved again but did not stretch his legs. Even with permission no one ever stretched their legs in the presence of a Shah. Mohammad read the hesitation in the man's eyes and commanded: "Stretch your legs or I will have them cut off." The Shaik thanked the Shah and obeyed his command. The Shah knitted his thin eyebrows and said:

"My mind can not rest at ease until the fugitive is caught."

The Shaik began to play with his long hennaed beard, pondered for a while and then looking straight into the expectant eyes that were fixed on him asked:

"Your Majesty, what if he asks for your pardon?"

Mohammad nodded his head in doubt and replied: "That proud, bold lad will never come off his high horse."

"Sire, what would you do if he did come off his high horse?"

"I will pardon his insolence, embrace him as a friend and give him a position suited to his rank."

"Your Majesty, will you allow me to write to him?"

A mocking smile appeared on the Shah's drawn face and rotating his index finger in the air he said: "Yes. But I wager that boy will never come to my presence unless in chains!"

"You might be right, sire. But then you have given him the choice. If he is wise enough he will decide prudently and if he doesn't then he has dug his own grave."

"As usual you are right, my friend," the Shah remarked and began to yawn.

This was a dismissal sign. The Shaik closed his open book, rose, kissed the Shah's stretched hand and back stepped out of the room.

The next day Shaik Jafar Tonekaboni wrote to Lotf Ali Khan.

In reply two letters arrived, one addressed to the Shaik, expressing gratitude for his concern and one to the Gajar. The Shaik read both letters, went pale, closed his eyes, swore at vanity and ran to the Shah's chamber. There he presented the two letters to his sovereign. The Shah asked him to read the letter addressed to him. The Shaik hesitated. "From the beads of perspiration on your forehead I know I have won my wager. Read. I am interested to know the way this boy's mind works."

The Shaik, unfolded the letter with a shaking hand, brought it near his myopic eyes and began to read.

"To the chief of the Gajars,

The Monarchy belongs to Zand dynasty and among the nobles of the Zand I stand superior. Hence Iran is mine to reign. Even if the Monarchy did not rightfully belong to us, we would never accept the sovereignty of a eunuch. Allegiance to a woman is more dignified than to a eunuch. We have heard you are a wise man. Therefore submit to our sovereignty and beg our forgiveness. I will pardon you and make you the chief eunuch of my andaroon."

The Shaikh stopped, pulled his handkerchief out of the pocket of his aba, and wiped the sweat beads from his forehead. He kept his head down – too embarrassed to look at the burning eyes that were fixed on him.

Shaking his head Mohammad snickered and said:

"The boy lives in a dream."

The old man with his turbaned head still down said: "Your Majesty, I beg you to forgive my gross mistake. You are a better judge of character than I am. I am so very sorry."

"There is nothing to forgive, Jafar."

The winter ran its course, the snow melted and wild flowers covered the plains. In the gardens creeper roses dressed the high walls, the bulbous flowers opened their petals to the bees and the birds returned to sing their songs. Blossoms in all colours competed for attention and people joined nature to celebrate its rebirth. At the court of the Gajars the Norooz [76] of the year 1205, 1790 was celebrated with more glamour than the previous years because Isfehan and Shiraz had been taken by Fath Ali. To reward his nephew the Shah proclaimed him his heir and made him governor of Teheran. Mah Rokhsar became the first Mahd Olia [77].

After the festivities the Shah went to Shiraz, where he had wasted so many years of his life in captivity. He went to Karim Khan's Ark (castle) and thought of his late aunt Khadijeh and then he went and visited the small lodging that he had shared with his guards. He walked to Shah Cherag shrine, circled the crypt, grabbed two of the gold bars with each hand, kissed them and thanked God for his freedom. The next day by his order the estates of the entire Zand clans were confiscated and the inhabitants of the andaroon of the fugitive Lotf Ali were sent to Teheran. In Shiraz the Shah found the Zand's own fratricide had made his promise to Jayran obsolete. The only noble alive was in fact Lotf Ali Khan, who riding his famous white horse Gharan [78], had escaped and was going from one province to another in search of supporters.

In Shiraz, Governor Haji Ibrahim Khan Kalantar's spies brought news that Lotf Ali Khan had found an ally in the Governor of Tabas who had given him men and money. He immediately sent his fastest messenger to inform the Shah and then wrote to the governors of the

---

[76] Norooz is the Iranian New Year that falls on the first of spring. A Zoroastrian tradition, it celebrates the rebirth of nature.

[77] Title of the mother of the Shah.

[78] It is said that Gharan was the fastest horse in Iran.

neighbouring provinces warning them of the Shah's wrath falling upon those sheltering the fugitive.

In Teheran the night was deep and dark. Shaik Tonekaboni had already left the Shah's bedchamber. Agha Mohammad Khan was asleep and dreaming. In his dream he saw himself in Karbella. [79] Yet he could not find the shrine. A voice was calling yet he could not hear what was being said. Suddenly he found himself in Najaf [80] following a shadow that led him inside the shrine. Somewhere the shadow stopped and a voice commanded: "Build your house here." Then the Shah woke up perspiring – unable to fall sleep again. His mind raced and raced until it was able to interpret the bizarre dream. At dawn Agha Mohammad Khan performed his prayer before his valet arrived to dress him and spread the breakfast sofreh on the carpet. He found the Shah in a pensive mood. At such times no one dared disturb His Majesty. The boy left quietly and then returned with His Majesty's breakfast tray that he put on the sofreh. He picked up the tea pot and poured freshly brewed tea spiced with cardamom into a large tea glass and then left without uttering a word. The Shah sat by his tray, drank his tea and did not touch his simple breakfast of bread and feta cheese. He seemed agitated and nervous. He could not sit still so he decided to attend the Audience Hall earlier than usual.

The door of the hall was open to all. Although people shivered at his name, they thought of him as a fair Shah. On this particular day the first entrants to the hall were a group of Arab clergy representing the people of Karbella. At the time Karbella was part of the Sunni Ottoman Empire and the Ottoman Sultans showed no interest in the maintenance of Shia shrines. The people of Karbella knew that the Gajar Shah was a devout Shia. Therefore when the ceiling of the holy shrine of Immam Hussain [81] collapsed, the elders of the city decided to appeal to the Shah of Iran for financial aid.

The courtiers, arms crossed across their chests, stood on each side of the grand hall. The Shah, in his usual soldier's custom sat on the Peacock throne that had only recently been salvaged from Nader's Kalan fortress.

---

[79] The holy city of Karbella houses the shrine of Immam Hussain, the grand son of the Prophet who was beheaded fighting for justice.

[80] The holy city of Najaf, also in present Iraq, houses the shrine of Immam Ali, the cousin, son- in-law of the Prophet and father of Immam Hussain. Immam Ali was also killed fighting for justice

[81] Immam Hussain, after Ali is the most revered Immam in Shia Islam.

Erect and thin, with his famous balloon-like hat making his face even longer, he listened to what the leader of the delegation was saying. An unusual sensation invaded his heart and settled in a smile on his thin lips. At that moment he felt very close to God. The speaker finished his request and the Shah whispered something into the ear of his personal servant who had become his public voice. He hardly ever spoke himself – for all symptoms of his predicament had to be concealed. The servant stepped forward and announced that it was His Majesty's desire that a team of architects accompany the respectable elders of Karbella with orders to renovate the building of the shrine and surround the vault with 18 carat gold railings. Later the same architects were to build a tomb for the Shah, inside the shrine of Immam Ali in Najaf.

The city of Kerman was the capital of the province of Kerman and its new governor was Morteza Gholi Khan Gajar, a mean and cruel man. His commander-in-chief, another Gajar, was also unpopular. The two had successfully managed to create deep dissatisfaction with their administration.

Kerman was close to Fars and the nobles who were helping Lotf Ali Khan were advising him to capture it. Jahangir Khan Sistani, a close friend of Lotf Ali Khan was of the opinion that the city had strong walls and even if the Gajar besieged it, the bitter cold winter of Kerman would force him back to Teheran until the following spring. This would provide time for reinforcement and a successful capture of Fars and subsequently the rest of the Gajar domain.

In Shiraz the highly ambitious and very conniving Haji Ibrahim Khan Kalanter, for his own selfish purposes was plotting to replace the two Gajar dignitaries of Kerman with his own men. To this end he set out to discredit the Shah's appointees. Confused by rumours, unhappy with the Gajar representatives the people of Kerman united and threw the two Gajars out of their city. Then they sent a team of their elders to offer their Province to the Zand.

This officially made the citizens of Kerman rebels against the Shah. Nobles of nearby provinces followed suit.

Punishment for treason was blinding.

No sooner had the Shah received the news, commanding his army himself he set out for Kerman and sent Fath Ali to deal with the rest of the insurgents. His prompt action impeded the consolidation of the forces of the rebels. Fath Ali, a brilliant commander, quickly crushed the opposition and blinded their leaders. Many fled the fallen cities and sought refuge in the city of Kerman where they thought they would find safety. Before the gates of the city were sealed off, 9000 refuges had passed through its gates.

The Shah besieged Kerman and cut off its water supply by blocking the Ganats [82]. Then gave orders to fill the trenches that surrounded the walls.

Inside the city deep wells were being dug, food and fuel were stored. People did not seem worried as they believed the siege would end with the first winter gale. The city remained linked to the outside by an underground tunnel used to smuggle in food and fuel until an enemy of Lotf Ali Khan reported the location to the Shah. The tunnel was immediately sealed off.

Outside the city walls the eunuch gathered several builders and artisans from neighbouring cities to construct barracks that would shelter the soldiers and the horses from the same winter that the people of Kerman thought would be their saviour.

Winter arrived and people who daily gathered on the walls to throw insults at the Shah saw no sign of retreat. Time crawled away. Food and fuel became scarce. Famine spread disease and death followed. One day the elders decided that they did not have enough to feed themselves let alone the strangers who lived in their city. They went to Lotf Ali Khan and asked him to expel the refugees. The Zand obliged. Aware of the Gajar's respect for the clergy it was decided that the Shaik of Kerman should write a letter asking the Gajar to grant safe passage to the people expelled from the city. Once the letter was written the mullah went to a post on the tower and waving the letter shouted: "This is for the Gajar leader." Then he attached the letter to an arrow, and darted it down. A soldier picked the arrow up, detached the perforated paper and took it to Agha Mohmmad Khan. He read the letter and considered the consequences. Amnesty would make his siege longer but he had time on his side. The Shah's permission was conveyed with the same arrow. Hastily and with utmost brutality the refugees were rounded up and forced out as though they were to blame for the town's suffering. Panicked men, women and children, weeping, begged for mercy for none believed they would see the sun set. At one stage a short fight broke out but since no one had any energy it did not last long.

---

[82] Ganat is an outlet of subterrainian water. Until around 60 years ago, together with wells it was the only source of drinking water and means of irrigation particularly in towns.

The snow fell hard yet Lotf Ali Khan, in his sable aba, stood on the tower and watched, without any emotions, the wave of misery that drifted out of the open gate into a path bordered by soldiers that meandered through the white terrain reaching the enclosure of the eunuch's main barrack. Women holding tight to their babies, children screaming and men carrying what meagre possessions they had, stumbled on the snow – trembling more from fear than the dreadful cold. Resigned to a faith unknown they aimlessly moved forward, their shoes crushing the frozen snow that had hardened. They floated, slipped, fell, rose and floated until they reached and entered a huge roofed enclosure. Then Moaz's [83] cry of Allah Akbar momentarily broke their lethargy. Noon had arrived. But to the doomed it mattered not. Suddenly smells they had forgotten existed perforated the air and brought water to their dried mouths and spasms of pain to their empty stomachs. At first they thought they were dreaming. But once bowls of steaming rice began to circulate tears began to roll down their bewildered faces. Shaking hands held the bowls with such gratitude that those who were feeding them began to cry too.

In Kerman, the expulsion helped with the food ration but not the fuel shortage. Suddenly rumours began to circulate that Haji Ibrahim Khan Kalantar, Governor of Shiraz who owed a lot to the Zand, had taken it upon himself to mediate with the Shah. No one remembered that it was the same Haji that had initially betrayed Lotf Ali. In expectation the citizens waited in hope. Corpses kept littering the streets and the air became foul by the stench of death. People died of starvation, disease and cold and when the nobles saw the futility of their résistance they collectively appealed to the Zand to write to the Shah. Reluctantly he put pen to paper.

"To Agha Mohammad Khan Gajar.

I've heard that through the mediation of Haji Ibrahim Khan Kalantar you have agreed to break the siege. Should this be true my representative will discuss terms with your emissary."

Agha Mohammad Khan's reply to this letter was curt and to the point:

"The war will stop with your surrender, capture or death."

History has not recorded exactly how Agha Mohammad Khan managed to break the walls and enter the city. Once inside the Shah

---

[83] Moaz is a man with a beautiful voice who goes on the minaret of the mosque and singing the praise of Allah calls the faithful to prayer.

displaced all his pent up anger on the people of Kerman. By his order all the male population of the city were rounded up and blinded.

Lotf Ali Khan together with his friend Jahangir Khan Sistani managed to escape. They headed for Bam where Jahangir's brother Mohammad Ali Khan was the Governor. As Gharan's speed superceded that of any other horse, Lotf Ali found himself isolated from his companion. He rode the 180 kilometres to Bam non-stop and arrived there when the night was thick and the huge gate to the oldest mud fortress in Iran closed. He descended from his horse and knocked several times before the cast iron safety shutter clicked open and an angry voice asked for the name of the night.

"I do not know the name of the night. I am a friend of the Governor and need to reach him immediately. For this service I will pay you."

The gate was promptly opened and a small, bold, irritated man appeared on the threshold stretching his hand for the coin.

Lotf Ali, took the coin out of his coat pocket and put it in the man's open palm and then politely asked:

"Good man, what is your name?"

"I am Safdar, the carpenter, and am guarding the gate in place of my brother whose wife is bedridden. Sire, what is your business at this time of the night?"

Lotf Ali ignored his question and asked:

"Do you know where Mohammad Ali Khan Sistani lives?"

The small man thought for a short while – further reward might be in store for him. He smiled at his luck and said:

"Sire, everyone knows where the Khan of Bam lives. His residence is a way from here. You mount your horse and I will take you to his residence."

"I have been riding for a long time and prefer to walk."

Thus Safdar, walking ahead, navigated through the tight, wiggling, brick paved alleys that ascended the steps to the highest point where the Governor's residence, overlooking the entire environ sat – majestically. On their way, Safdar asked many questions and received brief answers. At the gate of the Governor's residence Safdar knocked a few times before the gate was opened by a tall confident man. In spite of the darkness the man instantly recognized the Zand. With reverence he bowed and said:

"Welcome, Your Highness. This is Ali Ghoshchi at your service.

Please enter and I shall go and wake the master up."

"You know me, Ali Ghoshchi?"

"Sire, I grew up in your father's household."

Lotf Ali Khan put his hand into his pocket, took another coin out and gave it to a beaming Safdar.

Inside the courtyard Lotf Ali Khan gave Gharan to Ali Ghoshchi and asked him to take good care of the exhausted animal and also not to wake his master up. Ali Ghoshchi took Gharan's rein and called a name. Soon another servant appeared and bowed.

"Take His Highness to the guest chamber and serve him dinner while I take the horse to the stable."

Lotf Ali Khan had finished his meal and was undressing when Ali Ghoshchi returned to give him his saddlebag.
"Could you please wake me up early? I need a bath before I leave Bam.
What time do your bathhouses open?"

"They open at dawn, sire. Praise to God that you are alive. I pray that Jahangir Khan is also alive and safe."

"We rode out of Kerman together. But because of Gharan I have arrived ahead of him. He will be here soon."

Ali Ghoshchi woke the Khan just after dawn and led him to the town's bathhouse. The bath keeper, recognizing Ali Ghoshchi took them to the section that belonged to the Governor. Persian baths were built skilfully for they were not only places for hygiene but also places where men from all walks of life met and exchanged ideas and information. The bath's interior was divided into four zones. Nobles, clergy, merchants and commoners each had their own porch. The decoration of these porches and the tiled ponds in which they bathed differed in accordance with the stations in life.

The Governor's huge, blue tiled porch was covered by an exquisite Kerman carpet and the turquoise pond was filled with pleasantly warm water that rippled down into a smaller pond in which feet were washed first. A stout man with a loincloth wrapped around his waist and one hand immersed in a coarse glove stood ready to scrub the nobleman.

That bath was the last indulgence Lotf Ali Khan was destined to enjoy.

Refreshed, with his long, jet black hair spreading over his broad shoulders and a tantalizing smile lighting his shapely mouth the Zand walked out into the street to be met by admiring glances. The merciless sun of the desert was already casting its rays on the round domes of the short mud buildings that crowded the fortress. Dust was everywhere. In contrast to the height of the buildings the baked mud wall that encompassed the fortress was prohibitively high and its wooden gate tall, thick and solid. That particular day no one noticed that the first to pass through the gate was the Governor's fastest dispatch galloping towards Kerman.

At the residence the guest was warmly welcomed by his fat, floppy host whose small grey eyes sparkled with treachery. In a patronizing manner he directed Lotf Ali to the military dining room where they breakfasted amongst other personnel. During the course of their meal they talked about the collapse of Kerman, the ugly Gajar Shah and the safety of Jahangir Khan who had not as yet arrived. Lotf Ali Khan, sure that his friend would arrive safe and sound, thanked his host for his hospitality and told him he intended to leave for Tabas before noon that same day. Mohammad Ali Khan, his mind racing, set forth several reasons why the Zand should remain until the arrival of Jahangir. Eventually, under persuasive pressure Lotf Ali Khan capitulated.

Next day, early in the morning he went to breakfast in the dining room. It was very crowded but there was no sign of his host. He decided to wait for him. His eyes roamed around the room and saw men murmuring and averting their eyes from him. By the entrance he noticed two guards throwing him suspicious sideway glances. The atmosphere seemed thick with intrigue. He became apprehensive. His body tensed, cold perspiration drenched his white shirt, and nervously he pushed away an annoying strand of hair from his short forehead. His host arrived. Everyone rose in respect. He motioned them to sit. They did. The Governor smiled at his guest. They embraced without warmth, talked without saying much and Lotf Ali listened without hearing a word. His mind had numbed. He waited until his host finished eating; then he excused himself and went to the stable, took Gharan and went out of the fortress for a ride around the orange groves. Suddenly he remembered that he had not taken his saddle bag in which were his jewels. Turning back towards the fortress he saw the same two fellows who had been eyeing him in the dining room tailing him at a distance. It dawned on him that he had become a prisoner. He could have fled and neither of the two chasers could have ever caught him. But he could not leave without his saddlebag.

So he galloped to the stable. There he had not yet dismounted Gharan when three hundred men, swords drawn, besieged him. He drew out his sword and they fought for eight hours until a blade wounded Gharan's leg. The beast and its mount capsized. Lotf Ali swiftly picked up his sword rose and fought until both of his arms were severely wounded.

Above, from the window of his office overlooking the huge red brick stable Mohammad Ali Khan watched without any campassion.

European writers have compared the strength and bravery of Lotf Ali to that of Greek Hercules and the Iranians to their hero Rostam.

Dusk had spread its copper wings across the sky and the ground of the stable was littered by the dead and wounded. The Governor, towering over Lotf Ali, mercifully unconscious, was examining his wounds. Relieved that he was still alive he ordered his men to take him inside, dress his wounds and put him on a stretcher so that he could deliver him himself to the Shah's envoy, Mohammad Vali Khan Gajar at Darzin and receive his reward.

It was spring of 1209, 1794, when Mohammad Vali Khan arrived at the barracks with his prisoner. Two men lifted the injured Lotf Ali, from the stretcher on which he had been carried. A man fixed a heavy chain to his trembling blood-stained hands and shoeless feet and a heavy metal leash around his neck. Two other men, each on either side held him up. His outfit torn and blood-stained, his long black hair grubby, his faith in humanity lost for ever he closed his eyes and let himself be dragged like a beast.

In the distance, surrounded by his nobles, Agha Mohammad Khan sat regally. His skin was pale, smooth, and hairless but his eyes, alive and glowing with triumph. For this particular occasion he had discarded his soldier's outfit. He had dressed in a white, linen shirt with buttons of large, shiny pearls, an embroidered, silk vest with gold buttons and a long, quilted silk robe tied at the waist with a jewel-studded belt that sparkled in the sun. From a distance he looked handsome and magestic.

The area was crowded by sycophants and spectators. In awe of the historical moment no one even moved. The only sound heard was the rattle of the prisoner's chains. To watch a brave noble in leash brought tears to the eyes of those with a heart. But none dared to let those tears loose – such had become the fear of the eunuch.

Mohammad Vali Khan, walking ahead of the prisoner, stopped

in front of the Shah, bowed and then side-stepped for the Shah to see the captive. This indeed was a very special moment for Mohammad – in front of him, standing in chains, was the proud lad who had so boldly challenged his sovereignty.

Loft Ali, weak and almost breathless, tried to straighten his posture without success. He could only manage to lift his head and look at the eunuch. Their eyes met – one's glittering with ecstasy, the other's burning with hate. They studied one another for a long time.

Shaik Tonekabooni, who was standing on the left of the Shah could not bring himself to set eyes on the pitiful figure that was twisting and turning with pain, shame and hatred. He began whispering verses from the Koran and when finished blew the prayer towards the captive, sent a curse to the demon called pride, turned his back and slowly walked away.

Mohammad Vali Khan stepped close to the prisoner and ordered him to kneel.

"I will prostrate only in front of God."

Mohammad Vali Khan raised his hand and hit him hard on the head: "Prostrate."

"I told you, I only bow to God."

This time Mohammad Vali Khan put his hand on the head of the prisoner and forced him down so severely that the man squatted on his knees. The hand kept pressing until the prisoner's chin touched his chest – giving the impression of prostration.

The Shah rose from his seat, went to the prisoner and looking down at him said:

"I see you have not lost your arrogance yet. We shall put your stamina to test."

Then he ordered the Zand to be taken to the stable and be kept with the horses without food, water and medicine.

The next day, Lotf Ali Khan was again dragged to the Shah who was encircled by even more of his nobles. The prisoner was so sick that he could not open his eyes and his head rested on the chain around his neck.

The Shah went close to him and said:

"Lotf Ali you are still dreaming?"

Lotf Ali Khan opened his eyes with pain and whispered:

"You castrated, ignoble, Turcoman dog, I am not afraid of you or what you can do to me. You will take the wish to receive my submission to your grave – you beardless ugly eunuch."

Only the guards holding the prisoner heard the exchange. Frightened they let loose their hold and swivelling the prisoner fell on his face as though kissing the ground on which the eunuch stood. The Shah whispered something into the ear of his servant, turned and retired to his chamber.

That night Lotf Ali lost both eyes.

Agha Mohammad Khan left Kerman for Shiraz where he appointed Fath Ali as the Governor of all the southern provinces and then left for Astarabad.

Fath Ali sent his personal physician to take care of the Zand and once a modest progress was made he was sent to Teheran and was lodged with his family in the citadel. His presence brewed fresh rumours and the Shah heard that people preferred a blinded Lotf Ali to a eunuch.

Lotf Ali was executed in the year 1209, 1794.

In Teheran at the Royal andaroon Mah Rokhsar performed her duties with the wisdom of a sage. Following Khatoon's advice she had taken many wives for her son and had undertaken the education of her grandchildren. Fath Ali, viral beyond imagination, was producing children almost every month. This delighted his uncle.

Agha Mohammad Khan was indeed an empire maker with a consistent and clear vision. In a country without an army he managed to create a potent war machine at the back of his own tribal forces and their allies. In a series of campaigns that took almost two decades of his life he managed to unify the whole of Iran under his banner. Thus he brought back security and peace to a country seriously hurt by everlasting civil war. His first step in helping the nation was to abolish the hated practice of "tax or head". Those provinces hit by natural catastrophes were tax-exempt and some even received grants from the Shah's personal coffer. His soldiers' payments were regular and generous. After the conquest of Shusha in Georgia he put a stop to the practice of massacring the male population of the conquered cities and put an end to looting of the cities by the soldiers. He was the first Shah to treat the wealth of the monarch as the wealth of the nation and it was during the Gajar's that for the first time the concept of the Crown Jewels was initiated. He practised his religion and respected the Ulama [84].

The Shah perceived his relationship with his subjects as a social contract; in exchange for the state's providing security and order, the subjects were expected to remain obedient and economically productive. The Shah stood at the top of the social pyramid and the ultimate exemplar within a hierarchy that replicated his patriarchal authority over all lower urban, tribal and familial levels. Every man of rank and authority – the ulama, landlords, chiefs of tribes, city wardens, chiefs of the merchants, masters of the guilds, and leaders of the Sufi orders – was expected to mind his herd and be responsible for its conduct. The ruler was the defender of the kingdom and administrator of justice within his kingdom. Through his demeanour and deeds, Agha Mohammad Shah won the genuine respect of his people. Reverence mixed with fear sealed their tongues. The eunuch was indeed their Shah and he deserved to be crowned.

Agha Mohammad Khan designed his own egg-shaped crown that was to be made of four and a half kilos of gold and gems. His coronation cloak was threaded with gold threads, studded with large emeralds, diamonds and pearls. To create a masterpiece the commissioned jeweller demanded the jewels Nader had brought from India which were now in the possession of the blind Shahrokh. So the Shah sent his messenger inviting Shahrokh to his coronation at the same time asking him to lend the gems for the crown promising their return after the coronation. Shahrokh used his blindness as an excuse to refuse the invitation and denied being in possession of his grandfather's jewels.

It was the first day of Norooz, year 1210, 1795. The scent of blossoms perfumed the air and climbing roses overwhelmed the high walls. Erected triumphal arches were colourfully decorated to suit the occasion. The citadel in Teheran, where the coronation was taking place was alive with the sound of music. Dignitaries clothed in magnificent robes, their swords in bejeweled cases hanging from their gem-studded belts crowded the grand hall – all standing hands crossed over their chests. Whispers were predominantly in Turkish – the language of the Gajars. Agha Mohammad Khan, having crowned himself, sat on Nader's Peacock throne patiently awaiting the end of the gun salute. Regality became him. At that particular moment, the

---

[84] Scholars of religion

happiest in his life, he was pondering upon the travelled path that had led him to the throne of Persia. Proud yet not conceited he smiled at his fate. From the tall windows rays of spring sun poured over the crown making the jewels sparkle like stars. At each corner, in swinging copper burners wild rue was burning evil eyes. The mullahs were chanting their prayers and the spirits of Fath Ali, Khatoon, Mohammad Hassan and Jayran danced in the haze of the penetrating light. For the first time in history a eunuch was crowned and that eunuch was their Mohammad.

Ten lambs for every year of the Shah's life were sacrificed. Kebabs from five hundred and fifty lambs fed the poor of the capital. To each noble who kissed his hand the Shah gave a gold sovereign minted under his name. This custom was followed by all the subsequent Shahs on the Salam [85] of the Norooz.

After the New Year holidays the Shah wrote to all the Governors commanding them to announce in all the mosques the rebirth of a unified Iran, then he set out for a pilgrimage to the shrine of Immam Reza in Mashhad, the seat of the blind Shahrokh. The news of the Shah's trip reached the Governors and nobles of the provinces on his route. These men hurried with their gifts to meet their king and to accompany him on his journey to the holy city. As the Shah and his entourage neared Mashhad news reached Shahrokh that all the nobles of Khorasan had joined the Shah and his advisors urged him to follow suit. Shahrokh refused and only went to meet the Shah at his camp outside the boundary of Mashhad. For his guide Shahrokh chose the most prominent clergy of the city.

The Shah received the grandson of the man who had murdered his grandfather with respect and much kindness. Then he took his shoes off and began his walk barefoot to the shrine. His nobles followed suit.

At the entrance of the shrine the Shah went on his knees and kissed the ground. Then he rose and entered the illuminated hall with mirror mosaic walls and ceilings. The gold surrounds of the crypt glittered, the mirrors multiplied the image of the barefooted, pensive eunuch whose soul was soothed by the spirituality that permeated from the vault. With his small hands he grabbed one of the gold bars, attached

---

[85] On Norooz day the Shah gave audience to dignitaries coming to pay him their respects.

his face to the cold metal and whispered his gratitude to Allah through Immam Reza [86]. For a while his whole entity was infused by the magnetic energy that comes to true believers. At that moment of absolute surrender he felt close to his creator.

Before returning to Teheran the Shah ordered Shahrokh to return Nader's jewels to the people of Iran. At first Shahrokh refused but under torture, two large chests were taken out of hiding and presented to the Shah.

(Those treasures are now in the Jewel Museum in Teheran.)

Two years passed in peace and then news arrived that Ibrahim Khalil Khan, the Governor of Gharebagh in Georgia had abstained from paying his taxes, proclaiming independence. Rebellions were infectious and had to be put down as quickly as possible. So preparations were made and just before the Shah left for Shusha: the seat of Gharebagh, his astrologer rushed to his palace, fell on his knees and begged him not to go to Shusha. His warnings fell on deaf ears as this Shah was not a man to be influenced by apocalyptic revelations. However, on the day of his departure, after his morning prayer he summoned Fath Ali and told him of the astrologer's prediction, warned him of the internecine conflicts that could follow his death. Then said to him: "If I die make Abass Mirza your heir and take Razieh Khanum, the daughter of Mirza Mohammad Khan Bayglarbagi Davalu for his wife so that his son, whom you should name after me, will descend from both houses of the Qajar. My uncle Sulayman Khan E'Tezad al-Dowleh Quvanlu has faithfully served us. Give one of your daughters to one of his sons, and the child of this union will bear a daughter who must be wed to Mohammad Mirza. The son who, God willing, will be born of this union will be your great-grandson from both sides. Then although united with the Davalus, all will be Ashaghebash Quvanlu."

None of Agha Mohammad Shah's wishes were followed so accurately as this ambitious scheme of genealogical engineering. The Shah also warned his heir to never trust Haj Ibrahim Khan Kalantar; the man who had betrayed Lotf Ali Khan.

Later he did betray the Shah and was boiled to death.

The war at Shusha was won, Ibrahim Khalil Khan escaped the city and amnesty was granted to the citizens and looting forbidden. The soldiers were rewarded from the Shah's own coffer. A subsequent

---

[86] The eighth Immam of the Shiat.

uprising in Shiravan also failed and the Shah returned to Shusha where the last chapter of his incredible life was to end.

During long journeys, particularly in wars, each participant had to provide for his own needs; from food to bedding. Although Agha Mohammad Shah ate very little and during the latter part of his life he became vegetarian, he still took most of his household staff with him. Usually the most trusted servants were in charge of the Shah's huge kitchen. All Shahs lived in fear of having their food poisoned and Agha Mohammad Shah was no exception. Working in the Shah's household was a lucrative and prestigious position. Being within the sight of the king had great advantages and many servants proved themselves capable enough of becoming Prime Ministers. One such man in the household of Agha Mohammad Shah was Sadegh Nahavandi. Raised in the household of the Shah's brother Hussain Gholi, he was highly trusted. Sadegh Nahavandi was not only ambitious but also very greedy. After the conquest of Shusha, disregarding the Shah's orders, with two of his subordinates they went to the house of one of the richest nobles of the city and hoaxed him to give them all his coins and jewels. The noble, thinking that Sadegh was acting on behalf of the Shah, obliged their demand.

The next day the nobleman went to the head clergy and complaint about the Shah's injustice. The Shaik, who knew the Shah well, advised the man to put down his grievance in writing giving a full description of the criminals and then give him the letter to deliver to the Shah. Agha Mohammad Shah read the letter and from the description set down suspected Nahavandi to be one of the thieves. He ordered the Shaik to bring the noble to his camp.

It was the morning of 18th Zihajeh of the year 1212, 1797, when in the presence of the Shah the Georgian described the event and gave a vivid description of the men who had robbed him. The Shah ordered him to pull down his hat, stand in a secluded corner and see if he recognized the man who was going to be summoned. Then the Shah asked for Nahavandi, who appeared and prostrated. The Shah asked him some irrelevant questions and then sent him off on an errand. When Nahavandi left the room the Shah asked the protester whether he recognized the entrant. The answer was in the affirmative.

The following day the Shah expressed his wish to have apricots for dinner. The best apricots were grown in a town some distance from Shusha. Nahavandi hurried to procure the fruit. An extensive search of his quarters proved his theft. Nahavandi's two accomplices witnessed the search. Petrified, they waited until Nahavandi returned and gave him the news. Sadegh Khan, who knew the Shah's character well assured them that he would forgive them if they returned the stolen goods to its owner. When Sadegh Khan took his large tray to the Shah he received nothing but admiration of the size of the apricots. The Shah ate what he could and ordered the rest to be preserved. Nahavandi was taking the tray away when the door of the chamber opened and the wronged nobleman, following the Shaik, entered. Their eyes met, Nahavandi went pale, his bearded chin fell and his hands began to tremble causing some of the apricots to fall on the carpet. He bent, put the tray down, then kneeling by the feet of the Shah, with a quivering voice, confessed to the crime. Weeping, he pleaded for mercy. The Shah ordered him to go and bring the stolen goods. Thinking that all was forgiven he hurried to his quarter and together with his accomplices returned with their booty.

The Shah gave the owner a few moments to check the content of the containers and then asked if anything was amiss.

"Two hundred tooman is amiss, your Majesty."

"I shall reimburse you tomorrow myself after the thieves have met with their punishment."

The thieves' hearts began to thump, their faces paled and they exchanged meaningful glances.

The dusk had already spread its dark wings and no execution ever took place at night.

Nahavandi and his two friends were put in the care of the chamber master, who, out of friendship decided not to lock them up in jail and instead took them to a room and posted a soldier to stand guard by their door. The condemned knew that there would be no tomorrow unless they acted fast.

That night, very quietly they strangled their guard, tiptoed to the royal bed chamber, noiselessly strangled the two soldiers on guard and let Nahavandi saunter into the room. The Shah was peacefully asleep. Nahavandi was very swift with his dagger.

Agha Mohammad Shah died having gone through fifty seven springs. He was the Shah of all Iran for twelve springs. Had he not united Iran under a single dynasty, it would have been swallowed up by the whirlwind of European imperialism that subsequently devoured many sovereign nations and reorganized the map of the Middle East.

Fath Ali was in Shiraz, Mah Rokhsar in Teheran and many rebellious chieftains were on their way to the capital. As soon as Mahd Olia heard the sad news she called in the Prime Minister Haj Ibrahim Khan Kalantar, ordered him to mobilize the city's garrison and close the gates of the city until the arrival of the new Shah.

Agha Mohammad Shah's body was carried to Ray near Teheran and was put to rest at the shrine of Immam Abdol Azim until the necessary arrangements were made with the Ottoman Sultan to take it to Najaf. Then shrouded in white, the body resting on a howdah accompanied by two Gajar nobles, two prominent clergy and sixty Koran readers set off for its final destination – the grave he had built for himself at the Shrine of Immam Ali.

Chapter 8

Fath Ali Shah, during the thirty-five years of his reign generated a royal household of unprecedented size. He married Qajar girls, and virgins from all different walks of life. Black and Georgian slave girls, and a multitude of entertainers, eunuchs and others crowded his andaroon. Many of the marriages were out of expediency and the wives were often merely tolerated for their worth. His huge household happily settled in the vast andaroon of the Palace of Roses, under the strict supervision of Mahd Olia.

The palace, divided into male and female zones, was situated in the middle of the town. The andaroon was enclosed by high brick walls and referred to as "The Citadel." Inside, there was a large, extensive, brick paved courtyard, designed with flower beds in bloom, pools and ponds with dancing fountains, fruit trees and a large orange grove. On all sides of the building rooms had been built along the perimeter, one connected to another, two floors high. At the centre of the courtyard stood a three-storey building, closed in by a blue fence. This was the private sleeping quarters of the Shah. The care of the building was entrusted to the chief eunuch. He held all the keys to the royal quarters and to the harem doors. This eunuch was also in charge of the andaroon's affairs. No one entered or left without his permission. Under his supervision worked forty other eunuchs each with an assigned responsibility.

The adjoining apartments were distributed among the ladies related to the Shah. Some of the interior courtyards had outer sections which also contained residences. The Shah's main wives and Sighehs, each had their own maidservants and domestics. The number of women in the harem of Fath Ali Shah thus reached some one thousand. Only a woman as strong and willing as Mah Rokhsar could manage such an establishment. They all had to adjust to palace living, abandon speaking Turkish and learn Farsi.

While the Gajars in Iran were adapting to civil life and strengthening the central government, the French Revolution produced Napoleon Bonaparte. Elsewhere, ambitious European powers were making their mark on history. Commercial and battleships crowded the waterways of the globe and the colonization of less advanced countries was gathering momentum. Avaricious eyes were on the Middle East and the Orient. Iran, because of its proximity to Russia and India was attractive to all. Napoleon had already become an ally and the British, to protect India from his claws, were sending emissaries, diplomats, teachers and doctors to win the favour of the Gajar Shah – and spy on him. Wives of these people found their way into the royal andaroon and set in motion the current of change – albeit slow at first. Foreign doctors and teachers were employed and imitating the foreign ways became a fascinating pastime. Mah Rokhsar decreed that the grandchildren of the Shah from Gajar wives had to be brought up under her supervision. Thus she could mould their characters and arrange their marriages. To follow her late husband's scheme she chose Fath Ali Shah's daughter, Baygum Jan Khanum to marry Amir Ghasem Khan; the son of Sulayman Khan Quvanlu, a faithful ally and a cousin of Agha Mohammad Khan. The bride, only thirteen, with long curly black hair, large black eyes and ivory skin was a goddess of beauty. In stature she was petite but in intelligence she was enormous. Her groom, ten years her senior was a commander in the Shah's army. In 1220, 1806, Shahzadeh Baygum Jan gave birth to a robust baby whom the Shah named Malek Jahan [87]. The infant grew into a vigorous but plain looking girl, with a mind of her own, air of a queen and intelligence of a sage. In her shrewdness and vibrancy Mah Rokhsar saw another Khatoon and set to work on her training.

Amongst Fath Ali Shah's sons, Abass Mirza, from a Gajar mother, was Mah Rokhsar's favourite. He was tall, slender, handsome, benevolent and brave. His mates adored him; his jealous brothers hated him. He was tutored by 'men of pen', as well as government officials. Abass Mirza was a warrior who commanded respect and loyalty. His bravery was a source of inspiration for his soldiers and admiration for his enemies. To follow Agha Mohammad Shah's order for his first wife he took Razieh Khanum, the daughter of Mirza Mohammad Khan Bayglarbagi Davalu, who in the year 1808, gave him a son he named Mohammad after the founder of the dynasty.

On the other side of the Caspian Sea, Alexander succeeded Catherine and the hostilities with Russia in the Caucasus, which had

---

[87] Jahan means universe.

been intermittent since 1805, resumed.

The Russian raids in the Caucasus, a failed landing on the port of Anzali, the insubordination of a few vassals that were manipulated by the Russians in Georgia, in the north of Azerbaijan and in Armenia drove Fath Ali Shah to react strongly. He amassed a large army under the command of Abass Mirza and he took the war to the Russian border. It lasted ten years. The Iranian army was defeated after many bravely fought battles.

On 13 September 1813 a treaty was signed in Golestan by which Persia ceded Georgia, Darband, Baku, Sirvan, Shaki, Gana, Qarabagh, Mughan and part of Talish to Russia. This treaty also opened the way to the intervention of foreign powers particularly in the matter of the succession to the throne. By Article 4 the Russian Tzar undertook for himself and his heirs to recognise the prince who should be nominated as heir apparent and afford him assistance in case he should require it to suppress an opposing party. Through the Tzar's personal insistence Abass Mirza, whom he greatly admired, was appointed the heir to the throne of the Gajars. This infuriated his older brothers.

In order to counter further Russian ambitions, the Shah appointed Abass Mirza the Governor of Azerbaijan. It then became a tradition to give the governance of this province to the heir apparent.

Many European travellers passed through Tabriz, and visited the court. Through interactions with these people father and son realised the need for modernisation but Iran did not have the resources to acquire modern artillery. At the time Iran's economy depended on agriculture and the national coffer was filled either by taxes or lootings after conquests. Oil had not as yet been discovered.

Abass Mirza saw the necessity for his court to change its nomadic educational system to one that would expose his children to the subtleties of Persian civil life and proper governance. To this end he employed government officials and scribes to teach Mohammad Mirza and his brothers numerous diverse subjects.

Through the suggestion of the shahzadeh the Shah himself set to further his own education and proved to be a talented poet, living behind a Divan [88].

Then Abass Mirza set out to modernize Iran. Young Iranians were sent to Europe – to Austria, France, Prussia, and England, to study

---

[88] Collection of poems.

modern science and warfare techniques. At the same time foreign instructors, mostly Austrian were hired. Abass Mirza had the first printing house set up in Iran; he considered the publishing of a newspaper and ordered a few translations of some rudimentary technical books. He ordered the tutors to introduce his sons to foreign literature and history.

Amongst Abass Mirza's twenty-five sons Mohammad Mirza proved the least ambitious. He was remote, shy, taciturn, gracious and very humble. His eyes were large, slanting and dark; his smile kind and his posture relaxed. He was brave yet hated war and confrontation. His soul was pure and his nature loving. Yet he fought side by side his father in every war.

An enlightened prince, Abass Mirza presided over a period of cultural revival, and reforms. His court honoured literary talent whose teachings produced several scholars amongst the prince's sons.

In Tabriz around the year 1822 Mohammad Mirza formed a mystical attachment to a Caucasian émigré, turned mullah by the name of Haji Abass Iravani. Attachment to this eccentric dervish had a profound influence on the life of the Shahzadeh.

In the year 1819 Fath Ali Shah ordered the marriage of Malek Jahan and Mohammad Mirza – she was fourteen and he twelve years of age.

A magnificent wedding ceremony at the Palace of Roses bonded the cousins in what was to become a doomed union. Mohammad Mirza and Malek Jahan were poles apart, in character and outlook. Mohammad was soft natured and gullible. She was bright, lively, domineering, and shrewd. Her heart was as hard as stone; her tongue as sharp as a razor's edge and her judgement sound. The young girl could already read the Koran in Arabic and write poetry. Her only outstanding feature was a pair of black slanting eyes that enthralled. After her marriage she quickly acquired certain becoming European styles and incorporated them into her traditional customs and appeared far superior to those blessed with beauty. Her manner was immaculate, her demeanour highly feminine and her poise regal. Wherever she went her presence inspired awe. Mah Rokhsar, in the autumn of her life tirelessly worked to prepare this grandchild for the position of Mahd Olia. And one day, she summoned her into her private quarters, sat her on the armchair which was a gift from the French envoy and gave her Khatoon's journal, and jewels. Then she unrolled a long skin and spread it in front of her on the ivory inlaid table. The young girl staring at the scroll saw fading brownish stains over some signatures.

Mahd Olia saw the awe in the girl's wide black shining eyes, smiled and said:

"Azizam, I am going to entrust into your care this sacred document left for the Shahs of our dynasty. This is the will of our great matriarch Baygum Khatoon, which we must respect. It was her belief that for the Gajars to survive only the son of those from Gajar wives could rule the kingdom. Blood of non-Gajars will bring bad luck to the dynasty and cause its collapse. Make sure that this rule is observed. Should it be your destiny to become the next Mahd Olia your duty will be to look after the interests of your husband and your son whose four permanent wives must be Gajars.

In worldly matters trust no one for self-interest always prevails. Take preventative measures and put yourself at no one's mercy except God. Foreigners are here to enslave us. Play at their games – pamper them and use them against one another in a way that will create a balance that would shield Iran and the dynasty from their greedy claws. Never trust them but learn from them. Their ways are different – some are good – adopt them. Some are bad – ignore them. But always respect their views for we are all products of our cultural values. Khatoon, God bless her soul, told me this. She was right in everything she said." Mahd Olia stopped, took a fresh breath and continued: "Jahan your husband is not as strong as you are. Look after him and accept him for who he is. That is your duty as a loyal wife. Women contribute more to society than men do for they are mothers as well as wives. As mothers we are responsible for the upbringing of the men who rule our world. So a good mother will contribute to the betterment of society. I want you to understand that a Mahd Olia plays a greater role in our society than the Shah for the Shah is the product of the principles of the Mahd Olia."

Mah Rokhsar stopped again, looked into the black eyes of the girl who was absorbing her every word. The old matriarch smiled, for in the burning eyes that were fixed on her she saw fire. Malek Jahan rose from her chair, went and knelt by the chair of her grandmother, took her hand and kissed it several times. Then she looked up into the kind eyes she loved so much and said:

"Bibi joon, I will make you proud of me."

Mah Rokhsar smiled, pulled her hand away, stroked the bent head and asked her to rise and look at the document. The girl obeyed.

"Do you see the brownish stains?"

"Yes, Bibi joon. Are they blood stains?"

"Yes, Azizam. They are the blood stains of the signatories – your ancestors. Take the pen from the table and sign your name."

While Malek Jahan was signing Mah Rokhsar took the dagger with jewel handle that was resting on the table next to her chair and asked the girl to give her hand to her. Malek Jahan put the pen in its stand and opened her palm upwards. Mah Rokhsar gently took the small soft hand and lightly pierced the tip of the girl's index finger and commanded her to mark her signature with her blood. Thus Malek Jahan became the keeper of Khatoon's legacy.

Mah Rokhsar, having fulfilled all her responsibilities, died soon afterwards. History remembers her with respect and fondness.

Twelve years passed and Malek Jahan failed to give birth to a son. All she produced were female infants who died shortly after birth. This added to the existing tension between the man and wife. Once a week he visited her chamber to perform his procreative responsibility – without love and with reluctance. His heart was occupied by Khadijeh the Sunni Kurd. Malek Jahan knew this and suffered deeply. Her only hope was to give him a son. Perhaps then he would love her. She wished.

Within the andaroon malicious tongues continuously waggled – adding fuel to the fire. Soon rumours began to circulate that the Prince intended to divorce Malek Jahan.

Suddenly sorcerers and soothsayers found their way into the andaroon. The Court's English doctor attended Malek Jahan daily and the Iranian alchemists sent in their various herbs and potions. Then something worked and Malek Jahan became pregnant again. No one except her immediate family, particularly her eldest brother, Amir Aslan Khan became happy. Nine months passed in utmost seclusion. Every drink and every meal was first tasted by Zahra Khanum the wet nurse. Amir Aslan Khan visited his sister frequently and each time murmured secrets into Zahra Khanum's ears. This cross-eyed woman was closer to Malek Jahan than her own mother. She had breastfed her and was privy to her secrets. Regarding Malek Jahan's affairs her lips were sealed, her eyes blind and her ears deaf. She had kept count of her lady's missed periods and knew the approximate date of the confinement, which was to be soon. One Thursday evening when she knew the mosques would be jam-packed she took the sack of gold given her by Amir Aslan Khan from its hiding place, put her chador [89] on and tiptoed out of the andaroon. From mosque to mosque she went in search of pregnant women in their late months. Three she found, and whispering in their ears, she gave them a gold coin each with promises of more to come. The next day she persuaded Malek Jahan to leave the andaroon for the cool of Kohnamir a village about fifteen miles south of Tabriz. One Friday before dawn, when the inhabitants of the andaroon were fast sleep, Malek Jahan's small caravan sneaked out of the city in the direction of Kohnamir. She was tucked in a curtained horse drawn palanquin that moved very slowly.

At Kohnamir they were lodged at a house belonging to a friend of Amir Aslan Khan. Three other pregnant women arrived at Kohnamir from different directions and were housed nearby. The next day, the sun had not yet set when Malek Jahan's pains began to strike. Zahra first summoned the midwife then sent her son to fetch Amir Aslan Khan who was hiding in the nearby village. He arrived in time to witness the auspicious birth of his sister's son – the eunuch's predicted pure Ashaghehbash. That moonlit night in the village of Kohnamir two other infants were born. Hence began the insinuation that Nasser Al-Din was not the son of his father.

The news delighted Fath Ali Shah. He sent the court's fastest dispatch to take the news to Abass Mirza and Mohammad Mirza, both of whom were fighting the tribal warlords of north-eastern Khorasan. They arrived in time for the formal presentation of the infant to the nobility.

It was a brilliant day and the air cool. They came in resplendent garb, each gentleman surrounded by his own guards and pages, their horses – tails painted red – clad in embroidered silks and golden bridles. Two guards rode in front of the nobleman. A third and most trusted guard rode behind.

Outside the Palace, royal pages in bright red uniforms with elaborate headgear awaited the guests. They led the princes and the nobles through the palace gates into the Garden of the Marble Throne, cooled by the splashes of fountains dancing in the midst of a long narrow turquoise pond. The nobles began to whisper. The terrace, usually cloistered by an immense curtain, was open to view. On it was a gigantic throne, carved of green marble, its legs life-sized

---

[89] Islamic cover worn in Iran.

statues of fairies.

When all the nobles had assembled in the garden, Fath Ali Shah's favourite eunuchs stepped onto the terrace. They were five, all white, dressed in long coats tight at the waist and with long, flared skirts, their heads bearing balloon-shaped felt hats. One eunuch stood beside each pillar of the throne. The fifth and the eldest took his place in front. In his hands he held a jewel-studded cushion on which rested the Shah's bejewelled sword that had belonged to the eunuch Shah.

The royal page appeared.

"Make way!" he cried.

"His Imperial Majesty – The King of Kings – The Shadow of God on Earth, the Shahanhah of Iran!"

Trumpets blew. Drums roared. Fath Ali Shah appeared, wearing a splendid robe. He had on a long coat made of green velvet embroidered with paisley motifs studded with huge emeralds. He wore a matching crown of emeralds, diamonds and pearls, a jewelled dagger, shoes embroidered with precious stones, necklaces and rings and bracelets of emeralds and pearls. In his arms he held a bundle of white embroidered silk from which protruded a tiny black head. Behind him walked his son in a much less elaborate garb but with the confidence of a god and then his grandson Mohammad Mirza in a simple robe – appearing more like a dervish than a warrior. He had a subdued smile on his sombre face and no sparkle in his eyes. In his heart he felt shame.

In the garden the nobles were prostrating in unison.

The Shah stopped on the terrace and in his pleasant voice laced with a Turkish accent announced: "Allah has blessed my house with a great-grandson that will Enshallah carry the burden of kingship after his father. You have been summoned here to pledge your loyalties to him, whom I have named Nasser Al-Din Mirza."

He stretched his hand further. The baby boy, his black eyes slightly open, remained composed.

A loud murmur of Mashallah and Enshallah rippled the tranquil water of the blue pond and made the goldfish jump with joy.

In the andaroon Malek Jahan was on her knees praying for the safety and survival of her son. His birth had introduced a new dimension to her life. No longer in love with her husband he had become the focus of her affection and key to her happiness and success. He would become a King and she his partner in power. To this end she befriended all who could be of use. By nature hospitable, she opened her andaroon to the wives of foreign dignitaries, particularly the British and the Russians. It was during one of these visits that Lady Campbell, wife of the British envoy, presented her with a gift, heavy in weight, wrapped in a silk embroidered cloth carried by a eunuch. Malek Jahan Khanum thanked her guest and had the eunuch unwrap it. To her surprise she found a black, cast-iron safe with a rotating disc upon which numbers were printed. Instructed by Lady Campbell she opened the box and in it she found two small bottles filled with a yellowish liquid. She looked at the gifts without comprehending their significance. Lady Campbell, in her broken Farsi explained that the box was a secure coffer that could be opened only by turning the knob on the preset numbers only known to the owner and the liquid in the bottles was transparent ink used for secret messages. The box was for valuables and the ink was to be used if the Khanum [90] needed to communicate in secret with the envoy. Suddenly it dawned on Malek Jahan that the English Lady had come on a mission. An acknowledging smile lit her elongated face and communicated to her visitor that she had comprehended the message well. When Lady Campbell left she went straight to her carved wooden box that bore the signed scroll and Khatoon's journal. She was not surprised to find that it fitted well into the safe.

"So the British spy network had reached the confines of the royal andaroon." she thought with dismay. But the relationship could become of mutual benefit, she thought smiling at fate's hidden hand. A few days later using the invisible ink she wrote a thank you note to Lady Campbell, tucked it inside a silk pouch in which sat a ruby ring and had her eunuch deliver it to the Mission House.

Many years passed. Nasser Al-Din hardly ever saw his father and when he asked for him, he was told that shahzadeh was either away fighting or busy praying at the Khanegha. At times the little, shy boy felt like a poor orphan. No love, no attention and no present ever came to him from his father. But his mother was always there and his uncle. His beloved uncle! They shared a secret – him and Amir Alsan Khan. Oh how much he loved it when he whispered into his ears where to find the gold coins left for him. He had to be very careful in looking for the coins. He dared only to pick them up at night. No one had to know about them – if discovered his uncle would be banned from visiting him.

Had it not been for Amir Aslan Khan's fathering, Nasser Al-Din

---

[90] Lady of rank

would have gone through several bitter Tabriz winters without warm clothing – such was his father's neglect of him.

At the beginning of the 1820's, a man by the name of Sayyid Mohammad Mojahed, a fanatical and fiercely anti-Russian religious leader, launched a violent popular campaign to retrieve the provinces that had been lost in the Treaty of Golestan. He declared a state of Jihad.[91] Abass Mirza advised his father to calm the mullah instead of fighting the Russians. Fath Ali Shah not only ignored his suggestion but made him the commander-in-chief of the army. The Iranians fought with a bravery that even surprised the enemy but their bravery didn't count for much against the Russian modern guns. Iran was defeated. On 21st February 1828, at Turcomanchay a peace treaty was signed by which Iran ceded Erivan and Nakhjivan to Russia. Under Article 7 of this treaty, the Russian Tzar acknowledged Abass Mirza as successor to the Gajar throne and vowed to consider him the legitimate sovereign from the moment of his accession. Subsequently through extensive correspondence, the British and Russian governments acknowledged the appointment of Mohammad Mirza as heir to Abass Mirza and expressed their desire to act together in the maintenance of the internal stability, independence and integrity of Iran.

Soon after the war Sayyid Mohammad Mojahed disappeared. The Shah's spies brought news that he was in Moscow enjoying a luxurious life. He had, indeed, been a Russian agent.

Abass Mirza took the total burden of the defeat on his proud shoulders. His anguish was so severe that even the potions of the English doctor sent by the British envoy failed to cure him. He died at the age of thirty-four; some believe by the same English potion that was sent to cure him.

As far as history is concerned, he was the first Iranian leader to take up the challenge of modernization, and reforms.

Abass Mirza's death officially made Mohammad Mirza, a grandson, heir to Fath Ali Shah who had many sons each with their own aspirations.

Two years later when Fath Ali Shah was terminally ill the English doctor informed his master, who in turn using the invisible ink warned Malek Jahan in Tabriz of the impending death. Happy with the birth of her daughter Malekzadeh Khanum, she summoned her brother

---

[91] Holy War

Amir Aslan Khan, honoured him with the charge of her children, then in company of trusted friends headed for Teheran. On 23rd October 1834, Fath Ali Shah on his way to Shiraz died in Isfehan. He had gone through sixty-five springs.

Ascension to the throne did not come easy for Mohammad Shah. He had to fight several of his uncles and tribal chiefs. Then he had to obtain the approval of the two powers for the nomination of Nasser Al-Din as his heir. During a solemn ceremony the decree of the nomination was read to an assembly of army chiefs and provincial officials in Tabriz. Nasser Al-Din, tall for his age, thin, and extremely shy, wore with surprising dignity the Kyanid ornamental robe of the Eunuch Shah, his dagger, the armlets that were studded with the Daryae Noor and Taj Mah Diamonds and the decoration of the Lion and the Sun; the official state emblem. For the young prince this was a great change from the dismal days when he had to find Amir Aslan Khan's hidden coins.

Mohammad Shah nominated his tutor Haji Mirza Aghasi as his Prime Minister. This enraged Malek Jahan. To her Haji was a conniving impostor set to ruin Iran and curb her influence on the running of the affairs, which she did without her husband's knowledge.

Nasser Al-Din was an intelligent boy with an unhappy face. His large black eyes were shaded by long, straight eyelashes and his arched, joint eyebrows gave the impression of a perpetual frown. His straight nose was on the large side and the shadow of a moustache above his shapely mouth graced his olive skin. According to many foreigners he was very handsome yet withdrawn; he bore himself with dignity and spoke with a voice that was pleasant and authentic. He loved out-door living, hunting and later in life became an amateur painter, poet and writer. He inherited his mother's shrewdness and presence of mind. He was the apple of her eye and she his pillar of strength. Isolated from the outside up to the age of seven, he was confined to his mother's residential quarters, where a host of eunuchs, maids, and playmates compensated for the lack of paternal love. An Abyssinian eunuch slave, Bashir Khan, was in charge of the prince's wellbeing. Bashir was kind and a capable manager who later became Nasser Al-Din Shah's chief eunuch. All the young prince's childhood attendants were treated with kindness and Zahra, the cross-eyed wet nurse from Tabriz, was later honoured to be the mother of his first Sigheh. Her daughter Iffat al-Saltana [92] bore the Shah his most powerful and capable son: Masoud Mirza Zill al-Sultan.

Intimacy with maids and servants and their children, who were his playmates, taught him values of friendship and loyalty. Nasser Al-Din didn't go through the normal stages of growing up. In fact having had no peer involvements he did not go through the important learning and adjusting phases of adolescence. The political demands to behave majestically obliged him to adopt grown-up behaviour that could only be put aside in the private company of the andaroon's intimate residents. He had to grow up fast and that he did at some cost.

Finally, after five years of being separated from his father, in the summer of 1839, he was summoned to Teheran only to be deprived of his governorship of Azarbaijan – something very unusual. He spent the next nine years in Teheran with his mother at an andaroon; hostile to both. During this period all efforts, by opposing parties that included Aghasi, and Prince Bahman Mirza, son of Fath Ali Shah, a protégé of the Russians, were made to deprive the young prince from his right of succession.

Mohammad Shah's andaroon was much smaller than any other Shah. He had only seven wives and nine children. Khadijeh, the Sunni Kurd, his sogoli [93]; was crafty but devoted to her husband. When she gave him a son the Shah's total attention diverted to the newborn infant whom he named Abass Mirza and titled Naib Al-Saltaneh [94], an honour reserved for the Crown Prince. This led to speculation that the Shah doubted the legitimacy of the birth of his heir and wanted to choose Abass Mirza in his stead. Shrewd as she was, after having examined all avenues Malek Jahan made a deal with Aghasi to grant him the charge of the affairs after the present Shah's death in lieu of his support for her son.

Nasser Al-Din was fourteen and of marriage age. He was so good-looking that young girls of all classes waited on his way to catch a glimpse of him. Too young to notice such connivance, within the confines of the andaroon he spotted a beautiful cousin. In intimate relations with his French nanny he trusted her with his desire. Madam Golsaz, to favour his charge played the matchmaker. The girl's background pleased Malek Jahan and the Shah. Soon the young

---

[92] The Chastity of the Sovereign
[93] Favourite
[94] Vice Regent

Shahzadeh married his first primary [95] wife.

After the wedding Malek Jahan commenced extensive public relations in favour of her son's succession. The Shah was ill and anything could happen at any time. Ever since Lady Campbell's visit Malek Jahan had managed to maintain a valuable relationship with the British Mission and in fact had become a good friend of the British chargés d' affaires, Justin Sheil.

The Shah's gout was worsening and his health deteriorating fast. At the same time the young prince's support was rising and with it the power of Malek Jahan.

Nasser Al-Din had a great aptitude for learning. Faced with so many obstacles he quickly realized that he must employ all his faculties and resources, particularly in his dealings with the rival European envoys and Aghasi.

One day when the young prince was low in spirit, Malek Jahan took him to her large bedchamber, opened the English coffer and took out three letters; one addressed to Mohammad Shah, one to Nasser Al-Din and one to herself. She knew what went through his mind and why he always looked so sad. She blamed herself for all her son's internal turmoil. She gave him a loving look and asked him to sit by her on the large red velvet divan that occupied one entire corner of the room. He gave her an inquisitive glance. She caught it and smiling, winked at him. Then she handed the letters to him.

"Here are three letters from your late grandfather – one addressed to you, one to me and one to your father. I want you to read them all. In his letter to your father he gives him ample advice as how to be a good and fair ruler and asks him to make sure you follow the instructions he has given you in his letter 'diligently' because he believes your reign will last for fifty years!"

She stopped, swallowed the lump that was growing in her throat, smiled and looked deep into her son's moist eyes and pointing to one of the letters she said:

"Shahzadelh Abass Mirza sent this for you when you were only two years old. I also want you to read my letter. It is full of praise for you. If your father does not love you enough your grandfather did. Enshallah you will be the Shah and enshallah you will rule Iran for fifty years."

Then she knelt in front of her son, grabbed his lanky knees and began

---

[95] Moslems are allowed four primary wives and endless secondary wives.

to cry – something she hardly ever did.

Nasser Al-Din bent down and kissed her head that was covered by a white cotton scarf and gently said: "Mother, why are you crying? You are breaking my heart even more."

She lifted her head to look at him. Her wet eyes were swollen and her cheeks smudged by the black of her sormeh. [96]

"I cry because your suffering is my doing. Had I pleased your father, he would have loved you. God is my witness that I tried – I tried within the best of my ability. But that was not enough. Please forgive me." She paused to swallow her grief. Nasser Al-Din knelt down by her and put the letters on the carpet and embraced her with warmth. Then he gently unfolded his arms and without uttering another word crossed his legs, picked up the letter addressed to him and began to read it. His grandfather's words were just the elixir needed to lift his spirits up and lighten his heart. When he had finished reading them all, he handed the letters back to his mother, kissed her hand and thanked her for having kept them for him.

A few days later Nasser Al-Din was given back the governorship of Azarbaijan and was sent to Tabriz – this time without Malek Jahan.

In Teheran the night of 5th September 1848 was moonless and gloomy. The newly built Palace of Mohammadieh was hushed in a morbid silence. The Shah's stuffy bedchamber was lit by a faltering candle and the only sound that could be heard was of Khadijeh's weeping and the rhythmic breathing of Abass Mirza, the child of love, who was engulfed in his father's weak, cold embrace.

The Shah was dead. He had passed through forty more or less peaceful springs.

In Tabriz Nasser Al-Din had just returned from a hunting trip when he received the news of his father's death. He retired to his room, sat on his bed, hid his sunburnt face within the folds of his palms and began to cry. He cried and cried until all sadness and remorse was drained out of him. And then when the tears dried, his heart filled with light and his mind with determination.

In the capital, people and the foreign envoys feared instability that usually follows the death of a Shah. Particularly of concern was the continuous controversy regarding Bahman Mirza, the Shah's great uncle; the Davalu revolt in Khorasan and the existence of Aghasi backed by his

---

[96] kohl mascara

private Makuie troops.

In Tabriz the Shah, surrounded by capable men such as Mirza Taghi Khan Farahani was advised not to return to Teheran without an armed force. The Shah listened and while efforts were being made to achieve such an end, on the night of 14th Shaval 1264, 13 September 1848, in a ceremony attended by all the prominent officials, dignitaries, and military chiefs of Azarbaijan, Nasser Al-Din officially declared himself Shah, and coins were minted in his name.

The creation of the army needed money which was not in the Governor's coffer. However with the financial aid of the foreign powers and the gifts received from the nobles; the assiduous Mirza Taghi Khan (having been promoted to the rank of Amir Nezam, the commander-in-chief of the army) managed to form a respectable force that accompanied the new Shah to Teheran.

Mirza Taghi Khan Amir Nezam, thirty years older than the young Shah came from a village in the Farahan district, near Teheran. A son of the chief cook of the house of Ghaim Magham, he benefited from the education offered to the poor. He began his career as a bureaucrat in accounting and through his personal talent and zest managed to complement his bureaucratic and fiscal abilities with military skills. His meticulous efficiency and his contacts with both British and Russian representatives in Tabriz, secured him the secretariat of the European trained, modern Azarbaijan army.

When Nasser al-Din became the Shah, Mirza Taghi Khan was there to guide him. The young Shah was practical and open to good advice. During the three weeks' journey to Teheran, an intimate relationship blossomed between the young Shah and his Amir Nezam, to whom much authority was delegated. As a first step he excluded from the royal camp most of Nasser Al-Din's personal attendants thus intentionally insulating him in a crowd of mostly unknown and newly employed companions.

In the royal camp, through harsh yet necessary disciplinarian actions Amir Nezam created a sense of fear that produced order – hitherto rarely present.

By the time the royal camp reached Yaftabad (seven miles south of Teheran) and awaited the auspicious hour to enter the capital there was little doubt in the minds of those present as to who directed the Shah. Although the king himself was unaccustomed to such disciplinarian measures, he was intelligent enough to appreciate Amir Nezam's efforts that compensated for his own lack of experience.

In Teheran, after the death of the old Shah, dramatic steps were taken to maintain stability. While the old Shah was on his deathbed, Aghasi, aware of the general hostility towards him fled to his private summer residence.

Immediately after the death of the Shah, a council of the "Chiefs of the People" convened and declared itself the representative of all factions of the government. The council was supported by Mahd Olia as the representative of the Shah. All the decrees of the council had to be ratified by her. Effectively she became the Regent.

The council immediately sent two delegates to the British envoy to pledge its full allegiance to Nasser Al-Din Shah and emphasize its readiness to fight Aghasi. Upon the return of the delegates Mahd Olia issued a proclamation confirming Aghasi's dismissal. Subsequently the council persuaded the British envoy, jointly with Prince Dolgorouki, the Russian minister plenipotentiary, to send a note to Aghasi to remain in his summer residence and refrain from any political interference till the Shah's arrival.

Forever belligerent Aghasi, a few days later, commanding a small band of his Makuie guards, arrived in Teheran and took residence in his ministerial headquarters. To initiate open dissension he ordered the arrest of the Bayglarbagi Davalu; the mayor of Teheran. Enraged, the council, Mahd Olia and the foreign envoys reacted with such severity that Aghasi fled and took refuge in the sanctuary of Immam Abdal-Azim shrine, till the new Shah's arrival.

On 20th October 1848, at the most auspicious hour determined by the royal astrologer, the Shah entered a capital decorated with enormous triumphal arches and crowded by well-wishers who stood in his path clapping and shouting, "Long live the Shah." Handsome and majestic in his elegant army uniform the sovereign rode ahead of his impressive army and stole the hearts of all the onlookers; particularly the females. It seemed the whole population of Teheran including the princes of the royal family, the notables, tribal chiefs and members of the clergy had come to see the young Shah.

In the early morning of 22nd Dhu Al-qada 1264, 21st October 1848, in his first public appearance on the Marble Throne on the open veranda of the Palace of Roses, the Shah, only seventeen, his face composed, sat erect wearing the bejewelled Kaynaid crown of his ancestor, the two armlets studded with the Darya-y Nur and Taj Mah and the diamond-studded sword of Agha Mohammad Shah.

The Immam Jomeh [97] in his green turban and black aba, holding the Koran came near the throne, prostrated deep, so deep that his turban tilted to one side. The Shah's hand motioned him to rise. He stood erect, adjusted his turban, opened the holy book and commenced reading the verses that were to bless the reign of Nasseri. Then he stepped back to his place of honour, on the right of the Shah and allowed the nobles, in their splendid local and European outfits, each taking their turn in accordance with their rank, to come to prostrate and offer the Shah their allegiance and kiss his foot. Then came the foreign envoys led by the British representative.

On the same night Amir Nezam, tall and sombre, with his trimmed beard reaching his chest, wearing a pearl-studded robe of honour reserved for the Sadr-e Azam [98], was appointed to the status of Great Chief, (Amir Kabir), and was granted the honorary title of Atabake Azam [99]. A few days later the Shah issued a decree, declaring that all affairs of Iran were in the hands of the Sadre Azam and that he was held solely responsible for all the good and the bad that could ensue. For the first time in Gajar history all powers were vested in one official. The Shah's clever investiture of such enormous responsibility into the capable hands of the Amir Kabir prevented the possibility of a need for a regent for himself.

Nasser Al-Din, forever grateful, rewarded his uncle Amir Aslan Khan with two grand titles of Amid al Molk and Majd Dowleh [100] and gave his son Nasser Gholi Khan the title Amjad Dowaleh making him the Governor of Khamseh and marrying him off to Anvar Saltaneh – a granddaughter of Fath Ali Shah. My grandfather, Gholam Hussain Khan Ehtesham al Molk was the first fruit of this union. To Amir Aslan Khan's second son, Haji Reza Gholi Khan he gave a bride called Amir Zadeh Khanum. They are my husband's ancestors. And when Reza Shah Pahlavi made it compulsory for people to choose a family name ours became Amir Aslani – in honour of our great patriarch.

Amir Kabir's first and most fearsome foe was Mahd Olia, who viewed him as a dangerous threat to her authority and an intruder into the Gajar realm. She was offended to have a rival in power who was the son of a cook and was insolent enough to ignore her influence and

---

[97] The Friday Immam, who is the highest ranking clergy of Teheran.
[98] Prime Minister
[99] The grand tutor.
[100] Luck of the government.

treat her with unflattering aloofness. Malek Jahan believed that as the Mahd Olia she was her son's partner in reign. That fact had to be recognized and accepted by all. Unfortunately, Amir Kabir was a thorn amongst the flatterers who danced to her every tune. So tension grew between the two and became a serious nuisance for the Shah who for the first time was enjoying fatherly love from his devoted Atabak. He was torn between two conflicting loyalties. In Amir Kabir, he vested his hopes for good governance that would preserve his throne; in his mother he sought motherly care and protection from the spoilt Gajar nobility. This animosity was causing him much anxiety and he had to do something about it. To this end, in February 1849 he ordered his thirteen-year old sister, Malekzada, to marry the middle-aged Amir Kabir. To make his sister happy he gave her the title of Ezzat Dowleh [101].

The decision neither pleased Mahd Olia nor Amir Kabir who had to divorce his existing wife, as monogamy was the rule in any marriage with royal princesses.

Mahd Olia detested the idea not only because Amir Kabir was a commoner but because such a union would increase his power and influence. The rest of the royal family ridiculed the notion that the son of a cook should take the hand of their lovely princess. Nevertheless, none of the presented obstacles changed the Shah's mind. Nasser Al-Din had grown up with the servant class, and learned to appreciate their simplicity and devotions. So to him Amir Kabir's background did not matter. Besides, there were other more serious matters to deal with than the social background of his premier.

Between 1848 and 1850 the Babi (Bahai) movement, defying both the religious and secular establishments turned into uprisings in Mazandaran, Fars, and Zanjan. Bloody battles took place and it was not until Bab [102], the leader of the movement was captured and hanged that calm was restored.

During the same period, Hassan Khan Salar, the chief of the Davalu branch in alliance with some Turcoman and Kurdish chieftains, contested the rule of the Guvanlu's. Their uprising was successfully dealt with, too.

Still partially dependent on Amir Kabir, Nasser Al-Din Shah began

---

[101] The respect of the realm
[102] Bab was the initiator of the Bahai religion.

to seek various channels through which he could assert his own independence. Political maturity came to the young and energetic Shah quickly. He issued directives and decrees, demanded swift action, exercised justice, manoeuvred his way through a labyrinth of court intrigue and diplomatic impasses. He stood his ground against the unreasonable demands of the foreign envoys and played them against one another. The unloved, rejected child was dead and a confident youth had been born out of a will to survive, support of an ambitious mother and tutorship of a committed prime minister. Nasser Al-Din had an ambitious vision and a keen sense of diplomacy. He soon became concerned with history, with his own image in the eyes of posterity. He believed in decorum, in greatness, in wealth.

Amir Kabir's desire for joint control of the army and the administration, combined with his near total supervision over the Shah upset many; in particular Mahd Olia and her ally Mirza Agha Khan Nuri, Amir Kabir's lieutenant and partner in the government. Nuri, a scheming fellow, strengthened his ties with the British envoy who also disliked Amir Kabir's attempts to curb foreign intervention in Iranian affairs.

Mahd Olia's hatred for her austere son-in-law increased daily. She regarded him as the chief cause of her son's growing detachment from her. Having no intention of retiring from power play she believed the Shah's reliance on her could not be restored as long as Amir Kabir existed. She plotted against him and he against her. He spied on her activities and took the rumours to her son. He told him that her andaroon not only was a place of intrigue but of lavish entertainment. He feigned upon her love of music, dancing and unbecoming indulgences. He told the Shah that his mother's courtiers loved her brilliant mind, her extraordinary sense of humour and her sensuality. Discreetly he tried to make the Shah believe that his mother was promiscuous and unholy. Embarrassed, the Shah set his own spies upon his mother. They found nothing to report except that her quarters were always filled with Gajar relatives with grievances against Amir Kabir and that one of her protégés named Bibi-Khatoon Astarabadi had founded the first school for girls. [103]

Everything that the Shah heard, Mahd Olia heard too. Now "the

---

[103] Bibi-Khatoon Astarabadi, in 1895 published "*Failings of Men*", the first declaration of women's rights in Iran.

cook's son" was trying to get rid of her by tarnishing her reputation. That could not be tolerated – she decided.

The Shah visited his mother almost every night. At her quarters he could relax and enjoy the happy music of various musicians and dancers she patronized and laugh at her jokes and female gossip that always enthralled him. But now to his annoyance he found the atmosphere of her chambers sombre and her moods dark. In the mornings he had to hear Amir Kabir's complaints and at night his mother's whinges and threats against the Amir. Soon his patience ran out and he temporarily exiled his mother to Qum, a customary place for disfavoured royalty.

Maligned and scandalized, Mahd Olia saw her political survival and her reputation held ransom in a relentless power struggle that could have a tragic end. She wrote letters fiercely denying the accusations and blaming Amir Kabir for fostering the Shah's detestation of her. In her letters she pointed out that she was in contact with princes of the Gajar family and other elements in search of a unity within the tribe and that Amir Kabir had conveniently presented her interactions to the Shah as evidence of licentiousness.

Gradually the Shah's anger subsided. He forgave her and allowed her back. This time Mahd Olia had her own agenda against the "cook's son".

As time passed Amir Kabir's inflexibility and exacting attitude became unbearable even for the sovereign. He lost many supporters and became politically isolated. Due to his uncompromising dealings with the foreign missions, the envoys joined his opponents. The sole base of his power now was the Shah's trust and reliance on him. But the Shah had matured; he desired to present himself to the public as a responsible monarch. Therefore his premier could no longer dictate to him.

The rift between the two surfaced in the summer of 1851, during the royal visit to Isfehan, when the Shah's concerns for the security of his throne clashed openly with Amir Kabir's efforts to sustain predominance over the government. Insensitive to the king's dislike for his brother Amir Kabir requested the inclusion of Abass Mirza and his mother Khadija in the royal entourage. Since the death of Mohammad Shah, the young prince and his mother had been the subjects of recurring harassment by those who had loathed the special favours the late Shah had bestowed upon them. Fear of murder and insecurity had impelled Khadija to seek and obtain British protection. For unknown reasons Amir Kabir consistently advised the sovereign to act with leniency and kindness towards his half-brother. Their inclusion in the group infuriated both the Shah and his mother. Amir Kabir's closer association with Abass Mirza and his dubious conduct towards Khadija during the visit tainted the Shah's trust and increased his suspicions of the Amir. On the way back to the capital when the royal party was in Qum, the Shah appointed Abass Mirza the Governor of the city. Amir Kabir swiftly challenged the Shah's order and instructed Abass and his mother to leave for Teheran ahead of the royal camp. The enraged Shah ordered their return to Qum and reaffirmed the appointment. The Shah had sensed that since the recent death of his first heir Sultan Mahmoud Mirza, Amir Kabir was planning to make Abass Mirza the heir. The new incident assured and exasperated him. In spite of his anger he still felt a deep devotion to Amir Kabir and as yet could not think of his dismissal. But the faction against the Premier was strong and active and the Shah's paranoia deep. Gradually the Shah began to ignore Amir Kabir and talk to his sister Ezzat Dowleh instead. Amir's pleas for an audience were repeatedly denied. This frightened him and made him very nervous.

Two months later the Shah appointed Mirza Agha Khan Nuri as the new prime minister. Nuri's appointment was victory for Mahd Olia and Justin Sheil, the British envoy.

During this period many emotional letters were exchanged between the Shah and his ex-mentor. Finally the Shah granted him an audience during which the Amir unwisely reproached his sovereign by saying: "Is it fair that instead of rewarding me you now prosecute me as a criminal?"

The Shah's reply was: "You are a plebeian of humble origin who took pride in the high position that I conferred upon you. Having been in power for four generations, the Gajars are in no need of a peasant like you to put into order the foundations of their monarchy." Mirza Taghi Khan was stunned by these unexpectedly unkind words. Tears began to roll down his pale and drawn face. Humbled and broken in heart and spirit, shoulders and head bent, he left the palace to seek refuge in the devotion of his wife.

Subsequently Amir Kabir was offered various governorships which he refused. He did not want to give up his hold on the army and out of desperation he wrote to Sheil asking him to grant him protection should the need arise. Sheil, perceiving political advantage in such protection, granted the request.

Through Nuri's intervention and with the Shah's approval, Sheil agreed to persuade Amir Kabir to accept the governorship of Kashan. Sheil's assurances to Amir Kabir that his safety and that of his family and property would be protected by the British Mission and that he would govern with respect and without protestation, seemed to provide an acceptable alternative to Amir Kabir's request for asylum. Upon hearing the news of Amir Kabir's acceptance of the British offer, Prince Dolgorouki instructed the Cossack guards at his disposal to appear at Amir Kabir's residence (at the Citadel) and make him a counter offer of full and unconditional diplomatic immunity. His pride boosted, Amir made the biggest error of his life by deciding to opt for the Russian bid and not to leave Teheran for Kashan. This meant that he had disobeyed a royal order. Amir's decision nullified the British offer and infuriated Sheil. The unfortunate man did not know that Dolgorouki had acted impulsively without having had the official permission of the Tzar. The affair provoked the Shah's rage who perceived the Russian envoy's action as a symbolic violation of royal honour. Russian Cossacks had surrounded the royal premises in the Citadel where Shahzadeh Ezzat Dawleh, Mahd Olia and the Shah's wives were in residence. Besides the insult, the Shah was also terrified of the Russian protection of the Amir which threatened the survival of his reign.

A royal threat of reprisal forced Dolgorouki to retreat.

The following day Amir Kabir was stripped of all his positions, titles and privileges and the necessary steps were taken to remove all his diplomatic protection. Dolgorouki refused to oblige the Shah's request. Thus the Shah was forced to declare Amir Kabir a prisoner.

Resigned to his fate, Amir, accompanied by his wife who had refused to stay behind, and two infant girls; all hidden behind the curtains of a horse mounted palanquin which was surrounded by guards, drove out of the dusty capital and headed towards Kashan and the Royal Fin garden.

In the Palace of Roses, the Shah, forlorn, hidden within the solitude of his bedchamber was fighting hard to master the guilt within his crying conscience. On the screen of his memory were passing the images of a lonely, shy, vulnerable youth that had learned so much from a plebeian. In him he had found and lost the father figure he had never had. Perhaps it was the vengeance towards the real father that had displaced itself upon the man who had given much for the privileges he had earned.

The Shah's Farman [104] gave detailed instructions to the accompanying guards on the treatment of the prisoner and his family. To prevent an attempt to defect to the Russian mission, strict security measures were to be applied; however with utmost courtesy. Soon after their arrival at their new residence the couple became targets of harassment by ignorant guards and other officials. During the forty days in Kashan, to preserve his dignity, Amir Kabir hardly ventured out of his house, except once a day to report to the guards. Man and wife, alone and friendless, would spend hours sitting in the great eyvan [105] reflecting upon the course their lives had taken, the moments of happiness they had shared and the mistakes they had made. In spite of his initial unhappiness with his forced marriage Amir had fallen in love with his wife. Her love and respect had shielded him from the malice of the courtiers. Her pride in him had boosted his ego and her charm had warmed his heart. Now scared to lose him to the Gajar Coffee [106] she made it a rule to taste all drinks and food brought for him.

In Teheran the question of Amir Kabir's future was yet to be settled. His shadow still dominated all aspects of court and government life and made the contrast with the new corrupt and inefficient government more apparent. Nuri's nepotism and the sale of government positions gave cause for much worry. Order and discipline had vanished and those against Amir Kabir found no solace in the behaviour of the new premier who was too busy monopolizing all positions of power for himself and his clan. In his superciliousness he even forgot to pay Mahd Olia her due respect. The dissatisfaction with the new premier made the Shah see the mistake he had made in retrenching Mirza Taghi Khan. However, as bad luck would have it the arrogant prince Dolgorouki started boasting of the impending Russian Imperial protection for Amir Kabir. The news reached the Palace and re-ignited the Shah's paranoia. Nuri and Mahd Olia, independently of each other, encouraged him to order the termination of the Amir.

Amir Kabir's death warrant was issued on 13 January 1852. Ali Khan, the chief of the royal outer servant and Amir Kabir's old protégé

---

[104] Command

[105] Veranda

[106] The poisonous potion used to kill the enemies of the dynasty.

turned enemy, was given the decree and was ordered to go to Fin of Kashan and relieve Mirza Taghi Khan without pain. The decree specified that Amir had to be given the choice of the means by which he would be "relieved". The order was carried out with exceptional speed for Amir Kabir's enemies at court feared the Shah might change his mind – which he did but alas too late. Heading a small group of Royal servants Ali Khan arrived at Fin to hastily play fate's last trick on the fallen kingmaker. He was told that Amir was in the bathhouse. Ali Khan left the company of his associates and, by himself entered the steamed bathhouse where Amir had just finished bathing and his Dalak [107] was rubbing his back with oil of almond. He bowed and asked the Amir to relieve his servant of his duties. One look at Ali Khan and Mirza Taghi knew his end had arrived. With a gentle smile and kind words he thanked his Dalak and asked him to leave the bath house. The Dalak wiped his hand with the towel that was wrapped around his waist, bowed and tiptoed on the warm blue tiles, rinsed his feet in the foot pond and disappeared behind a maze of tiled walls.

"You have come to end my life, Ali Khan?"

Handing the warrant to the Amir to read he responded:

"Yes. All peacocks eventually fall."

"So I was a peacock to you, my man?"

"You were a peacock to all of us. Power blinded, you forgot that you were a peasant and through His Majesty the Shahanshah's grace you were elevated to the highest rank. Not only did he give you endless power, but he made you part of his noble house. And how did you repay him?"

"I was to him the father he never had. I taught him all that has made him great. Is that not enough for the privileges I earned?"

"I see you still like to ride your high horse. Shahanhah's kind order is to ask you by which means you want to be relieved of your useless life."

"I am sure His Majesty never referred to my life as 'useless'."

"It is useless now. Do you want your head cut off, or your veins?"

"Veins please. But first allow me to read the warrant." Amir, with a steady hand unfolded the paper and calmly studied its content, and then put the document on the tiles and resigned, stretched his

---

[107] The person who washes and massages in the bathhouse.

arm. The executioner knelt beside him, took out his dagger from its case, took Amir's hand and made a deep incision on his wrist. Then he requested the other hand. Amir, bearing the pain with dignity, obeyed. The second incision was even deeper. This time Amir smiled at his killer and whispered: "May God forgive me for having incited such hatred in you." Ali Khan ignored what he heard and dropping the bleeding hand ordered his victim to stretch his legs. This was not on the death warrant; nevertheless the dying man slowly untangled his legs from under him and stretched them out. There was no noise. The steam from the bath stank of death while, the blood of a plebeian dropping from the porch onto the tiled floor ran into the Khazineh.[108] Amir, pale and wheezing kept smiling at the busy evil man. Blood oozed out from the ankles too and spread over more tiles. Amir did not utter even a moan. This infuriated Ali Khan. He was expecting signs of human fallibility – instead he was witnessing magnanimity. (Later he told his mates Amir Kabir went to hell begging him for mercy.) Now he picked up Amir's white towel that was folded neatly, shook it open and ordered the dying man to open his mouth wide. Too weak Amir tried but failed. So the killer shoved his thick blood stained fingers into his mouth, forced it open and with his other hand shoved the towel into the mouth until Amir Kabir asphyxiated. Then, satisfied, he rose, kicked the corpse with his foot and then calmly descended the steps of the porch walked to the clean-foot pond and washed his hands, the sole of his shoes and dagger.

The next day Shahzadeh Ezzat Dowleh, in deep mourning, and her tearful daughters were taken back to the andaroon of the Palace of the Roses.

Nasser Al-Din never forgave himself for his mistake – nor did his sister forgive him for the murder of her husband. Subsequently she was ordered to marry four other men of substance but it was through her daughter from Amir Kabir, Taj Saltaneh, that the next Gajar Shah procreated his heir. Thus pure Gajar blood was mixed with that of a plebeian.

To Amir Kabir's credit, his achievements included his reorganization of the army, reform of certain aspects of government finance and fiscal practices; creation of Dar al-Funun polytechnic and the official government newspaper, Vagayi Ittifagaiyat.

---

[108] The pool, filled with warm water that served as the bath tub.

Nasser Al-Din Shah proved to be a survivor – with or without his Atabak. He was a man of many interests and had an eternal love of the outdoors. Horse riding, shooting and hunting were the means of releasing his pent up frustrations. August is the hottest month in Teheran. The heat and the guilt of Amir's execution were suffocating the Shah. So he decided to go on a shooting excursion in the valleys of northern Teheran where the air is cool, vegetation green and rivers roar with excitement. Someone's loose tongue brought the excursion plan to the notice of the editor of Vagayi Ittifagaiyat and the next day all knew that on the 15th of August his Majesty would be going on a shooting expedition.

In the early hours of the publicised date, the Shah left Niyavaran palace, situated in Shemiran, accompanied by a huge party of nobles and friends. Riding ahead of the rest, accompanied by a few attendants, he was approached by three seemingly, tribesmen [109]. One of the men holding out a petition insolently demanded rectification for the insult thrown at his religion by having hanged Bab, the leader of their faith. As the Shah drew near the trio, shots were heard. The Shah swivelled and fell off his horse onto the ground. Panic broke out. A fierce struggle ended with one of the attackers being killed and two captured.

The Shah was carried to the palace and his physician Hakim Toulousan, who was always on hand, nursed the wound which fortunately was only skin deep.

The attempt petrified Nasser Al-Din. He began to suspect everyone including Nuri. His spies set to work and those with the remotest connection with the Babi movement were brought in for interrogation or were put under observation. Included in the list of the suspects were Abass Mirza and Khadijeh. Their involvement was fabricated by their enemies but it suited the Shah to believe in their guilt. Therefore through a series of political manoeuvring Abass Mirza and his mother were sent off on a "pilgrimage" to Iraq – with an adequate annual pension to allow them a decent lifestyle. Eventually the British gave Abass Mirza an English passport and he lived safely within the Ottoman Empire.

During the rest of his reign Nasser Al-Din took charge as a

---

[109] The name of the three men were: Mirza Mohammad Nayrizi, Mohammad Sadig Tabrizi and Fathullah Qumi.

benevolent dictator, following the path of his friend Napoleon III.

The Shah believed in the necessity to modernize Iran and to learn how to do this he made trips to Europe during which he dined with European monarchs, enjoyed their ballrooms and ballets, viewed their armed forces and visited different scientific exhibitions. Having been to a Russian ballet he became enamoured with tutu and ordered many for his wives. Thus the shaliteh, a tutu-style, short, fluffy skirt worn over pantaloons became fashionable amongst the ladies of the royal andaroon.

In Teheran he hired artists and sculptors to beautify his palace, spent entire days posing for portraits where he would appear in royal costume, adorned with jewels and medals. Having imported from Europe the first camera and the art of photography, he kept a photographer on hand at the palace, and had him take photos of him amongst his nobles, wives, family members and attendants. He paid biographers and historians to keep records of his reign, and having read Khatoon's journal he wrote detailed accounts of his own trips to Europe. He maintained prodigious correspondence with other heads of states to make sure no one would forget him. His favourite penpal was Napoleon III whose ideas of a benevolent dictator strongly appealed to him. He held court for foreign emissaries and flourished upon them generous hospitality. The Shah's visits abroad, although costly, were to represent Iran and speak on its behalf. He even established a dialogue with America – hitherto an unimportant country.

In private life Nasser Al-Din was a homely man who enjoyed the basic pleasures of life. He never drank alcohol but he loved food. He had a great sense of humour and loved those who could make him laugh. He always had a "Funny Face" around him. In the andaroon he was surrounded by his women who adored the ground he stepped on. Yet in his heart he felt lonely. And after having two of his heirs die in infancy the question of succession continued to play on his nerves and make him absolutely miserable until finally something miraculous happened to him.

In the auspicious year of 1851 he fell in love – in our modern sense of love: private and individual.

The daughter of a villager from Tajrish in the north of Teheran, Jayran was tall, slender, and vivacious and with a pair of eyes so beautiful that one could not but worship. She was brought to the andaroon to be trained as a female musician and singer. One night, when dining at his mother's elaborately decorated dining room, he noticed her among the musicians who were playing for his pleasure. For a moment their eyes met and his heart melted. She blushed and he crimsoned without removing his tender gaze from her. For the first time in his life, his heart began to palpitate for a woman; desire encapsulated his entire body and a feeling of anxiety gripped him and he lost his appetite. All he could do was imbibe her with his eyes. The sharp eyes of Mahd Olia noticed everything and his interest in the girl delighted her. Now she could use Jayran to regain her son's devotion. So discreetly she provided more opportunities for him to enjoy the soothing voice of the young maiden from Tajrish who soon found herself lodged in the andaroon as a secondary wife with the title of Forough Saltaneh [110].

Attractive, bright and outspoken, Jayran shared with the Shah an everlasting love of nature, riding and hunting. In the saddle, complete with boots and a man's outfit and wrapping her roobandeh [111] around her forehead, she was a novelty in comparison with the serious and submitting ladies of the andaroon. In her the Shah found a sympathetic wife; a loving and exciting energetic companion and a passionate lover. No one so far had shared his bed during the entire night. Jayran found her way there and became his sogoli, hence the most influential woman of the andaroon, overshadowing Mahd Olia herself. The Shah could not live without her and she knew it. She loved the Shah but she also knew her limitations as a secondary wife. Jayran, like all the other intelligent women of the court, had her own agenda.

Often during royal hunts (almost daily), accompanied by a large retinue of gamekeepers, falconers, and servants with her own falcon on her wrist, and riding her horse Ahu, Jayran would take the lead, galloping away from her husband and then returning to boast her prey, delighting the Shah and his companions. Jayran was very popular amongst the Shah's hunting mates. That pleased him immensely and made him proud of her. He loved her for who she was and for him she was perfect. They shared many interests and more importantly they enjoyed the simple pleasures of life, hitherto unknown to Nasser Al-Din. She was daring, outspoken and smart. He never dared to take her for granted. She kept him at a distance, always yearning for her. By being who she was – honest, caring and funny, Jayran put the

---

[110] The sun of the Sultan.
[111] Facial cover

Shah in touch with his human side; a novelty for a hereditary monarch. She made him feel like a man – not an idol. He gave her everything she wished for. She occupied the most luxurious of the apartments at the andaroon and had more servants than the others. Amongst her maids, was one given to her by the Shah himself named Zobaida. She was a poor Kurdish girl with a deformed face brought to the harem at the age of ten in the year 1850. So capable and cunning was this girl that within months she became her lady's personal attendant, governess to her cat Barbi Khan and a secondary wife to the Shah [112]. Nasser Al-Din trusted her so much that he gave her the title of Amina Agdas [113].

When the Shah took other wives, they were sent to Jayran to be trained. One among these new arrivals was Fatimeh Sultan, a peasant girl from the district of Immama. She was given the title of Anis al-Dowleh [114]. Only thirteen she was of medium height, plain looking and very gentle. Her skin was olive, her eyes narrow but bright. She had no beauty but she was intelligent, enigmatic and charming. Her gaze was soft but commanding, her words kind but meaningful. Sometimes her presence overshadowed that of Jayran herself.

In 1852 Jayran, to the delight of her husband gave birth to a son whom the Shah named after his maternal grandfather Amir Ghasem Mirza. Jayran was only a temporary wife and her son could not become an heir. The Shah's love for Amir Ghasem Mirza was so immense that he thought of him and no one else as his heir. However in the midst of unfriendly relations with the British, who favoured the exiled Abass Mirza and, with the Russians, who pampered Bahman Mirza, now enjoying a life of luxury in Garebagh, the Shah faced numerous obstacles to his wish. In addition to Amir Ghasem there were three older boys with the third, Mozaffar al-Din, from an unloved Gajar mother.

Determined to have her son the heir, Jayran began a tireless campaign. In this both Anis Dowleh and Amina Agdas helped her at the cost of infuriating both Nuri and Mahd Olia, who now found in Jayran a formidable rival in power.

Nuri soon realized that he could not fight Jayran. So he decided to

---

[112] It was customary for the Shahs to take maids as secondary wives so that they could become Halal and have access to the royal chambers.
[113] Trustee of the blessed sovereign.
[114] Friend of the realm

work for her. With the Shah's permission he consulted and negotiated with the representatives of the two meddling powers and eventually persuaded them to agree to Jayran becoming a full wife so that her son could inherit the throne. The Shah already had four primary wives so he had to divorce one. That happened very quickly.

A lavish wedding was organized and invitations went out without the customary signature of Mahd Olia, who was repulsed by the idea of having such a low creature as a permanent wife of the Shah. In her place the Shah had his sister Ezzat Dowleh sign the cards. This break with tradition angered the entire Gajar nobility. On the night of the wedding, Mahd Olia who hardly ever cried, wept from the heart, opened her safe, took out the old skin on which the blood stains of its signatories had withered away and burnt it – it had become obsolete.

In September 1857 the Shah nominated Amir Ghasem his heir apparent.

To work within the Gajar tradition the officials created a pedigree that connected the peasant Tajrishi father of Jayran to the Gajars and beyond to the Sasanian!

The couple's happiness was very short lived. Soon they noticed that their son was losing colour and tiring quickly. Doctors were summoned and remedies prescribed. In spite of all efforts the child's condition deteriorated rapidly. His temperature rose high and pain paralyzed his diminutive body. He became so weak that he could not open his sunken eyes, nor swallow anything. To the anguish and horror of the parents the doctors' cumulative efforts proved fruitless and the child died in his father's arms.

It was June of the year 1858.

The cause of death was diagnosed as brain fever, in modern terms meningitis. The death of the six year old boy devastated both parents – the Shah more than the mother. Such was his anguish that he would not eat nor receive anyone. He would just sit on his chair and stare at nothing. At nights he would lament till the breaking of the dawn when he would rise to pray and complain to God for having taken away the light of his eyes and the love of his life. Even Jayran could not comfort him.

The sudden death of the heir apparent heightened factional hostility in the court and within the andaroon could not be accepted as a coincidence. Even before Amir Ghasem's death, Jayran had viewed her son's illness as the outcome of a conspiracy hatched by Nuri and his agents to destroy her and her son.

To prevent their evil influence from taking its full effect, she had refused to allow the Prime Minister or any of his allies, including physicians connected to him to come near the ailing boy. The doctors who treated the child all fell under suspicion for their connections with different factions. Rumours were whispered and many involved Nuri. Both Jayran and Mahd Olia capitalized on the conjectures and turned the susceptible mind of the Shah against the Premier. Investigation into the affairs of the Premier proved him guilty of immense corruption. He was dismissed and exiled to Esfehan.

Having lived through so many turbulent years the Shah emerged as a confident ruler. An avid reader and a good listener, he became conscious of the new phase in the Anglo-Russian competition for supremacy over Central Asia. He began to appreciate the advantages of European-style governance. Within his court there were many experienced men with European experience whom he used. Europe itself was undergoing change. In Russia Alexander the II was introducing many reforms including abolition of serfdom. In Germany and within the Ottoman Empire reform measures were also being taken. In India an unsuccessful revolt caused the transition of the Indian government from the East India Company to the British crown. British relationships with India's neighbouring countries became less threatening and more amicable. Murray, the replacement of Sheil, became more sympathetic and advised the Shah not to delegate all the responsibilities of the state to one individual and maintain the power in his own hand. The Shah, attracted to the idea of ministerial responsibility and division of labour under his own direct supervision, issued a decree to divide up the responsibilities of the government among ministries of the interior, foreign affairs, war, finance, justice and pensions. All ministers would be directly answerable to the Shah himself. They were organized in Showraye Dawlat,[115] which would meet to deliberate the affairs of government.

In addition to the Council of the State, the Shah also introduced the Majlise Maslahat-khani[116]. This was a surrogate legislative body the Shah created at the outset of his reform period. The Majlis was to deliberate on all domestic issues that were expedient to the state and

---

[115] Council of State
[116] Assembly of the House of Consultation

promote development of the country. All men of wisdom were invited to present their ideas to the twenty-five-member assembly of the experienced notables and civil servants. Not only could the Council hear from members of the public and deliberate on matters related to the growth of trade and agricultural development it was also empowered with legislating estimable laws that aimed to improve the life of the citizens and the infrastructure of the country. A majority vote was to determine the Consultative Council's decisions, which later were to be presented to the Shah for approval and implemented by the State Council.

In January 1860 while the Shah was busy with his reforms, disaster struck again. Jayran fell ill, her colour became pale, her beautiful eyes lost their lustre and her verve evaporated. Her irregular coughs became frequent. Not to disturb his sleep she left his bed for her own at the andaroon. Anxiety about Jayran's health became so hard to bear that the Shah increased his hunting excursions. It was during one of these hunts when he accidentally killed a gazelle which he had vowed never to kill. In Turkish Jayran means gazelle. His heart filled with apprehension and he hurried back to the andaroon only to find Jayran dead in her bed. The Shah's grief was beyond measure. The andaroon fell into deep mourning – not for Jayran but for the Shah's grief.

She was buried in the shrine of Shah Abdul Azim. The Shah did not have the heart to attend her funeral. That would have meant acceptance of her death. He could not bear that. For him she never died – only passed to another dimension of life where he hoped to join her when his time came.

Jayran's quarters and all her possessions were given to Anis al-Dawla. Gradually this peasant girl's wisdom, charm and sensibilities wiped away the dust of grief from the Shah's heart and she became his soul mate and advisor. She was the most honest critic of her husband and he listened to her more than he had ever listened to his mother or Jayran – for he knew that her comments and criticism were unbiased and accurate.

Anis al-Dawla made sure never to cross paths with her illustrious mother-in-law. A woman of great taste, etiquette and influence she turned her quarters to a European-style court at which, during festive and formal occasions the wives of foreign ambassadors were admitted into the Shah's presence. All the influential and noble families and all the wives of ministers and other functionaries were also received at her court. Most petitions were submitted through her because when she presented them to the Shah they were accepted. In essence she became the queen of Iran wearing tiaras over her embroidered head covers. Even at the apex of her power she remained a protector of the weak. She never wished to become a permanent wife. Unfortunately, Anis al-Dawla failed to provide her husband with a child.

Amina Agdas was all that Anis al-Dowla was not; conniving, ambitious and cruel – yet extremely loyal and dedicated to the Shah. Playing on the Shah's weaknesses and indulging his many emotional cravings, she allied herself with Mirza Ebrahim Amin al-Sultan, the Shah's trusted butler who had been promoted to the rank of confidante and Court Minister, and later with his son; Ali Asghar Amin al-Sultan, who would become the Shah's last Prime Minister. As a secondary wife and the governess of Barbi Khan she endeavoured to make the cat the focus of the Shah's love and attention. Soon the cat was clothed with all manner of fine, expensive trimmings and fed with delicious food. Waited on like a human being, it had servants and attendants who looked after him day and night. Amina Agdas' little, ugly, dirty nephew was the cat's playmate. As this pet reached the height of its happiness and glory, the women found their husband more occupied with the poor creature than themselves. Growing jealous and resentful, they paid someone handsomely to seize the cat and hurl it to its doom in a deep well. With the cat dead, to the disappointment of these ladies, Amina Agdas lodged the love of its playmate, in the heart of the sovereign. To the annoyance of the entire court Malijak was given the hefty title of Aziz al-Sultan [117] and became the Shah's constant companion. Pleased with Amina Agdas the Shah placed the supervision of the royal treasures and gifts in her custody and gave her a hefty pension, and a huge private property. Although not of the same calibre as Anis al-Dowleh she was highly influential in the politics of the court and instrumental in the rise of Ali Asghar Khan Amin al-Sultan. Suffering from cataracts, she lost one eye before she was able to visit Vienna for treatment in 1891. Shortly after her return she died of a stroke.

The andaroon celebrated her death.

---

[117] Beloved of the Sultan.

Chapter 9

The andaroon was unusually quiet. Anis al-Dowleh had forbidden any merriment within the citadel because Mahd Olia was seriously ill in bed. Foreign and Iranian doctors were visiting her daily but nothing they did relieved the chest pains that came particularly during the night. With all her foes dead and her son totally emancipated from her web, life had lost its lustre – she had nothing else to live for. She knew he was busy struggling against the prevalent forces of imperialism. Without a matching army and limited resources he had no choice but recourse to diplomacy. And that he was doing with considerable mastery. At times he had to give concessions and if necessary retract them. In her heart she cursed the day she had met Lady Campbell. The English were to blame for all the misfortunes of the world. It was the foreign influence that was changing their lives and making it so difficult to adjust to. She was just too old and too tired to face any more changes. Now rooms were lit by electricity – far brighter than the flickering of candles and there was something called telegraph that made communication fast with St Petersburg and London. Both these inventions pleased her. In view of her bad sight she could read better by the electric lamp and she liked telegrams because her spies could send her news fast. "But to what avail?" she thought wistfully. Disappointment and pain had killed her spirit. And now anxiety had been added to all the other ailments. News from the streets was disturbing. It seemed people had acquired a voice and dared to criticize the Shah's modernizing steps. Pamphlets were being circulated, and agitators were poisoning citizens' minds. Her son had turned the capital into a great metropolis with grand buildings, a university, a hospital and several secular schools with proper teachers instead of the mullahs. In the city, there were conduits and streams to direct the underground waters, and good roads linked the capital to major cities. The road to Europe had been opened by the Shah himself.

People of means travelled beyond the shores of the Caspian Sea and some even sent their children to French, Russian or English military academies to study and learn the foreign tricks. Within the andaroon, princesses were taught French, violin and piano. Foreign books were being translated daily and were being read and discussed by the ladies of nobility. The Shah patronized art and literature and he, himself, had become an accomplished artist. On good days he would come to her quarters and make her pose for him – against her vociferous objections. She knew she had never been beautiful but now with all the wrinkles and a dull complexion she had no wish to be eternalized on a canvas.

Nothing pleased her anymore. Not even going to *Tazieh*[118]. Her son had true faith in Shia Islam and patronized the Tazieh that commemorated the martyrdom of Immam Hussein[119] and the sufferings of his followers. These plays were performed during the holy month of Muharram in a mixed spirit of mournfulness and amusement. Mahd Olia, as the first lady of the andaroon, always attended the Palace Tazieh but this year she preferred the comfort of her bed to the noisy gathering and decided to lament for the martyrs in the solitude of her bedchamber.

In her bed and often, by her own order, alone, she reflected upon her life and wondered why she had failed to impress upon her son her devotion to him. All her schemes had been to preserve his sovereignty. That was the advice given to her by her beloved Mah Rokhsar and she had followed that advice to the best of her ability. As strong a person as she seemed to be, inside, she was sensitive and vulnerable. She felt the pains and pleasures of human interaction like everyone else. But because she was so capable and potent no one ever had any sympathy for her. Her pride never recovered from being rejected by a husband she had set out to love but failed to please. Perhaps her pursuit of power was an unconscious endeavour to prove her worth. She was too intelligent to be fooled by sycophants and took everything for what it represented in terms of her ultimate goal – to keep her son on the throne. Inside she felt empty and insecure. However amidst all the grey and gloom a slight matter had lately pleased her and that was the nomination of Mozaffar al-Din Mirza as the heir apparent. This

---

[118] The Shiat passion play.

[119] The third Immam, grand son of the Prophet who was martyred in Karbella.

grandson was married to his own cousin Taj al-Molouk, Amir Kabir's oldest daughter from Malakzadeh. The marriage had been instigated by the Shah himself who had told his sister that he wished for Amir Kabir's blood to be running in the veins of the future Shahs of Iran. The sickly unloved boy from Shahzadeh Shokooh Saltaneh was now in Tabriz away from his father – waiting for his turn.

Gradually as she fell deeper into depression; her pains increased and then one night her large heart stopped beating.

It was the year 1873 and she had gone through sixty-five springs. She was given a grand funeral and was buried in Qum. At the time the Shah was in Europe.

The Nasseri Era was of change and progress. Naturally some people were happy and some not. After all there are always those who are never happy anywhere. One among these people was a clergy by the name of Sayyid Jamal al-Din Asadabadi; known as the Afghani who had a personal vendetta against the Shah and was openly calling for his downfall.

A well-known political activist and advocate of Pan-Islamism, he was born a Shiat Moslem in northwestern Iran. He adopted the nomenclature "Afghani" after being expelled from Kabul in 1869. The presumed Sunni identity brought him wider acceptance in Sunni countries. Chastised by the conservative Ulama in Istanbul for his outspoken revolutionary views, and in 1879 expelled from Egypt by the British who feared his mischievous activities he went to India and then to Europe. In order to appeal to a more diverse audience, he modified both his political and religious messages but he remained consistent in his opposition to the British and in his Pan-Islamic call to regenerate Islam as a political force to combat imperialism.

In 1889 Afghani was invited by Prime Minister Amin al-Sultan, to return to Iran to aid Iran in her negotiations with Russia. However, wary of Afghani's criticism of the regime, Nasser Al-Din Shah expelled him to Ottoman Iraq. The humiliating experience hurt him deeply, and from Iraq he began an intense campaign against the Shah. He called upon the Shiite leaders to denounce Nasser Al-Din for granting a damaging tobacco concession to foreigners. He circulated sinister literature that generated dissent. On the invitation of the Ottoman Sultan "Abd al-Hamid", Afghani returned to Istanbul in 1892, primarily to advocate the Sultan's claim to the

Islamic Caliphate. There Afghani continued to attract dissident Iranian intellectuals and laymen amongst whom was Mirza Reza Kermani; an impoverished petty merchant turned agitator enraged by the wrongs he had suffered at the hands of the Shah's favorite son, Kamran Mirza's henchman named Agha Bala Khan. Kamran Mirza was the Naib Saltaneh [120] and the Minister of War. Afghani decided to use Mirza Reza to avenge himself against the man he hated so much.

While all this was going on, in the year of 1878 a peasant boy was born in the northern village of Alasht, six thousand feet above sea level, in a thatched roof mud shack that clung to the edge of a precipitous slope. The winters were cold in Alasht, the summers arid. This boy was named Reza. He was only a year old when his father died and his destitute mother, Nush Afarin Khanum, wrapped her son in a bundle of straw and tucked him in the pocket of a donkey saddle. She rode the donkey through the hazardous paths of the inhibiting Alborz Mountains to the safety of her brother's small hut in the periphery of Teheran. She found another husband, remarried, and left Reza to the care of his uncle who in turn, gave him away to a friend – Amir Tuman Kazim Khan, a general in the army, who was wealthy and well connected. Reza grew up in Kazim Khan's house but he always remained an outsider. He had a room of his own, food to eat, and a chance to study with Kazim Khan's children. But he was conscious of his humble status – an orphan boy, half-guest, and half-servant, ill at ease among his benefactors, resentful of his fate. He was an intelligent boy, capable of great thoughts and deep understanding. For a while he tried to study with the tutors who came to the house. But he was older than Kazim Khan's children, and they laughed every time he made a mistake. Patiently swallowing his pride he studied with the tutor until he could read, then he quit his lessons. In 1893, when he was fifteen, he enrolled in the first group of the Cossack Cavalry Brigade at Teheran and left Kazim Khan's house to live with his regiment.

Lonely, he devoted himself entirely to his training. He had grown tall, handsome, with a thick moustache and a pair of eyes no one dared to look at. He had impeccable discipline, and unbending

---

[120] Regent

determination. Almost immediately he distinguished himself among the Cossacks, and earned promotions. Both his inferiors and superiors admired and respected him. There was something awesome about this orphan, semi-literate youngster that impressed his peers.

The Persian Cossack Brigade had been created in 1888, under the leadership of a Russian commander by the name of Baron Moadel whose mission was to protect the Shah and the foreign legations in Teheran. It had been established at the request of the Shah, who in Russia had been impressed by the Cossack regiment guarding Alexander II. Nasser Al-Din Shah had asked the Tzar to create a Cossack unit in Teheran. Reza disliked the idea of having a Cossack unit in Iran, whose primary allegiance was to the Russian Tzar, an enemy of Iran. He voiced his objection to his mentor only to hear that the Shah was a great man and he was modernizing the country and bringing it out of the dark ages. Kazim Khan told Reza that the Shah's travels to Europe were to bring home the latest in progress, that the Shah had given Iran its first university, and modern hospital; that he had introduced art, theatre and photography to his nation. Reza always disagreed because he thought the Shah was buying progress at a high cost and he was paying more than he was procuring. He would add that the Shah's concessions in the name of progress were giving the mullahs reason to condemn every monarch as an imposter – a usurper of the position entrusted by God to them. And one day at the end of such an argument Kazim Khan became so angry and shouted at his impertinent protégé that "a king has a duty to protect his kingdom's integrity – without a king this country will be destroyed by the mullahs who would not hesitate to hang you, Reza." Shuddering Reza kept his silence and never argued with his mentor again.

The summer was sizzling hot and the Shah had camped by a river rushing down from Mount Alborze heading south. The smell of wet earth was soothing and the sprays of the river rush refreshing. The Shah was in a dire mood so he decided to take a solitary walk along the river. He walked a long way without noticing how far he had gone. Two armed attendants shadowed him from a distance. Suddenly His Majesty stopped to look at a pair of shapely legs that were teasing the water of the river. He tiptoed behind the trunk of a nearby tree and stood to watch. The legs dipped into the water and slowly a rather plump girl with long, wavy, black hair, pulling her long skirt up emerged from the fold of the trees. She had a happy smile and her large black eyes glowed with pleasure. At first she began to wash her face; then she looked around to see if there were any intruders; relieved that none were spoiling her privacy she unbuttoned her white shirt and revealed two glorious breasts as large as melons with cherry red, erect nipples. She threw her shirt and skirt on the turf and delved into the water shouting with exhilaration as the icy water cut into her soft skin. Shivering she sat on the floor of the riverbed letting its currents pass over her and spray her rosy cheeks with droplets that rolled down her long white neck like diamond pieces. Behind the tree the smiling Shah felt a burning sensation in his loins. That made him extremely happy for it had been a long time since he had desired to bed any of his wives. His infertility of recent years had been a source of embarrassment to him and malicious whisper amongst his courtiers. With his hand he gestured the attendants to turn their backs to him and he stayed hidden until the girl rose, dressed and humming joyously strolled away.

The next day Amid Hosor, the Shah's trusted eunuch found the identity of the girl whose father was a prominent merchant of Teheran Bazaar and went for Khasegari on behalf of the Ghebleh Alam (Mecca of the world). Honoured by the proposal, Valla Khanum, only fourteen, found herself in the royal andaroon with the grand title of Mahboub Saltaneh [121]. Unlike the arrogant inhabitants of the andaroon, Mahboub Saltaneh was down to earth, kind, sociable and very amusing. Her cheerful nature endeared her to all.

To the Shah's delight Mahboub Saltaneh bore him two daughters; the youngest of whom; Khadijeh Khanum, titled Ezza Saltaneh [122] was born in the summer of 1890.

Shahjoon, [123] as we were to call our grandmother, was only six-years-old when her father was preparing to celebrate the fiftieth anniversary of his reign with a nationwide jubilee.

Mahboub joon, as my mother would call her grandmother was full of stories about her life with Shah-e-Shahid [124] particularly what

---

[121] Love of the realm
[122] The respect of the realm
[123] Short for dear princess
[124] The martyred king.

all his wives did in preparation for the jubilee celebrations.

According to her (and history) during those happy days, the Shah was so ecstatic that his smile never left his face. He had become so kind and generous that he granted everyone's wish. At nights, to have a good laugh at the ladies he would arrange ridiculous events. For example he would urge everyone to walk about in total darkness. Having previously equipped several page boys and eunuchs with masks, they would appear suddenly and frighten the ladies who were already aware of their husband's trick. Everyone would pretend to be frightened and act in a silly manner to give him his laugh. Gambling sessions were held almost every night after dinner. He would pull new money out of his pocket, and distribute it amongst the ladies before the start of the game. To please him everyone tried to lose to him. Ecstatic to be the winner he would return his spoils and leave with a triumphant smile – as though he had conquered the world. From the crack of dawn everyone would preoccupy themselves with the preparations for the jubilee, and people's joy knew no bounds. The only topics of discussion were the celebration, the dresses, the ornaments, and the jewellery. Despite all this exuberance there were certain nagging feelings in the air, the reason for which remained elusive.

One night the Shah surprised everyone by ordering the eunuchs to bring in the clothes he was to wear on the day of the jubilee. They were made of the finest black felt and studded with large pearls. The clothes were accompanied by a beautifully designed crown, covered by pearls and precious stones. The ladies, having examined even the minutest seam of the clothes, complimented His Majesty's choices. He beamed with delight. Everyone was in an elated mood except Anis al-Dawla, who silently watched His Majesty with a profound trepidation.

This dedicated woman had become suspicious of the Grand Vizier's dealings with certain dubious elements of the society and had extended her investigations into his activities, never letting up in her efforts to gather information. Thus she had discovered that after having left the country for a while one of the victims of Agha Bala Khan had returned to Teheran on the orders of the cursed Afghani. This man's name was Mirza Reza who had been jailed and tortured by Agha Bala Khan. Somehow the return of this particular man with a deep grudge against the monarchy and at this historical moment worried Anis al-Dowla beyond comprehension.

The Court astrologer had chosen 2nd May 1896, as the most propitious day for the celebration. Governors of all provinces were invited to come to Teheran and all regiments, warriors, tribal, and Cossacks were ordered to march in the parade. In thanksgiving for his long reign the Shah exempted all farmers from two years of taxes and all prisoners were freed.

In Teheran, triumphal arches were erected on every street, shop-owners decorated their stores, the royal kitchen began to feed the poor and new clothes were given to needy children at orphanages.

The night before the eve of this auspicious day, a tearful Jayran came to the Shah in a dream asking him not to come and visit her until after the celebrations. The Shah had never seen Jayran destitute and that made him very unhappy particularly on the eve of his jubilee. He was going to Shah Abdol-Azim that same day to thank God for his blessings and would go to Jayran's grave, as was his habit. To set his mind at ease he called for his dream interpreter and told him of his dream. The man went pale but said nothing for a while and then took the Shah's hand, kissed it and said: "It is said that the dead know the riddles of life better than we mortals. Your Majesty the unknown will be revealed when due." The Shah saw no sense in what he heard and angry, asked for a better explanation.

"I can say no more, Your Majesty. Enshallah when you return from your Ziarat [125], I shall know more."

As soon as the dream interpreter left Anis al-Dowla, who had been waiting to see the Shah, asked for a private audience. Granted they went into a room where, throwing herself at his feet she pleaded:

"I beg you don't leave the palace. My astrologer has predicted that the next three days will be ominous for you. Be merciful to yourself and your nation. Cancel your Ziarat today. You can go after the celebrations."

The Shah's heart sank and his jaw fell. The coincidence was frightening. He pondered for a while and then raised his head and said: "Anis al-Dowla if my subjects look at my reign with fairness, they will see that I have not been a bad king. Throughout my reign I

---

[125] Pilgrimage

have not fought unnecessary battles with neighbouring states. I have not wasted the nation's wealth nor have I usurped people's property. Today the national treasury is rich, and the royal vault is full of jewels and gems. I have managed to maintain my nation's sovereignty. Now with all the plans I have drawn up and all the provisions I have made for my subjects – giving them rights to voice their grievances, abolishing their taxes, convening a consultative assembly for them, admitting regional delegates to represent them – I don't believe their welfare lies in my death. Suppose all my services went unacknowledged and they truly intended to murder me. If I don't go out for three days, they will kill me on the fourth day when I do step outside. So let them do it. I am sure after my death they will realize what a good servant of my people I have been." The Shah stopped and then as though he remembered something else he added:

"I'm not afraid at all. But I feel sorry for my people, because my son is incapable of being a good ruler. All that I have saved for Iran's rainy day he will squander in a few years."

Tears filled his eyes and he wiped them with a handkerchief. Anis al-Dowla whispered: "My Sovereign why do you cry with all the power that lies at your hand?"

He replied: "No, Anis al-Dowla. It's not for me that I feel sad. It is for this land."

Anis al-Dowla looked deep into her husband's wet eyes and said: "My lord! Don't accuse the people. They all love you. The enemy is he who has been the beneficiary of your own generosity. This worthless worm that Your Majesty has raised to such rank that he now dares to plot against you is only but one individual. One man's transgressions don't stain an entire nation."

After a long pause the Shah said: "If you're referring to Amin al-Sultan I have planned his dismissal to take place after the jubilee. But since you insist, I will do it tomorrow."

"Cancel your ride today: first attend to this matter, then go for the Ziarat next week."

"No. I am the sovereign I cannot be intimidated by the slightest sign of danger."

Anis al-Dowla rose, took the soft, small hand of her husband to kiss. The Shah drew her to himself, pressed her to his heart and kissed her on the forehead. That was their last farewell.

The pilgrimage was scheduled for half past one in the afternoon. All the way from Teheran to the shrine, the road was jammed with men and women, walking, riding mules or horses and some in carriages heading towards the shrine so that this once when the holy place was declared to be not off limits during the royal visit, they could see their Shah. With a national life expectancy of only 49 years Nasser Al-Din had been their Shah throughout their lives.

At noon, a horseman galloped towards the shrine and announced to the Cossack leader in charge of the area, that His Majesty's cavalcade was near. Immediately the shrine was cleared of all pilgrims just for the duration of the Shah's prayer.

Outside the shrine all the nobles were waiting for the Sultan and as soon as the royal coach halted, Prime Minister Amin-al Sultan ran forward to open its door. Two nobles held His Majesty's hand and helped him alight. He was smartly dressed in a grey tunic, decorated with various medals, over his black trousers and soldier's boots. He had a leather belt studded with diamonds and a lambskin hat tilted to one side. A cape hung from his shoulders over his outfit.

The Shah greeted all with kind words and then proceeded to the shrine. Once inside and alone he grabbed the gold grill surrounding the sarcophagus, rested his forehead against the cold metal and began to murmur his prayer and thanks. He sent a prayer for his grandfather, Abass Mirza who had predicted the length of his reign years ago and then he turned to head for Jayran's grave when he faced a clergy with a drawn and pale face holding a petition. As the Shah stretched his hand to take the petition the man, with his other hand that held a gun, fired at point blank range, several shots. The Shah fell, his blood running over the marble floor towards Jayrans's grave. The Cossack leader and the royal guards charged the attacker, took away his gun and tied his hands. The man smiled at his captors for he had acted as the sword of justice – according to his master – the Afghani.

Amin-al Sultan ran to the Shah, knelt and shaking him hard, pressed an ear to his heart. He heard nothing but the sound of the crowd outside – the people, having heard the gunshot, panicked, had burst into a frenzy of cries and questions. Then he heard the Shah whisper: "Bury me next to Jayran."

During the chaos that followed Amin al Sultan, a seasoned

politician, unreasonably suspected by the ladies of the andaroon, decided that the death of the Shah had to be kept quiet for the moment. He calmly stood up, his face pallid but remarkably composed. He looked at the assassin and instantly recognized him as Mirza Reza Kermani, the agitator with grievances against Kamran Mirza and strong links with the Iranian clergy. Calmly he ordered the Cossacks holding the assassin to keep him inside the shrine, then walked outside and, facing the crowd raised his hand commanding silence and said: "Praise to God, His Majesty the King of Kings is alive and unharmed." A heavy sigh of relief went up and frightened away the pigeons that had taken refuge on the golden dome of the mausoleum. The Prime Minister praised God again and then re-entered the shrine. There he quickly ordered Mirza Reza to be taken to Teheran and then he called for the royal chair. He picked up the Shah's corpse, and arranged it on the chair so it was sitting straight, the eyes still open. With the aid of a Cossack he held the corpse in place and waited for it to harden. Then he ordered the Cossack to hold the Shah's hand and talk to him while the chair was being moved. Thus the Shah, now placed in his carriage was carried to Teheran.

Nasser Al-Din Shah went through sixty-five springs and reigned peacefully for half a century, less one day.

History has judged him a benevolent Shah.

Late afternoon of the same day there was a major commotion in the andaroon. Despite Amin al-Sultan's explicit orders for silence one of the younger eunuchs, unable to bear his anguish, tears running down his beardless face, had rushed to inform the ladies that the Shah had been fired upon. Suddenly a storm of emotions broke out. All the women, with awestricken faces, dishevelled hair and without their veils rushed out of their lodgings and ran to the government house. Screaming they demanded to see the Shah. The head eunuch, his face ashen, presented himself and with a quivering voice announced that the Shah had been wounded and was being taken care of in the White Hall. The women's screams turned into shrieks. Another eunuch emerged with the news that His Majesty was well and would soon enter the harem from the main entrance. The women rushed to that entrance. Weeping hard, they waited until dusk, which vanquished their hopes of ever seeing their husband again. That entire night one could hear nothing but the sad hum of deep sorrow. No one had any respite till the morning when all the ladies gathered in Anis al-Dowla's quarters to resume the outpour of their grief and wait for her guidance. Anis al-Dowla bore her sorrow with admirable poise and tried to console the others. It was hard but she managed it anyway.

Outside the andaroon quickly and efficiently official announcements were made, the new Shah declared and the royal burial organized.

Two days later the Shah's body, having been washed and shrouded at the palace was carried to the Shrine of Shah Abdol Azim and was ceremoniously buried next to Jayran's grave. Later his figure was carved on a single piece of white marble that was placed on his grave. That stone was removed by the revolutionary guards and is now in the Palace of Roses. Only God knows what purpose this serves.

Until the arrival of Mozaffar Al-Din Shah the Prime Minister was in charge of the state affairs. For the first time in recent history, succession was taking place without being contested. The Shah's two powerful brothers, Zelle al-Sultan, the all powerful Governor of Isfehan, and Kamran Mirza Nayeb Saltaneh, had already pledged their loyalty to their brother.

The Palace of Roses, once filled with exuberance had stumbled into a dreadful, agonizing sobriety. Clothed in black all those pretty faces were drawn, the complexions clouded, the eyes swollen and their hearts bleeding. The happy days of the past just seemed like a sweet dream.

But life went on.

After the royal funeral an extensive interrogation of Mirza Reza Kermani revealed his association with Afghani and the Ottoman Sultan Abd al-Hamid. Having told his master of his grievance against Kamran Mirza and his imprisonments Afghani had read to him from Rumi's Masnavi: "The fish begins to stink at the head and not the tail." Afghani cleverly managed to convince Mirza Reza that the Shah posed a major obstacle to the long-cherished dream of Pan-Islamism, which Afghani wished to see fulfilled under the auspices of the Ottoman Sultan. Apparently the Sultan had said to Afghani: "By reason of the long duration of his reign and his esteemed age, Nasser Al-Din Shah has acquired a power and prestige such that, if he is firm, the Shiite Ulama and the people of

Iran will not move to support our ideas or accomplish our aims. We must therefore think of some plan for dealing with him personally."

Mirza Reza Kermani, the tool of the Afghani and the Ottoman Sultan was subsequently hanged in public – believing that he had been the sword of justice.

The Ottoman Sultan, soon awakened to the true nature of Afghani, put him under house arrest until he died – cause of death unknown.

The new Shah's arrival did not face any unforeseen problems. His father had left him a stable monarchy. His small family of seven wives and a dozen children noisily settled at the Palace of Roses. The Shah's marriage to Taj al-Molouk had not lasted long. After giving him a son the marriage failed to bring happiness. Of strong character, Taj Al-Molouk could not tolerate her husband's weaknesses. Once their relationship became violent Nasser Al-Din Shah granted permission to divorce and Taj Al-Molouk and her son Mohammad Ali Mirza were returned to the andaroon of Nasser Al-Din Shah until Mohammad Ali Mirza was twelve years old. Nasser Al-Din Shah, who loved his grandson dearly, arranged for his marriage to his cousin Malek Jahan, daughter of Kamran Mirza. After a grand wedding ceremony the couple were sent to Tabriz to live at the court of Mozaffar al-Din Mirza the Vali-Ahd. And now Mohammad Ali Mirza the Vali-Ahd, had to remain in Tabriz.

After the coronation an edict came down from the Shah demanding the ladies with adult children to leave the andaroon for Sarvestan, the house of Monir al-Saltana; Kamran Mirza's mother who would now be living with her son. Those who had small children were permitted to remain at the Palace. Only a few had children, amongst them was Mahboub Saltaneh. Shahjoon and her seven step-sisters and two brothers – all very young – were left to make the best of their new position. They had already met their sovereign brother who had shown them affection – but in their little hearts they all missed their father who used to play with them and spoil them rotten.

Anis al-Dowla died soon after her husband's assassination.

Mozaffar Al-Din Shah was a very simple, kind, soft-hearted man. He was also gullible, week-willed and without any charisma. His family lacked court refinement and his courtiers were mostly upstarts, Turks eager to fill their pockets. However he was prudent enough to allocate all powers to the capable hands of his father's Prime Minister who was now his.

Mahboub Saltaneh made friends with the new Shah's wives and Shahjoon found herself a beneficiary of her brother's attention and generosity. Years passed in such blissful tranquility and Shahjoon grew up to be a shy, dignified Shahzadeh with large black eyes shaded by long straight eye-lashes and a smile that won all hearts. She was of medium height, slender and always very smart. Her nature was sweet, her heart large and she was as down to earth as her mother. From the ladies to the servants, they all adored her and her mother worshipped her. She was wise, shrewd and talented. She spoke fluent French, wrote poetry and played the piano well. Daughter of a Shah, sister of another Shah, suitors were queuing for His Majesty's permission to wed her. Among those was Gholam Hussain Khan, Ehtesham al-Molk, the oldest son of Nasser Gholi Khan Amjad Dowleh, the Governor of Khamseh and the grandson of Amir Aslan Khan; Nasser Al-Din Shah's favourite uncle. Gholam Hussain Khan, in his twenties was one of the wealthiest, most accomplished nobles of the dynasty. Tall, slender and erect he was extremely handsome, charming and generous. Having been to Russia and France he clothed himself in European clothes and hats. He carried himself with exceptional dignity. A sportsman he favoured hunting, shooting and women! The latter worried the Shah. So before accepting Amjad Dowleh's Khasegari His Majesty ordered Gholam Hussain to take a temporary wife and sire a child. The Shah's concern was not for Gholam Hussain's infertility but gonorrhea or syphilis. Soon Gholam Hussain took a Sigheh [126] and nine months later a robust girl was born and named Fakher Taj [127] Khanum. The Sigheh was given the choice of accepting a hefty sum of money and taking the baby with her or remaining as the nurse to the child or taking the money and leaving the child to be brought up within her father's household. The prudent lady took the money and left the child in the care of the nanny employed for the purpose.

The groom's health proven, the Khasegar was accepted with the condition that the marriage would be consummated after Ezza

---

[126] Temporary wife. These wives were contracted in marriage for a certain duration of time.

[127] Pride of the crown

Saltaneh's puberty. The astrologers determined a few dates and the Shah gave Mahboub Saltaneh five thousand toomans for the trousseau. The inhabitants of the royal andaroon became busy preparing for the Aghad [128] ceremony. The smile did not leave Mahboub Saltaneh's face. She had seen her future son-in-law and also his father who was as handsome as his son and recently widowed. Shahjoon took all the excitement with her usual calm and then one day she saw blood. All celebrated the sign of puberty by singing and dancing and informing the groom that he could indeed take his wife. On the day of the wedding Shahjoon was taken to the bath house with her wet nurse, two maids and Amid Hosor to teach her female crafts and beautify her body. First the hair on her body was removed by the criss-crossing of two fine strings held between the two fingers of her wet nurse. The woman had enough sense to bring a bloc of ice to numb the bride's private part before epilation. Men liked it white and hairless. Even with the ice the excruciating pain brought tears to her large innocent eyes, which were shed without a whine. Then she was bathed in goat's milk perfumed with rose essence. Looking and smelling like a blossom about to open its petals she was returned to her mother's chambers where one of her attendants plucked and shaped her joint eyebrows, powdered her cheeks, rouged her lips and coiffed her hair with a gold threaded cloth sent by the Shah. She was dressed in white silk brocade with gold threads and pearls. Then a thin lacework veil fully covered with gold embroidery shaded her small, smiling face. Around her head was tied a headpiece, consisting of cloth and cotton: two long artificial ears inlaid with gems and covered with glossy gold coins. Once the toilet was finished, Mahboub Saltaneh went to her daughter, put her arms around her, looked at her with pride, kissed her forehead and wished her luck. Two women appeared with their wild rue burner, whirling it over the bride's head to burn the evil eye.

At the great Hall of Mirrors all the Gajar nobility had gathered to wait for the bride. The guests at this Hall were all men sitting cross-legged on the carpet in front of gold platters and trays of confectionery and fruits that they could not touch in the presence of

---

[128] Aghad is the occasion during which the couple are united by the marriage contract which has to be signed by witnesses. A cleric blesses the unity.

the Shah. Music was playing, dancers dancing and page boys circulating gold trays of steaming tea and cold sherberts [129]. The Shah, unaccustomed to the court etiquette of his father wondered why no one was sweetening their palates. Upon enquiry, astonished, he broke his father's rule by permitting the guests to treat themselves with the cornucopia of delicacies that was prepared for them.

Mahboub Saltaneh, accompanied by a small band of musicians and singers singing 'yar mobarak bad' – the wedding song and amongst the hubbub of the other ladies and their children led her daughter to the Shah, whose feet they both kissed and then the ladies settled themselves in the adjoining hall. There the bride sat on a stool studded with all sorts of sparkling gems, her young heart beating with anxiety. In front of her lay a conspicuous sofreh Aghad [130] embroidered with gold threads and pearls. On the sofreh were laid several gold platters of sweets, coloured eggs, bread and bouquets of herbs and flowers. Facing her was a huge gold-framed French mirror and a pair of crystal candelabras. A volume of the Koran encased in green velvet on which was embroidered the Gajar crown, her name, and the date of the wedding, sitting in front of the mirror.

In the great Hall of Mirrors the Shah granted his permission for the groom to enter the lady's hall. As he walked in and Shahjoon saw his reflection in the mirror her fears vanished and a delightful sensation squeezed her heart. For her it was love at first sight.

The Immam Jomeh read the appropriate verses from the Koran and then asked the bride whether she accepted the groom as her husband. Tradition dictates that the bride has to be asked three times before she says 'yes'. But Shahjoon said "yes" after the first inquiry. This thrilled her husband and endeared her to him for the rest of his life. Immediately handfuls of gold coins mixed with sugar candy and jasmine petals were thrown over the head of the couple while in the next hall the marriage contract was being signed by His Majesty and Amjad Dowleh. As wedding present, a village by the name of Bousar, in Rasht was signed over to the bride. The festivities continued for seven days after which Shahjoon, mounted

---

[129] Sweetened fruit juice

[130] In Iranian tradition an embroidered table cloth is laid on the ground on which are set all the elements that bring luck to the marriage. The most important items are a mirror, and a pair of candelabra

on a white elephant-driven howdah, followed by twenty camels carrying her trousseau was taken to her father-in-law's palatial residence at the most prestigious residential area of Teheran called Amirieh. With the Shah's permission Amjad Dowleh invited Mahboub Saltaneh to take up residency with her daughter.

A couple of months later Amjad Dowleh, enchanted by Mahboub Saltaneh's sense of humour and charmed by her sensuality asked the Shah for her hand. Mahboub Saltaneh married Amjad Dowleh, in a very private Aghad and became step-mother of her son-in-law.

Amirieh became the core of happiness for all its inhabitants including Fakhar Taj Khanum and her wet nurse. Soon both Mahboub Saltaneh and Shahjoon became pregnant and in due course presented their husbands with healthy infants. Mahboub joon named her daughter Nosrat Agdas and Shahjoon named hers Ghodsed Dawla. We all referred to Khanum Nosrat Agdas as Ameh Khalleh. [131]

The relationship between Shahjoon and Agha Mamani [132], as we would call our grandfather was one of respect, sincerity and devotion. Nevertheless, living within a society with double standards, Agha Mamani (who had to remain monogamous) made his wife the queen of his heart while discreetly satisfying his sexual desires with other women – particularly the Europeans. Among those who had affairs with him were two of Shahjoon's sisters. My very patient grandmother knew of all her husband's infidelities yet to maintain her dignity never once reproached him. He knew that she knew and she knew that he knew that she knew! Nevertheless this dual standard exists in all male-dominated cultures particularly in the present Islamic Republic of Iran.

The house at Amirieh, which Agha Mamani inherited after Amjad Dowal's demise, accommodated two hundred domestics. This included wet nurses for the children, cooks, gardeners, Abyssinian slave women who had been freed but had chosen to remain within the household and several eunuchs including Amid Hosor, Nasser Al-Din Shah's favourite. Since Amid Hosor was the most respected member of the staff he was allocated the lucrative position of the

---

[131] Ameh in Farsi means aunt from the father's side and Khalleh means aunt from the mother's side.

[132] Father of mother.

"matchmaker".

The house had its own andaroon and Birooni. Several springs fed the pools and irrigated the fruit orchards, orange groves and herb gardens.

Shahjoon gave birth to fifteen infants although only six survived the prevalent childhood diseases that killed ruthlessly. After my aunt Ghodsed Dowlah, God gave her my uncle Hussain Gholi, to whom the Shah granted the title of his great-grandfather; Amid Al-Molk, my aunt Nayer Agdas, my mother Monir Agdas, my uncle Amir Hushang and my aunt Victor.

My aunt Ghodsed Dowlah married Shahzadeh Nosrat Sultan and aunt Nayer Aghdas married Nosrat Sultan's brother Farokh Dawlah. The two princes were sons of Kamran Mirza, Shahjoon's brother and Mohammad Ali Mirza: the Vali Ahd's brothers-in-law.

While the Amir Aslani family lived in ultimate comfort the nation was rising against dictatorial rule of an ineffective Shah. Mozaffar Al-Din lacked his father's political and administrative capabilities. Besides, he had given free reign to his Azerbaijani courtiers who were hungry for power, position and wealth. Their excesses together with the Shah's frequent visits to Europe soon brought the government to the verge of bankruptcy, as his father had aptly predicted. The massive foreign debts incurred had to be paid by the sale of concessions and mortgaging customs and other revenues. The bazaar, the heart of the business in Iran became nervous about the economic state of the country and the average man hit by a devastating plague that had killed indiscriminately was livid. This gave the clergy their opportunity to voice their own grievances and unite with the nationalists against the Shah and ask for constitutional Monarchy through which they planned to exercise their power. Suddenly in Teheran, and especially around the bazaar, where the mullahs had the greatest influence, people spoke of limiting the Shah's powers. From overseas people had learned the idea of nationalism – of a people bound together by a common border; of the duty of kings to protect their country's soil and integrity. Secular-minded nationalists and the clergy in unison demanded the establishment of a parliament and the writing of a constitution. Each group had a distinct and opposing goal: the nationalists envisioned a law based on modern secular thought; the clergy planned a constitution drawn from the Koran, one that placed the clergy above the Shah. Nevertheless, they joined forces against the monarchy. Two of the most respected clerics of Teheran; Seyyed Behbahani and Seyyed Tabatabí joined the movement and gave it the extra strength it needed. The following civil unrest compelled the Shah to agree to a constitutional monarchy. However, to the chagrin of the mullahs the Constitution that was accepted was based on the Belgian model of 1830 that granted all citizens equal rights before the law. It pledged specifically to defend the life, property, and integrity of all Iranians, regardless of religion or race. It prohibited the existence of ghettos – the forced exile of any person to a particular place or neighbourhood, and the refusal of residence to anyone based on religion. No sooner had the constitution been ratified than the clergy declared it null and void. Having found themselves written out of the country's new laws they called on the believers to avenge them. But people were satisfied with their new liberties and were in no mood for vengeance particularly on behalf of the mullahs. Two months after the signing of the Constitutional Decree, Mozaffar Al-Din Shah died.

That was the year 1906. He had gone through 53 springs; ten of which were on the Peacock Throne.

In spite of all his weaknesses Mozaffar Al-Din Shah was receptive to modern ideas and institutions. He was a benevolent man with an open mind. Through his encouragement, education and the press were modernized, modern schools were established, the publication and translation of Western literature into Farsi [133] was encouraged; greater freedom for religious minorities, particularly the Jews, was granted, and a greater access to Europe's educational institutions was made possible by his benevolence and urge for modernization. It was during Mozaffar Al-Din Shah's reign that oil was discovered by Australian William Knox D'Arcy and, in 1909 the Anglo Persian Oil Company was formed. The terms of the agreement granted D'Arcy the right to exploit natural gas, petroleum and asphalt throughout the country, except in the Northern provinces which were the Russian zone of influence. Initially when D'Arcy asked permission for his explorations everyone thought he was mad! That was why he was given such a generous contract.

Mohammad Ali Shah began his reign with a hatred for

---

[133] The language of the Iranians

Parliamentary Constitutionalism. Greatly influenced by his extra-conservative Russian tutor he wished to re-establish absolutist monarchy on the model of Russia. Although he signed the supplement to the Constitution, he remained suspicious of the radical revolutionary societies. This was reaffirmed when in early 1908 an assassination attempt was made against him. Determined to abolish democracy he summoned General Lyakhov, the Cossack commander, and ordered him to besiege the house of Parliament on a day when it was in full session and blow it up. His order was obeyed. Casualties were many and the outcome fatal for the Shah. Lyakhov was promoted to military commander and Teheran was placed under martial law.

In the city of Tabriz a man by the name of Sattar Khan took arms against the monarchy. This man had been raised on horseback, a rifle in his hand since he was a child. As he grew he became famous for his marksmanship and his bravery. He had been drafted by the royal guard into Mozaffar Al-Din Shah's army, and he had served until his brother was killed by a government official. Bruised, Sattar Khan swore to revenge his brother's death, escaped the royal guard, gathered hot-blooded youths and became a bandit without a cause. Soon the band's fame spread throughout north and northwest Iran. And when Sattar Khan heard that Mohammad Ali Shah had bombed Parliament in Teheran, to restore democracy became his cause. He occupied Azarbaijan and found himself fighting the Russian troops sent by the Russian Tzar to aid Mohammad Ali Shah in his fight against the revolutionaries. Tabriz was besieged and supplies cut off. Cold, famine and disease took many lives. Sattar Khan lost most of his followers and was about to relinquish hope when the siege broke off. Sattar Khan found himself the hero of Tabriz. He joined Samsam Khan, the chief of the Bakhtiari tribe and together they rode to the capital and joined forces with the Constitutionalists. To save his life, Mohammad Ali Shah and his family, taking what they could of the crown jewels, took refuge at the Russian Embassy. The National Council deposed the Shah and through an intermediary, negotiation commenced to determine the Shah's departure from Iran. Eventually after several weeks of wrangling the Shah agreed to leave Ahmad Mirza, his twelve-year-old Vali Ahd to replace him on the throne as a constitutional monarch. He accepted an annual salary of close to

£17,000 and agreed to live in a palace in Odessa.

In July 1909, the Shah, Queen Malek Jahan, (Malek Jahan was the first recognized queen of modern Iran), their children and a huge entourage left Iran for exile. Subsequently, backed by the tzarist regime, Mohammad Ali launched two unsuccessful anti-revolutionary campaigns and soon after the Bolshevik revolution he left for Istanbul and then France. He died in Italy in 1925 and was buried in the shrine of Immam Hussain in Karbella.

Mohammad Ali Shah's granddaughter Toran Dokht married my cousin Shahzadeh Khosro Mirza; the son of my Aunt Godsed Dowla and Shahzadeh Nosrat al-Sultan Kamrani. They have two sons.

During all these upheavals Reza Khan was advancing in his career and expanding his political horizons. A curious man, he had recourse to all foreign current events, in particular the westernizing reforms being attempted by the Young Turks; a political party led by Kemal Ataturk.

After the departure of the deposed Shah Teheran fell into chaos. The government had no clear leadership and no plan of action. All seasoned politicians were already dead. Having reached Teheran victorious, Sattar Khan and his followers refused to surrender their arms. During the campaign that followed Sattar Khan was severely wounded and died soon afterwards.

On the day of his coronation Ahmad Shah was only twelve-years-old. His heart was aching for his mother and his large black eyes were swollen and red from tears. When the emissary of the National Council went to take him from the Russian Embassy to the palace of Sahebgaranieh he found a dignified, short, plump boy with straight black hair and a round face dressed in a military uniform and a Turkish fez patiently waiting for him. The little boy was the last of the Gajars to be crowned.

At the same time another little boy, named Ruhollah, (the Soul of God) who had been born at home, in a small, mud brick shack in the rural town of Khomein was learning to read the Koran. His father was a poor but respected and vociferous mullah. This little boy spent his childhood amid the tumult of the constitutional revolution. In 1921 he went to Qum to study theology. There he heard of a Cossack soldier by the name of Reza Khan who had risen to the highest rank in the Iranian army. Ruhollah had no liking either for the Cossacks or the Monarchy.

Chapter 10

In 1914, World War 1 broke out and, within a short period, Iran was divided between the Russians, the British and the Turks. Eventually, two events occurred in Iran's favour. The plague took care of the Turkish army, and the October Revolution caused the disintegration of the Russian forces. The country was left to the British and, in August 1919, an official accord deemed Iran a British Protectorate.

Five years of war had beleaguered the country with famine and misery. As though this was not enough the Bolsheviks, in pursuit of the Russian army which had tried to seek refuge in Iran, landed in Enzeli on the Caspian Sea and formed an alliance with a local rebel named Kutchek Khan. Together, they created the Socialist Republic of Gilan.

Meanwhile Colonel Reza Khan had formed a close and opportune friendship with Sayyid Ziaeddin Tabatabai; a young, cultured journalist who was experienced in politics. Tabatabai, son of a mullah, had easy entrée into influential circles. In order to realize their political ambitions in a country divided between two occupying armies they had to make a choice. That choice was the British, who were particularly opposed to Ahmad Shah. In February 1921, as a result of a successful coup d'état against the government, Reza Khan was promoted to general and war minister and Tabatabai was made the new prime minister. Within a few days, the Russians signed a treaty with the new government renouncing all concessions and zones of influence and promising to respect the country's independence. Shortly afterwards, the Republic of Gilan was liquidated and the British pulled back to the Persian Gulf where lay the country's rich oilfields.

At some stage after that, the alliance between the two men faced a conflict of interest. Tabatabai, was found to be a British agent, and fearful of the general's wrath, he fled to Mesopotamia.

The 1919 Accord was repudiated by Ahmad Shah and the British were forced to accept the Shah's decision. In the process of aggrandizement the all-powerful Reza Khan proclaimed himself the prime minister and, quite audaciously, suggested the young Shah take a trip to Europe. Ahmad Shah named Prince Mohammad Hassan Mirza, his eldest brother, regent and left the country for France – never to see it again.

Meanwhile, Reza Khan, planning to establish a republic, submitted a proposal to the parliament. He faced no objections there, but the top Shiite clergy fiercely opposed his project. The people favoured Ahmad Shah who had proved himself a real constitutional monarch, but the young Shah, afraid of a civil war, did not return to Iran. Eventually, on October 29, the parliament deposed the Shah and handed power to Reza Khan. A few days later, Mohammad Hassan Mirza, together with the Shah's immediate family was shipped to exile in France. Ahmad Shah died in 1930, a heartbroken monarch – a fate, so it seems, that neither of the Pahlavi Shahs were able to avoid, either.

After the departure of the Gajars, well-monitored elections were held to set up a new assembly and, on 21st December 1925, the members unanimously handed the Peacock Throne to General Reza Khan and thus the infant who had been driven on the back of a donkey through the mountainous paths of Mazandaran became the Shah of Shahs, empowered to shape the history of modern Iran. Reza Shah chose the name Pahlavi for his dynasty.

The new Shah, inspired by Ataturk, the President of Turkey, commenced the westernization of Iran. His first reform was to abolish native dress. His greatest opponents, the clergy, protested loudly but without success. To get rid of the chador, Reza Shah at an official inauguration presented his wife and daughters wearing western clothes and hats. He had them photographed and ordered all Iranian women to follow suit. The mullahs and the merchants, whose offices were in the bazaar which was and still is the commercial section of the city, resisted and faced savage retribution. It is said that the police made the rebellious mullahs drink their own urine. In fact, the government did everything possible to denigrate and crush the influence and the power of the clergy. Soon the chador became an absurdity of the past.

Meanwhile, Reza Shah also changed the name of the country from Persia to Iran, which means 'the land of the Arians'. Persia had been the name given to the plateau by the ancient Greeks and, later, by other Europeans. Iranians had always called their country Iran.

The Shah also made it compulsory for people to adopt a surname and apply for a birth certificate.

In spite of all the political upheavals and the collapse of the dynasty nothing really changed in the house at Amirieh. Agha Mamani had always shied away from political life and had lived on the income from his twenty villages around Rashat. Shahjoon was busy with her unmarried children who were in their teens now. Both her sons-in-law, Nosrat Sultan and Farokh Dowla had lost their government positions and were living on their inheritance from their father Kamran Mirza. Shahjoon's third daughter, Monir Agdas had just recovered from smallpox which had mildly dented her soft skin but luckily spared her beauty. Her sweet nature, kind heart, patience and prudence had made her a favourite of her mother. Shahjoon was very attentive to her needs particularly since the recent plague had killed Monir's wet nurse to whom she had been attached. In those days wet nurses were like surrogate mothers who lived in the household until their dying days.

While Reza Shah was imprisoning or killing the Gajar princes with the remotest claim to the throne my grandparents were spending their summer holidays at the mansion in Bousar where they could laze by the gorges and the river that wiggled through the lush estate. Bousar, with its endless rice fields, tea plantations, herb gardens and cool air was a true paradise. Agha Mamani also had goats, sheep and cows grazing on his pastures and a poultry farm. For nutrition, Bousar was self-sufficient. Gardeners were always busy providing the cooks with fresh produce from the garden. In the kitchen there was a charcoal oven for bread baking. So there was plenty to keep everyone industrious.

The women flourished in their new-found freedom. There was always some sort of rumour keeping them curious and lively. Female staff, to enhance their position and salaries looked after the gentlemen far more attentively than the ladies. Often during those hot summer months a quick wedding or two, amongst the staff was arranged and paid for by the Lord of the Manor. Celebrations were joyous with guests fully aware that the bride had already been deflowered either by the master or a guest – hence the wedding. In such marriages both the groom and the bride smiled at their fortune for my grandfather was a very generous man.

While ladies took strolls around the estate and occupied themselves with nature's offerings, their men went out hunting or shooting. In the jungles of Gilan there were plenty of tigers, reindeer, boars and various game. All the well-known landlords of the Northern Provinces were wealthy and their favourite gathering venue during summertime was the great hall at Bousar with its french windows that opened onto a large south-facing balcony. It had french furniture and a huge Bohemian crystal chandelier that illuminated their card table. At home they played Chemin De Fer. In the absence of gambling chips they played with gold coins.

My grandparents were hospitable and generous. Ehtesham al-Molk was the Agha of Rasht and benefactor of the impoverished peasants. Everyone loved and respected him.

In Rasht also lived another Agha, but of common blood, by the name of Mohammad Izadi Gilani Navad Deux. Navad Deux means ninety-two. All famous entrepreneurs of Gilan had a number attached to their surname which signified their importance and credit in the bazaar. Mohammad Izadi Gilani was number ninety-two from a hundred which made him a well-respected individual in his sphere of influence. Mohammad Agha was also a director of the Imperial Bank of Iran, established in Rasht by the British. This made him even more prominent than his peers. He exported rice and tea to Russia and imported various Russian goods to Iran. He had two sons and two daughters. His youngest son was called Hassan. He had been sent to Dar-al-Fonoon; the highest academic institution in Iran at the time. Hassan Agha, besides being educated was handsome and chic. All the women of Rasht were in love with him – and he with them. Rasht, because of its proximity to Russia and the commercial interactions between the two countries was far more modernized than Teheran and Rashti women were known for their sexual liberation.

Hassan Agha and Amir Hushang Khan; my youngest uncle and Amin Divan Safari, who was son of the most eminent landlord of Lahijan were inseparable mates and through Amir Hushang had entrée to the house at Bousar. On one of the occasions that Hassan Agha had come to tea his eyes fell on a beautiful maiden who passed him by too quickly. His heart sank, his loins ached with desire and he told himself he must have her. But aware of his inferior social standing in comparison with Amir Aslani's he did not dare to enquire about the identity of the girl. Fortunately he was aware of the old Amin Hosor's function in the household. It cost him two Pahlavi coins to discover that the girl with mesmerizing black eyes and shapely, slender figure was Monir Agdas, Shahzadeh's third daughter. She was seventeen-years-old and of the sweetest nature. Another fistful of gold coins saw Amin Hosor informing Agha-e-Ehtesham al-Molk of the excellent qualities of Navad Deux's youngest son. The information interested Agha Ehtesham al-Molk beyond Amir Hosor's belief. With a bit of manoeuvering he discovered that His Excellency's overseer had been stealing without shame and had to be replaced by an honest man – rarely available to an absentee landlord. A Rashti son-in-law could resolve this problem. Thus the Master of Bousar ordered his eunuch to make further inquiries about this young fellow. Agha also made a mental note to see Hassan for himself. A few days later what he saw pleased him.

Hassan, by now smitten, took his dilemma to his father who curtly advised him to forget the girl and find someone in his own class. The inaccessibility made Hassan even more eager. He increased his visits to the Amir Aslani house, hoping to see the girl and perhaps establish some sort of connection with her. Destiny was at work. One day upon his arrival at the house he caught Monir chatting with her brother, Amir Hushang. Their eyes met again. His heart began to race and she blushed. He bowed. She nodded and then turned to leave when her brother, who had sensed Hassan's fascination for his sister, held her arm and told her he wanted to introduce her to his best Rashti friend. Monir turned back, their eyes met again. He smiled. She returned his smile. He bowed again. Keeping her smile she invited him to take tea and guided them to the table which was set for that purpose in the veranda. They walked in silence. Neither knew what to say. Then Hassan turned to his friend and said: "Hushang joon, what about a carriage ride in the Boulevard after tea?"

"That is a great idea and we can look at all the Rashti beauties promenading there!"

Hassan blushed, avoided the curious glance thrown at him by the subject of his desire and said: "I meant to go for the ride so that we could buy ice cream."

"We can do both."

Monir found the conversation beyond virtue so she got up and left without a word. Hassan regretted his mistake.

Two days later Amin Hosor bribed Monir's personal maid to deliver to her a note from Hassan. She took it and ran to her secret place in the garden – in the trunk hollow of an ancient tree facing a river that hardly flowed during summers. She kissed the paper and unfolded it. She read: "If I am right, mahe'man (my moon), your feelings for me are as strong as mine are for you. If I am right, mahe'man, meet me by the second gate of your garden at three in the afternoon. I await you in my carriage. I am alive only for you – do not keep me waiting too long or I will die."

Blood rushed to Monir's face, her heart increased its palpitation. She took the letter to her heart and then to her mouth and kissed it several times. The invitation was daring and the act sacrilegious. If they were discovered Agha would kill her with his own hands. The danger made the challenge even more tantalizing. She did not dare to write back. Instead she found Amin Hosor and told him to tell Hassan that his invitation was accepted.

Three in the afternoon was a perfect time to disappear without being noticed as the household would be taking their siesta. Monir had no appetite for lunch. So she retired to the bedroom she shared with her younger sister Victor. Victor was her father's favourite and usually took her siesta sleeping on the floor next to the bed of Agha. So Monir could get ready without being noticed. She changed into her best clothes, rubbed her face and hands with coconut oil and some orange blossom essence and pinched her cheeks several times to make them pink. Then in order not to be recognized she put her black chador on and tiptoed out of the building and disappeared amongst the trees. She met her man waiting by his carriage. Hurriedly she was helped into the enclosure and Hassan ordered the coachman to drive to the Boulevard. At first neither could utter a word. Then Hassan dared to take Monir's soft hand. She felt his warmth and smiled. They rode in silence. Words were not necessary. They were already in heaven.

The secret rides went on for five days then Victor's wet nurse became suspicious and followed Monir to the gate. The carriage took off and the nurse headed for the Shahzadeh's room. When Monir returned to her room her mother and the nurse were waiting for her. Shahjoon ordered her to take her underpants off, lie on the carpet and open her legs. Then she ordered the nurse to check if she had been violated. Embarrassed, blushed and shivering Monir obeyed her mother's orders. The nurse's examination proved her intact. Then Shahjoon dismissed the nurse, slapped her hard on both cheeks and without raising her voice said: "If this man's intentions are honourable why doesn't he ask for your hand?"

Monir took her mother's hand kissed it and whispered: "He doesn't dare."

"Why? Agha would be more than happy to have a Rashti son-in-law whom he could trust with his affairs."

"Shahjoon joon, do I have your permission to tell this to Amin Hosor?"

"I will tell him myself."

One month later Monir Agdas Amir Aslani married Hassan Izadi Gilani Navad Duex in a wedding that went on for seven days and seven nights. Several camels carried her trousseau to her new rented home near her in-laws' great house.

Two weeks later Rasht saw another elaborate wedding – that of Ameh Khalleh and Amin Divan Safari. Mahboub joon gave her daughter the village of Foomen, which had been given to her by her late husband Amjad Dowleh. These weddings were the last festivities the family would enjoy for a long while.

World War II broke out in 1940 and Reza Shah, a pro-German, proclaimed Iran's neutrality. Germany's role in the country's foreign trade was massive and its influence on Iran's army crucial. Thousands of German engineers and technicians were working in Iran. They had helped in the construction of the trans-Iranian railroad that connected the Persian Gulf to the Caspian shore.

On June 22, 1941, Hitler invaded Russia and it became apparent that the allies wanted to use the Trans-Iranian railway to get supplies to the Russians. This meant another invasion of Iran. In late June, the British and Russian ambassadors suggested that the Shah expel all German nationals and open the railway to the allies. The Shah refused. A month later, the government was forced to co-operate and, shortly afterwards, the Russians and the British again divided Iran into three zones: the North went to the Russians, the South to the British and the narrow band in the middle to the Shah. Forced by the Allies, Reza Shah abdicated on the 15th of September 1941 in favour of his son Mohammad Reza. The old shah was exiled to South Africa and, three years later, died in Johannesburg.

Iran became fully occupied and the Tripartite Treaty of 1942 was signed to clarify the allies' position in the country during the war with Germany. The treaty respected Iran's territorial integrity, sovereignty and political independence and guaranteed the evacuation of foreign forces from the country within six months of the end of the war. While in Iran, the British and the Russians did whatever they pleased, from looting to rape. They even went so far as to replace unsympathetic elements in the government with their own partisans. In the north, the Russians replaced the Iranian governors with their loyal political commissars and, through communistic propaganda, were able to create the Tudeh, a party of the masses. In a matter of months, the entire Russian zone became a separate region making secession from Teheran inevitable – a real threat to national unity.

Mohammad Reza Shah's saviour was Franklin D. Roosevelt, another interested politician in the affairs of Iran. Roosevelt saw the communist threat and realized the importance of saving Iran which was the most strategic zone between Russia and the Persian Gulf. A special command was created and, during the course of 1942, thousands of Americans arrived in Iran. Now the country had three occupiers, each with its own particular interest and intelligence network.

In late 1944, the Tudeh triggered a general rebellion. Azerbaijan in the north fell. The Shah appealed to the British and the Americans, who had already honoured the Tripartite Treaty and evacuated their forces from Iran. The Russian forces left Iran only after US President Truman issued an ultimatum to Stalin and Iran's ambassador in Washington pleaded Iran's cause before the United Nations Security Council.

In December 1946, Azerbaijan was recaptured from the Tudehs. The cold war was on and Iran's importance for the West undeniable. So, Washington granted Iran a huge credit to help arm its troops.

Chapter 11

Once the excitement of married life cooled down and the reality of living within a strange society began to reveal its cold façade, the two young brides found themselves miserably unhappy. Left alone in the midst of their Gilaki [134] in-laws, whose dialect they could not understand and their garlic-saturated cuisine they could not appreciate, they began to whisper – only to one another, about their nostalgia for home and for the lunches and dinners they were missing by living in boring Rasht where no one seemed to be interested in making their acquaintance. Monir Agdas, the wiser of the two soon realized that here they were looked upon as royals thus more or less untouchables. Quickly it became obvious to her that the natives shied away from social interaction with them, fearing their uncouthness could be perceived as rudeness. This in-law aloofness hurt both of them deeply. At first, each within her capacity tried to break the ice and then when all efforts failed they decided to confront their husbands with their desire to return to Teheran. To their delight they found their spouses as willing as themselves.

The autumn leaves had not yet been swept away by the icy wind from the north when the two families arrived in Teheran at the Monirieh house. There each was allocated an apartment until the men could find suitable lodgings for their wives.

Hassan's reputation as a shrewd business man had preceded him to Teheran and upon his entry into Teheran society he was offered a partnership in a printing company with new machinery that could print in colour. He began his business with a bullish determination. Within four years he was able to buy his wife and two little boys a beautiful two storey house with a paved garden; in the midst of which was a fish pond shaded by a huge persimmon tree whose branches in winter bent under the weight of its large, pink fruit.

---

[134] People from the province of Gilan.

Amin Divan and Ameh Khalleh lived in a huge mansion. He never worked in his life. Their marriage was blessed with five sons, four of whom died early in life. Their eldest son, Nasser Safari survived his parents to become a tycoon living between France and England.

Ten years passed before Monir became pregnant again. Hassan wished for a girl and Monir always wanted to please her husband. To this end she went on a pilgrimage to the shrine of Immam Hussain in Karbella and begged him for a daughter. It seems, since Hassan was Sayyed, [135] the Immam heard her plea and granted her wish. On Sunday July 7th, 1946, Monir Agdas gave birth to a daughter with a head full of black hair – me. To celebrate my birth, Agha joon, as we called our father, gave a gold Pahlavi coin to every visitor who came to see his beautiful Lily. My name was chosen by my oldest uncle the Amid al-Molk, Dr Hussain Gholi Amir Aslani. He had just returned from his diplomatic post in Belgium and thought I should have a name that foreigners could pronounce with ease!

By the summer of 1947, Father's printing business was flourishing and he was the wealthiest son-in-law of Agha Mamani and the object of envy of my aunts. Agha joon's character was completely devoid of complexes and the airs and graces of his royal in-laws never seemed to bother him. He knew that they were jealous of his financial success. In fact, he had become their bank, from which they often borrowed money for their extravagant journeys to the gambling and spa centers of Europe. Very few of the Gajars ever worked. They usually lived off the income from their land, or pawned their valuables for ready cash. Those with the remotest claim to the throne had already either been exiled or killed, and the rest had to make do with what was left to them by the very rich late Pahlavi Shah, who had confiscated whatever had caught his fancy.

Luckily, Agha Mamani's villages were not by the Caspian shore, the area most coveted by Reza Shah, so his rice fields and tea plantations were safe for now.

In his house also lived two of Shahjoon's destitute brothers, Shahzadeh Salar Saltaneh and Shahzadeh Yamin Dowleh. When Nasser Al-Din Shah died he had nothing of his own so none of his children inherited anything from their father. Agha Mamani loved his two brothers-in-law and took them with him on his frequent tours of

---

[135] Descendents of the Prophet are referred to as Sayyed, a title that bears much respect.

Europe, which took months. My grandparents loved Paris and they visited the city often – every time with an entourage of ten to fifteen, which included their cook. In Paris they usually rented an apartment at Avenue Foche, bought a car and hired a temporary driver. The car was to take them to the casino at Deauville and Shahjoon shopping at Avenue Montaigne. Shahjoon was particularly fond of Chanel suits and handbags and Louis Vuitton suitcases. In Iran we waited for their return impatiently because we knew we would receive plenty of European gifts non-existent in Iran.

It is customary to visit family members who return home from a voyage. My grandparents had just arrived and all my aunts and uncles and cousins were at their house to welcome them and receive their gifts. Shahjoon's personal maid, Ashraf Sadat, the "key keeper", was at the height of her element. She always wore a leather belt from which hung all the keys of the house and trunks. Naturally when she moved one could not but hear the jingle of her keys. That day we had gathered in my grandparents' huge bedchamber. Shahjoon sat on her very special comfortable chair and Agha Mamani, as was his habit lay on his bed with his night cap tilted to one side. The grownups were sitting on chairs and we the children cross-legged on the floor waiting. Suddenly to our delight we heard and then saw Ashraf Sadat come in followed by two men servants, each holding an end of what seemed a very heavy patterned trunk (LV). They placed the trunk in front of the Shahzadeh and Ashraf Sadat immediately produced the correct key with which she opened the trunk. My cousin Bahram was closest to the case; he elongated his thin neck and took a look inside, screamed and started to cry. We all rushed to the trunk and in it saw nothing but what seemed a hairy, black, dead animal. Shahjoon darted amusing glances at us, smiled, turned to my aunt Nayer Agdas and said: "There is a mink coat for each of these children. Take them out, and let me see them wear them." Now I really became frightened.

"Shahjoon joon I am not going to wear this. It is a dead animal," I complained, beginning to cry too.

"Don't be silly, Lily joon. This is a fur coat to keep you warm in winter. Once you put it on you will love it, azizam." So they fitted each of us with a mink coat too big to fit properly. Commutatively we looked like a herd of black sheep. That winter, at first none of us liked to wear our coats as people would single us out and laugh at us. Then gradually we got used to the laughter and began to enjoy the warmth.

Agha Mamani found travelling to Bousar every summer too tiresome. After months of search in partnership with two of his friends, Mokhber Saltaneh Hedayat and Mohaseb Mamalek Shaibani, they bought Darous, a village in the North of Teheran at the foothills of the majestic, snow-capped Alborz Mountains – where Agha Mohammad Shah had chosen his first home. Agha Mamani's only source of cash was my father, who was always willing to lend him money as long as the interest rate was high enough. In those days, there were no banks to borrow from. The only people with cash ready to lend were the bazaaries, who did it discreetly – usury being forbidden in Islam.

Father was not an orthodox Muslim. He performed his daily prayers regularly, helped the poor, never lied and believed in having fun. My mother was the same and their marriage was as solid as a rock.

The family spent Thursday evenings and the whole of Fridays (the Muslim weekend) at Agha Mamani's house. The evenings usually began with the older generation sitting together reminiscing about the good old days. The younger ones would challenge one another in a game of Bakara, while listening to live musicians playing romantic music and singers crooning sad songs, and the children – we lived in a paradise devoid of any restriction and much spoiling. Then our parents wised up and saw the necessity to send the elder children to European boarding schools. Masoud and Mahmoud, my two brothers were the first to go to a private boarding school near Norwich in Norfolk. At the time, Masoud was 13 and Mahmoud, 11. Neither knew any English. The brave little boys were dressed in their best and sent to London, a city drastically hit by the war and still on food rations.

Peace in Iran has been intermittent for centuries. However troubles change forms according to time. In 1949, while attending an event at the University of Teheran, the Shah narrowly escaped an assassination attempt. The assailant, Fakhr Arai, a young member of the Tudeh party, was shot on sight taking to his grave the secret of the daring plot. Martial law was imposed. Most of the known agitators with USSR ties were rounded up and jailed. The communists went underground. And meanwhile, people poured into the mosques to thank Allah for their king's escape. The Shah took advantage of the emotions surrounding the event and made a series of political moves consolidating his power. These initiatives included passing a law limiting freedom of the press, curtailing the powers of parliament by making the senate, the parliament's inactive chamber, equal to the elected and active Majlis. Half of the senate would be appointed by the Shah, who would have the right to dissolve both houses singly or together by a farman; a simple decree. The curfew was lifted once order was restored.

The Shah's new strength, and his success in crushing the Tudeh, impressed President Truman enough to persuade him to grant Iran a huge amount of financial aid. Elated by his new position of power, the Shah met and fell in love with Soraya Esfandiary, an 18-year-old beauty from the Bakhtiari tribe. They married on Monday, February 12, 1951. Unfortunately, Soraya could not bear children. The marriage ended in 1958 and Soraya, given the title of Princess – and, apparently, a generous monthly allowance – left Iran for Europe.

1951 was an auspicious year both for the Shah and Iran. It was in this year that Mohammad Hedayat Mossadegh, a Gajar aristocrat born sometime around 1881, pushed through the nationalization of Iranian oil. Mossadegh had entered politics early in life, dedicating his career to fighting against corruption. A devout nationalist, he had turned his attention to addressing the problem of the country's oil and stirring up violent attacks against the British. In 1922, he became minister for finance.

During Reza Shah's reign, he was frequently jailed, the awful conditions of prison permanently impairing his health. After the war, he formed the National Front, a party with only nine deputies. In April 1951, when he became prime minister, this handful of men succeeded in imposing the law which nationalized Iranian oil. The nationalization infuriated the British, but in our house there was great jubilation. Everybody loved Mossadegh. Shahjoon was the aunt of his wife with whom she was in constant communication.

I was Shahjoon's favourite grandchild and she took me everywhere with her, including to Mossadegh's residence. I spent every summer with her at the new palatial house which had been built at Darous. A well-kept lawn shaded with weeping willows surrounded the house and a bubbling spring ran into a blue-tiled pool; in the midst of which danced a happy fountain. The garden was sheltered by three hectares of fruit and nut trees.

Besides me there were fifteen other children of around my age who belonged to the live-in servants, nannies, cooks and gardeners. My cousins often visited but never stayed the whole summer.

One June day, Shahjoon had the car summoned for us to go

shopping at the Istanbul bazaar. I was too young to understand what was happening, but I noticed people buying lots of dried provisions like rice, lentils, tea and cooking oil. The town had an air of excitement about it. Small groups of people were gathered, talking and arguing, at street corners, in shops and by electricity poles. The police seemed unusually vigilant. On the walls of every shop I noticed pictures of Mossadegh hung side by side with the Shah's. Shahjoon spent a long time shopping – so long that I got through three ice-creams purchased for me by our chauffeur. It was dark when we arrived home to find my Aunt Victor and her husband Mohsen Khan sitting with Agha Mamani, speculating on these latest political events. Gathering to discuss politics became a routine custom that summer.

As autumn approached, the air grew cool and the leaves on the trees began to change colour and fall. The family left Darous for their house in Kushk Avenue, while I went home to my parents. Agha Joon was happy to have me back and Maman, practical as ever, was preoccupied with filling our own basement with food. I loved the excitement, especially now that I could play my favorite game 'supermarket' with real food and not toys. I also began to develop the habit of inspecting mother's wardrobe, going through her bags and pretending they were mine. On one occasion I discovered something new, bright and shiny. A sack full of gold coins! I emptied the sack onto the floor, making pretty patterns with the coins on the carpet. Unexpectedly, Maman entered the room and, seeing the coins on the floor, her eyes widened and she screamed hysterically, "What are you doing? Where did you find them?"

"I found them in your wardrobe, behind your shoes, Maman." Sensing retribution, I began to cry.

'Put them back in the sack at once, and don't tell anyone – not a single soul – about what you found!' she scolded with angry eyes.

Obediently, I picked up the coins and dropped them back in the sack, secretly enjoying the jingling sound of the metal mounting up in the container, and oblivious to the meaning of my mother's hysterical reaction. Those coins were father's security in case of trouble. Now, looking back, I admire his sense of foresight. Trouble came. The rial lost its value, gold went up and high inflation followed. When Mossadegh nationalized the oil, Britain sent paratroopers to Cyprus, gathered the troops she had based in Iraq on the Iranian border, and asked the International Court of Justice in the Hague to appoint an arbiter in the oil dispute and impose an economic blockade on Iran. She also appealed to the United Nations and, on September 30, the Security Council voted to look into Britain's complaint against Iran.

During this critical period, the Shah was politically inactive and indecisive. However, Mossadegh wasn't. On the morning of October 7, the prime minister, thin and pale, and with his ever-running nose, left Mehrabad Airport for New York accompanied by his advisers and leaving behind a crowd of supporters chanting 'Allah Akbar' (God is great). Once in New York, he was taken to New York Hospital where he feigned illness until the Security Council voted to postpone examination of Britain's request until the International Court came to a decision regarding the issue. A few days later, the fully-recovered Mossadegh met with President Truman in Washington and asked for financial aid. He received only a very small loan.

The economic situation in Iran was deteriorating rapidly and the country was on the verge of bankruptcy. Nevertheless, on his return to Teheran, Mossadegh was greeted with hysterical joy. For the first time in modern history a leader had given Iranians a sense of identity. Although in a miserable economic situation, Iran owned its own natural resources, its own wealth and had a prime minister who stood by the rights of his nation. Iran had found a defender in the person of Mohammad Hadayat Mossadegh.

To manage the money problem, he floated a loan of two billion rials and started printing money. Inflation followed, but the people supported and stood by him. Mohsen Khan was one of his most active followers and a member of the National Front. In an attempt to solve the country's political problems, the prime minister asked the newly re-elected Majlis for six months of absolute power. This request was granted. He also asked for the portfolio of war minister, but the Shah refused to oblige. Mossadegh resigned. Riots broke out. Four days later Ahmad Gavam, the Shah's newly-appointed prime minister resigned and the Majlis voted for Mossadegh's reinstatement. He became war minister, took over the crown's budget and exiled many of the Shah's friends and meddlesome family, including Princess Ashraf, the Shah's shrewd twin sister.

Tension was ruling the nation. The grown-ups were all concerned about the political situation. Many couldn't decide whether to be self-concerned or patriotic – whether to choose the Shah, whom the powers seemed to be backing, or Mossadegh, the hero of the common man.

Rumours began to circulate that Mossadegh was going to sell the country to the Russians (as Iranians always called the then USSR.) The Tudeh Party was beginning to resurface – and nothing scared the average Iranian more than the threat of communism, especially at times of economic crisis.

The youngsters were left to their own devices but were infected with the same mass hysteria: Shah or Mossadegh. Our games were all based on politics. We would form into two groups, those who were pro-Shah and those who were pro-Mossadegh. I always chose the Shah because of Soraya. We would each take the longest stick we could find in Shahjoon's garden and chase each other around pretending to fight for our hero. Usually a real fight would break out, someone would get hurt and, sulking or crying, he or she would run to the servants' quarters to be comforted.

Mossadegh's popularity began to decline and with it, Iran's chance of ever attaining democracy. When Churchill became prime minister of England and General Eisenhower was elected American president, the two men sided with each other to put pressure on Mossadegh and bring about the catastrophe which eventually followed.

By the summer of 1953, Teheran's population had proliferated and the town was beginning to sprawl towards the North, where the climate was cooler and the environment green and lush. Avenue Kushk had lost its prestige as a residential area and was becoming increasingly commercial. Foreigners were pouring into Teheran and there was only one luxury hotel to accommodate them: The Park. One of Shahjoon's nephews had just returned from Europe, full of fresh business ideas and keen to persuade Agha Mamani to turn the Kushk residence into a modern luxury hotel. My grandfather succumbed to the idea and, when summer came, the family vacated their house to take up permanent residence at Darous. I was ecstatic about this decision as it meant I could take my Norooz holidays there too.

Norooz is the Iranian New Year, which begins on the first day of spring after the stroke of the equinox (March 20 or 21). The festivities continue for 13 days. Norooz is an ancient celebration of the rebirth of nature. The ceremonies represent the two ancient concepts of End and Rebirth, Good and Evil. A few weeks before the New Year, people thoroughly clean and decorate their homes, buy new clothes, bake pastries and germinate seeds as a sign of renewal. On the eve of the last Wednesday, (Shab-e Chahar Shanbeh Soury, The Red Wednesday) bonfires are lit and people leap over the flames, believing the blaze will burn the bad luck, sickness and unhappiness of the year to come. A day before the actual turn of the year, a sofreh is spread either on the floor or on a table and is decorated with goods representing the seven symbols of life, rebirth, health, happiness, prosperity, joy and beauty. These symbols, which begin with the letter 'S' are: Sabzeh (represented by sprouts), Sib (apples), Samanou (a wheat germ dish), Sonbol (hyacinths), Senjed (fruit of the Jujube), Seer (garlic), and Somagh (sumac). Also placed on the sofreh are a copy of the Koran, some coins (usually gold), a bowl of water, painted eggs, a mirror, candles, plates full of pastries and pictures of the family members not present.

At the stroke of the equinox verses of the Koran are recited and the family, including the servants all gather by the sofreh, hugging and kissing and exchanging greetings and, of course, presents. Families and friends visit each other in accordance with age and social standing. On the 13th day people picnic in the fields and by the riversides and throw away their sprouts, thus removing bad luck from the house where they were grown. Norooz was the best time of the year for us children. It meant gold coins from the grandparents, money from the rest of the family, new clothes, lots of delicious pastries and above all being together.

The house in Darous was huge, a square building on three levels with 14 bedrooms, mirrored halls and marble bathrooms. A turquoise pond with a leaping fountain took prime position in the grand hall. During the day, sunbeams penetrated the hall through the french windows, creating colourful patterns on the marble floor. The rays were so bright that thousands of floating particles of dust could be seen suspended in them. A crystal chandelier lit the hall at night. Chaise longues were set on each side of the pond, perfect for reclining on and dozing off during the long, hot summer afternoons. A separate row of rooms lodged the servants and the retainers.

My uncle Mohsen Khan, much-respected by Agha Mamani for his French education, law degree and modern ideas, convinced his father-in-law to turn his share of the village into a modern suburb by subdividing the land into residential acreages to be sold to friends and relatives. Within a year the plan was approved by the municipality of Shemiran and the wheat fields had been turned into a well-planned suburb bearing Agha Mamani's name, Avenue Ehteshamieh. Each son received six thousand square metres, each daughter three thousand and each grandchild one thousand. The avenue connecting my mother's lot to Ehteshamieh was named after me, Avenue Lily.

First to build on his lot was Mohsen Khan himself. His house was a simple, Swiss-style cottage with a large swimming pool in which he later taught every one of us to swim. Soon, the others followed suit, including Agha joon. Though he had no intention of moving house as yet, he believed that once the political situation stabilized, foreigners would flood the country and the cost of rented accommodation would rise. Agha Joon was always right. The problems did get ironed-out, foreigners did flood the country and rents rose sky-high.

On July 6th 1953 Kermit Roosevelt, grandson of Theodore Roosevelt, an agent of the Central Intelligence Agency, and a specialist in Middle East affairs entered Iran to tackle the Mossadegh menace. Only three people knew of the plot: the Shah, General Zahedi, and his son Ardeshir. Zahedi was to act on behalf of the Shah from an underground position. The initial plan was for the Shah to initiate a decree to remove Mossadegh and replace him with Zahedi.

On August 10th the Shah decided to leave Teheran with Soraya for a short holiday at Kalar Dachte in the mountains. Colonel Nematollah Nassiri, commander of the Imperial Guard, was elected to deliver the dismissal decree to Mossadegh.Through a leak, however, the prime minister became aware of the plot. Nassiri was arrested but Zahedi, warned in time, escaped. Early the next morning, Mossadegh went on radio and broadcasted the news of the unsuccessful coup détat against his government. The entire press attacked the Shah, pronouncing him 'the foreign puppet'. At Kalar Dachte, the royal couple panicked and hurried to Ramsar where the king's aircraft was waiting for them. They fled to Baghdad, where they requested and were granted asylum.

On August 17th, 1953, the fall of the Shah of Iran made international headline news. The Iranian ambassador in Iraq demanded the Shah's extradition, but King Faizal refused and the couple left for Rome where Mohsen Khan's eldest brother, Nezam Sultan Khadjenouri, the Iranian Ambassador, and a friend of Mossadegh did not welcome the Shah to the embassy. He was to pay a heavy penalty for this slight. Back in Teheran, the conspirators, who had been lying low, were regrouping, biding their time for the right moment to set their plot into motion. The following events all worked against Mossadegh. First, the Tudeh resurfaced singing communist songs; then rumours began to spread that Mossadegh was selling the country to the Bolsheviks; and finally, Teymur Bakhtiar, the chief of the Kermanshah garrison, in support of the Shah allied himself with Zahedi.

In Darous, scared to death, everyone including the servants was sitting around their radios waiting for news. Conspiracy was in the air – though of course, at that time, no one was aware of the CIA plot which was only revealed decades later. Nevertheless, the atmosphere was electric with anticipated trouble. People loved Mossadegh, but feared the Tudeh. They also loved the Shah. For as long as they could remember they had had a king. It was part of their culture, part of their heritage. Now he had fled and left them fatherless. To hell with the foreigners: the British, the Russians and now the Americans! What did they care for the Iranian people? For the peasants who toiled the land, sleeping hungry at nights? For the bazaari whose credit was diminishing? And for the landowners, whose land was being confiscated? The foreigners did not want to help Iran. They wanted to exploit it. The Shah had already gone. Mossadegh, the old man, was he really planning to betray his country to the Russians?

During those history-making August days everyone was restless, unhappy, anxious, indecisive and tired. No doubt it was this confused state of mind that induced the people to turn from Mossadegh to the Shah. On the 17th, a deal was struck between Roosevelt and a man nick-named 'Brainless' – an athlete and leader of a gang of louts from the south of Teheran. This group was to supply Zahedi with enough men and tanks to make another attempt at a coup on the 19th.

On the morning that the Americans were plotting to change Iran's destiny, Shahjoon and I were shopping in Avenue Islambul again. Small groups of men, shouting 'Long live the Shah!', were slipping ten rial notes bearing the Shah's portrait under the windshield wipers of cars as they passed by. People, cautiously at first, then boldly, began to cluster around them frantically stretching out their hands for a ten rial bill. This was creating a terrible traffic jam. Cars could not move. Our driver had gone white with fear and tears were running down Shahjoon's normally composed face.

I was petrified, even though I was unable to comprehend the gravity of the situation. The crowd was turning wild. Everybody was waving the notes around, shouting hysterically, 'Long live the Shah! Long live the Shah!'. All the streets converging on Parliament Square, including the one we were in, now swarmed with masses of moving black heads and outstretched arms waving the notes like flags on a joyous occasion. Except that this occasion wasn't joyous at all. It was a time to be remembered with shame and regret. It was the time that the first Iranian attempt towards experiencing true democracy was crushed by the will of those who proudly call themselves advocates of democracy.

Mossadegh supporters were now mixing with the demonstrators and were snatching the notes and tearing them up. Fights broke out between the different factions. The situation deteriorated and I became so terrified that I buried my face in my grandmother's lap and began to weep, silently, scared of attracting the attention of the crowd. Eventually our car escaped the jam and we headed speedily towards Shemiran.

At home that night we heard from one of the servants who had been caught up in the riot that, around noon, a gang of disguised roughnecks had crowded into Parliament Square. Suddenly, throwing off their disguises, they had taken out guns, revolvers and clubs, forced their way into the ministerial offices, beaten and thrown out the occupants and locked the doors. Soon afterwards a tank carrying Zahedi and his aides appeared, dividing the crowd into two groups – on one side the Mossadegh people and on the other the CIA. As the tank approached, a collaborator shouted 'Long live Zahedi!' and 'God protect the Shah!' In Rome that same day the Shah was informed that his people wanted him back.

The Shah returned, welcomed by the cheering, flag-waving crowds which had lined up along his route from the airport to his palace, lulled into believing that they genuinely wanted him back. A few days later Mossadegh, the man who had defeated the British in nationalizing Iran's oil, the man whose aim had been to eradicate corruption and injustice and rule within a true constitutional monarchy, was arrested and placed in a cell with common thieves. His house was looted and ransacked.

Mossadegh's era ended swiftly. Yet the spirit of the old man has survived the demise of the Pahlavi dynasty and will be remembered with pride. The key players in the coup were handsomely rewarded by the Shah but, with the exception of Ardeshir, none of them escaped the curse of Mossadegh.

Chapter 12

General Teymour Bakhtiar, an attractive man in his late 30s was the military Governor of Teheran in charge of tracking down Mossadegh's escapee supporters.

Bakhtiar wasted no time in filling the Ghar prison with Mossadegh's former ministers, known supporters and Tudeh members. In Teheran alone, many caches of red propaganda, secret arsenals and crates of ammunition were found.

Bakhtiar imposed a curfew and harsh restrictions on consumer goods, resulting in public dependency on the black market. A period of repression followed and once again the country was on the verge of bankruptcy. This time, the Shah acted swiftly and appealed to President Eisenhower for aid. He was granted millions of dollars. Diplomatic relations with Britain were re-established and after protracted negotiations an international consortium consisting of American, British, French and Dutch companies was created to replace the former Anglo-Iranian Oil Company. Money began to flow into the country causing an economic boom. New movie palaces, department stores and commercial buildings mushroomed all over the city. Shemiran, with its sumptuous villas, nightclubs and restaurants became a millionaires' retreat and imported luxury cars became the new status symbol.

To maintain the country's security with the technical help of the Americans, Bakhtiar created SAVAK (Sazemane Atelaat va Amniate Kechvar – The Organisation for Information and Security of the Country). Gradually, SAVAK grew to become one of the largest secret services in the world. It was everywhere. Every high-ranking official was followed by a SAVAK shadow that monitored his every move. The same held true for all the country's large business enterprises, in particular the National Iranian Oil Company and the universities, where every dean of the students was expected to cooperate with SAVAK.

At Darous no one really cared much about what the government did so long as peace was maintained. Mohsen Khan had become the Member of Parliament for Shemiran and uncle Doctor as we called our eldest uncle, had recently married the granddaughter of Bahman Mirza (Nasser Al-Din Shah's uncle who had fled to Georgia). Our new aunt, Azar joon was very tall, beautiful and elegant. The two were now in Madrid where uncle Doctor was the Iranian Consul General. My father was busy making money and the rest did not work; only kept Agha Mamani's company. Every day together with Agha Ehtesham al-Molk they went to town organizing the grand opening of the hotel. The construction had been completed a month earlier and the decorators were now busy furnishing it.

The holy month of Moharam had arrived and the inauguration of the hotel had to wait until the end of the mourning months. Every Thursday evening, during the holy month, my grandparents' kitchen cooked for the poor. On one Thursday morning, when Ashraf Sadat was sitting comfortably on the floor beside her large board cutting freshly-kneaded pasta into hair-thin strips for the charity meal, she invited me to sit by her. Delighted, I did and asked her for the reason. She told me that she knew I did not know much about the holy month and she wanted to educate me. I kissed her bony cheek, crossed my legs and sat to listen. She cleared her throat and began her lecture about Moharam, the month when Iranians commemorate the martyrs of Karbella.

She began by saying, 'Many hundreds of years ago, on such a month, 72 brave men led by Immam Hussain, the son of Immam Ali, the Lion of Islam and the grandson of the prophet, went to war against the massive army of the ungodly Caliph Yazid, successor of the usurpers of Caliphat from the line of the prophet. Outnumbered, these men of God fought bravely until they were martyred by the army of Satan. These men gave their lives to save humanity from corruption on earth."

Exhausted, Ashraf Sadat paused to take a deep breath and, with moistened eyes looked into my bored eyes and asked me if I had understood why I had to love these martyrs. To please her I shook my head. Then, smiling, she promised to take me to the mosque that same evening which was the eve of Tasua, the night of the commemorated event for which she was dressed in black.

After dinner, covered in our chador, we headed for the mosque which had been sponsored by an endowment from Agha Mamani. At the entrance we took off our shoes before entering. The interior of the mosque was divided into two levels; the lower level accommodated the men and the upper level the women. A white-bearded turbaned mullah standing behind the altar was recounting the story of the war. With sorrow in his tone and sadness on his countenance, he repeated each sentence at least twice in order to play on the emotions of the listeners. The story told, the mullah sat on the floor, giving the platform to a younger man who had stepped forward calling for his slain Immam: 'Ya Hussain, Ya Hussain!' After a sudden commotion, all the men stood up and began beating on their chests to the rhythm of the chant. Gradually the chanting became more excited, provoking a frenzy of hysterical emotions in the Dasteh (the flagellating group).

Women watching the scene were equally aroused. They were crying and under their chador were gently beating on their chests to the same rhythm. Intermittently the flagellation stopped. The participants would sit on the floor, wipe the perspiration off their faces with black handkerchiefs then take a cup of tea and a piece of date served by a donor. After a short recess, the mourning would resume. This continued until the time came for our congregation to leave for the mosque in the next suburb of Gholhak.

Outside in the street, the Dasteh started off in an orderly procession. The men were chanting, beating on their chests and waving the green flags of Islam and banners proclaiming 'Ya Hussain, the slain of Karbella!' The women and children followed. On the road more people joined in the procession and the procedure repeated itself until, at midnight, the last designated mosque (usually the largest in the district) was reached. Then, well-satisfied with their performance of religious duty and assuming all sins to have been forgiven, the worshippers broke up to gather again the following morning, the sacred day of Ashura. On Ashura all activities in Shiite communities come to a complete standstill. It is a true day of commemoration, tears and prayer. Ashraf Sadat and I returned home after our Dasteh left for Gholhak.

That was my first experience of 'fanatical faith'.

Ashraf Sadat and Nanny were my first religion teachers. Their faith was absolute but blind. All they knew of Islam was what they had heard from the clergy who themselves were as ignorant. The Koran was read in Arabic, with some verses being memorized to be whispered at times of trouble. The majority of people didn't even know the meaning of their daily prayers. As time passed, people became more educated. The Koran was translated into Persian and the clergy had to attend a Divinity College before they could preach. Very slowly, blind faith became a thing of the past.

With only a fragmented knowledge about Islam, at the age of 12, I was thrown into the world of Christianity to learn and comprehend the concept of the Trinity! It took me many years of living in doubt, searching for the truth, fearing the fire of hell and the acquisition of two university degrees before I could choose my path to God. I chose Islam because in its philosophy I found an appealing sense of equality, justice and, above all, simplicity in the relationship between man and his God. Having lived most of my life more among non-Moslems than Moslems, I have come to the conclusion that the aim of all religions is the same. It is the culturally peppered directions they take to reach the ultimate goal of "being a deserving creature" that differs. Unfortunately, we find it within the pages of history books and we see it in the actions of fundamentalists that religion is the sharpest sword in the wrong hands.

As I grew older, I became more immersed in my studies. Agha joon expected me to excel in everything. I tried – sometimes I succeeded and sometimes I failed drastically.

Weekends were a welcome relief from hard scholastic work. Every Thursday afternoon Shahjoon came to collect me from school. On Fridays, as usual, the family gathered in her house for lunch and a game of cards. The success of the family hotel was the main topic of conversation and a recent pastime was to spend the evenings lounging in its busy lobby. We usually sat in a prominent position, feeling important as the owners of such a grand establishment, expecting respect and demanding immediate service from the waiters who spoilt us with trays of caviar on toast and glasses of chilled Smirnoff vodka.

It was during one of these gatherings that I found myself being whispered about, but however hard I tried I could not hear what they were murmuring. On the way back to Shemiran, I asked Shahjoon why I had been the subject of discussion. At first she feigned ignorance, but eventually my persistent pleading and sulking persuaded her to divulge the news of the appearance of a Khasegar, wishing to take me as a wife.

The parents of a young man from a prominent family had telephoned my mother for an appointment. They had told her that they had been searching for a suitable wife for their eighteen-year-old son Mansour, and a mutual friend had suggested me as a perfect match. This friend, knowing which school I attended, had brought the young man in question there one afternoon as I was leaving and had pointed me out to him. After seeing me, and having then followed me to school repeatedly, Mansour had fallen in love with me and wanted to marry me and take me to America, where he intended to further his education. His parents were thrilled with his choice and wanted to see me at the earliest opportunity.

I was horrified. To marry at the age of twelve! I began to cry. Shahjoon began to laugh. It gave me courage. I wiped my eyes with the Kleenex tucked into my sleeve and asked her:

"Shahjoon, surely Maman won't want me to get married at the age of twelve?"

"No," she replied. "I don't think so. I believe your parents are planning to send you to England to study." Shocked again I asked:

"Why, Shahjoon? What have I done wrong that Maman wants to send me away?"

Tears started to fall again.

She looked at me with kind eyes, pulled me to her large bosoms, kissed my head and answered in a matter-of-fact tone, "You have done nothing wrong azizam. It is because they want to give you the best education possible. You are a very lucky girl to have such thoughtful parents. It is a great sacrifice to be separated from your children."

The following day, as soon as my parents arrived for lunch, I asked them about the Khasegar and England. Agha joon looked at me with teasing eyes and said: 'Lily Khanum, we are going to marry you off to a good-looking boy who is going to take you to America.' I shivered at the thought and began to cry. Maman came to my rescue and reprimanded him for teasing me. She explained that she had refused to grant an appointment to Mansour's parents and assured me that an arranged marriage was out of the question. However, they were planning to send me to England to a private boarding school. There, my brothers would supervise my affairs and look after me. Relieved that I was not to be forced into marriage, I went into the garden where my cousins were playing. They had already heard about my marriage proposal and, spotting me, they began to make joking remarks. I joined them in laughing at the idea.

The task of finding a suitable school in England had fallen on Masoud's capable shoulders. He was a young man now and had finished his first year of studying medicine at the University of Durham. He was a hard-working student, a first-rate athlete and a responsible elder son. In spite of our age differences and separation I had grown to love both my brothers dearly. During the summer holidays that they had spent in Teheran both had shown me a lot of affection. They were good-looking, sociable and smart and I was very proud to be their sister.

Soon we received news of a school in Cardiff, South Wales which took foreign students and undertook to teach them English. Arrangements were made for Maman and me to travel to London at the beginning of the summer. My father was to join us later.

While we were preparing to leave, the Shah took a new queen.

Farah came from a respectable family. Her father, Sohrab Diba, was a diplomat and Farah had been born in Romania where he was posted. Sohrab died of tuberculosis in 1948. Not wealthy, Mrs Diba had to work, something quite unusual for a woman at that time.

Working hard, Farah won a scholarship to study architecture in Paris. At a student gathering at the Iranian Embassy, she met her future husband and impressed him with her bold criticisms of the way overseas student scholarships were handled. Subsequent private meetings were arranged by Ardeshir Zahedi, the Shah's son-in-law, and the couple married on December 21.

During the two decades she spent as Shahbano (Empress) of Iran the country benefited immensely from her conscientious fulfilments of royal duties. Farah was passionate about everything Iranian. Her tireless efforts initiated a revival in Iranian culture and arts. Museums were enriched, neglected historical monuments were restored, and artistic talents were sought and patronized. However, as was the nature of the system, it did not take long for Farah's family to ingratiate themselves with the royal couple, demanding respect and favours. The Diba clan, with the exception of Sagatdouleh Diba and one or two others, were unrenowned with little merit of their own except their royal connection. Her Majesty committed the unforgivable sin of allowing them to take full advantage of her name in making deals, and winning lucrative contracts.

The day of our departure for London arrived. Once packed and ready, Maman and I bade farewell to the rest of the household. Shahjoon, sad but sedate, accompanied us to the airport. As we kissed goodbye she told me she would miss me much. I hugged her tight, praying to God that she would have a long life and that I would see her again.

At Heathrow Airport we were met by my welcoming brothers who then jammed us into Masoud's small Saab and headed for Cambridge, where Mahmoud was studying at Trinity College. He was an excellent athlete. The mantlepiece of his college room was filled with trophies he had won in different competitions. From Cambridge, we drove to Newcastle where Masoud was studying medicine at the Royal Victoria Infirmary. We spent a couple of weeks in Newcastle and then when the summer holidays commenced we drove to the South of France where my father was waiting for us. That summer, we travelled along the entire coast of the French Riviera. I was not looking forward to returning to England as it meant separation from my parents. Our wonderful holiday ended too soon and, two days after our return to England, I was packed and ready for school. I spent my last night in bed with Maman. None of us slept. We wept all night – even Agha joon. The next day, just before I climbed onto the train he held me tight and said, "Lily joon, remember this sacrifice is for your future. Life has many faces. One day our inheritance may not be enough to see you through life – but your education will." How right he was!

St Peter's School in Cardiff, South Wales lodged one hundred students, many of whom were foreigners enrolled to master the English language. In the early days I found my new life very difficult, but gradually my determination to learn got me through.

St Peter's was a Catholic school, with compulsory chapel attendance twice a day and one hour of church every Sunday. I reasoned that if I was to venerate Christianity and attend prayers the school should, in return, respect my faith and allow me time to practise it. To this end I made an appointment with the school's headmistress. With my rudimentary English and non-verbal means I made her understand that I wished to perform my daily prayers and needed permission to enter my dormitory during the free period after lunch. (The students were not allowed to enter the dormitories during study hours.) I intended to perform my morning and noon prayers together. This way I would not disturb my roommates at dawn.

The headmistress gazed at me for a while then, with the shadow of a smile on her thin lips, nodded her permission. From the expression on her face and her gentle pat on my shoulder I knew I had won her respect.

Letters were my only means of communication with the outside world and, recently, they had been bearing good news. Agha joon, in partnership with a friend, had leased a large, modern hotel in the heart of the commercial centre of Teheran. Together, they had named it The Mar Mar. Based on Mahmoud's brilliant suggestion they had built an English pub, the first in Iran. And it had become a money-printing machine – for both the partners and the barmen.

Another important item of news was that, on the morning of October 31st, 1960 Farah had given birth to a long-awaited heir to the Pahlavi throne. He was named Reza.

The second year in England commenced with my enrolment at Felixstowe College, a public school in Suffolk. All in all, scholastically and mentally the years at boarding school were tough and at times very frustrating. Nevertheless with my brothers' help I managed to survive and as a result became a very independent person.

Having finished school I asked my father to allow me to return to Iran for my summer vacations. He was hesitant because the political situation was once again volatile; this time stirred up by Ruhollah Khomeini, a hitherto unknown cleric who was attempting to launch a religious coup. Khomeini had violently opposed the Shah's agrarian reforms and the emancipation of women. His vociferous sermons attacking the regime had agitated the faithful out of the mosques and into the streets where they shouted anti-Shah slogans. Because Islam is a theocracy, religion has always been a strong political force as well as a form of nationalism in Iran. Shi'ism, a political necessity, was first introduced in 1501 by the Safavid dynasty, as the state religion to create a national identity separate from the then threatening Ottoman Empire's Sunni-ísm. To preserve this identity the constitution of 1906 required all legislation to be examined by five learned clergy. Nothing offensive to Islam was to be included in press, laws and education curricula; the Shah, his prime minister, all the members of the government, and judiciary had to belong to the Twelver branch of Shiá Islam. Although the principles of Islam were well woven into the new constitution, the secular reforms created a western-style democracy that disillusioned the clergy.

By the age of seven, gifted with extraordinary ingenuity and talent, Ruhollah had already completed reading the Koran. At adolescence, much concerned with humanitarian issues, he surprised the elders of his family with fiery debates. In 1925, an ascetic youth, having spent most of his time studying theology, logic, and literature he qualified as a mullah with a surprising penchant for poetry!

By the 1930s, Khomeini had quietly and methodically begun his campaign against the regime, limiting his forum to the mosque and the Qum seminary where he taught. The focus of his sermons was the nature of society. He believed no new society could be created in a vacuum without a true understanding and appreciation of its past. He stressed that in Iran neither the influences of a 25-century-old culture nor of Islam, the dominant religion for thirteen centuries, could simply be wiped out by modern reforms. Therefore, to succeed, reforms had to take into consideration all social, cultural and religious values of the community they were to serve. A rigidly disciplined Khomeini, with his absolute dedication to his version of Islam, managed to build a grassroots network among growing numbers of estranged seminary students and the devout – who decades later succeeded in toppling one of the eldest monarchies of the world.

In his late twenties, Ruhollah married Ghods-Iran, a teenage daughter of a Teheran ayatollah, sharing with her his regimented austere life. In spite of his dislike of Reza Shah, Ruhollah never found an opportunity to confront him. At the age of forty Ruhollah began to write theses on different social and religious issues making various political statements. He perceived faith to be a form of belief that compels man to action. Furthermore, he emphasized that it was the religious duty of the individual to seek the rectifications of contemporary political and social problems. His obsession, throughout his life was the survival of Islam not merely as a religion but as an all-encompassing way of life. In his eyes, man's evil acts were the bitter fruits of estrangement from Islamic values. Khomeini fully understood and utilized the qualities unique to Shi'ism that provided means to counterattack social injustice. Notable among these idiosyncrasies are first the mobilizing power of the mullahs, who are empowered to interpret religious law and duty (Ijtihad); second, Shi'ism, an idiom of social protest, which stands for the fight against injustice. Once a year, on the day of Ashura, Shiá Muslims of the world commemorate the events of Karbala where thirteen centuries ago, the brave 72 men of Islam embraced their martyrdom, establishing the precedent of dying for belief rather than living with injustice. From then on, in the history of Shiá Islam, revolt against tyranny and martyrdom became a duty to God. For Khomeini every day was an

Ashura and every place a Karbella. He consistently argued that whatever the cost, the clergy should stand up and fight against injustice represented by the monarchy. Moreover, he believed that religion should direct the life of the individual, the community and the state, not only in Iran but in the entire Islamic world.

During the unrests, in the holy city of Qum, Khomeini was arrested and the news had led to further demonstrations, turning Teheran into a battleground. The army had intervened and the demonstrators, in their frustration, had set fire to the bazaar. Martial law had been proclaimed and the SAVAK had become busier than ever.

In spite of my father's warnings when July came I went to Teheran, to our own house in Darous. We now had two properties, one in Avenue Lily recently built and rented out, and the older house where my parents now lived. This substantial house sat in the midst of a beautifully landscaped garden that was dominated by a large, blue, swimming pool. A unique feature of the garden, placed next to a lovely weeping willow, was a huge, square timber bed with four ornamentally carved legs and a set of steps leading to its timber base. This unusual piece of carpentry had been Nasser Al-Din Shah's summer bed. It had been a present to Maman from Shahjoon.

That summer I spent many memorable moonlit nights on that bed, its wooden surface covered with a thick carpet and spread with comfortable cushions, sometimes alone, sometimes sitting with my family. We would drink vodka, eat yoghurt mixed with cucumber, listen to Persian music and simply enjoy the moonlight and the balmy air of those peaceful summer evenings.

Iranians love the moonlight, and the Teheran sky before the city became smog-ridden was idyllically beautiful; a clear, deep blue dotted with gently drifting milky clouds which passed over a galaxy of huge twinkling stars, and everything bathed in the golden light of a large moon. I often miss those nights sitting on the bed; alone, relaxed, without a care in the world. I would savour the cool evening breeze and gaze at the sky trying to find God to thank him for my life.

The holidays passed quickly. All of my cousins, like me, were in Teheran for the holidays. Mamal Khan Bahram's oldest brother was home from England and was planning to go to America to Utah State University; Bahram was to join him there when he had finished high school. Afsaneh was back from Switzerland and was to go to London after the break. God had given Khalleh Victor another cute girl whom she had named Masoumeh. The baby of the family, she was so spoilt that no one dared to approach her without either being spat on or hit by her little fist. And Feri was home from Germany where she had been studying. Shahjoon was ageing, but her spirit was as strong as ever. Now we were next-door neighbours and I visited her daily.

Life was just perfect – those days.

Chapter 13

I left Felixstowe at the end of the '65 school year and began a course at the St James' Secretarial College in London. My father had bought a lovely, four-bedroomed house in Fulham and my brothers and I were living there. Mahmoud was working for a petrochemical company and Masoud was working at Guy's Hospital. I hated secretarial work. I had wanted to go to university but my parents had considered the idea ridiculous. The only ambition they had for me was that I should find myself a suitable husband. We had fought; I had lost – but not totally. They had agreed to let me take a modelling course in my free time.

I enjoyed modelling and for a part-time worker I earned a considerable amount of money. Gradually I became in demand and landed myself with a part in a film named *Deadlier than the Male*. The excitement lasted until my agent informed me that the part had been re-allocated to an Indian girl with a proper work permit. I was devastated, my parents pleased. A film career would have killed my chance of ever marrying a respectable Iranian man and to put an end to what they conceived to be an embarrassing situation, they decided I should return home immediately.

I found Teheran changed for the better and sensed an overwhelming feeling of progress and prosperity, which pleased me.

Both of my family's hotels were doing extremely well and Father was building three new houses, one for each of us. There was no prospect of a career for me in Teheran. It would have been deemed below my dignity to become anyone's secretary. So I was forced to become a lady of leisure, waiting for my Prince Charming. Extremely hyperactive, it did not take long for me to become restless and I began searching for something useful to do. Khalleh Victor was my shining example of an achiever, interested in a variety of sports, politically active and heavily involved in charity work. She was the head of Shemiran's Red Lion & Sun Organization. I volunteered to help with her community work, and together we supervised many fund-raising activities. Soon I became quite a socialite, invited out every night. Men found me attractive and females found me amusing and very assertive, which at times cost me dearly. I was at the right age for marriage and needless to say I had many suitors. My heart did beat for some who were not destined for me.

In spite of the Pahlavi era, the one thousand ruling families only associated with one another keeping away from the parvenus that were mushrooming with a speed of thunder. We followed the traditional rules and for all of us, in spite of our freedom, the concept of virtue and family honour still counted. Most of us went into our husband's bed still a virgin. That concept was to become obsolete after the Islamic Republic made temporary marriages in mode again. Each of us circulated in a hand-picked group and the group did everything together. Those days my closest friend was Shirin Etehadieh, who has now become a famous artist in Iran. I tried to matchmake her for my brother Masoud, who had now become a Fellow of the Royal College of Surgeons and was in Teheran practicing Urology. But my endeavours proved futile. Shirin married a handsome Khan and Masoud married someone else. In the meanwhile Mahmoud with his Master's degree from Cambridge was working for the Plan Organization and courting Kokoli Fallah.

My activities led me to the School of Social Welfare where I was employed as a bilingual interpreter for Iranian students and their American lecturers. The school had been founded by Satareh Farmanfarmian, a distant relative who had been the first educated social worker in Iran.

During my free time, I continued helping Khalleh Victor in her extensive charity work. Realizing how the 'have-nots' lived had made me more socially conscious. The gap between the living standards of the rich and those of the poor was enormous. Surely a regime which sustained such social injustice could not survive? There again, I thought, how could it fail while protected by America?

I increased my charity fundraising by constantly appealing to the benevolence of my own family members. Maman and Shahjoon were my most generous donors.

Shahjoon had become almost bedridden, but her spirit was as strong as ever. Every afternoon, her bedroom became a gathering place for the family to drink tea and chat. From the flock of household staff who had served her over the years, only ten remained.

After Agha Mamani's death from a heart attack, my two uncles who had inherited most of his wealth sold the grand house at Darous and Shahjoon moved to the house she had built for herself at Avenue Ehteshamieh. Dai [136] Hushang lost the bulk of his enormous inheritance at the gambling houses of Europe and was left with very little. He was now living in an apartment at a corner of Shahjoon's garden. She was supporting not only him, but also his two children. To his dying day in Paris in 1988, Dai Hushang never earned a living – and yet his apartment was always open to those less fortunate than him.

Mohsen Khan was now an elected senator, vociferous in his criticism of the corruption of the regime. His attitude had so displeased His Imperial Majesty that he was banned from court. And the rest of the family was waiting for Mahmoud's wedding – the talk of town.

On the auspicious day, at three o'clock the handsome groom, dressed in a smart suit, left home for the Fallah residence. We followed him half an hour later.

At the gate we were greeted by the bride's father. Inside, an assortment of roughnecks were mingling with the elegant guests – a sure sign that many government officials were to attend.

The venue was overflowing with enormous baskets of exotic flowers, exquisitely arranged. In the main salon musicians were playing happy songs, and the waiters were circulating trays of drinks, caviar and other cocktail savouries. Mrs Fallah, plump and short was attired in a Dior outfit studded with diamantés. A pair of dangling emerald earrings complemented her olive skin. She was talking to Loretta Young, the Hollywood actress who was her friend. The bride, standing by the groom, looked striking in her short dress of French lace.

A little while after our arrival, Prime Minister Hoveyda and three ex-prime ministers honoured the couple by being the witnesses for the Aghd. (Islamic law requires only one witness from each partner but Mrs Fallah insisted that if only one of Their Excellencies had been asked, the other three would have been offended.) The religious verses were to be recited by the Immam Jomeh, who had performed the wedding rites for the Shah.

Sharp at five Mahmoud and Kokoli were married. Mrs Fallah could not stop smiling and nor could my mother. Both were very happy

---

[136] Uncle

but for different reasons. The party went on till the early hours of the morning, when exhausted, the couple was driven to a suite reserved for them at the Royal Hilton Hotel.

From the start it became apparent that the relationship was tempestuous and stressful for both partners. Each saw the world from a different perspective. However, for eight years they tried and when no solution presented itself they parted. The fruit of this union is Nilofar, my lovely niece who is now a successful photographer working in Europe.

Thirty years later Mahmoud remarried and found happiness with a capable and compatible lady named Shaida.

By 1967, Teheran was growing fast. It had become a paradise for foreign businessmen and tourists. Pavement cafés flourished along both sides of the tree-lined Pahlavi Avenue, which joined the prosperous north to the poverty-stricken south. Elegant nightclubs in Shemiran entertained the Westernized Teheranies and downtown cabarets featuring Iranian singers and belly dancers attracted the louts, as well as the new, middleclass businessmen with cash bulging out of their pockets. But the trendiest entertainment centre in Teheran was the Bowling Club, a grand set-up with twenty bowling alleys, a brasserie and a cinema showing films in English. Shirin and I were in the habit of going there every Sunday night to have dinner and see a film.

One evening, just as we were leaving the restaurant, I noticed my cousin Bahram sitting at a table with a handful of his friends and went over to say hello. Seated next to him was an extremely handsome man with a bright, attractive smile. He flashed a quick glance in my direction then dropped his head and began fiddling with his fork. The rest of the boys were undressing me with their eyes. I lingered a little longer than necessary, to see if the attractive young man would pay me any more attention. He did not, and feeling crestfallen and slightly ashamed I left for the cinema.

The next day, just as I arrived home from work, Bahram called to see if I would like to go to his house for a game of Pasour, an Iranian card game. Feri and a friend were already there, he said, and they needed a fourth player. I told him I would join them after I had changed into more comfortable clothes.

I took a shower and, feeling refreshed, I decided to walk to Bahram's house which was about ten minutes from ours at the top end of Ehteshamieh. Near the front entrance of the house stood an old blue

Comet, which looked as though it had been driven by many bad drivers, so many dents did it have on its side panels. Suddenly, a sixth sense warned me that my fate was somehow connected to this old dented car. Was it possible that it belonged to the good-looking man I had met at the Bowling Club?

Feeling excited, and at the same time a little nervous, I rang the doorbell. Bahram's nanny opened the door and showed me to the family room where my relatives and – yes – the man from the Bowling Club were sitting comfortably chatting. As I entered he rose and was introduced to me as Mehdi Monadjemi. We shook hands. His were very soft, and his bright smile was so enchanting that I fell in love with it at once.

The group had been waiting for me to arrive to start the game, so without more ado we sat down at the card table and drew cards for partners. The cards decided that Mehdi and I would play against Bahram and Feri. We chose to play for dinner at the Kolbeh, a restaurant and nightclub in the mountains on the outskirts of the city. As we played, I was conscious of Mehdi's surreptitious glances in my direction, quickly followed with a lowering of his head as he pretended not to be interested. I was enjoying his discreet game.

Mehdi and I won the round and I left to go home and change into something more formal for dinner. Feri was Bahram's next-door neighbour and Mehdi lived in far away Karadj, where his father was a professor of physics lecturing at Karadj University. He had come prepared to spend the night at Bahram's.

At home, I groomed myself carefully and put on my newest gown. I was going to indulge in a little competition with my cousin who was trying to win over the attention of the stranger. At eight-thirty the door bell rang and I went outside to join the others. Since I was going out with family members, the usual rule did not apply and I did not have to be chauffeured in our own car. True to my premonition, the blue Comet did belong to Mehdi and my feeling of excitement grew as I climbed in.

As we chatted on the way to the restaurant, I discovered that he was, in fact, a distant relative. I also discovered that he had just graduated from Utah State University in economics and was holidaying in Iran while trying to decide whether to return to America for post-graduate studies or find a job in Teheran. He, like everybody else, had to enrol for compulsory national service and this he wished, by hook or by crook, to avoid.

Kolbeh is situated halfway up a hill just before the ascent becomes too sharp for cars to go any further. It is a picturesque venue. Waterfalls gently spray the surrounding rocky escarpments before merging with the river and rushing downhill towards the south and the mingled sounds are like music to the ears. The evening air is always cool and pleasant in Darband and, on that particular night, it was chilly. I was shivering and Mehdi gallantly took off his jacket and draped it around my shoulders. However, during dinner he amused himself with my vivacious cousin, completely ignoring me. She was sitting beside Mehdi, while I was seated across from him. Feri is talkative, sociable and without any inhibitions. They seemed to be enjoying themselves. So I decided to turn my attention from the two and listen to Bahram's plans for a trip to Paris where he could be with his beloved girlfriend.

After dinner, annoyed and bored, I suggested leaving for home; at this, Mehdi interrupted his flirtation and suggested that we go to a party at his aunt's house. He had been invited and had promised to call in after dinner. Both Feri and Bahram agreed and, since it would have been very rude and unsociable of me to refuse, we left the restaurant and headed for the party.

On the way, I discovered a little more about Mehdi's background. It seemed that his mother was my mother's third removed cousin on Agha Mamani's side. So we shared the same great grandfather! His grandfather had been a prominent lawyer who had owned a lot of land; he had divided this between his children – hence his family, like mine, lived in the same street.

Mehdi's aunt's house was full of people when we arrived, mostly the 'nouveau riche'. The host and hostess and their son Kambiz already knew Bahram and, when Feri and I were introduced to them, they extended a warm welcome to us. The majority of the guests were much older than us and within a short while all the younger people present gathered round us, no doubt bored with the company of the older folk.

We were listening to the boys' conversation about their lives in the United States when Mehdi, who had disappeared, returned accompanied by a short, plump and smiling lady whom he introduced as his mother. A tall, silver-haired, pleasant-looking gentleman followed. He was Dr Monadjemi, Mehdi's father, and I took an instant liking to him.

It was getting late and I was worried that Maman would be waiting up for me so I insisted that, this time, I must go home. In the car, I found out that Mehdi liked playing tennis as much as I did. I found it rather strange that he seemed to be preoccupied with Feri while remaining fully aware of me; but, I told myself, it did not really matter.

I felt strangely elated that night and somehow knew that the next day would have a surprise in store for me. I was right. Mehdi called, inviting me to play tennis. I accepted and told him I would book a court at Veisies, a nearby club.

Mehdi and I played tennis every afternoon for one month. Every time he came from Karadj, his car was full of artichokes which had been grown at the Karadj agricultural centre. He knew I loved them and his gesture displayed a thoughtfulness and simplicity I was unaccustomed to. I was having fun with Mehdi and there was plenty of positive energy between us. For the first time, I really enjoyed being with a man without feeling nervous or worried. His tranquil nature had a calming effect on me. There was a quality of pure kindness and a gentility about him that instilled a sense of trust, respect and peace in me. At nights I went to bed without a care, knowing that I would be woken by his soft voice on the telephone wishing me 'good morning' and wanting to know my plans for the day.

Mehdi's uncle, Dr Moshir Fatemi, a grandson of Shahzadeh Zell al-Sultan, was my mother's cousin and a good friend of my father's and this gentleman took it upon himself to play matchmaker. One day, Father called from The Mar Mar to inform Mother that Dr Moshir Fatemi, had called and wanted to make an appointment for Mehdi's grandparents, parents and the aunts and the uncles to come to our home for Khasegari. This must have been the best news that Mother had heard since Father's proposal to her. I had guessed this was coming, as Mehdi had mentioned to me that his grandmother wanted to visit my mother – though he had omitted to mention anything about Khasegari. I had got to know my man a little better. He was modest, honest and obstinate, an introvert with a very composed temperament. Always immaculately dressed, he had a cultivated taste in almost everything. It was most unfortunate that he had no money. On the other hand, money had never really been an issue in my life. Agha joon had always made sure that I had everything I wished for and he would continue to do so whether I was married or not. So why worry?

My parents were very happy that at last I had managed to find a decent man from a decent family to marry and they went out of their way to celebrate the occasion. I was their only daughter and the apple of my father's eye. He was so proud of me that he gave me a grand engagement party as well as a lavish wedding celebration, both on the roof garden of the Mar Mar Hotel with Mahasti, the celebrated singer entertaining the guests. We married on 14th September 1967.

Our celebration was not the only one in town. The Shah's coronation was set for October 28. The Iranian constitution lacked provision for a regent in the absence of an adult heir so, during the Shah's absences, provisional power was vested in a commission. Considering all the attempts on his life, the Shah needed to appoint a trusted regent till his son came of age. Accordingly, he had certain points of the constitution modified so that only he could designate the regent. The right choice was Farah, but first she had to be crowned.

On the morning of the 28th, Maman, Mehdi and I watched the historical event take place on the television in Shahjoon's bedroom – our small, private world looking on at history being made.

In the great Hall of Mirrors at the Golestan Palace, the Shah sat on the Peacock Throne. Seated one on each side of him was Farah in a Dior white satin dress and the young prince in his uniform. Suddenly, the trumpets blared and the Imperial flag was hoisted above the throne. The Immam Jomeh, chanting Koranic verses, stepped forward and handed the Koran to the monarch to kiss. Then the Shah put on his belt, slung Reza Shah's sword into it and placed his father's jewelled mantle around his shoulders. A group of dignitaries then marched forward and offered the crown to the Shah, who took it and crowned himself.

The attendants who were carrying Farah's crown and jewelled mantle then approached the throne. The queen knelt before her husband and the attendants draped the mantle over her shoulders. The sovereign crowned his wife then, turning to his son and pointing to the assembly, he pronounced young Prince Reza as his heir.

Shahjoon never learned to accept the Pahlavies and once the ceremony finished she remarked: "I hope Mohammad Reza will not run away again – in the face of adversity!"

"Shahjoon joon what adversity can befall such a powerful man?" I asked in a teasing tone.

"Megalomaniacs are often their own greatest enemy," she said turning the television off.

Our married life began with the usual period of adjustment, which at times seemed very hard. In character we were poles apart. Mehdi was soft, patient and forever content. I was totally independent, assertive, ambitious and a workaholic. Had it not been for our sense of dedication to traditional family values our marriage would have not lasted the test of time. To avoid National Service, Mehdi applied and was accepted at the University of Southern Illinois in Carbondale to take a doctorate degree in economics.

We spent our last evening at the Persian Room, where Masoud threw a farewell party for us. The guests were all close friends, with the exception of a petite, elegant and very beautiful young woman who had arrived with one of Masoud's friends. All evening she kept darting alluring glances at her host. Mehdi noticed this, too, and remarked: 'Soon you might have a new sister-in-law, Lily!' I shook my head in agreement. Two months later they were married, alas without our parents' blessings.

We left Iran for New York on the 20th of February 1968. There we bought a navy-blue Mustang convertible and set off on the long drive to Carbondale which was a very small college town.

Every morning, Mehdi went to university and I was left alone to do the housework – which amounted to virtually nothing. At the end of the first term, my husband achieved high enough marks to qualify for an assistantship, which added a bonus to our monthly allowance and provided for a comfortable lifestyle.

After a while, the monotony of this lifestyle led to frequent irritability on my part which was not pleasant. So I decided to apply for a degree in social welfare, with which I could contribute to my society. I had seen what poverty could do to people, and I wanted to do something about it. True to form, I acted on my decision immediately and whole-heartedly, and the pursuit of knowledge in my chosen subject, once a hobby, now became a goal. Life became more pleasant as we each sat on our favourite chair and studied in the evenings. Our conversations became more academic and we competed for excellence in our fields. For a while, life was pretty much perfect. Then I became pregnant.

Maman arrived in Carbondale shortly before the baby was due. It was wonderful to see her after two long years. Once she had recovered from her jet lag, she enthusiastically took charge and ordered me to rest. Her presence, her help and support, were like a precious gift to me. She was the very essence of motherhood – loving, generous and selfless.

My daughter, a healthy baby with rosy cheeks and a head covered with black hair, was born at 1 am on the 18th of February, 1969. For a newborn baby, her features were well-defined, promising great beauty. Mehdi was disappointed at first. He had been hoping for a son to perpetuate the family line. But Betsabeh was so gorgeous, that nobody could help but adore her, not least her disappointed father. My mother stayed with us until I could manage the baby by myself.

Back in Teheran, Masoud had sought Shahjoon's assistance to act as mediator to mend the rift between him and my parents. Through her, he asked my parents to forgive him and to accept Chista as his wife. My parents had been waiting for such an appeal; they loved Masoud deeply and, in spite of the fact that he had hurt them, they were ready to embrace him again. Reconciled, my parents gave him the key to the house they had built for him. Chista's gifts to our family are Amir Khosrow and Keyvan, two lovely boys who have made their father very proud. This marriage also did not last.

A year after his divorce Masoud married Mahtab, a lady with an everlasting smile. She gave the family a girl named Sarah.

In Carbondale with Maman gone, it seemed to me at first that I would never manage. Taking care of a baby, along with domestic chores and a full load of credits per term seemed impossible, but with meticulous planning and lots of hard work, I managed to establish a convenient routine. Sometimes happy, sometimes wretched, overworked but successful, we studied and saved money. We toured the length of the United States by car, brunched at Nickelson's Farms, gambled at Las Vegas, lunched at Fisherman's Wharf in San Francisco, dined at the Russian Tearoom in New York, stayed at the Hilton on the Michigan Boulevard in Chicago and, finally, in late 1972, graduated with honours and returned to serve our country.

We moved to the house my parents had built and furnished for me. Soon Mehdi, with his doctorate in economics, procured a lecturing position at the National University of Iran.

Through Masoud's influence with the Minister of Health and Welfare, I became the principal social worker at the Reza Pahlavi Hospital in Shemiran. It was there that I witnessed first-hand the farce of the regime's propaganda, which bragged about the benefits bestowed upon the nation by the Pahlavi regime. Reza Pahlavi Hospital was a government institution with a social work ward, the function of which was to provide home care for children from poor families. On my first day at work, I presented myself to the assistant of the president of the hospital, who was to introduce me to the social work team. After offering me a cup of tea, which I refused, she got up and led me into a long corridor, at the end of which was the social services office. In this room sat a young girl who immediately rose from behind her metal desk to greet me. The assistant introduced her as Miss Shirazi, the principal social worker.

Assuming that she was leaving her job and that I was replacing her, I asked her the reason for her departure. Cautiously, she hinted that I was replacing her not because she was leaving, but because of my US degree, and that she would be working under my direction. Her words and her resigned attitude embarrassed me. Trying to be as natural as possible, I assured her that we would work as a team. I told her that I would appreciate her support, welcome her suggestions and needed to draw on her experience. This approach seemed to break the ice a little, because she became less tense and friendlier as she briefed me on the duties and functions of the office. As she explained how the system worked, she stressed that most of the patients' needs were financial. She pointed out that some people abandoned their sick children to the care of the hospital, while others were so poor that they could not take care of nor feed their children in convalescence. In the former cases, the social worker had to find the parents and persuade them to collect their children, and in the latter she had to determine which patients qualified for a token for the dried provisions available for the purpose. I was horrified at the thought of mothers abandoning their beloved children because they could not afford to feed them.

Miss Shirazi took me to the ward where the bulk of our patients lay. The large room was packed with children of all ages, some suffering from malnutrition, some from burns and many from infections caused by lack of hygiene. She told me that when there were no available beds, the gardeners often found breathing bundles which had been left inside the hospital grounds. My introduction to the job ended. At home that afternoon, I took the longest shower of my life, scrubbing myself as though to wash away the social guilt I felt for being affluent.

The next day I was to look after my first case. The patient was ten-years-old, semi-recovered from severe diarrhoea, and her mother had disappeared after learning of her coming release. My task was to locate the mother at an address given as: near the silo in Javadieh. Javadieh was the concentrated slum area in the south of the city, where there were many silos. How was I to find this woman?

I was told that I could use the hospital van, but a telephone call proved the driver to be on an errand for at least another hour. While I was waiting for him to return, sheer luck brought the mother into my office. She was a thin, haggard woman dressed in rags. Her face, though not old, was heavily weather-beaten and her blistered hands told of much hardship. I greeted her warmly and asked the janitor whose responsibility it was to serve tea to look after my visitor. At the sight of the biscuits I offered her, she brightened up and patiently I let her enjoy the entire box. After she finished her tea, she sat looking at me meekly, as though waiting for a reproach. I returned her gaze until she became uncomfortable enough to begin talking.

Sixteen years ago, she told me, she had married a peasant and given him three daughters. Two years ago the family, like so many others, had left their village and come to the city in search of a better life. After one year of trying without success to find permanent work, her husband had left their room one morning and never returned. It did not take too long for the unpaid landlady to learn of the flight of the breadwinner and throw the family out into the streets. Not knowing what to do, the young mother had taken her children to the nearby silo site in search of work. The foreman there had taken pity on her and offered her employment. Her wage was dependent on the number of bricks she collected – ten rials (about seven US cents) per hundred bricks – and as an incentive to start work immediately he had allowed her to collect enough bricks to build a shelter for herself and her children. With the help of her oldest daughter, she had erected four walls and roofed it with a sheet of tin given to them by the foreman. Their dwelling, which she referred to as a tin hut, was without any means of sanitation or water. Their drinking water was either joob water (water from the gutter) or was drawn from the nearby well. Their toilet was a hole in the ground which she had dug outside the hut. When finances permitted, she took the children to the neighbouring public baths.

Her oldest daughter, aged fifteen, was also working at the silo. Her second daughter, fourteen, had been sold for five thousand rials to a pimp from Shahreno (the red light district). He had promised her the girl would live well and wear good clothes. Now she did not know what to do with the third one, who was in hospital.

The story was heart-rending. What could I offer this woman? What would truly benefit her – Freudian counselling, or a couple of kilos of lentils? How many hundreds – indeed, thousands – of such desperate souls existed in our society?

Suddenly, my thoughts were interrupted by the woman, who was asking me what I could do for her. I apologized and told her I must see her room before I could make any decisions. I had to make sure she was telling the truth. I called the driver again. He was in. I led the woman to the parking lot, where we got into the van and headed for what can only be described as the shameful underworld of the Pahlavi paradise. After one and a half hours of driving in the horrific southern Teheran traffic, we reached the site. It was a huge shambles of a place which most human beings could not conceivably imagine to exist in a modern capital city of an oil-rich country. Scattered rows of tin huts provided shelter for the people who scraped a pathetic living from the silo. The stink of human waste permeated the air, and swarms of flies were feasting on dung everywhere. A few diseased dogs, thinner than the people they were watching over, were scavenging around on the barren land. A handful of children were playing next to one of the huts, and a couple of babies were crawling with bruised knees on the muddy, contaminated ground. A little baby girl was sitting in a corner trying to suck at a broken brick.

The woman guided me to her so-called home. The encompassed area was just large enough to accommodate four bodies stretched on the floor side by side. The inside was immaculately clean. The ground was covered with an old, faded, many times mended kilim. A thin mattress lay folded up in a corner. The only cooking apparatus was a gas burner, next to which some tin and plastic bowls and plates were neatly stacked. Some tin cutlery and a wooden spoon filled an old shoe box. This was her share of the Pahlavi paradise.

I could not control my tears. The woman looked at me as if I was mad and asked me why I was crying. I stared back at her, not knowing what to say. Then it dawned on me that this individual had accepted her fate and was trying to make the most of it. Such was the lot of those who were not caught up in the whirlwind of the march towards the Great Civilization. On the way back to the hospital, I told her I would make arrangements for her to receive five thousand rials in cash per month, plus ten kilos of rice and lentils, if she took her daughter with her when we returned to the hospital and rented a decent room. The look in her eyes was worth a million rials. For the dried provisions, she was to go to the hospital each month; for the money she was to go to the reception of the Mar Mar Hotel and ask for Mr Izadi.

The next day I resigned. The social problems in Iran did not need social workers with US degrees. They needed a system which aimed at eradicating the problems from their roots up. They needed a revolution. The woman remained on my payroll until she found herself a bricklayer husband who could take care of her and her children. In spite of her abject poverty, she had enough dignity to refuse our meagre handout when it was no longer absolutely essential.

My next job was at the National University of Iran, as an English lecturer in the Department of Psychology of the School of Humanities. The Head of this Department was Dr Cyrous Azimi, the most respected psychologist in Iran. He was Mehdi's cousin and liked me very much. Each department had an English course that aimed to enable the students to read their English texts.

Initially, those students registered at the university had been from the higher income groups who were able to pay the annual fees. As time passed, and Iran prospered, the government took the positive step of abolishing this fee. Naturally, the socio-economic backgrounds of the students changed as the original students went abroad and vacated their places to applicants from the lower income groups. Interestingly, I noticed that the number of girls in Hejab was rapidly increasing. This meant more women were becoming educated. That was good. However, I also noticed that SAVAK vans had become a permanent feature in the campus parking lots. From whispered rumours, I gathered that any dissent among the students was severely and savagely punished. In retaliation, the students would look for the slightest excuse to start a riot, and often took their anger and frustration out on the university windows. It was not unusual for us to go through an entire winter with a piece of cardboard covering our class window as a substitute for the broken glass.

Nevertheless, life for the majority seemed prosperous and not many took student riots seriously. The Mar Mar was always full and Agha joon had bought a beautiful waterfront property on the shores of the Caspian Sea. Masoud had become the head of the Reza Shah medical complex, and Mahmoud was living in London at a substantial property Agha joon had bought at Rutland Gate in Knightsbridge. He was director of a British petrochemical company.

My cousins, who I saw frequently, were all doing well. Bahram, now married was a board member of the Omran bank; Mamal Khan, a director at the Ministry of Electricity; and Afsaneh had married Tooraj Etehadieh, who with the help of his father-in-law had become a successful and wealthy contractor. Mohsen Khan, senator by royal appointment, was busy turning one of his villages near Galandoak into a modern residential suburb and I had become owner of a large block of land in Galandoak.

Meanwhile, our Shah was exultant at his success in masterminding the oil price rise of 1973. Massive capital was being injected into the economy. The inflation was rising. Teheran, already overcrowded with cars and people, was buried under a thick cloud of pollution. The city was pulsating with activities of all kinds: construction, commerce, festivals and conferences. It had become a city of neurotics searching for wealth and success. The relaxed traditional customs and courtesies were being wiped out by the onrush of civilization – that is, the Shah's idea of civilization. Yet, contrary to expectation, people did not seem to be happy; nor were they enthusiastic about the transformation of their society, or the fact that Iran had become more than just a spot on the world map and there was no unemployment. Labour was being imported.

Foreigners were greatly impressed by the Shah's total dedication to turning Iran into a Western industrial state. But to his detriment, as he became more prominent on the international scene, he also became more isolated from his people. The strict demands of protocol, together with the tremendous security measures which surrounded him, shielded the monarch from direct contact with his subjects. His SAVAK had become ubiquitous and repression of the people had intensified. We only ever heard the Shah's helicopter fly over our heads.

Even we, a class which lived in perfect affluence, felt the wrongness of it. Yet whether we liked it or not, we were living in a land of bewildering contrasts, going through a process of dynamic economic, social and cultural change which influenced every aspect of our lives. We were part of a gigantic wave sweeping across the country, crushing all obstacles in its quest to become part of an ocean of prosperity. Now we even had a minister for women's affairs. Divorce laws were being changed, their Koranic origins being discarded to give more rights to women. No longer could men divorce their wives simply by saying 'I divorce thee' three times. There were family courts to protect the women's rights and women were becoming a huge and remarkably efficient force in the labour market.

Almost everybody I knew was employed, with two or three different jobs. Mehdi had become an executive board director of a government bank, with a good salary and a chauffeur-driven car. 'Workomania' and progress were the moods of the time.

I was teaching extra hours myself. The two Filipinos I had employed in place of the Turkish housekeeper were managing the house very efficiently and looking after little Betsabeh. Now aged five, she was growing tall, slender and very alert. We had enrolled her at an International school where she was learning both Farsi and English. Our happiness became more profound when I became pregnant again.

The Shah was at the pinnacle of his power committing mistake after mistake. Now by his order our calendar from its Islamic origin of Hejrat; the Prophet's emigration from Mecca to Medina, had been changed to the twenty-fifth century of the Persian Empire. This silly whim meant that all legal documents, beginning with one's birth certificate had to be changed. The decree was a bureaucratic blunder and a direct affront to Islam which, quite rightly, infuriated the clergy. However, fearing SAVAK we could only complain about the Teheran traffic.

The Empress, as active as ever on the cultural scene, was patronizing the controversial annual International Cultural Festival at Shiraz, where talent from all over the world entertained royalty and those who could afford the tickets. The citizens of Shiraz and most of the audience found the avant-garde nature of the programs offensive to Iranian traditional sensitivities.

The Shah, meanwhile, had introduced another ploy in the guise of an industrial reform. A decree had been passed which compelled all industrialists who owned plants over a certain size to sell forty-nine per cent of their ownership to their workers within a certain time limit, with a greater share to be sold to the workers in nationalized industries. This sudden reform led to panic and uncertainty among the entrepreneurs, who became reluctant to invest any more capital in Iran. They began to send their money out of the country, and by 1977, billions of dollars had left Iran. The workers, lacking faith in the authorities, did not welcome the reform; nor did they take advantage of the generous offers of share acquisition in place of cash wages. Through lack of trust, this reform, too, failed to have the desired effect.

Agha joon, like most people, was getting worried about all these unpredictable changes. Cautiously, he too began to send money out – for a rainy day, as he put it. Parissa, my second daughter was born on May 14th 1975. She was tiny but gorgeous. She hardly ever cried, or bothered Fe, her nanny. I enjoyed being with my children for the duration of my maternity leave and when I recommenced lecturing I noticed that the classroom environment had changed; the normally polite students had become impertinent. The cafeteria in which I sometimes lunched seemed fuller, noisier, the tables occupied by lively groups of students involved in heated discussions – which always changed to small talk when anyone in authority appeared on the scene. The almost threatening expressions on their faces made me uncomfortable and I stopped going there altogether.

Mehdi had been appointed dean of the students. One evening, over dinner, we began to talk about the changed atmosphere of the campus. He divulged that SAVAK had intensified its vigilance, and that their representative had asked him for his co-operation in identifying dissident students. I was horrified and asked him whether he was going to resign or co-operate. He replied that he was going to do neither; instead, he would try to protect the students who were being picked up daily and sent to SAVAK headquarters; some returned, others disappeared for ever. Many of those taken to headquarters could be helped, Mehdi said. By using his influence he could act as intermediary and try to secure their release. The suspicious looks, the anger and the hatred now made sense.

Naively, I had been wondering why the students were so against the regime, which seemed to offer them so much more than before. All the reforms targeted at the rich were to make the poor people's lot better. Wealth would trickle down, wouldn't it? Education was expanding, entering the remotest areas. University fees were being abolished and many of the students received grants. There was so much work that skilled labour was being imported from overseas. People could travel freely. Iranians did not need visas for most countries. There was no exchange control; many people had apartments and houses all over the world and for those who did not wish to shop abroad most consumer goods could be purchased in Iran. Why, then, were these young people – who owed their education to the Shah – so against him?

Mehdi had a completely different view of the situation. He did not believe that the majority of people were content. He believed that the oil money was the worst calamity that had ever hit Iran, and that it would have serious repercussions for the regime. The result of the boom was an annual inflation rate of around twenty per cent. The Shah's dreams were unrealistic and most of his projects too grand to realize. Many companies, and the government, too, had indulged in excessive imports of all sorts of goods, whose transfer from port to city was impossible because of inadequate roads, fragmented rail links and limited means of transport. The infrastructure simply was not ready to absorb the pressures of an overheated economy.

The boom had also created a wide gap between rural and urban incomes, a situation which had persuaded many farmers to sell their land and drift to the already overpopulated cities, like Teheran, which could not accommodate them. This state of affairs not only damaged agriculture, but also worsened the spread of the city slums. To make matters worse, villages on the outskirts of the capital were being bulldozed to make room for modern towns, leaving the inhabitants homeless. The majority of them had no choice but to seek refuge in the poverty-stricken areas like Javadieh.

High wages and rising expectations tended to make the urban working classes, particularly industrial and construction workers, volatile in their political and social attitudes. Their lot had definitely improved. Now they were eating take-away pizzas and drinking Budweiser for lunch, instead of their usual bread, goat cheese and Coca Cola. The influence of American culture, once detested, was now embodied in the hamburger shops and pizza parlours which mushroomed on every corner. A chain of Kentucky Fried Chicken restaurants was installed, though without a legitimate franchise. The colonel definitely looked like an Iranian.

A kind of social vacuum was engulfing the populace, especially in the larger cities, threatening to endanger the existing social order. Everything was changing, but in the absence of logical goals, rational planning and trained human resources only God could predict the results.

Mehdi forecasted a gloomy future. I knew he was right, but I did not want to admit it. What concerned me most at that particular time was the shortage of onions. The greengrocers were complaining that all the onions were rotting at Khoramhahr (the major Iranian port) because there were not enough trucks to carry the goods to the cities, and to aggravate the situation the government was trying to enforce an impossible price control in order to curb the embarrassing inflation. Needless to say, this situation had created a black market.

I did not let the lack of onions, an essential ingredient in Iranian cooking, bother me for long. Instead, I hunted the supermarkets for dried onion flakes and bought the entire stock of the local supermarket. I felt relieved about the eradication of this minor problem. To be on the safe side, I began storing imperishable goods like rice, cooking oil, canned and bottled essentials. Both freezers in my kitchen were filled with meat and frozen vegetables. I was only half-conscious that I was preparing my household for trouble.

Norooz, the New Year, was approaching and my parents decided to take their vacation in the villa by the Caspian. I loved going there where I could swim and sunbathe all day, and gamble away the evenings at the casino in the Hyatt Hotel. This hotel had been built by the Pahlavi foundation, which had been created by the Shah in 1958 and which boasted its own bank, the Omran, to utilize the revenue obtained from the sales of crown land. The foundation invested in all areas, from industry, to hotels, to offshore investments. Initially, its profits were to be used for social services, but in truth the foundation acted independently of the central government. Its managing director, a Dr Rumm, had been chosen by the Shah himself from among his most trusted servants and appointed by a royal decree, putting him in charge of investing the Pahlavi wealth in the most lucrative businesses in Iran and abroad – especially in the United States.

The Omran Bank, the channel through which these financial transactions were made, was expanding under the management of Dr Rumm and had become the fourth largest commercial bank in Iran. One of the aims of its managing director was to infuse the board with new, western-educated professionals. A hunt was initiated and one of the preyed-upon was my husband. He was offered a generous package including a brand new, chauffeur-driven Mercedes Benz. The offer was promptly accepted.

The bank's most recent investment was the creation of the ultramodern Shahrak Gharb, a new suburb on the outskirts of the Evin Hills, spreading out from the west wing of the city. Naturally, the land belonged to the foundation and different international developers were contracted to construct residential complexes on the site. The apartments were advertised to be sold off the plan. It seemed like a good investment and we decided to buy two apartments, one for each child, from the Omran Techlar Complex which was being constructed by a Greek company.

The happiest and most secure year of my life was probably 1976. I had everything I had ever wanted and was living in the most exciting country in the world. Iran was preparing to celebrate fifty years of Pahlavi rule and, through the university, we were invited to attend the main ceremony at Reza Shah's mausoleum in the holy city of Ray, near the shrine of Immam Abdol Azim. This is an isolated yet magnificent place situated on an arid desert plain. From the main road, one sees only a long, wide avenue leading to the main building, which is surrounded by nothing but dry, stony earth.

On the day of the celebration we got up very early. Women were to dress in long, formal gowns and the men were to wear black ties or uniform. Mehdi had to wear his black university gown. By nine-thirty in the morning we were both ready to leave for the hall at Teheran University, where we would be picked up by special security buses and driven to the site. Bayat, our new driver, arrived right on time to drive us to the university. I felt pleased with myself: riding in my new chauffeur-driven Benz, all dressed for a royal occasion.

The hall was full of excited academic dignitaries robed in their black gowns, which billowed around them when they moved; their wives wore long, chic, custom-made dresses and stood by their husbands feeling important, making intellectual jokes, trying to corner those who were more important then themselves and avoid those with lower ranks. At ten thirty it was announced that it was time to set off on the hour-long drive to the mausoleum.

When we reached our destination I was stunned. The dry desert had been transformed into a garden filled with flowers. Stands were erected on each side of the avenue leading to the steps of the building. Pot plants were dug into the ground to create a make-believe green border, and carpet runners smoothed the path for their majesties. Many important people from the upper echelons had been invited to celebrate the occasion: cabinet ministers, generals of the armed forces and diplomats shone in their uniforms, which were ostentatiously decorated with stars, medals and ribbons. The crowd made a magnificent sight. Here, rivalry, snobbery and sycophancy went beyond the imagination.

When all the buses had arrived and the numbers had been matched to the SAVAK's list, the guests were asked to take their places at the designated stands. Placement was in accordance with rank; the most important officials and diplomats were seated near the building and the lesser souls were allocated stands in accordance with their ranks. Our position, to my surprise, was not very far from the mausoleum.

The sound of helicopters announced the arrival of their majesties. I could not see their aircraft from where we were sitting, but a few minutes later a burst of applause and the movement of people rising told of their approach. The Shah, very erect, looked immaculately elegant, but the empress appeared sullen. I was so excited, and clapping so hard, that I could not feel the cold which a few minutes ago had been making my bones ache.

The imperial couple, followed by their entourage, were nearing our stand and the crowd's excitement was rising. As they passed us, I caught the sovereign's hypnotic glance for a split-second and was mesmerized by its magnetic force. During that euphoric moment a surge of pride touched my heart. With smiles and waves of the hand they acknowledged the spectators' salutations as they walked the length of the path to mount the steps and enter the mausoleum. After a short while, they returned to their helicopter and flew back to their palace. This was to be the last grand imperial event to take place in Iran.

That night, we watched the ceremony on television. I was astonished to see the Shah and the empress driving in an open, horse-drawn carriage for what seemed like many kilometres, waving to what seemed like thousands of cheering people. When had they driven in the carriage? Where had been the crowds of such apparent magnitude?

I concluded that the mass media and the propaganda machine had been at work again. An electronic montage had been cleverly created to give the impression of a popularity which simply did not exist. Such a gross lie felt eerie and I regretted my jubilation of only hours ago. I felt manipulated and naive. What deception! And why?

Chapter 14

In November 1976, Carter became the President of the United States. Democrat presidents had not favoured the Shah in the past, as their foreign policies had frowned on corruption. President Carter's public devotion to the cause of human rights in third world countries, and his emphasis on the need to reduce the volume of sales of military equipment to them, gave the Shah ample cause to worry and led to a period of uncertainty in Iran-American relations.

The Shah, in order to endear himself to the new president, initiated a considerable liberalization of his regime, albeit haphazardly, again. This breeze of greater political freedom was refreshing at the university campus.

Newspapers were becoming more readable and openly signed letters from respectable citizens such as lawyers, academics and members of the old National Front Party began to circulate. These letters were critical of the policies and performances of the regime but surprisingly, no arrests were made. Friday mosques became crowded with the impassioned clergy using the occasions to voice their hostility towards the Shah's modernizing moves.

One Friday we heard that a prominent Ayatollah was to speak at Ghobad, a well-known mosque not far from us, so we decided to attend. After dinner we walked to the mosque. Cars were parked for kilometres on either side of the narrow road leading to the house of worship and a huge crowd had gathered outside to listen to the sermon, which echoed from the loudspeaker. Wrapped in my chador, I held tightly to Mehdi's hand. Near the entrance, an elderly man turned to me and said: "Sister, women are sitting inside." I asked him what time he thought the preaching would finish. He replied: "At ten." I looked at Mehdi, who politely thanked the old man and told me to go inside and meet him by the entrance after the sermon.

Inside, the mosque was crowded with elegant women chadored in black silk, sitting cross-legged on the carpeted floor listening intently to the speaker. Their made-up eyes twinkled with excitement and the scent of their French perfumes fused with that of the mosque's usual rose water gave the solemn interior a surrealistic aura. Clearly these women were not the usual mosque-goers of Ashura nights. Immediately I spotted two of my university colleagues. Luckily, they did not see me.

The well-informed Ayatollah, standing erect behind his Manbar (pulpit) was professionally stirring up the audience by criticizing the regime's anti-corruption policies – the way in which honourable merchants and poor street vendors were being rounded up and jailed for selling overpriced merchandise, while the government was powerless to stop the Pahlavis and their cronies from ransacking the country and so on and on. Then the Ayatollah, having exhausted the malaise of political policies, arrived at the shameless absurdities of the annual Shiraz International Cultural Festival. Apparently, the vulgarity of the artistic events of the 1977 festival had been an affront to all decent values. An actual rape scene had been enacted on a pavement in a shopping centre.

The crowd in the mosque was now highly aroused and looked as if they were ready for a bloody battle.

The sermon went on until ten when the Ayatollah's "Allah Akbar", in unison with that of the congregation, shook heaven and earth with its power. Then, the preacher, satisfied with his conquest, lifted the ends of his long black flowing robe, gracefully descended the steps of the altar and disappeared behind a door that was held open for him by a worshipper. The excited crowd rose too and began to swarm towards the sole exit. The passageway immediately became jammed and people began to struggle to get out.

It was a frightful experience. The constant movement from all directions was making me dizzy and nauseated. A sudden shove from behind threw me outside into the street where bodies, cars, motorcycles and bicycles mingled together trying without much success to move. Mehdi was nowhere in sight.

As the road was one-way, the general push of the crowd was towards the north, in the direction of Avenue Ehteshamieh. Suddenly, I caught sight of my husband's raised head trying to locate me amongst the wave of women spilling forth from the mosque. I was just lifting my hand from under my chador to signal my whereabouts, when someone stepped on the fabric from behind, pulling it off my shoulders and onto the ground. I bent to pick it up and, suddenly, felt a heavy weight crushing me. Before I knew what had happened, I was lying on the ground on my right side with the paralyzing weight of a motorbike resting on my left leg, its cold metal handlebars jamming into my chest. For a moment I was stunned, and then I felt an excruciating pain in my leg. Many heads were bent towards me, and hands stretched to lift the bike off me. After what seemed an eternity, the weight was lifted and a kindly hand grasped mine and helped me to get up. At the same time, someone grabbed my shoulders from behind, intensifying my terror. In a state of shock I tried furiously to free myself, and then I heard a gentle voice asking me if I was all right and realized it was Mehdi.

Fortunately, in spite of the dreadful pain in my leg, I was able to walk. Mehdi acted as my support and, slowly we headed for home. Safely there, Aniana helped me into a hot bath where I lay for a long time. The heat soothed my pain and cleared my head. Lying motionless I had time to reflect on the events of the evening. Ghobad Mosque was in Shemiran, an area which housed the most affluent sections of society. Why had it been so crowded? Clearly, the people I had seen were not the discontented poor. What reason did they have to support dissent? Were we perhaps in the throes of a revolution?

All of what had been said at the mosque made sense. Was this sudden liberation movement by the regime logical, or was the Shah playing with fire? Why had SAVAK stood by and allowed the Ayatollah to say what he wanted? Was he perhaps going to "disappear" in the night? Could it really be that the Shah, after so many years of autocracy, was going to let the people voice their grievances? Was he going to acquire a listening ear, even though he was not prepared to relinquish any power? After all, people just wanted to have a say in the issues which concerned their lives; nobody wanted drastic change or a revolution which involved bloodshed. Perhaps now the Shah will listen to the message of his people, I told myself, and before getting out of the bath I implored God to help Iran. But neither God nor the monarch listened to the voice of the Iranian people. Sooner than was expected, SAVAK's physical attacks on the moderate elements drove them underground again. But what SAVAK could not control was the resurgence of religious traditionalism. Recently, there had been several disturbances at Teheran University, with threats being made against the female students for their choice of provocative Western dress. There had also been a strike against mixed cafeterias for the students. I had not visited ours lately, so I was not sure what was happening there. But I became cautious with my choice of clothes.

In our circle, life went on as normal. We were all patiently waiting for America to resolve the problems of our country! But that did not happen. Strikes began. The lights went off and the lines at petrol stations became longer and longer.

The cold season lashed at us with unprecedented severity. Yet, people seemed to be coping with the power failures and all the other small difficulties which presented themselves daily.

Gradually, the atmosphere in Teheran changed to that of unrelieved sombreness and many people began to liquidate their assets, with the intention of leaving the country. Most of my friends were going to take long vacations overseas, particularly those with second homes in Europe and or the United States. Fortunately, my relatives stayed in Iran and Shahjoon's house remained a centre for the latest gossip. Mohsen Khan had not been reappointed senator; like many other long-serving citizens he had been whimsically discarded. Happily, because of his unblemished reputation, they could not accuse him of corruption so he had not yet been jailed. Now he spent most of his time in Galandoak, writing his memoirs.

On Christian New Year's Eve, I had Anniana cook whatever was customary in the Philippines and the domestics joined us in the formal dining room to eat. After dinner I released them from their duties so that they could spend the evening with their friends. The children went to bed and we sat in the television room waiting for the news. President Carter and his wife were in Teheran celebrating the occasion royally, at the Niavaran Palace. Nothing was broadcast that evening, but the next day the newspapers gave extensive coverage to President Carter's after-dinner speech. The Democrat president had called the Shah's Iran "an oasis of peace and stability in a troubled region", and had confidently stressed the popularity of the Shah among his subjects.

This was the news we were waiting for.

That night Mehdi and I, after many sleepless nights slept soundly.

The next day, like every other day after breakfast, the two of us scrutinized our daily paper. Mehdi started first and then passed the paper to me. Today we were sitting in the television room waiting for the news, when Mehdi threw his newspaper on the floor and exclaimed furiously: 'What infamy!' Taken by surprise, I asked him what it was that was infamous enough to raise such a fury in such a calm individual. Grudgingly, he picked up the paper and handed it to me to read. On the front page was a long article by Daryoush Homayoun, the minister for information, detailing Ayatollah Khomeini's personal background, private morals and religious credentials and boldly discrediting the man. I was devastated by the abusive tone of the article and frightened of the consequences of such an attack on an idolized deity that he was becoming to the populous. I wondered whether or not I should send the children to their school, which was located next to Niavaran Palace. What if there was a march towards that area, or worse, an attack on the palace itself? In desperation, I turned to Mehdi for advice; he assured me that security in that vicinity was tight and that we should not panic.

The following day, nothing untoward happened, except that tension mounted in the campus. Most classes were half-empty and those who were present were inattentive. Small groups of students whispered among themselves as they hurried from one building to another, their coat collars turned up, and knitted scarves protecting their faces from the lashing wind which whipped through the snow-covered hills. There was a feeling of foreboding in the air.

When my lectures were finished, I set off for home without returning to my office. I spent a few hours with the children, and then took a brisk walk to Mohsen Khan's house. Inside, his male domestic greeted me and ushered me into the formal sitting room. My uncle, looking haggard, but as elegant as ever, was sitting on a comfortable chair next to the fireplace where limp flames burned dejectedly. I kissed him, and then sat down on the armchair facing him. Our conversation almost immediately turned to politics. I wanted to know what he thought of the present crisis and what he thought the future held. I knew that he disliked the Shah, and I also knew that he was not religious. I asked him what he considered to be the best solution to the present problems. Without hesitation, he replied that the Shah must go.

"Go where, Mohsen Khan? If he goes, we will have anarchy."

"What do you think we have now?" he asked sarcastically.

"I don't know. But why doesn't he act like a sovereign?"

He retorted with bitterness: "He is waiting for his master's orders."

"The Americans or the British?" I asked.

He rose, took a piece of wood from the antique brass tray and placed it on top of the last burning log. Then, with a poker, he played with the smoking ashes until a blaze began to flicker. Satisfied, he rested the instrument against its stand and returned to his seat.

Impatient with his silence I continued, "I don't think the British are for him. The BBC (Persian language service broadcasts) is supporting Khomeini. Everybody in the country is listening to the channel's nightly broadcasts, which are definitely biased against the regime. Radios with FM receivers have become as rare as fresh meat." (Fresh meat had become a scarce commodity. Apparently, a ship full of livestock from Australia had been thrown into the Persian Gulf because it had been impossible to unload it. Later I was to meet the Australian cattle owner who had consequently gone bankrupt.) "The British are very clever. They know the Iranian mentality and they know who to back."

As though I had been talking to the wall Mohesen Khan cut in, "An alternative for the Shah is to choose a prime minister from among the National Front Party."

"So you know of such a person – someone who is willing to forgive and forget the past and help him?"

"Yes Khanum, there are still people who prefer the constitutional monarchy to the rule of the mullahs. But they are not willing to co-operate with the Shah while he is still in the country because they believe His Imperial Majesty will never give up his autocracy." I realized that my uncle definitely knew something. I heard someone enter the room and turned to see my aunt approaching, followed by the servant with a tray of freshly-brewed tea. He placed this on the table next to her chair. I rose and kissed my aunt. I loved her very much. She was my role model, and I admired her strength and prudence. The Shah used to call her "Victor Khan" not "Victor Khanum" (Lord Victor). She took her seat and enquired about Mehdi and the children and, once satisfied that they were well, she handed us our cups of tea and joined in the conversation. She was in total agreement with her husband, holding the view that the Shah must hand over the executive power to a democratically elected prime minister and leave the country – at least until the dust settled.

What she said made sense, but seemed unrealistic. Once the Shah had gone, he could never come back, and without him there would be no cohesion within the government. For the past thirty-seven years, he had been the sole decision-maker, purposely creating division between the governing forces so that no section would become strong enough to challenge his authority; in his absence, surely, all would fall apart. I was surprised at the extent of my aunt's sensitivity towards the monarch. I did not agree with my aunt and uncle, but neither was I qualified to argue with them. Suddenly, I realized that it was already dark and I had to walk home. My aunt offered to drive me, but I refused. The streets were still safe and I enjoyed walking.

On January 9, in retaliation to the infamous newspaper article insulting Khomeini, serious rioting broke out in the holy city of Qum. Troops were called in and a bloody confrontation led to the loss of hundreds of lives. This incident shocked the entire country, leading to irreconcilable hostility between the religious leadership and the government. The religious leaders proclaimed the observance of the customary forty-day mourning period for the martyrs of Qum and immediately their followers covered in shrouds began demonstrating in the streets.

A deceptive lull followed, during which life resumed its normal course, until exactly forty days later when riots broke out in Tabriz, the capital of Azerbaijan and the home base of Ayatollah Kazem Shariat-Madari, the most respected clergyman in Iran. Groups of rioters stormed out of the mosques, burning and destroying anything and everything that was symbolic of Pahlavi modernism – banks, cinemas and liquor stores. The town's garrison was called in and the many killings at the hands of the army led to another forty-day mourning period. More martyrs. Soon, bloody riots in all the major cities became an acknowledged part of life.

One day, when Agha joon had had enough of the tension and mounting problems, he decided we should all take a break in London. Obediently, we packed and the whole family, including Fe, flew to London. Under the circumstances, and after what seemed like a century, this family reunion was a tremendous morale booster, especially for the children, who loved being together again. Agha joon was enjoying himself more than anyone else – living in London, the city he loved, and bestowing generosity upon his offspring, especially his favourite, the effervescent Parissa.

First thing every morning he and Parissa, hand in hand, headed for the local corner shop to purchase doughnuts and newspapers, both Iranian and English. At home, the papers were studied for news of developments in Iran. The Shah, it appeared, was diligently pursuing his anti-corruption campaign, and a new order had prohibited all bank directors from leaving the country without a pass from the Clearance Committee of the institution for which they worked. This decree applied to Mehdi and meant that when we returned to Teheran he would not be able to leave the country again unless cleared by the bank's committee. The next day we read that the Cinema Rex in Abadan had been set on fire, incinerating 400 people. The regime blamed the incident on the opposition, while the opposition accused the government. This news shocked us deeply. It seemed the situation was more serious than we had thought, so we packed and returned to Iran.

One afternoon, we were gathered at our parents' house for tea when Taghi, the cook, entered the room, obviously excited and bursting with some kind of news. Mother asked him where he had been all day.

He replied, "Khanum, I rode to town this morning to do your grocery shopping. On the way back, when I was crossing Avenue Shah Reza, I was held up by a huge demonstration. When I discovered that the march was organized by the clergy, and that it was for Islam, I got off my motorcycle and joined in. From the man walking next to me, I learned that the demonstration had started off from the Shahyad Square and was heading south."

He stopped to catch his breath, and then continued: "Khanum joon, I must admit they were very daring with their anti-Shah slogans. But what was so wonderful was that they were so friendly towards the soldiers who were standing by their tanks watching us. Many people were holding carnations and on various occasions, with my own eyes, I saw them place their flowers in the barrels of the soldiers' rifles and call them 'brothers'. Khanum, I swear by Immam Ali that I have never been as proud in my life as I am now. With Islam in power, all will be well again." The emotionally aroused servant stopped to wipe away his tears.

What a clever ploy, I thought, as I realized the meaning of the events he described.

"Taghi, why are you crying?" I asked.

He stared at me wide-eyed, as though questioning my sanity for asking such a ridiculous question and then, without uttering another word, he turned and left the room – something he would never have done before all these upheavals started.

The next day an edict was issued banning further assemblies without prior authorization. Two days later, on September 8, I was woken up at about 5 am by a voice announcing something on a loudspeaker. Anticipating trouble, I listened hard, but could not quite make out what was being said. Hurriedly, I woke Mehdi and asked him to listen, too. Frightened, he jumped out of bed and opened the window. The voice was proclaiming martial law.

"Why martial law?" I asked.

"What could have happened last night, Mehdi?"

"I don't know. But something must have."

We sat in bed, drowned in thought, waiting for the next radio broadcast at 7 am. Right on time I turned the wireless on. The newsreader announced that during the night, in defiance of the government's edict, another demonstration had taken place without permission. Therefore, to bring law and order to the city, martial law was proclaimed for Teheran under General Ovissie's capable auspices. Well, at last the government was showing a sign of strength. Martial law had been declared to stop these weird processions. I was confused, but relieved. Nevertheless, I kept wondering why the Shah gave freedom one day and took it away the next. Then, to my horror, I realized that perhaps he really doesn't know how to deal with the problem.

That day, a Friday, we decided that instead of going to my parents' house we would take the children for lunch at the Imperial Club. We had not finished eating when a friend entered the restaurant and came over to our table to say hello. After the usual exchange of niceties, he began to smile broadly as though he had conquered the world. Mehdi asked him what was making him so happy during these troubled times. He seemed surprised at our ignorance and, with a big, sinister grin lighting his face, asked, "Don't you know what is happening at Jaleh Square at this very moment?"

"No, we don't," replied Mehdi.

"Well, you'll be happy to hear that at last His Imperial Majesty has decided to have the army burn the roots of those recalcitrant mullahs and their followers. The troops are killing them like ants in the square because they defied martial law and gathered for another demonstration." He stopped talking, but retained his grin in expectation of an approving response from us. To his disappointment, he did not receive any.

Unable to control my disgust at what the man had described, I glared at him with eyes full of hatred and said, "Slaughtering unarmed citizens is not a matter for rejoicing. What if a brother or sister of yours was present in the square? Would you be laughing still?"

He was insulted by my question and shouted, loud enough for all to hear, "My kin wouldn't be seen dead with those dirty black devils." Chin up, he shot a contemptuous glance at me, and without saying goodbye to either of us, he turned and left. We did not stay for tea, and after taking care of the bill we drove to my parents' house, hoping Taghi would be there and would know what had really happened.

Arriving at the house, I found my parents resting in bed watching television. I told them the story and asked where Taghi was. Apparently, he had gone out that morning and had not yet returned. Mehdi sat on a chair and I took my shoes off and climbed onto my Mother's bed, cuddling up against her. There was so much worry in our hearts that the only soothing thing was the warmth of unconditional love. Mother stole a quick kiss from my head and made room for me in her single bed. I loved her so much. Feeling safe, we waited patiently for our informer to show up.

At around five in the afternoon he arrived. The man looked like a resurrected corpse in his bloodstained clothes. Mehdi asked if he had come from Jaleh Square. The trembling man began to sob. "Yes Agha, I have come from hell itself."

"Taghi, why did you go to Jaleh Square when you knew that there was a martial law prohibiting assemblies?" I asked, terrified of what I might hear.

"Last night after the evening prayer, Agha (the mullah) informed the congregation that there would be a demonstration at Jaleh Square (south east of Teheran) and that it was the duty of all good Muslims to participate."

He stopped to clear his throat, and then continued, "I try to be a good Muslim, so after my breakfast, even though I had heard the news about the martial law, I rode to the square. After parking my motorcycle in a secluded corner, I saw the troops standing around. I didn't take much notice of them because, like everyone else, I assumed that this march would be peaceful like the previous ones and that, as usual, the soldiers would stand aside watching us. None of us thought the soldiers would shoot at us. When the square became crowded, the sound of helicopters began shaking heaven and earth. At first, we thought the Shah was coming to watch us from his flying machine, but then we realized that the helicopters belonged to the air force."

"As the choppers were circling the sky, loudspeakers began ordering the demonstrators to disperse. No one paid any attention, because no one believed that the soldiers would shoot at unarmed people. Suddenly, all hell broke loose. The troops on the ground, and those from above, began firing into the crowd. Bodies fell like autumn leaves savaged by a sudden storm. The blood of the martyrs running on the asphalt sanctified the square." Taghi was moved to eloquence.

"The sound of machine guns, the wail of those going to heaven and the chant of 'Death to the Shah, Khomeini is our leader' thundered through the air. Those still alive, never having been faced with such ferocious retaliation, desperately tried to disperse, but the soldiers wouldn't stop. They kept on firing and firing and firing."

Taghi stopped again, the lump in his throat preventing him from continuing. The man was shaking. I got off the bed, took Father's glass and poured some water from the water jar which he kept on his bedside table. I gave it to Taghi and asked him to sit down on the floor. He took the glass, drank the water, thanked me and sat down, crossing his legs.

Taghi had survived because when he had heard the sound of the first shots, his legs had given in and he had fallen into a nearby gutter. When the noise had subsided, he had tried to move, only to find that he had been buried under a corpse. Horror had made him collapse again, but eventually he had managed to gather enough courage to push the body away and pull himself up. Then, oblivious to his surroundings, he had run as fast as he could to where he had parked his motorcycle. Luckily it was still there.

We were devastated by his tale. He must have detected our fear because he turned to Mother and said, "Khanum, you and Agha should go to England. This country won't be safe for you anymore."

Mother immediately replied: "Taghi, we are Iranians like you. This is our country, too – and besides, we have never done anything which should make us afraid. Why should we leave?" Taghi shrugged his shoulders, rose from the floor and, again without permission, left the room. Islamic brotherhood was catching up fast.

After a short period of silence, Father shook his head and said, "He is right. We should go to London."

Mother asked: "And live on what?"

"We could sell this house, and my apartment building which will be finished soon," replied Father. He was building a block of twelve apartments in one of the best residential areas of the city.

I disagreed. "Why should we sell two prime properties because people are daring to stand up against corruption? If any changes take place, there is no reason to believe that they will be for the worst. The dissidents are not communists; they are ordinary people fighting for their rights. I am surprised that the soldiers did fire into the crowd. They are of the same rank and file as the dissidents and I cannot believe that they are going to fight their brothers for long. Then, with no army, there won't be any bloodshed. Some sort of civil solution will save the country, if not the Shah."

I was still blind to what really was happening. The tide of the revolution had not reached Avenue Ehteshamieh. My territory had not yet been threatened.

My mother was wiser than me. Within a couple of months she sold the house and came to live with us until, at the end of her tenant's lease, she could take over her rented property in Avenue Lily. I did not have any cash savings, and I had to think about liquidating some of my assets. I suggested to Mehdi that we should try to get our money back from our two apartments at Omran Techlar, but he immediately rejected the idea, declaring that he would never do anything illegal. I pleaded with him, but to no avail. Nobody was in a buying mood, so there was no chance of selling any of my blocks of land. The only alternative was to sell my carpets. I had never sold anything in my life before, so I consulted my Father, who was still in touch with the carpet dealer he had dealt with for many years. When he heard my request to be put in touch with the dealer he became very angry. To him, selling part of my dowry was demeaning. He forbade me to talk about it and offered to help us should we ever be in need. My husband and I were grateful for the gesture, though neither of us ever intended to take him up on it.

The only alternative to selling the carpets was to take some of them to London and leave them with Mahmoud at the house in Rutland Gate. I shared this thought with Mehdi who approved of the idea, and a trip was planned for the coming university holidays.

Meanwhile, even nature seemed to be against the regime. In mid-September, a tragic earthquake at Tabas, near Mashad in the Eastern desert, almost erased the town from the map killing close to 20,000 people. The army was put in charge of the relief operations but the mullahs, the theological students, and the students from the University of Mashad rushed into the devastated area and began working non-stop to supply food and shelter for the survivors.

Allah had really cursed the plateau. With the speed of lightning, violent demonstrations spread throughout the country and strikes crippled both the private and public sectors. The worst strike was that of the workers and technicians in the National Iranian Oil Company. It meant there would be no petrol and, for those who used oil heaters, no fuel for the coming winter. Long lines began to form at all the petrol stations as people sought to fill their car tanks and stock up on bottles of petrol. The queues at the bus stops became longer and longer, and walking became the surest means of transport.

Gas for cooking purposes had to be purchased in containers and since the gas company had stopped delivering these, they had to be collected from their outlets. In desperation one day, I asked my driver Bayat how many we could carry in the car. He told me four. We immediately set out for town, and after procuring the four containers and putting two in the trunk and two on the back seat, I asked him to drive me to the fruit market at Behjat Abad. We also had to collect Father from the Mar Mar later on.

At the intersection of Avenues Ferdowsi and Zahedi, we came across a small, excited crowd sticking Khomeini's pictures onto the windows of cars which were waiting at the traffic lights. I was terrified. With four containers of gas in the car, what would happen if they decided to get violent? We could not turn back, so had to continue in the same direction. As our car stopped at the lights, two teenagers jumped onto the bonnet, and a third stuck his head through the open window and ordered us to say "Death to the Shah". We had no choice but to comply. Then he stuck a black and white printed picture of the Immam on the windscreen. When eventually the light turned green, the two teenagers sitting on the bonnet jumped down and I heard Bayat sigh with relief. We collected Agha joon, forgot about grocery shopping and headed for home.

On October 7, the BBC announced that Khomeini had flown to Paris, where he had been joined by Abol Hassan Bani Sadr, Sadegh Ghotbzadeh and Ibrahim Yazdi, three of his most devoted followers. I had never heard of any of them. I wondered why he had chosen France. Perhaps the French and the British had decided he would be better off under their noses. Paris, the centre of liberalism to the world, would provide him with an excellent public platform from which to continue his campaign against the Shah. In Europe, he would also have access to all the resources of modern communication.

At the university the autumn term had started, but hardly anyone attended classes. Joined by high school children, teachers and some professors, the students were too busy demonstrating in the streets. Within the government, the prime minister was attempting to dramatize the anti-corruption drive by putting Hoveyda's ministers in jail. Some of them were our good friends. Even General Nassiri, the former head of SAVAK and presently the Iranian ambassador to Pakistan, were called in to face a military tribunal. Liberalizing policies were being passed daily but, unfortunately, nothing seemed to work. Khomeini, from his platform in Paris, was stealing the show with his simple message: 'Mohammad Reza must go'.

The most recent rumour was that the military had become irritated by the guaranteed freedom for the press and was planning to take severe action against the revolutionaries. It seemed that the government had become a divided body. For the first time since the torrent of revolution had begun sweeping the country, the Shah appeared on television talking about liberalization and, in a way, apologizing for the past mistakes. He seemed aged and dispirited. His confidence and arrogance had evaporated. The speech was so low-key that the appearance did not generate any confidence in him, or in what he was trying to do. In the past, he had never even tried to create trust in his subjects. What made him think that his promises were now going to be believed and trusted? I felt very sorry for him. His dreams for Iran had been too grand and too unrealistic.

My parents' last dinner in Teheran was eaten at the Mar Mar's restaurant. Early the next morning, I drove them to the airport and pensively stood on the balcony of the departure building watching the jet fly them to safety.

November saw the peaceful demonstrations throughout the country turn violent. Some people believed that this was because Zbigniew Brzezinski had contacted the Shah to assure him of the United States' support for his regime. Apparently, this reassurance had encouraged the army's generals to push for a military coup. Many people supported the notion of a military takeover and thought of it as the only effective means of dealing with the uprisings.

Every morning, we woke up expecting disaster. I was anxious about the safety of Mehdi and the children. Leaving the house was not safe anymore, although Bayat our driver was very loyal and careful and yet the dangerous location of the school worried me. The vicinity of Niavaran Palace was not an enviable location anymore. The Omran Bank was also dangerously situated in the middle of the city, where demonstrations frequently gathered momentum. This bank, which belonged to the Pahlavi Foundation, was the perfect target for a frenzied mob with a penchant for arson. Fortunately I was safe, because the students had taken their angry outbursts to the streets and, for the moment, the campus was empty.

I was glad about this. Going to work had become nerve-wracking, and witnessing the change in my colleagues abhorrent. Most of the lecturers were now trying to link themselves with the dissent. As a kind of tokenism, the men had put aside their neck-ties and grown beards, while some of my sophisticated female colleagues had taken to covering their hair with scarves from Dior or YSL. Once, I asked one of them: why the change? The reply was that the chador was to support the anti-regime movement, and that it would be worn until the country was rid of the "old vulture". My guess was that she counted on the fundamentalists winning and wanted to keep her job once they took over. I do not think many of the women who supported the revolution believed that they would be reduced to second-class citizens after the victory. A good number were educated, westernized females like me. I think they tried to look Islamic purely out of pragmatism.

As time passed, most of our family and friends left Iran. Our evenings were spent at home, or with those of our relatives who were still in Iran. Shahjoon's residence, our only link with a glorious past, was our favourite meeting place and we visited her every afternoon. Aunt Nayer was looking after the hotel at Avenue Koshk and Mar Mar had a new manager.

I had given up going to the city after that horrific day when we were caught in the demonstration with the gas containers in the car, but one day a friend of mine persuaded me to join her in a shopping spree at Avenue Manuchehri, where the antique shops were bursting with rarities. We planned to make a day of it by first having lunch at the Mar Mar and then walking the short distance to the shops. The date was set for November 5. I also made an appointment with my hairdresser for the same day, to save petrol and another trip to town.

On the morning of our date, I arrived at my hairdresser's salon, which was situated in the Avenue Takhte Jamshid near the American Embassy, gave my shopping list to Bayat and instructed him to shop for me and to then go to the Mar Mar for lunch. I told him I would walk the few blocks down to the hotel and meet him there.

My hair was finished by 12:30 and, after taking care of the bill, I descended the flight of stairs and opened the door to leave. To my amazement, I was confronted with an ocean of people – men, chadored women and children making their way along the street side by side in an ordered procession. I hesitated for a moment, trying to decide whether to leave now or wait for the marchers to pass. I estimated that with the number of people involved it would take hours before the last of them passed me. The crowd was very dense, but fortunately it was moving in the right direction for me, so I joined in.

With my make-up and coiffured hair I looked odd and conspicuous in the midst of the chadored crowd, so to avoid trouble I surreptitiously pulled a tissue from my bag and rubbed it over my lips to remove the signs of sin. I did not have to worry about my eyes as they were covered by my large, tinted spectacles.

Gradually, after my initial fear wore off, the mob identity took over and I became part of the tidal wave pushing ahead. This feeling of unity lasted until I became conscious of the glance of the man walking next to me. I read hate in his face and intent in his expression. When my eyes met his, he thrust his head close to my face and whispered: "You whore."

God forbid. My legs began to shake like jelly. Frightened, I kept quiet and pretended not to have heard him. I doggedly fixed my gaze on the throng ahead. Ignoring my silence he said again, "You whore."

I began moving faster in a bid to lose the dreadful man. Suddenly, I realized I was passing the intersection of Takhte Jamshid and Avenue Zahedi, where I had to turn left. Hastily, I made the turn, stealing a quick look to see if the aggressor was following me. Thank God, he was not. Avenue Zahedi was just as crowded, and this time I had to move against the flow, which was very difficult. Eventually, after half-an-hour of pushing and squeezing, I reached the entrance to the hotel where Bayat, looking worried, was waiting for me.

Inside, I made my way to the lobby and collapsed into a chair. When the receptionist saw me, he left his desk and came over to give me the message that my friend had cancelled our lunch appointment. I was so relieved because I was in no mood for socializing after my ordeal. I decided to have lunch by myself in Father's empty office, hoping that the streets would be cleared by the time I had finished eating. A flash of memory brought Agha joon's kind face to my mind and tears to my eyes. He had always loved it when I had lunch with him here. Now he was gone, and I was lonely. So lonely. But thank God he was safe.

I was still eating at around 2 pm when, suddenly, the building began to shake and the sound of several explosions shattered my peace. It sounded as though a bomb had gone off. I jumped from my seat and ran towards the broken window. The street was empty of demonstrators, but small groups of young men were feeding a large fire in which two cars were burning. Some other men seemed to be leaving the hotel, pushing armchairs out into the street.

Where was Bayat? Where had he parked the car?

Was it my car they were burning? I looked hard. No, it was not.

Why were the demonstrators in the hotel? I opened the window and fragments of glass crashed to the floor, the sharp edge of one shard cutting into my skin. I did not feel the pain. Numbness! Oh God, it is sometimes so good!

I rushed downstairs to the lobby, where angry men were dragging whatever they could find outside and throwing it onto the ferocious fire. The hotel employees were just standing aside letting the vandals do whatever they pleased. Petrified, I joined the observers and watched. To my surprise, none of the violators was interested in the cash register. These were no thieves, and they knew exactly what they were doing.

From behind, Bayat's familiar voice whispered: "Khanum, don't worry – the car is safe."

Happy to hear him I murmured, "Thank God for that."

Gradually, the rioters' fever subsided and they left the hotel. The spectators gathered in groups to discuss the event and I ran to the telephone to find out whether or not my husband was safe. He was. I then called the school to see if there had been any disturbances in that area. There had not, but we only had twenty minutes to get to Niavaran and pick the children up.

Half-running and half-walking, Bayat led me to the car, which he had parked in a narrow lane a couple of blocks up the street. Safely in the car, we set off for the school. As we turned into Avenue Takhte Jamshid, I realised where the sound of the explosions had come from. Columns of smoke were rising from carefully selected buildings to the north of the American Embassy. As we drew nearer I saw that two banks, a cinema, a couple of office high-rises which belonged to prominent businessmen, and a supermarket had been turned into fiery rubble. Fires were still blazing everywhere. A large pile of paper money, probably salvaged from the burning bank, was fast becoming a mound of ash. The flames were burning the symbols of the Pahlavi regime.

Who was responsible for this atrocity? Who in the name of heaven was responsible? Further up the street, frenzied men were plastering the crawling cars with stickers which read "Death to the Shah. Our leader is Khomeini."

Very slowly, we left the crowd behind and entered the Old Shemiran Road. Free of the congestion, Bayat sped towards Niavaran where, half-an-hour late, we reached the school. My beloveds, looking anxious, were waiting at the gate holding hands. As the children glimpsed the car, they made a move towards the road, but were pulled back by the school janitor. I got out of the car, ran towards my daughters and with one arm around each, pressed them to my heart and began kissing them as though they had been lost and I had found them again. "Thank you, God, thank you!" was what I was whispering to myself. On the way home, driving down Niavaran Road, I saw the black smoke rising to join the smog that hid the long-forgotten blue sky. The city was still burning.

At home, I took a shower and went into my bedroom, spread my prayer mat on the floor, put on my chador and prayed. I prostrated myself on the floor, pleading with God to save my family and my country from disaster.

The next day, General Azhari was appointed the new military prime minister. The appointment gave rise to the suspicion that the city had been set on fire by the armed forces to justify a military government. Why else had the soldiers stood aside and merely watched? Nobody knew what to believe anymore. There had been no loss of life and no looting – only arson.

On the afternoon of the 6th I decided to walk to my Aunt Victor's house again. I felt more secure with a military government in charge. Faced with the army, the strikers might return to work, and some sort of political compromise might bring about national reconciliation. One had to be positive or else the doom was too dark.

At the house I was received cordially by my aunt and uncle. Tooraj was also present, and the three were discussing the Shah's latest televised speech during which he had told the nation that he had heard their message and had appealed for calm. He assured us that the days of corruption and tyranny were past; that in the future everything would be done according to the constitution of 1906; and that free elections were to be held in the immediate future. Tooraj was very excited about the speech and believed it was about time the Shah showed some sign of sovereignty and took charge of his country again.

I agreed with him, but his father-in-law did not. The old politician was as gloomy as ever and looked sick. Apparently his stomach was troubling him. Mohsen Khan believed that the military government was no solution at all and that Azhari was a poor choice of leader. He argued that a military government was a thorn in the eyes of the people. It would simply aggravate them further and lead to more uprisings.

I had come hoping to hear good news and was disappointed. It seemed that nothing would satisfy my uncle except the Shah's departure from Iran. I did not hold to this view. Without the Shah there would be no army, and without the fear of the army there would be anarchy. The Shah could not run away again. He had to stay and if necessary die for Iran – the Iran of which he was the king – had he not proclaimed during the celebration of the 2500 years of Iranian monarchy: "Cyrus, sleep in peace for I will safeguard your legacy with vigilance." Had he lied? I loved him too much to believe that.

Miserably agitated I could not stay long, and when Tooraj rose to leave I asked him for a lift. In the car I enquired after Afsaneh and the children. He told me that they had rented a small flat in Knightsbridge near the children's school, and were waiting for him to join them. He, however, did not want to leave Iran because of his vast financial involvements with the government. Besides, like me, he believed that the Americans would save the Shah. He dropped me off at home and went to my cousin Sharzad's house, which was near us.

Mohsen Khan was right. The new government proved as powerless as its predecessors. Turbulence and strikes proliferated, especially in the provinces. The Central Bank became paralyzed and people were queuing to take their money out of all the banks. What small savings we had were at home, wrapped in a nylon bag inside a large metal box which had been placed in a bucket and lowered into the well.

As the military government's ineffectiveness became more apparent, the Shah's obsession with persecution of his officials intensified. General Nassiri, the man who had helped him to power during the 1953 coup, and who had subsequently headed SAVAK, was arrested together with General Khademi, the head of Iran Air. The latter was said to have committed suicide in dubious circumstances, but rumour had it that he was, in fact, murdered by his captors because he was a Bahai. Then Hoveyda was arrested. When, a few months later, the Shah departed from his country he took his dogs with him, but left his loyal prime minister, who had served him for thirteen years, behind bars in Evin Jail.

Most of the Shah's loyal servants, including Hoveyda, were executed shortly after the victory of the revolution.

The situation was deteriorating by the hour and I was becoming increasingly worried about the future, so I decided to take a week off and go to London, taking with me a couple of carpets and my jewels.

On the day of my departure, just to be on the safe side, I sewed the jewels into the lining of my mink coat. Luckily, the custom officers were too busy to check anything or anyone very thoroughly. The trip was short and pleasant.

Back in Teheran, I noticed that the city had changed, even in the short time that I had been away. Walls were defaced with slogans like: "Yankee go home", "Death to the Shah", and many obscenities addressed to the Shah and Farah. Avenue Ehteshamieh was deserted. Most of the residents had left the country, leaving their houses in the care of their servants. The only people I saw in our vicinity were some construction workers excavating the pavements for gas pipelines. To my surprise, I discovered that these workers were Kurds.

It was encouraging to see something constructive going on, especially during this time of unending destruction and misery. Selective power cuts plunged Teheran into darkness daily. Pressure was building up against foreigners – particularly Americans – and there had been some killings in the provinces. The economy was in ruins and the foreigners, whose technical expertise was essential to the running of Iran's various industries, were starting to leave the country. Parliamentary sessions were being televised and the prime minister was submitting all government measures to parliamentary debate. Members of parliament seemed to have found their long-lost tongues and were expressing radical opinions.

During one of my frequent visits to my avuncular political mentor, I heard the first good news in months. Mohesen Khan had been asked by the Shah to contact his old friend Dr Shapour Bakhtiar, a respected member of the National Front, to see if he would form a government. Serious negotiations were underway, but one of Dr Bakhtiar's conditions for accepting the appointment was that the Shah must leave Iran indefinitely.

With hope we all waited, while praying for a safe passage through the month of Moharram, which would start on December 21st. The days of Ta'sua and Ashura would create the greatest challenge to the authorities. Given the history of these two holy days, the emotional background would provide the most opportune time for a powerful religious drive to initiate the decisive push against the shaky structure of the Pahlavi regime.

Some time in late November, fully aware of the martial law, Khomeini issued instructions to the people to hold the ceremonies and defy authority of any kind, indicating that Moharram was a month of blood and vengeance. In retaliation, the government banned public processions and instructed that religious ceremonies would have to be confined to the mosques and that a curfew would start at 9 pm every evening.

On the eve of the first of Moharram, we went for a short walk in the direction of Ghobad Mosque. It was full, and even though it was cold and wet, people were standing outside listening to the sermon. The sky was thick with black clouds and the atmosphere seemed ominous. To avoid the possibility of another entanglement, we immediately turned back towards home. Shortly after we entered the house, the electricity went off. Inside, it was cold and quiet. To keep warm, Fe and Anniana slept in the same bed. Betsabeh and Parissa slept together on the floor of our bedroom, warmed by an electric heater – that is, when there was electricity. Fortunately, I had lots of blankets; otherwise we would surely have frozen that bitter winter. The children were already asleep, and with no electricity, there was nothing else to do but go to bed.

In the middle of the night I was woken by the sound of chanting in the distance. I concentrated hard in order to hear better and after a time I made out the words "Allah Akbar", continuously repeated. The chanting seemed to be becoming louder by the minute. Hastily, I woke Mehdi and told him to listen. Trying not to disturb the children, we got out of bed quietly, put on our dressing gowns and slippers and went outside into the garden. It was very cold. I shivered. The black clouds had cleared, but the sky was lacklustre and there were no stars.

The chanting was getting louder and louder. Mehdi said that he would go up to the roof to see what was happening. I followed him. Apart from the twinkling lights of the city, nothing could be seen. But in the distance, we heard the sharp report of machine-gun fire. We stood there in silence, the wind pelting our faces. I no longer felt the cold; fear had numbed my senses. We stayed motionless until the chanting and the sound of the machine-gun had died down.

The next day, the radio announced that in a clash between the authorities and the defying demonstrators, some people had been killed, many more injured and hundreds arrested. However, Taghi was of the opinion that the government was lying and that the incident had resulted in more than 1,000 casualties. No one could pinpoint where the chants that had been simultaneously heard throughout the city had come from, but the general belief was that, at a designated time, the revolutionaries had gone onto their roofs and cried: "Allah Akbar". A one-day general strike followed and the schools were closed until after Ashura. Night after night the same scenario repeated itself. The cry of "Allah Akbar", mixed with the sound of firing machine-guns, became our bedtime lullaby.

On December 2nd, in a communiqué issued from Paris, Khomeini called on all soldiers to leave their barracks and join the people. He expressed his gratitude for the general strike and ordered the strikes to continue until the government was paralyzed. He also called any politician who planned to form a government under the oppressor Shah "an opponent of Islam."

The latest rumour was that it had not been real people who had been shouting "Allah Akbar" from their roofs; the nightly chants had come from amplified tape recordings played through the loudspeakers of the mosques. Ezat Khanum and my brother-in-law laughed at the insinuations, because every night both of them were going onto their roof to sing, "God is great".

The nation was anxiously waiting to see what would happen during the two holy days. To everyone's relief the authorities lifted the ban on processions in order to allow the Ta'sua and Ashura marches to take place. On these two occasions the troops were to be withdrawn from the streets.

On the day of Ta'sua, I asked Mehdi to accompany me to Avenue Pahlavi to watch the procession, which was to make its way towards Shahyad Square, a modern monstrosity which had been built near the airport. He would not hear of it so I resigned myself to watching the event on television. From what was televised, it seemed as though the whole city was on its feet. From early morning, crowds had set off from their various starting points and begun heading towards the square. All streets feeding to the main route of the procession were overwhelmed with disciplined marchers carrying banners with different slogans: "Death to the butcher Shah", "Khomeini is our leader" and "Islamic Republic". The sheer number of the demonstrators was awesome, and they seemed to be brilliantly organized. Men and women carrying babies, or holding the hands of their children, walked side by side in orderly fashion.

The turmoil had changed to a tide, pushing the nation into an unbelievable unity between the forces of the extreme right and the extreme left and, in between, swallowing the moderates.

Even I, sitting in the safety of my home watching what was going on outside through the lens of the cameraman, felt proud of my brave countrymen. They certainly had more courage than we did, standing as they were against what they believed to be evil with nothing but a simple cry of "Allah Akbar". I felt ashamed that I did not have the guts even to observe the march from a street corner.

Contrary to the authorities' expectations nothing went wrong on that day.

On the following day of Ashura, when the procession reached Shahyad Square, a mullah climbed up the steps of the monument and read out a seventeen-point declaration on behalf of all opposition groups and parties, each of which was mentioned by name. The most important points stressed were that Khomeini was the leader, the Shah must be overthrown, strikes must be supported and the army must unite with the people. Ashura also passed in peace. However, the next day we heard that there had been a shoot-out at the headquarters of the Imperial Iranian Ground Forces. Some soldiers had shot at the guards. This was a very serious situation; it meant that the armed forces were divided among themselves.

Uncertainty continued.

Our only hope was Bakhtiar, who had by now become the black sheep of the National Front. The constitutionalists were waiting for him to be appointed the new civilian prime minister. Rumour had it that the Shah had agreed to appoint a Regency Council and leave the country. The crucial question was whether or not the army would back

Bakhtiar in such a situation. We also heard that Ardeshir Zahedi was back from Washington, where he acted as His Majesty's Ambassador, as the emissary of Brzezinski. His mission was to try to dissuade the Shah from leaving the country and to encourage him to take severe military action against the revolutionaries.

On December 31, it was officially announced that Bakhtiar would form a government and that the Shah would go overseas for rest and medical attention.

At last, what I had been waiting and praying for had happened. With Bakhtiar in power, the nation would reconcile and all would be well again.

Chapter 15

Shortly after Bakhtiar's appointment, secure in the thought that rosy days were ahead of us, Mehdi and I decided to take the children to London for a short holiday. The sleepless nights, constant anxiety and pressures of daily life had affected both of us. I was experiencing bad headaches and he was suffering from insomnia. However, to our surprise Bakhtiar was not to be the saviour I had been praying for. To our chagrin the strikes intensified. The queues for petrol and kerosene grew longer. Often it took a whole day of waiting in the queue before anything could be procured. Bayat was responsible for the purchase of petrol for both of our cars. He would drive the Mercedes to the petrol station at 6 am and return, if he was lucky, at 4 pm with a full tank and several large bottles which he had filled for the Fiat.

Mehdi was very unhappy at the bank and was toying with the idea of resigning. I was against the idea. If he resigned, we would lose Bayat, the Mercedes and a good income. With Father gone and the hotel making virtually nothing, who would support us?

On the afternoon of January 3rd, Mehdi had just arrived home from his office when he received a telephone call from a well-wisher, informing him that he would soon receive a message asking him to return to the bank to co-sign a cheque for release to an important general. The sum involved was one million dollars. The money belonged to the people, said the informer, and if Mehdi valued his life he would not answer the call.

Horrified, we decided to do as the man advised.

Ten minutes later the call came. I picked up the receiver. It was the secretary of the bank's managing director, wishing to speak with Dr Monadjemi. I informed her that my husband had not yet arrived home. She told me that his presence was urgently required at the bank. I assured her that as soon as he arrived I would convey her message to him. Mehdi did not return to the bank that evening; nevertheless, the General left Iran the next day – with his funds safely transferred to his Swiss bank account.

On the same day, I received a call from Mohsen Khan, wanting to know if we would mediate with one of our well-known university friends to accept a ministerial position in Bakhtiar's Cabinet. Mehdi refused. I asked him why. He replied that he had chosen to remain apolitical. He believed that what was going on in the streets of Teheran was determining the future of the country. The parliament had become obsolete; the Constitution of 1906 was dead. People did not want democracy. They wanted another idol to worship and the cry was for Khomeini.

I agreed with my husband, especially in view of the conference which was taking place on the Caribbean island of Guadeloupe at which, it was believed, the leaders of the United States of America, Britain, France and Germany were deciding the political fate of Iran. The future of Iran depended on their decision, not on anything Bakhtiar did. In fact, the signs indicated that their support was for the Immam. The presence of General Huyser, the American Deputy Commander of the NATO Forces in Iran also pointed to the fact that the Americans were very much involved in what was going on. It was believed that his mission was to ensure that the decision of those present at Guadeloupe would be carried out.

On January 6th, Bakhtiar presented his cabinet to the Shah and, soon after, the media news confirmed the Shah's intention of departing from Iran. Now all we could do was to wait for the 16th, to see if the free parliament would confirm the new government.

In the meantime, the food shortage had become acute. One day, quite by chance, I came across a smuggler who sold me three kilos of Beluga Caviar. Sturgeon fishing and the distribution of caviar was the monopoly of Shillat, the government fishing organization which was managed by the Davalu Gajar family. Amir Hushang Davalu was my mother's cousin and one of the Shah's best friends. He had already left Iran. It was against the law for ordinary fishermen to fish for sturgeon; however, some did and sold the caviar on the black market. Ludicrously, for two weeks we had caviar on toast for dinner. I often thought of the poor who could not afford the black market prices and who did not have freezers in which to store their food. From what Taghi told me, I gathered that the young people and the mullahs were taking care of feeding the needy. The food was distributed in the mosques, subsidized by money from the bazaar – the section most estranged by the monarch's policies. Street activities indicated that the people themselves were in charge. Few police were seen and all one saw of the army were soldiers sitting on their tanks, smiling and waving at passers-by.

On the morning of January 16th, 1979, Bakhtiar's cabinet and programme were approved by both houses of parliament. That same day, at around 10.30 am, I heard the familiar sound of helicopters flying over our roof. This time, however, there were many, not the usual two or three. I ran to the roof just in time to witness a tragic historical moment. The Shah – the King of Kings, the Shadow of God on Earth – was leaving his land to become a wanderer. I kept my blurred gaze on the helicopters until they became mere black dots on the horizon. The king was running away again.

Very slowly, I descended the steps to the patio, went to my bedroom, put on my cloak and walked to Shahjoon's house. The sorrow I felt was too intense to bear alone. Ehteshamieh was even more deserted than usual. Suddenly, a colossal black cloud which had been following the helicopters burst into a downpour, and a savage wind whipped through the leafless branches of the gnarled trees. It was as though nature, too, was weeping for the fallen monarch – or perhaps for us, a class which was about to become extinct – a sex that was to become subjugated.

When I entered Shahjoon's bedroom, she was sitting in her bed with her lunch tray on her knees, unaware of what had happened. Her dear, beautiful face brightened when she saw me. I bowed, kissed her hand and then her face, and told her that the Shah was leaving the country. She shrugged her bent shoulders and retorted that the Pahlavis had got what they deserved. Her maid brought tea, and at my request, turned on the radio. The 2 o'clock news announced the Shah's dramatic departure from Iran.

Within a few minutes of the announcement, the sound of honking car horns drove us out to the gate. The street, which had been deserted only a short while ago, was filled with cars, flashing their headlights, their drivers shouting, "The Shah has gone!" I could not share in the jubilation and went back inside where I stayed with my Shahjoon for another hour before walking back home.

The days that followed saw nothing but a deterioration of the situation. Statues of the two Pahlavi Shahs which had adorned most city squares were pulled down, smashed and urinated on. Strikes were rife, most of the shops were shuttered and closed and there were demonstrations everywhere. The whole country was rebelling. SAVAK nests were being discovered, ravaged and burnt and the soldiers had begun to fraternize with the revolutionaries. A couple of cabinet ministers had already resigned.

Gradually, Mehdi and I began to realize that people wanted Khomeini and only Khomeini. From what we read in the newspapers, it seemed that the opposition's provisional government was made up of reasonable men – men like seventy-five-year-old Mehdi Bazargan, a European-educated secular leader who had been a faithful adherent of Mossadegh, and who had been imprisoned on many occasions by the Shah for his leadership of the old National Front Party. Bazargan was a good Muslim and, hence, highly respected by Khomeini and the bazaar. With people like him governing the country and with Khomeini, a man of God, acting as the spiritual leader of the nation, the Iranian revolution would surely be remembered as the most peaceful, disciplined, orderly movement of its kind in the history of the human race.

A democratic secular government working within an Islamic framework, we told ourselves, would bring about the desired social justice, equal opportunity and general prosperity for which so much blood had been shed. We had nothing to fear from the future. There would be no more killings – especially now that the Shah and his family were safe in Egypt.

This is what we told ourselves and each other. In times of extraordinary crisis, the human mind becomes cunning. It desires to create positive visions which are crucial to its survival. Under such dismal circumstances one cannot live without hope – however remote, however unrealistic. So, we hoped.

Every morning, we woke up to a new rumour. One day it was a military coup, the next, Bakhtiar was flying to France to meet with Khomeini – and so on, and so on. On January 29th, at a press conference, Bakhtiar announced that the airports, which had been closed, would be reopened to permit Khomeini to return to Iran. I immediately called my travel agent and booked three tickets on British Airways for London departing on February 3rd, and one on the 11th for Mehdi, who could not leave the bank before then.

Passports had to be submitted to the office of the SAVAK three days prior to departure for a security check. To save time and travelling, I took

Mehdi's as well, and handed the four passports to the travel agent who was responsible for the submission. On the date of travel, the documents would be returned to us at a special section of the customs area, after our tickets and luggage had been checked in.

On February 1st, we stayed at home, sitting by the television, ready to witness yet another historic event – the return of the architect of the Iranian revolution. The Ayatollah, his advisors and many journalists arrived aboard a chartered Air France 747. In the aeroplane, he was interviewed by one of the reporters and asked the question: "What do you feel about returning to Iran in triumph?" the Imamm did not even look at the reporter. With an expressionless face and a gesture devoid of any emotion he replied, "Nothing."

If the leader felt nothing, the crowds certainly felt something. Khomeini was greeted by jubilant mobs in their millions. All the streets leading to the route were full of people dancing with joy. The procession moved very slowly, the soldiers standing back and allowing the security to be handled by the revolutionary forces. Somewhere along the way, Immam got out of the car and climbed into a helicopter which took him to Beheshte Zahra. The cemetery too, was a sea of living souls who had gathered to welcome their hero, the Idol Smasher, Bot Shekan.

Khomeini took up residence in a small, inconspicuous school building in the south of the city. He was to prove to be everything that the Shah was not – humble, true to his word and devoid of worldly interests. He was to give Iran a new identity – whether it was good or bad, only time would tell.

On February 3rd, I went to visit Shahjoon to bid her a quick farewell. She cried, and forecasted that she would never see me again. I promised her that this was going to be a short trip and that I would be back in no time at all. We left the house for the airport, Mehdi driving. We drove through the empty, littered streets which had witnessed so much in such a short time, past walls scarred with posters and slogans, past The Mar Mar with its shattered windows, and the squares with their broken or headless statues, and we passed the Shahyad Monument; the rostrum of the revolution.

The airport was packed with excited, unruly people, each carrying more than the allowed weight. No revolutionary spirit was to be found here – just the anxiety, impatience and fear of people on the run. At the counter where we were to collect our passports, two elderly men in front of me were denied theirs. They had become prisoners in their own country. I dared not think of their fate.

The flight was on time both at take-off and on arrival, and at Heathrow Airport we were welcomed by my brothers and my parents. It was an unforgettable moment of delight. For one week we had a happy, even carefree, time. Then all hell broke loose. On the evening of February 9th in Iran, the Homafars, the western-educated air-force technicians (non-commissioned officers), who were in charge of the maintenance of the most sophisticated weapons systems at Doshan Tappeh Air Base on the Eastern outskirts of Teheran, demonstrated for Khomeini. Fighting broke out with the troops of the Imperial Guard and additional troops were brought in, escalating the fighting. Some time before morning, the Homafars broke into the base armoury and seized thousands of rifles, most of which they tossed over the fence to the revolutionaries outside. A curfew was imposed and ignored. Bloody demonstrations spread throughout the country.

Communication with Iran broke down. I had no news of Mehdi. For four days I sat by the telephone trying to dial home, and when I became exhausted, one of my brothers or the children took over. Desperate fear for Mehdi kept me numb, but focused. The televised news was horrific. Fighting between the revolutionaries and the army was bloody, and there was no information about the whereabouts of Prime Minister Bakhtiar. For two days the shooting and killing continued, until the military withdrew to its barracks proclaiming its 'neutrality' in the political conflict.

At 3 am on February 15th, after ten hours of dialling our number, I got through. Mehdi's gentle voice answered. I kept crying: "Are you really alive, my darling? Are you alive?" For a few minutes, we both wept with relief, and then we calmed down and began to talk sensibly. As we were exchanging news, I could hear the sound of shooting in the background and asked him where the noise was coming from. He told me that the revolutionaries from the Ehteshamieh Committee were shooting at suspects or into the air. I asked him what a 'committee' was. He chose not to answer and began telling me how he and his father had narrowly escaped death a few days beforehand.

On February 10th, guessing that the airport might close again he had decided to go there to collect his passport. He had picked up his father from his house, and they had driven to Mehrabad together. At the entrance, they had seen a large sign which read: "The airways are closed to the thieves who want to run away." Empty-handed, they had set off for home, and on the way had been caught in a shoot-out. Luckily they had not been hurt, but back at the house the trauma had taken its toll. Mehdi's father had suffered a heart attack and had been hospitalized.

After thanking God that he was still alive, I asked my husband what he wanted us to do. He replied that we should stay in London until it was safe for us to return to Iran; otherwise, he would find a way to join us. We said goodbye and I promised to telephone him every day.

Over the next few days, the regime of Immam Khomeini was recognized by all heads of state and the Iranian revolution hailed. I was stunned. How had an inchoate reform movement turned into a full scale revolution in a country like Iran? A country with a sovereign like the Shah, protected as he was by such a formidable security organization as SAVAK?

Well, now the events had taken their course and there was nothing for me to do but hope that this man of God would declare a general amnesty and bring about the paradise the Iranians had fought for. Two weeks later, Mehrabad Airport re-opened and we were on the first flight home to Teheran.

There were only a few passengers on our plane, so disembarkation was quick. At the bottom of the aircraft's mobile steps, we were met by a row of soldiers with machine guns who were patrolling the route to the airport building. Inside, bearded, tieless revolutionaries were in charge.

We met Mehdi in the visitors' lounge, and together again, headed for our car. Feeling rejuvenated, I asked Mehdi why he had not brought Bayat to help him with the luggage. He fell silent for a while then, looking guilty, admitted that he had resigned from the bank. This news was traumatic for me and I did not know how to react without hurting my husband, so I did not dwell on the subject.

At home, our domestics received us with affection. Anniana served a delicious Philippino dish and Mehdi opened a bottle of wine. In pouring the drink, however, his usual generosity was not apparent. He told me that there was a ban on alcoholic beverages and the Passdaran Enghelab, the revolutionary guards, were attacking the liquor stores and breaking the contents. We only had a few bottles left in the house and these were to be kept for special occasions like tonight.

I asked Mehdi who the revolutionary guards were. He explained that komitehs, or local revolutionary committees, had blossomed throughout the country on the morning after the revolution. Many of them, it seemed, were extensions of the neighbourhood committees which had been formed around the mosques in 1978 to organize strikes and demonstrations, and to distribute food and kerosene to the needy. After the final fall of the regime, any sense of discipline had vanished. The young people who made up the majority of the Komiteh members became fully armed, taking their weapons from the thousands of rifles and submachine guns which had been seized from military arsenals on February 10th and 11th. These committees were serving both as local security forces and as agents of the revolutionary authorities against the members of the old regime. In short, they had become a power unto themselves.

I asked if we had a komiteh in our neighborhood. It seemed that we did. The guards, in fact, had already been to the house to check if the owners were in Iran, and demanding to see the deed to the house. Mehdi had told them that the house belonged to his wife, who was overseas and would be returning soon. They had given him a month to present both the deed and his wife to the komiteh, otherwise they would confiscate the property.

The next morning I called Shahjoon, who sounded well and was impatient to see me. I promised to visit her in the afternoon, then tried Mohsen Khan's house with no success. It was a fine day. Spring was just around the corner and my weeping willow was beginning to turn green. The climbing roses were blooming and the violets, in their different shades of purple, covered the borders around the pool. The sparrows had returned from their winter holidays and were chirping cheerfully. I suddenly felt very happy and decided to walk to Mohsen Khan's house and surprise him.

Avenue Ehteshamieh was as soulless as before and the abandoned villas looked forlorn without their inhabitants. Most of the shops appeared to be empty and some were still closed. The streets were devoid of traffic and the occasional passers-by looked glum. There were very few women around and, of those, most were in chador. Only one or two were bare-headed like me. There was a peculiar sadness in the air. Clearly, the revolutionary euphoria had vanished.

I walked briskly across Saltanatabad Road and entered the Golestan

10th, at the end of which was my uncle's house. Even from this distance I could see that the gate was closed and I took this to be a security measure. As I drew closer, however, I saw that there was a board attached to the gate. This was unusual. I quickened my pace. The gate was padlocked and the wooden placard informed me that the house belonged to the Foundation of the Disinherited. 'Disinherited' now-a-days referred to the poor. What did this mean – I wondered? A solitary revolutionary guard holding a submachine gun was standing at the corner, picking his nose and watching me. I continued to walk, passing the house without looking at it, and when I arrived at the first crossroad, I turned right. My mind was a muddled blank. I could not think clearly.

Still in shock, I continued walking for some time, then decided to change direction and return to the house. When I reached the crossroad I saw that the guard was still standing on the corner. I was certain all of a sudden that he was watching the house. I approached him and asked: "Brother, what is the meaning of this sign?"

Without looking at me he replied, "This house belonged to an undeserving Corruptor of Earth. It has been confiscated for the Foundation of the Disinherited and soon it will be put to good use."

"Yes, I am sure you are right. Justice must be done. God be with you, brother."

"God be with you, sister," he replied, still looking down at the ground.

I almost ran home. I called Mehdi at the university and demanded an explanation. He informed me in carefully worded sentences that on the night before my arrival from London, Mohsen Khan, who had just had a stomach operation, had been seized from the hospital and taken to Evin Prison. The house had immediately been confiscated. Aunt Victor had been allowed to pack her necessities into one suitcase and had then been forced to leave. She had been staying with Tooradj ever since. Shahjoon did not know of the arrest, Mehdi stressed, and was not to be told.

Mortified, I replaced the receiver then, without a second thought, I ran out of the house and walked as fast as I could to Tooradj's house. My aunt was there. She looked aged, spiritless and very thin. Her aristocratic nose looked longer and her domineering eyes had lost their glitter. It seemed that she had no energy for talking. I went to her, gave her a hug, and we both began to cry silently. Prudence had not deserted her, however. She whispered in my ear that I should not ask any questions, nor mention any names. Obediently, I moved away from her and sat on a chair nearby. We began to talk, touching only on trivialities. On the opposite wall I noticed a large picture of the Immam. His penetrating eyes seemed to stare right through me.

I had not actually understood the necessity for precaution until I heard Tooradj's boisterous voice in conversation with someone else. The two men entered the room and Tooradj introduced the stranger as Ali Agha, a guard from the Darous Komiteh who was in charge of their safety. I greeted the young man and froze in my seat. So, they were under house arrest. Mamad, the cook, brought a tray of tea, and in silence we occupied ourselves with sipping the hot drink. I was impatient to find out what had happened, but obviously this was impossible in the circumstances, so I invited my aunt and Tooradj to have dinner with me and politely extended the invitation to Ali Agha. He, fortunately, thanked me but refused.

Around 7.30 pm my guests arrived. My aunt looked more at ease, less nervous and willing to talk. She told me that, one afternoon, a group of guards bearing a command from the revolutionary tribunal had entered her husband's hospital room and taken the patient to Evin Prison. No reason had been given, no crime mentioned. One of the group members had accompanied her to her home where she had packed her suitcase and left, leaving all her possessions behind her. The next day, their bank accounts had been seized and all their properties, including Galandoak, confiscated. She had been told to appeal to the office of the prosecutor-general (Dadsetan-e Kol), and the Foundation of the Disinherited to establish what property and possessions belonged to her and what was her husband's. Anything she had inherited from her father would be returned to her.

She and her son-in-law had already contacted some of their old friends from the Mossadegh era for help, and Tooradj was optimistic that he would find a way to secure his father-in-law's freedom. Their positivism lifted my spirits and we began planning how we could expedite matters. Before taking their leave, Khaleh Victor asked if she would be able to stay with us if need be. I welcomed the idea.

That night I could not sleep. All I thought of was my uncle, who during his life had not hurt a soul and had given so much of himself to the country he had served so loyally.

The new university term started, but for the first few days I found my classes without students. Dr Azimi had left Iran and a small committee of students had undertaken to do the planning for the faculty. The janitors had become the link between the student committee and those lecturers like me who had not gone into Islamic cover or had not yet lost their neck-ties.

One day, feeling particularly frustrated, I asked Abass Agha, my favourite janitor, why the students were not attending my classes. He told me that they were boycotting them. I asked why. He gave me a friendly shrug and suggested I ask Dr Ahmadi, the new head of our department. Worried, I went to Dr Ahmadi's office and knocked on the open door. The bearded revolutionary rose from his chair and politely pointed to a seat. Without beating about the bush, I told him the reason for the visit and asked him if I was being 'purified'. He assured me that this was not the case. My dossier had been studied thoroughly and it was clean. However, the students had accused me of being a 'dictator' and 'in the habit of dressing inappropriately'. Neither of these was a crime for 'purification'. The problem was simply that the students of the School of Humanities had decided not to attend my classes, he went on. I had either to present myself and debate the issue, or find another college within the university where I could lecture. I accepted the challenge of a debate first, and told him that if the result was futile I would apply to another college. He acknowledged my decision as sound and saw me to the door.

Through Abass Agha, I made an appointment with the student body to defend myself.

The situation was humiliating and nerve-wracking, but under the circumstances pride had to be swallowed and nerves soothed by tranquillizers. For the five years that I had been involved with the university, I had done nothing but my best for the students. My lectures, I believed, were interesting, well-prepared and targeted to the cognitive level of my students, the majority of whom had entered American universities without any difficulties and had sent me thank-you letters. True, I had failed without remorse those who had not studied enough, and those I had caught hiding text books under their chadors during examinations. It was, of course, to these students that I had been a 'dictator'.

I was a stubborn fighter, and a stickler for principles. Both qualities, if not properly understood, might be mistaken for a domineering trait. With a clear conscience I had nothing to fear from the student committee and, if necessary, I was prepared to fight them.

On the day of my so-called 'trial', dressed in my usual choice of clothing, I entered the room, sat at the lecturer's pulpit, gazed at my judges and, defying their authority, smiled at them. I asked them, one by one, to give me their reasons as to why they refused to attend my classes. There was no mention of 'dictatorial behavior', or 'provocative dressing.' They must have realized that they could not discredit me with accusations which they could not substantiate.

The sum total of their objections was that I had no qualifications to teach at the university and that my position had been acquired through favoritism. Thrilled that I could prove them wrong, I asked one of the students to be kind enough to go to the personnel officer at the employment bureau and ask him for my file. A chorus of muttered objections hummed through the cold room but, eventually, one of the students rose and left for the bureau. After half-an-hour of uncomfortable silence, the door opened and he entered with a thick green manila folder tucked under his arm. He handed the file to the student who had been acting as their leader, who proceeded to extract my degrees from among the other papers. He read each out loud then, satisfied, nodded his head, apologized for the group's mistake and rose, indicating that the session was terminated. I rose too. Looking directly at him I said, "I hope I will see you tomorrow for the nine o'clock lecture."

I received no response from the students. The silence was morbid. In the cold of the classroom, I was burning with degradation and hatred for all that happened to us. Eventually, the leader found his tongue and replied maliciously, "Dr Ahmadi will inform you of the outcome of this meeting. Until then, there will be no classes."

With my chin up, and forcing a quivering smile, I left the room, beads of cold perspiration running down my back and forehead now. For the first time, I realized that logic counted for nothing with these young revolutionaries. It was, after all, a time for pure and utter vengeance.

Without wasting another minute, I headed for the office of the Head of the School of Economics. Having been ushered inside, I told the head of the department my story and asked him if he could find me a position. I was counting on Mehdi's popularity with the faculty and the students to persuade him to help me, and I was right. Fortunately, they did need an English lecturer. He asked me if I had enough knowledge of economics to be able to prepare and deliver the lectures. I replied that learning had never been a problem for me and that, after all, their best professor was my husband. We both laughed and this broke the ice. He assured me that as far as he was concerned the position was mine – but, he warned me, he had to discuss the issue further with the student body. He said that he would let Mehdi know of their decision.

Light-heartedly, I left his office and began to descend the three flights of stairs which I had climbed so anxiously only an hour ago. For the first time, I noticed the pictures of the different communist leaders, from Marx to Mao, which hung on the walls of the college. Small wooden tables stood next to the portraits, with stacks of books written by those leaders for sale. A couple of students stood by each desk ready to propagate or defend their ideologies.

Whoever would have dreamed that such freedom could exist in Iran?

At home, I told my husband of what I had done. He admired my audacity and made no objection to my working at his college so long as I watched what came out of my mouth!

The next day, Mehdi was informed that I could start my classes from the following Saturday (the first working day in Muslim countries). I had one week to prepare my economic lectures in English. Mehdi gave me the appropriate text books and I was well-prepared and fully organized for my first class. The students, unlike many of their peers, who generally started fidgeting fifteen minutes or so before the class was finished, stayed until after the bell rang then gathered around my chair, inundating me with questions. Soon, I had earned for myself a reputation equal to that of my husband's and the students became my friends.

Young people are very observant. It did not take them long to realize that I was not a Hezbollahi, a fundamentalist. The leftists, identifying themselves with modernism, thought of me as a sympathizer – yet I was far from being a communist. Nevertheless, I found talking with the leftists easier, and their arguments more rational than those of their religious counterparts. That was probably why they liked me.

Gradually, I began to favour the Kurds in my class. They were a courageous tribe for whom I had always had the greatest respect and sympathy. Their lot was worse than all the other minorities, as they were a group which inhabited four different countries – none of which really wanted them. Now, agitated by the revolutionary leftist elements, they had initiated a movement for autonomy in Kurdestan. To crush their uprising, the central government was fighting them fiercely and with a cruelty which was unbecoming to a regime which called itself Islamic. The Kurds were also very poor. I still disliked the Tudeh, and never associated with my very active brother-in-law.

Mehdi's office was the meeting place of all the factions. The students loved and respected him. They had not forgotten how he had helped them in their dealings with SAVAK. He was the only lecturer with a known affiliation to the Pahlavi Foundation who had not been 'purified' – as yet.

The process of 'purification' was becoming very common these days. Every institution had a committee which was 'clearing' the organization of the criminals of the old regime. Within a short period, hundreds of educated technocrats, engineers, doctors, professors, and, in particular, military officers lost their jobs, some for real but most for fabricated reasons. Personal grudges were being used to damage neighbours, business partners, employers, superiors, friends and family members. Even the prime minister had confessed to a state of social disorder. He had called Teheran 'a city with a hundred sheriffs'. There were parallel governments of the revolutionary committees, courts, guards and the government of Bazargan all trying to rule according to their own perception of what was right and what was wrong – or rather, what should be right and what should be wrong. Security had collapsed. Society was on the verge of polarization and we all had to fend for ourselves.

It is amazing how human beings learn to adjust to change. In the absence of Bayat, I had to collect the children from school and do the shopping myself. Food was scarce, but if you had enough money it could be found. I established good relations with the owners of the various shops in my vicinity, and occasional tips saw to it that I obtained the best available goods. Walking to the shops replaced walking as a form of exercise, and I enjoyed my afternoon strolls to Shahjoon's and then to the bakery to purchase freshly-baked Sangak bread for dinner. Foresight was paying off. I was well-stocked with frozen meat and out-of-season vegetables and was proud that, in my household, no one felt the hardship that had been imposed on others. Imported goods were almost non-existent. The price of electrical appliances had increased tenfold and everybody was seeking freezers and refrigerators. Music tapes and videos could be purchased only from the black market. Female singers and actresses were either in hiding or had already left the country. Mrs Parssa, the first woman cabinet minister, was executed and the talk was that soon everybody would have to go into chador.

One afternoon, when I returned from collecting the children from school, Fe handed me a letter which had been delivered to the house by a member of the local Komiteh. It requested donations for the families of the martyrs of the revolution. I gave the letter to Mehdi and we decided to make a monthly contribution. This meant that we had to go to the Komiteh ourselves, which presented a good opportunity to take the deed of the house to establish my ownership, and to let them know that I had returned from overseas and was residing in my own house.

For this occasion I had to look Islamic, but I was determined that I was not going to wear the chador. The next best attire was my blue cloak, with a white woollen hat which covered all my hair. Long boots and thick stockings would take care of my legs.

We walked to the Komiteh headquarters, where two armed youths in khaki parkas stood guard at the entrance. As was the traditional custom, Mehdi entered first, while I followed, pretending to be a meek, obedient wife. I was laughing secretly at the whole charade. Inside, we were asked the purpose of our visit. As per habit I began to answer, but the man ignored me and looked at my husband. I had to learn to control myself. The new order was totally male-dominated and women were expected to accept their second class citizenship. This was something I would never learn to do!

We were ushered to the main room, in which wooden chairs were set out for visitors, and a distinguished-looking old man with white hair and a white beard was sitting on an aluminum chair behind a large aluminum table littered with papers, manila folders and an ashtray full of cigarette butts. Four unshaven, untidy-looking roughnecks were standing near him, carefully examining a pile of coloured photographs and making derogatory comments.

We took the two chairs closest to the table and sat waiting to be attended to. I was curious to catch a glimpse of the pictures which were attracting so much attention. Unobtrusively, I tried to steal a glance at the photographs which the man standing nearest to me was holding. Coincidence had him throw them on the table, well within my view, which unfortunately, was a little hazy without my glasses. When I could not control my curiosity any longer, I leaned towards the table and took a good look at the photograph on the top of the pile. It was a picture of the empress and ten other women standing in a row dressed in bathing-suits, the tallest at one end and the shortest at the other. I guessed that it had been taken at the Noshahr royal residence by the Caspian. Excited, I addressed the old man humbly and asked if I, too, could look at the pictures. He picked up the pile from the table and handed them to me.

I knew most of the women in the photographs. One of them was my second cousin from my Mother's side. She and her husband were successful architects, and her father had been the first radiologist in Iran and a president at Teheran University. The family was well-respected. While looking, I was also listening. The guards, in their door-to-door inspection of the district's houses, had come across my cousin's residence which, in their absence, was being looked after by an old caretaker. To save his own skin, he had let them in and the inspectors had ransacked the house. The pictures were from her album and proved her connection with the court.

Now the men were debating whether or not the photographs were evidence enough to warrant the seizure of the property. After a long discussion, the resolution was that the husband and wife were guilty and that the house should be taken for the Foundation of the Disinherited. Suddenly, I became very frightened.

After the roughnecks had left, the old man introduced himself as Haj Sabaghi. I realized he was the father of one of Bazargan's cabinet ministers. Very politely, Mehdi introduced himself and me to the man and handed him the deed to the house, along with my birth certificate which we had brought in case they questioned my identity. The old man took the documents, examined them carefully and, satisfied, handed them back. He asked Mehdi what his occupation was and when he learned that he was a lecturer, the old man's tone became friendlier.

Encouraged, Mehdi began expressing sympathy for the families of the martyrs of the revolution and offered a monthly contribution of 5,000 rials. He laid the envelope he had been holding on the table. The old man opened it, took the cheque out, looked at the sum and then praised Mehdi's generosity. He asked us if we wished to have tea. We declined and politely took our leave.

Outside, a thin, pale moon hung in the sky. Young men, mostly in their teens and clutching machine guns, were being dispatched to their posts at the crossroads. Their mission was to stop and search every car that passed, looking for anti-revolutionaries, drugs – especially opium – and breath-smelling for alcohol.

These youths were responsible for the shootings we heard nightly, the shots sometimes aimed at people, and sometimes no doubt simply a means of entertainment for the bored Passdaran.

At home, we both knew what to do first. We took our photograph albums out of the library and searched through them thoroughly. Any possibly incriminating photographs were taken out and, one by one, torn into tiny pieces. Then the remains of our cherished memories were flushed down the toilet. Not even the garbage bin was safe enough.

At dinner, I found Betsabeh excited. She couldn't wait to tell me that her new teacher, an American married to an Iranian, was from Jackson County in Illinois. This made her and Betsabeh fellow countrywomen. Betsabeh was her pal and she had been given a packet of American bubble-gum.

Suddenly, I remembered that I had to renew her American passport. After dinner, I took the document out of the safe and saw that it had already expired, so the following day I went to the US Consulate to have it renewed. There was a long queue at the entrance and I cursed myself for having neglected this task. Patiently, I waited five hours for my turn to be seen.

Tired and hungry, I arrived home to discover that Anniana wanted to hand in her notice. She had decided to go and live in Paris. I could not blame her, but I was aggravated by this additional source of frustration. One by one, the agents of comfort were deserting us. The trimmings which had made our life easy were disappearing. The good times were dying, and with them, a part of us. I was amazed at my own calm. A short while ago, I would have considered Anniana's resignation a major disaster. Now, it was simply a nuisance to be shrugged off.

The next bad news was that seven families of the Disinherited had taken occupancy of Father's unfinished apartment building in the city. I could do nothing about this as I had no power of attorney from my father. I called London to give him the news. He replied that he and Mother would return home at once to claim the property, but I advised against their return. Comfort and safety were more important for an elderly couple than possessions. Agha joon listened to me carefully then told me that he had done nothing in his life which warranted hiding. I explained that no one knew anymore what was right or wrong; the new values had not yet been established, and a society undergoing such dramatic changes was not safe for an elderly couple to live in. He should wait until the fervour for vengeance had subsided before he returned. Finally, he agreed to heed my advice.

Two days later, Mother called from London informing me that a man named Kaman had contacted her and had offered to get her money out of Iran for a thirty per cent commission on the total value. This was a good rate in view of the government's strict exchange control. Mother asked me to contact the man's representative, stressing the need for utmost secrecy. Smuggling money out of the country was a criminal offence which incurred the death penalty.

I refused. She became angry. I grew angry in return, then eventually gave in. She gave me the name, address and telephone number of the man in question and instructed me to call his representative, Javad Agha, immediately for an appointment. Both on the telephone and at the meeting I had to repeat a coded message for identification. When Mehdi came home, I told him of the telephone conversation. At first he was upset, then he was cautious, and finally he agreed to accompany me to meet the man.

The next day I called Javad, introduced myself and repeated the coded message. An appointment was made for the following day at 11 am. At around 10 o'clock we set out for the meeting, which was to take place in the heart of the city. We both felt more than a little apprehensive about the whole affair. Mother was putting us in a dangerous situation. A pang of resentment passed through my heart. They, living in London, were safe and secure. They had no right to jeopardize the safety of our lives for their money. Now it is Mother's money, next it will be someone else's, I told myself.

I regretted agreeing to see this agent. How did we know whether or not we could trust him? Would he remain discreet if his operation was discovered, or would he divulge our names to the authorities?

Somewhere between Shemiran and the city I suggested we return home. Mehdi was also in two minds about the situation but, somehow, the blood bond overcame our fear. We parked the car a block away from our appointed meeting place and walked the rest of the way to the office, which was located on the fifth floor of an unobtrusive building. The lift was out of order and we had to use the stairs. The door was open and we entered the empty room. An unshaven man in a khaki parka came to see who had ventured into the premises. He looked like a Pasdar. I felt cold and apprehensive.

After a few moments, Mehdi, looking extremely pale, gathered the courage to ask for Javad Aga. The man told us to wait. He disappeared into another room and, after ten minutes, a giant of a man, also unshaven and dressed in a khaki parka, presented himself and asked us to follow him into a small conference room. He closed the door, giving the impression that he did not feel safe in his own premises. Mehdi introduced us and repeated the coded message. The man smiled and asked: "What can I do for you, Agha?"

In a semi-whisper, Mehdi informed him of the purpose of our visit. The man listened, watching us carefully as though trying to assess our worth and then declared that he would have to get in touch with Mr Kaman before any arrangements could be made. Mehdi asked him how they were able to get the money out in spite of the exchange control.

He replied, "It is very simple, Agha. Mr Kaman is a businessman and has secured a foreign exchange line of credit with the central bank. Every time he wants to transfer funds, he presents the necessary commercial documents to the bank to secure foreign exchange for the purchase of imported goods. Once the fund is released to him he can do whatever he wants with it."

"Doesn't the government hold him responsible for the goods which are not imported into the country?" asked a surprised Mehdi.

"Agha, don't worry," the man replied. "Mr Kaman has a good many of the customs officials in his pocket."

The procedure recommended itself to an economist.

I asked the representative how he would require the money and what security we would have that the money would be transferred. He replied that he would need the money in cash and that our security was our trust in Mr Kaman.

As we walked back to the car, Mehdi and I discussed whether or not we felt it was safe to go ahead with the deal, and also whether we should sell something of our own and send that money out, too. After examining the pros and cons of the matter, we decided to wait and see how this deal went. If all went well, we would sell the rest of our carpets and send that money out.

Three days later, Javad called and asked us how much money we intended to transfer. I told him the amount and he instructed me to put the money into a suitcase. He would pick it up from my house at an agreed time when no one except myself or my husband were at home.

A day before the appointed date, Mehdi and I, carrying four large shopping bags, entered the branch of the Bank Meli and cashed the cheque given to a trusted traveller to deliver to us. Bundles of 10,000 rial notes were put into the paper bags. The cashier was looking at us suspiciously, probably guessing that the money was about to leave the country.

Trying to look like ordinary shoppers, bent under the weight of the shopping bags, we walked to the parked car on the other side of the street, keeping as close to each other as possible. We placed the bags on the back seat and drove straight home.

At the gate, Mehdi honked and Fe appeared, opening the garage door. Mehdi drove the car inside and we both got out. Assuming the bags contained groceries; Fe began opening the car door to remove them. Hastily, I stopped her, telling her that they were to be delivered later to the Princess's house. She closed the door and went inside the house. I whispered to Mehdi that I would go in and ask her to come down to the basement with me to get some meat from the freezer. While we were down there, he should take the bags up to my bedroom and hide them in the closet.

The next day, an hour before Javad Aga was due to arrive, I sent Fe and the children to see Shahjoon. Ten minutes before his arrival, I stood gazing out of the kitchen window, which overlooked the street and, in the distance, the Alborz Mountains. The snow had melted; only a white cap remained. How I loved those mountains.

Right on time, a blue Volvo drew up in front of the house and Javad Aga got out. He looked round carefully, then rang the bell. I ran downstairs to open the garage door and he climbed back into his car and drove inside. I ushered him into the house. He stood completely still as though awestruck. I asked him what had caught his attention. He replied: "This must be the most beautiful house I have ever seen in my life. You are a lady of great taste, Mrs Monadjemi."

I thanked him, shrugged my shoulders and remarked: "Yes, the house is beautiful, but I have become its prisoner."

He asked me what I meant. I told him that I could not leave the country because I had no money outside of Iran. I could not even take a holiday because, if I left the house, the komiteh would assume that I had run away and would confiscate it. So, I was its prisoner. He said nothing.

We entered the sitting room. He sat down on the light green armchair next to the marble fireplace, refusing my offer of a cup of tea. His eyes were darting here and there around the large and very bright room, admiring the antique paintings on the walls and the Gajar ornaments on the tables. I left him to appreciate my treasures and went to the bedroom to get the red suitcase containing the money. I brought the heavy case in, placed it on the carpet and opened it. I told him what sum it contained, assuming that he would trust me. I was wrong. He sat down on the carpet with his legs crossed, licked his finger, and began taking the bundles out and counting every note, one by one.

God Almighty, I thought to myself. He is going to be here for hours. Jokingly, I remarked: "Don't you trust us?"

Without lifting his head he replied, "Mrs Monadjemi, I am only an agent."

Fair enough. I sat next to him and began counting, too.

Two hours later, he left the house with the suitcase in the boot of his car. The money was to be in Mother's bank account within seven working days. Nine days later, a call from London confirmed the completion of the transaction.

The referendum to decide the post-Pahlavi political system took place on March 30th and 31st. We were sure that no matter what went into the ballot boxes, the Islamic Republic would win with a 99 per cent majority; therefore, on the afternoon of the 31st, we walked to our district polling centre, voted for the Islamic Republic, then went to visit Khalleh Victor.

By the time we arrived at Tooradj's house, it was late afternoon. I rang the doorbell and immediately, as though a guest had been expected, Mamad opened the door. He looked pale. I asked him what was wrong and the old servant replied: "This morning at 11 o'clock they took Tooradj Khan to the Komiteh for questioning and he has not yet returned."

We rushed upstairs and found my aunt in the sitting room. The poor lady looked like a breathing corpse. Her long, thin fingers were trembling and her eyes were moist with tears. We kissed her and sat down, waiting for her to tell us what had happened. After a minute or two, she whispered, "They must have taken Tooradj to Evin."

Mehdi, in an attempt to console her, said, "Victor Khanum, he might still come back."

I asked, "Khalleh joon, do you know which Komiteh the guards have taken him to?"

"No, I don't know. I only know that the summons was from the prosecutor general," she replied tearfully.

"Khalleh, perhaps Ali Agha, the man who was posted to guard you, might know."

"Oh, yes. I had forgotten about him. But he hasn't been here for the past two days."

I suggested that she contact him for assistance.

The shaken woman rose, went into her bedroom and returned with a small piece of paper. She sat down, took the telephone from the side table, placed it on her lap and began dialling.

Ali Agha himself answered the phone. She told him what had happened to her son-in-law and asked him for help. From the change in her colour I guessed what Ali Agha was telling her. Tooradj was indeed in Evin Jail.

We invited my aunt to come and stay with us for a while and the distraught lady accepted the offer with the nod of her head. That night I told her about Kaman, anticipating that one day she might wish to employ his services herself.

That night, too, I asked myself: Why all this hatred towards the members of a dead society? Was it a crime to live and work in your own country? It was not our fault, I told myself, that we had been born under the Pahlavi regime. Surely being born into affluence was determined by destiny, not choice. Islam does not frown on wealth, as long as it is earned with honesty and as long as one's religious dues are paid. So why were we being ostracized and persecuted like common criminals? Then I remembered that the revolutionaries were not all Hezbollahis; they were also from the Mojahedin, the Fadayan, and the Tudehs – all leftists who would love to gather us together in Shahyad Square and shoot us.

It was two months before Tooradj was released. His cunning nature had found an ally in one of the revolutionary guards who, for the love of money, had helped to facilitate his freedom.

The reign of terror which had begun only months before was becoming more evident by the day, and it was obvious that the revolution was not leading us towards the promised paradise. Two of the most respected, democratically inclined Ayatollahs were already in their graves. Talegani had been found dead in his bed in suspicious circumstances and Motahari, a distinguished professor of Islamic philosophy at Teheran University's Faculty of Theology, had received as his gift from the revolution an assassin's bullet.

While the revolution was devouring its most distinguished children, Ayatollah Khalkhali was taking great pleasure in the group executions of hundreds of men, women and children. Rumour had it that he had once been an inmate at the Chehrazi Mental Institution because of his bizarre hobby of hanging kittens. Now he was hanging the Kurds and opium smugglers by the dozen. Ironically, in some shops, his portrait hung side by side with that of the Immam.

The unity that had spanned twenty-five centuries of monarchy was disintegrating. Factions were killing and discrediting each other, and even in the classrooms tension and rivalry were rife. I was beginning to fear for our safety.

The Mar Mar had been confiscated and the house by the Caspian was under investigation. I had already presented myself twice to the town's Komiteh with the deeds of the property, and had informed them that my parents were in England for medical reasons. They had given Father six months to present himself or, they said, they would confiscate this property, too.

Construction on the OmranTechlar apartments had been stopped because the Greek contractors had disappeared; so, too, had their bank guarantees which had been placed as security for their performance. There was a rumour circulating that the Omran Bank director in charge of the affair had stolen the bank guarantees and given them to the Greeks in exchange for a handsome sum of money deposited in his overseas account. He, too, was missing.

I felt sorry for Mehdi more than the rest of us. This apartment was the only possession he owned in the world. There again, I told myself, he only had himself to blame for its loss. I had asked him on numerous occasions to pull some strings to release the large deposits we had paid for the flats, before it was too late. But each time, he had rejected the idea. He was too honest for his own good.

Luxury had not only become taboo, it had also become a burden. In all likelihood I would soon have to take down the portraits of my ancestors and hide them in the basement with the suitcase my aunt had left with me when she had returned to Tooradj's.

My aunt had always been very reticent, but since her husband's imprisonment she had become very close to me, and one night she divulged that his trial was coming up shortly and that, for the first time in the history of the prosecutions, he and two other prisoners were going to face a public trial.

This news was a relief. It seemed to be a move in the right direction and we believed that there would now be a good chance that they would be pardoned. At 63, my uncle was the youngest of the three senators; the others being 72 and 80 years old. The trial was to take place in three weeks' time.

In the meantime, my aunt had been allowed to visit her husband once a month at the jail. I loved my uncle and I asked if I could accompany her on her next visit.

Evin Prison is situated on the outskirts of the Evin Hills on the upper-west side of the city. From outside the prison, only a large iron gate and high walls are visible. That afternoon, the vicinity was packed with parked cars and visitors of all ages who had formed a long line which stretched down the hill. Only immediate family members were allowed to see the prisoners and I was to pass as my uncle's sister. After an hour and a half of waiting, we arrived at the identification kiosk where I was required to show my birth certificate to prove my identity. My shattered nerves made it easy for me to produce calculated tears. Pleadingly, I addressed the guard: "Brother, misfortune has brought me absentmindedness. I forgot to bring the document with me. Please, for the love of your own sister if you have one, be gracious enough this once to allow me to see my brother. I have not seen him for the past two years as I have just returned to Iran from India."

He looked at me for a while and then, without uttering a word, quickly stamped two passes and handed one to each of us. I thanked him profusely. At the gate, Aunt Victor handed the parcel she had brought for her husband to the jailer to be inspected and delivered. Then we submitted our passes to a guard, who ushered us into the corridor of a single-storey building containing several rooms. Each room had a glass partition down the middle with a telephone on either side of it. The prisoners talked with their visitors through these bugged telephones.

We entered a cell and I saw my beloved uncle standing behind the glass partition waiting for his wife. He was dressed in a white shirt and brown trousers and it seemed as though he had aged a hundred years. His beautiful grey hair had turned white and his thin, lined face, though still handsome, looked little more than a skull.

Man and wife exchanged simple endearments.

My heart was bleeding. I was having difficulty controlling myself but, somehow, I managed. I did not have the heart to deprive my aunt of so much as a second of her brief communication with her husband; consequently, I did not utter a single word to the man I respected so much. I just stood there looking at him, crying inside numbed by the tragedy surrounding me – innocent men behind bars – their lives depending on the mercy of unmerciful men. After a short time, a bell indicated that our time was up. My uncle looked at me, his kindly eyes communicating his appreciation that I had come. I blew him a kiss, then the old couple said goodbye and we departed in silence – each in thought – each praying for a miracle.

For several days, the front page of every newspaper was covered with pictures of the three senators on trial. No lawyers were to attend, and the accused had to defend themselves. The proceedings were taking place behind closed doors and only the press were permitted inside.

We read the printed reports and listened to the news. Khalleh Victor was optimistic and Shahjoon, having been told, had bought a lamb to be sacrificed; the meat to be given to the poor in gratitude for the freedom of her son-in-law.

On the night before the end of the trial I had a peculiar dream. I dreamt of my grandfather, who seemed very happy. I asked him what was the cause of his happiness and he laughed and said: "Child, don't you know that my dearest son is free? As free as a bird, and is about to come to me. I am waiting for him."

Elated, I woke up with heart palpitations. The dream had not seemed like a dream. It had seemed very real. I began to shake Mehdi to wake him up. He groaned. I shook him again. "Mehdi! Tomorrow Mohsen Khan will be set free!" I told him excitedly. He groaned again and told me to go back to sleep, but I kept on shaking him until he listened to me. "I dreamt of Agha Mamani," I went on, "and he told me my uncle will be freed tomorrow. When I was a child, Ashraf Sadat told me that if you dream of dead people and ask them questions they will reveal the truth. It is true. My uncle will be free. You will see."

By now Mehdi was fully awake and replied, "Lily, I hope by God your dream will come true."

"Enshallah," I said looking at him with love. "I am going to have breakfast. Would you like me to bring your tray?" my husband asked in his usual calm way.

"No thanks. I am not hungry at all." I replied and pulled my cover over my head and went back to sleep.

In the morning, I dressed quickly and drove to the university. In my euphoria, I forgot to switch on the radio for the news. As I entered the staffroom, I noticed that two of my colleagues started whispering and thought that perhaps the students had been creating more trouble for me. In the corridor on the way to my classroom I saw Dr Ahmadi, who was exceptionally gentle and friendly. But I was in such a hurry to get through the day that I did not pay much attention to what was being whispered around me.

I finished my lectures and, at around four, I left the University for home, hoping to catch a newspaper vendor somewhere on the way. At a crossroad, a young boy carrying a stack of Keyhans under his arm approached the car. I took out the ten rial coin which I had ready in my coat pocket and gave it to him. He handed me the paper. The traffic light was still red. I put the paper face up on the front seat and saw the large black heading: "The execution of the three Corruptors on Earth, and the Enemies of God, took place at 3 am." the pictures of the executed senators were printed in a row under the headline.

I screamed in disbelief and began beating my head against the steering wheel. No...No...No, I repeated over and over to myself. It cannot be true. It can't be! Where was justice? What, after all, was the difference between this regime and the previous one? Which holy religion sanctifies the execution of three old, innocent men? The Koran says it is better to leave vengeance to God. So why did this new Islamic order take so much pleasure in bloodshed – killing, and killing, and killing?

The honking of cars behind me made me realize that I had caused a traffic jam. With trembling hands, I changed gears and drove off like a maniac. Suddenly, memories of my dream of the night before came back to me. Free! Free! Agha Mamani had been right. His favourite son was free. Free from this cruel world which was devoid of humanity.

Somehow, I found myself at Tooradj's house. At the door, a sorrow-stricken Mamad informed me that everyone was at Dai's house. I drove there. The number of cars parked outside the gate indicated that there were many mourners present. They must all have heard of the execution on the morning news, which I had missed.

The gate to the garden was open and I walked up the drive to the house. Inside, the house was full of relatives close and distant, all attired in black. Khalleh Victor, red-eyed but composed, was sitting on a sofa next to Shahjoon. As she saw me, she stretched out her thin, quivering arms. I ran to them and we both began crying. Shahjoon's soft hands stroked my back gently. She was crying, too. Azar joon, one of the kindest ladies in the world, came and helped me up and led me to another room. My teeth were chattering and my body was shaking uncontrollably. The servant brought me a cup of sweetened chamomile tea and I sat drinking the herbal concoction until the shaking subsided. Then I left to go home to change into black. At the gate, I met Mehdi who was just leaving the house. The sight of him released the pent-up anger I was feeling towards the world and I began shouting and screaming at him, scolding him for not informing me of the news in the morning. He stood there patiently until I had calmed down, then hugged and kissed me in an effort to comfort me. He waited until I had changed then, together, we drove back to my uncle's.

At least one hundred visitors paid their respects that afternoon and evening. Many stayed for dinner, which had been prepared by a catering service and paid for by Shahjoon. Khalleh Victor had joined the ranks of the disinherited.

After dinner, when the distant relatives had left and a semblance of life had returned to the widow, I dared to ask how she had been informed of the news. Apparently, at 1 am, a telephone call from a guard had ordered her to present herself at the jail immediately. At first she had thought the call was a bad joke. To make sure, she had rung the prison to check the validity of the order and was told that if she wished to see her husband for the last time she had better hurry to the prison. Tooradj had driven her to Evin, where a guard at the gate had taken her to her calm and resigned husband. My uncle had begged her to have courage. He had given her his watch but had not parted with his wedding ring. They had said goodbye, then one guard had taken him to the firing squad while another had accompanied her to her car. She had heard the shots being fired.

For a few awful days, we became lifeless souls. Our brains functioned and our hearts pumped the blood round our bodies, but it was as if we were only half-alive. We also had a major problem which required immediate attention; this was to secure Uncle's body and give it a proper burial. The corpses of the 'Corruptors of the Earth' had been deposited in the morgue, ready to be dumped into a mass grave. Some families of the executed had even been billed for the bullets.

We unanimously decided that we had to find a way to give our dead relative an Islamic burial. A few years back, when the Behesht Zahra cemetery had been built, a number of rooms had been sold to various families, to be utilized as eternal resting places for family members. Father had bought one of these halls for us and I now offered to give my grave to my uncle.

Agha Reza, a trusted employee, was present at this family meeting. He told us that he knew the morgue's doctor and offered to find out what this good man could do to help. The suggestion was welcomed by all and the loyal man left immediately.

I decided to spend the night at Azar joon's, where the mourning widow was staying. At around midnight, Agha Reza returned and brought the good news that the doctor would co-operate and let us have the body. We had to go to the morgue the next day at 12 noon, which was when the guards usually left to attend their prayers at the nearby mosque. The plan was that Agha Reza and Tooradj would go inside, find the body among the hundreds of corpses which had been thrown together, then carry it out to an ambulance which would be waiting for them outside. Of course, the ambulance driver would have to be handsomely paid off.

Early the next morning I went home, collected the deed and the key to the burial hall and returned to my aunt's. The house was again full of visitors. Just before noon, Khalleh Victor excused herself from the gathering, pretending to be suffering from a migraine headache. Then one by one, but at intervals, Tooradj, Mehdi, Khalleh Nayer, and myself left the house and headed out into the street. Tooradj joined Agha Reza in his jeep while the rest of us climbed into our car.

When we arrived at our destination, Mehdi parked some distance from the entrance. Tooradj and Agha Reza parked near the building and walked inside. An hour later, an ambulance passed us and honked its horn and Mehdi, alert for this signal, started the car and followed. It was a forty-five minute drive to the cemetery but, luckily, the traffic was not heavy and we were able to move quickly. We passed the slums of Javadieh and the silos. Nothing had changed. The tin houses were still there, but there were no women gathering bricks. The factories had closed.

We entered the cemetery and the ambulance stopped at the mortuary. Tooradj got out and ordered us to remain in the car until he returned. The two men opened the back doors of the ambulance and gently pulled my uncle's body out. He had gone to his death in his white shirt and brown trousers. There were many bullet holes in his chest. His handsome face was white and his eyes were closed and the expression on his face not of pain – but of peace.

My aunt, courageously in control, stepped out of the car and very composed walked towards the body, which was now inside the small building. I sat, transfixed, trying to imagine what the poor, innocent man must have gone through while waiting to hear the judgment of the jurists (not the jury).

How did he feel when he heard his sentence? Did he at once regret his connection with the Court? Or had he been executed because of his relationship with Bakhtiar? Why had he not left Iran when Dr Bakhtiar disappeared? What a silly question, I chided myself. My dear hero was a true nationalist. He had loved Iran and he had died for Iran.

Tooradj's loud voice interrupted my thoughts, telling me that we could go in and pray for our dead. In the room the body, cleansed of the stamp of human savagery, wrapped in a white shroud and sprayed with rosewater, had been laid on the carpet facing Mecca. My aunt, seated by his head, was crying soundlessly.

I sat at his feet, stroking his stiff, bony legs and began to pray for his soul. Then the mullah stood facing Mecca and commenced the death prayer. Our men stood by him and the women behind. I mused that the mullah was truly a good man. He had engaged in the prohibited task of washing and blessing the corpse of an 'Enemy of God' – something for which he would be punished if discovered. After the ceremony, he advised us against burying our dead in the cemetery. He told us that the guards frequently checked new graves, and that if they suspected one to hold an executed body, they desecrated it, removed the corpse and burned it. It seemed that there were spies everywhere.

Khalleh Nayer was in charge of the upkeep of Agha Mamani's mausoleum. She suggested a visit to the caretaker. We drove to the Shrine of Immam Abdul Azim through heavy traffic and reached the site just before dusk. Khalleh Nayer and Tooradj got out of the vehicles and entered the mausoleum. After a long half-hour they returned. The caretaker had agreed to co-operate with us but had demanded two million rials for his services. In the circumstances we had little choice but to agree to his demand.

While we waited in the mausoleum, the man went home to fetch the equipment necessary to remove the single, marble stone on which Agha Mamani's figure was sculptured, and to open the grave. At last, he returned with a large spade, a drill and some other tools. Our three men took off their jackets, rolled up their sleeves and began their laborious task. After three hours of non-stop labour our beloved was safely buried.

Later on, the revolutionaries bulldozed all the mausoleums that surrounded the shrine – trying to wipe out history – as if they could!

Happy, Agha Mamani! His favorite son was indeed free – and they were together now forever.

Chapter 16

The husband having been killed; the wife now became the prey. The hunt began precisely forty days after the execution. Fortunately, the messengers of death knocked at her door when she was out of the house and a God-loving neighbour, who happened to be outside at the time, heard their conversation with Mamad and placed a warning call to Tooradj. The family and a few trusted friends hid Khalleh Victor while she prepared to escape.

I was feeling deeply angry with the recent course of events and the non-stop killings. I wanted to strike back, but I did not know how or at whom. Then one day, one of my Kurdish students came to my office, and asked for permission to enter. I invited him in and asked what his problem was.

He smiled, nodded his head and said: "Mrs. Monadjemi I never have any problems with your course. You are the best language lecturer I have had."

"So to what do I owe this pleasure, Mr Alizadeh?" I asked smiling at him. I liked him very much because he was a very good student and very polite – something that had become very rare.

"May I sit down, Khanum?"

I nodded my permission and pointed to the nearest chair to my desk.

He pulled the chair even closer than it was and in a low voice said: "You and Dr Monadjemi are good people and I thought perhaps you could help our people in the mountains. In Kurdistan, our brothers are being massacred both from the sky and on the land by Mostafa Chamran, the minister for defense. We need money and warm clothes urgently. Any help counts."

The unexpectedness of the demand froze the smile on my face. Suddenly, I was in a position where I had to make a politically dangerous decision – one for which I was not prepared. I thought for a moment and then I realized here was my chance to make myself feel good.

"Okay. But you have to let me discuss this with my husband. Come and see me tomorrow." The joy in his eyes warmed my heart.

That night Khalleh Victor was spending the night with us; she could not stay in one place more than one night in case her persecutors discovered her whereabouts. After dinner, when the children had gone to bed, I told her and Mehdi about the Kurd's request and asked them for their opinions. We agreed that we should help by donating money and warm clothes and my Khalleh offered to give me all her husband's clothing which was stored in our basement. Quickly between us, we collected a trunk full of clothes and blankets and also a hundred thousand rials in cash. Mehdi cautioned me not to give the Kurd anything in our own vicinity.

The next morning I told my student to meet me in his car at 5 pm in front of the hamburger shop in Avenue Ehteshamieh from where he should guide me to a safe area where a trunk full of essentials could be transferred from my car to his.

Just before five I drove by the shop. Alizadeh was there, sitting waiting in a Paykan, and when he saw me he started the car. I drove round the Marvdasht Circle and began to follow him. He rode up Rostamabad and made a left turn into Niavaran Avenue, heading for Tajrish. He passed the fruit bazaar, entered Pahlavi Avenue and took the turning which led to Evin and the prison. Suddenly, it crossed my mind that I might be helping the wrong person. What if he was a spy, sent to discover anti-regime elements? What if he was taking me straight to the prison with the condemning evidence in my car?

I began honking at him hysterically and indicated that I was going to stop the car. The Kurd slowed down and parked some distance ahead. He got out of the car and walked back in my direction. I felt cold and frightened. When he reached me he politely asked what the problem was. I replied that we had driven far enough, and asked if he would now remove the trunk from my boot. He glanced around quickly to make sure no one had followed us, then swiftly opened the boot, grabbed hold of the trunk handle and pulled it out. It was heavy, but he seemed to be managing the weight. He walked away towards his car. After a few minutes I ran after him and said, "There is a hundred thousand rials in an envelope inside. Please send a prayer for my uncle when you use the money."

He looked at me with his kind but tired eyes and said: "Khanum Monadjemi, God bless you and your relatives and damn those who murder under the name of Islam." I stood there, speechless, watching him as he tried to hurry carrying the heavy case to his car. The air was cold but I did not feel it. The sky was clouded, but I did not see it. I had become nothing – a mere robot, in the midst of all those senseless things that were happening around me.

In the car driving back home I realized that the animal instinct in me had momentarily got the better of my civilized nature and that I had reacted accordingly. In a jungle where wild, wounded scavengers reigned, the primary maxim was to survive, and that was what the robot was trying to do.

On November 4th, I was preparing to go to my class when Ahmad Agha, the janitor, came to my office. He told me that there would be no classes that day as the students were celebrating the occupation of the American Embassy – that "Nest of Espionage" – by the "students following the Immam's line".

I could not believe my ears. Anti-American sentiment was high, but I had never dreamed that anyone would ever attempt to occupy the embassy. This was tantamount to declaring war on America. Bazargan was a practical politician, and right from the beginning he had tried to maintain some sort of amicable relationship with the United States. The rumour was that only recently he had met with Zbigniew Brzezinski in Algiers. Who, then, was responsible for this daringly dangerous act? Was it perhaps a reaction to Washington permitting the ailing Shah, now dying of cancer, to enter the United States for medical treatment? What will happen now? I asked myself. How is Great Satan, America, going to retaliate to this insult? And what is Carter going to do?

In a way, I was glad. I hated Carter's divided administration. I believed that they were responsible for everything that had gone wrong in Iran. How could they let down the man who had served the world's interests in this fragile and important zone for more than thirty years? Did they not realize what would happen if Iran no longer maintained the rein of power in the middle East – where a Jewish state – out of the expediency for the west was planted at the cost of the Palestinians, among enemies? Were the people in power ignorant of Sadam Hussain's ambitions? The Shah of Iran represented peace in the area. One day America would wake up to its gross mistake and regret the mess it had created, not only for Iran, but the world.

I called Mehdi's office to see if he was free to come home with me. I did not dare to talk about the situation at the embassy on the phone. Unfortunately, however, he had a staff meeting to attend so I left for home alone. When I arrived at my house, I honked my car horn to ask Fe to open the garage door. Within seconds, the door was opened, but one look at her colourless face told me that something was very wrong. I drove the car in, parked it and then asked her what the matter was. She began to stutter then eventually, pointing to the basement, managed to tell me that there were armed men down there. I ran inside and quickly made my way down the stairs. My daughters were sitting on the bottom step, hugging their knees and shaking with fear. When they saw me, they jumped up, their arms clinging round my legs, and began to cry hysterically. I held my girls tight and kissed their little heads, trying to calm them: "Don't worry, my darlings. Everything will be all right. Mummy is here now."

Two mean-looking, unshaven young guards in khaki parkas, each holding a machine gun emerged, ghostlike, from the room in which Mohesen Khan's suitcase was. One of them came close and said: "Salam, Sister. We have come from the office of the Prosecutor General to collect what your aunt has been hiding here. Could you tell us which suitcases are hers?"

Without a word I went straight to the empty one and kicked it: "This is what my aunt has in this house."

The older of the two bent over and opened it.

"It is empty."

I gave him a sharp look and replied: "Of course it's empty! What did you expect to find in it? Your men supervised what my aunt took out of her house. This suitcase contained the clothes she brought with her in the hope that, one day her husband might need them again. I am sure you are aware of the fact that he is dead and so, not having any further use for them, she has given them to the needy."

Suddenly, I remembered that I had not checked their letter of authorization. I asked the man I was talking to if he could show me the document, and he immediately took a folded piece of paper out of his pocket and handed it to me. It was genuine and bore the proper stamp, authorizing him to search my basement for the executed man's possessions.

God almighty! I had a spy in my household! How else could they have known about the suitcase in the basement? I felt as though my heart was about to stop beating. I was having difficulty breathing and could not prevent my legs from shaking. Summoning all my self-control I handed the letter back to the man and waited to see what he and his cohort would do next.

If they decided to search the rooms upstairs, they would find the antiques and the Gajar paintings on the walls, all my parents' carpets, my silver and all my other treasures which were so carefully and beautifully exhibited. Even here in the basement, if they looked into the other room they would find the wine. Oh God, help me, please. If they find the wine I'll die under their lashes.

Unexpectedly, little Parissa began to cry again. I lifted her up and pressed her tiny head to my shoulder, kissing her long, brown curls.

The two men began whispering to each other.

Parissa's sobs had now grown louder and Betsabeh was still clutching onto my skirt, fear written across her face. Perhaps the sight of the children's fright brought compassion to the men's hearts, for the one who had been doing the talking suddenly turned to me and said: "Sister, there must have been some mistake. We were told you were hiding your aunt's valuables here. The informer must be your enemy. He will be punished."

Relieved, that they had not demanded to search the rest of the house, I replied: "Thank you, brothers. No need for apologies, you are only fulfilling your duties."

I turned towards the stairs, deliberately guiding them to the side door, and they left the house disappointed and empty-handed.

Betsabeh and Fe followed me to my bedroom. I laid Parissa on the bed and asked Fe how long the men had been in the house before my arrival. She replied that they had been there for ten minutes. I asked her if they had entered from the main entrance or the side door; luckily, she had had enough sense to bring them in from the side door. The decor of the main entrance was very impressive, and these days, dangerously condemning.

Contrary to the dictates of logic, at that moment I decided to let the house remain as it was. Nothing really belongs to us, I mused. We are only the keepers, though some people are luckier than others and live and die with what they have. We come to this world with nothing and leave it wrapped only in a white shroud. Everything belongs to God. He gives and takes for reasons unknown to the human mind. It is wise to become detached from the material world, I told myself. It hurts less when they take it away from you. I sighed. No more can I believe that man makes his own destiny. After all, how am I responsible for what has happened to me, and to my family and my country? A force beyond my control is shaping the future. Suddenly, I remembered our Behesht Zahra's private resting hall and began to laugh. What a joke.

I was certain that the men who had been here already knew about my antique collection. Even if I took everything down and hid it, they would know where to find it. Who was the spy? It could not be Fe – she was not a man. And Bayat had not been in the house since long before the suitcase had been brought in. It must be Nematallah, the gardener, I reasoned. But he had loved the Shah! On the afternoon of the day that the king had left the country, I had found him crying in despair. I had asked him what was bothering him and, still sobbing, he had replied: 'My Shah has gone. I love my shahanshah.'

I had cried with him.

How could he have changed so quickly? I made it my business to find out about his political inclinations next time he came to do some gardening.

Meanwhile, the presidential election was ahead and everybody was talking about the two most prominent candidates. Admiral Ahmad Madani, governor-general of Khuzestan province, was the favourite of the upper-middle classes and Abol-Hassan Bani-Sadr was backed by the masses. It would be interesting to discover who Nematallah's favourite was. A week later, I found him busy shovelling the snow from the garden path. As usual, I discussed the garden with him and talked about the annuals I wished him to plant for the following spring. Then, gradually and meticulously, I steered the conversation to Bazargan's resignation on November 6th and the coming election. Nematallah had definitely become a Hezbollahi, and a staunch follower of Ayatollah Beheshti. He was proud of the occupation of the "Nest of Espionage", as though he himself had participated in the event, and was very happy about Bazargan's resignation.

In the heat of the conversation, the gardener also informed me that his wife was pregnant again. I was stunned. He already had seven children. I asked him why the eighth. His answer was that he wished to offer Islam one more martyr. My God! How had they managed to brainwash this Shah-lover so thoroughly? No, I realized after a moment's thought. He had not been brainwashed. It was simply expedient for him to belong to the system. His class had put him in the heart of it, and it had lavished on him provision coupons and all sorts of other advantages; perhaps a large house confiscated from the

'Enemies of God'. I had to be careful. Very careful!

The first presidential election took place in January 1980 and, as was expected, Bani-Sadr became the first president of the Islamic Republic.

A couple of months later, it became obvious that there was a serious struggle for power between the president and Ayatollah Beheshti; the strongman of the Hezbollah. Now there was unrest everywhere. Hezbollahi club-wielders were breaking up Mojahedin meetings, and the Fedayan and the Tudehs were being called traitors and the 'Enemies of Islam'. My communist sympathizer brother-in-law was arrested and sent to Evin Prison, where he would remain for many years.

Most of our friends and all my cousins had left. My cousin Sharzad's husband had been 'purified' from the diplomatic corps and had gone to Geneva where he had landed himself a good job at the United Nations, but Sharzad and her son were still in Teheran. She owned a stud farm and reared Arabian horses. Khalleh Victor had, thank God, managed to escape in an aeroplane, though no one knew how. Most wanted people fleeing to Europe were taking the route to Turkey either on foot or on horseback.

The television programs now being broadcast were all Islamic. Night clubs and all the good restaurants had been closed and there was a ban on music and video tapes. In the absence of alcohol, housewives were distilling Arak (a home-made substitute for vodka) from dates, rice and raisins. Apparently, Arak made with raisins was dangerous and had been known to cause blindness and even death. Not daring beyond my less than profound cooking skills, we bought ours from an Armenian painter I knew.

Marijuana was being grown in most gardens. Adultery, in cases where one marriage partner was absent, had become common and almost accepted. Parties were given very privately, as there was no guarantee that the guards would not get wind of what was going on and come to raid the house, rounding up the sinners and bestowing upon them the appropriate penalties. One hundred lashes was a mild punishment for the smell of alcohol on one's breath, and hanging was the one due for smoking or smuggling opium.

During those crucial months, only hope for a national amnesty kept me from going insane. I sincerely believed that the people had revolted for a good cause under the leadership of a man of God. I believed that

Ayatollah Khomeini would see to it that Islamic justice would be restored to our society and that, under his auspicious guidance, the nation would begin a period of reconstruction. My beloved Iran would, after all, become the paradise for which so much blood had been shed. I had not yet realized that, like all other abstractions, the concept of paradise was subject to interpretation.

The vigorous rivalries between the hardliners and President Bani-Sadr, moved the American hostage crisis to the centre stage of domestic politics. Not only were Iran's demands for the Shah's extradition, the return of his wealth, and the admission by the United States to 'crimes' committed against the Iranian people not met by Washington but, in addition, the billions of dollars in Iranian assets held by American entities, banks and their overseas branches were frozen and imports of Iranian oil banned.

I gathered from the newspapers that President Bani-Sadr and Foreign Minister Sadeg Qotbzadeh were doing their best to solve the crisis. However, because the central government was divided in its strategies towards Washington, nothing seemed to work, and as the days passed, the 'students of the Immam's line' became bolder in their hold of the hostages, to the extent that they began threatening to try them as spies if Washington did not meet their demands. Bazargan's government was rendered impotent by infighting, jeopardizing the rule of the moderates.

Luck was on the side of the hardliners. Only a week ago, an American attempt to rescue the hostages had come to naught. Apparently, an aircraft and some helicopters had landed in the desert, west of Tabas. Two of the helicopters had failed to function and one helicopter and a C-130 aircraft had crashed, causing eight American airmen to be burned alive in the flames. The scene of the disaster was extensively televised and the failure of the mission was proclaimed as a miracle for the revolution. The lawn of the university campus was covered with the grizzly pictures of Ayatollah Khalkhali, inspecting the burnt bodies of the US rescuers.

This foreign intrusion caused a revival of fears of American, Royalist and Zionist plots against the regime and led to further purges and 'purifications', especially in the armed forces. Naturally, mass executions followed.

A few days after the American disaster, just before dawn, we were awakened by the excruciating sound of aircraft flying so low that I thought they might hit the roof. We were so frightened that I rushed everybody into the basement, expecting some sort of bombardment. Nothing happened, and the next morning the radio announced that the dawn's air traffic 'raid' had been an air force exercise. It was not an air force exercise and none of us ever found out what it really was.

It seemed that, these days, our state of mind was permanently one of bewilderment and numbness – that is, until shock brought us out of it. Every day witnessed a new and terrifying event that shattered the nerves of the people. For the silent majority, living during a revolution is like being a matchbox floating on the ocean waves. The box floats here and there until the force of the waves disintegrates it. Like many of my kind, I had become like the matchbox – but, somehow, there was something in my heart that was telling me not to give up, not to disintegrate.

What frequently happens in revolutions is that different extreme factions unite to bring down the hated old system, then, once that short-term success is achieved, the unity falls apart and the fight for power begins again until the strongest establishes its supremacy. This same process was now afoot in Iran. Unified hatred gave way to individual rivalries and confused goals. The extremism which had been vital for the initial revolution was now imploding. The leftist groups were pushing for radical measures, calling for sweeping nationalization, distributive justice, the cancellation of 'imperialist' agreements and the purging of people connected with the former regime. They were feeding the revolutionary turmoil and undermining the government of the moderates.

The leftists were everywhere, especially in the Komitehs and the universities. Thousands of young radicals would turn up at Teheran University to listen to Mojahedin-e-Khalq's leader, Mas'ud Rajavi, whose ideology was based on a classless, Islamic society; a potent tool with popular appeal. The campuses had turned into huge platforms for political debates.

The Hezbollahis viewed the leftists with animosity and thought of the universities as centres for agitation. They were pressing for the closure of these centres. The issue became so important – so hot – that it was taken up at a meeting of the Revolutionary Council, where it was decided to give the left-wing political organizations three days to vacate University buildings and grounds. Classes had already stopped and political meetings followed one after the other.

Most active lecturers were leftists and they were preparing to put up a fight. Mehdi and I, however, were as apolitical as ever, believing that some good would come out of all the change. Our immediate concern was with what would happen to our salaries should the universities close. We drifted naively, not acting, merely watching.

Khomeini was on the side of the fundamentalists, and frequently attacked the "westernized universities which are training our youths in the interest of the west". On many occasions, he had compared the intellectuals to 'donkeys carrying books on their backs'. Encouraged by the Immam's latest anti-university speech, the Hezbollahi club-wielders attacked the Teheran Teachers' Training College and lynched one of the students. As a result, bloody confrontations broke out in campuses all over the country, the worst of which took place on April 21st at Teheran University, where many lost their lives.

The following day, the Teheran University campus hosted Bani-Sadr and his followers celebrating the cleansing of the campus of its left-wing elements, and proclaiming the start of a 'cultural revolution' to 'Islamize' the universities.

Shortly after the proclamation, the universities closed indefinitely. As far as salaries were concerned it was announced that, after a thorough 'purification' of the undesirable elements, those acceptable to the system would receive their base wages, for which they would be required to work at government-designated institutions. The next step taken by the regime was to prohibit the employment of females not in Islamic wear. This meant the end of my academic career.

University salaries are low everywhere in the world, and no academic can maintain a comfortable standard of living without some kind of salary supplementation. We were no exception and now, with the closure of the universities and colleges and Mehdi's earnings from extra lecturing having ceased, I did not know how we would live. So I began selling the rest of my carpets and some of my gold coins. The price of gold had increased tenfold but, unfortunately, within a short period of time the property market crashed and I could not liquidate my lands. Rumour had it that soon, all uncultivated land would be confiscated and given to the disinherited.

One afternoon, when Taghi and his wife returned from Galandoak, he came to my house bearing bad tidings. Mashallah had set fire to the beautiful garden I had created and of which he was a gardener. I was aghast. Why on earth would he burn my trees? I asked myself.

Mehdi and I drove to Galandoak at once to see for ourselves. We found the garden barren, dotted here and there with black ash where once had stood the trees. I knocked at Mashallah's door. He opened it, greeted us politely and invited us in. We refused and remained standing outside. I asked him what had happened to my trees.

He began scratching his grey head and replied, "Khanum, I was not here when it happened. When I arrived home, my sons told me that some guards from the local Komiteh had come and set fire to the trees, thinking the land belonged to Afsaneh; the daughter of the cursed Mohsen Khajehnouri."

I could not believe my ears. This so-called faithful retainer was cursing the man for whom he had worked for thirty years and because of whom he had educated his children and had become the owner of the house in which he lived.

"Mashallah, your wife is always at home and your sons themselves are in the Komiteh. Surely they could have protected the garden?"

"Khanum, I am not responsible for what my family could have done, or have not done. The deed is done. Why don't you go to the Komiteh and complain, rather than accusing me of negligence?"

I was getting very angry. Mehdi saved the situation: "Khanum, Mashallah Khan is right. The deed is done and we cannot do anything about it now. Perhaps Mashallah can plant new trees for you."

"Yes, perhaps." Having agreed thus, I turned and got into the car, slamming the door behind me.

Mehdi stayed behind a little longer.

"He is as guilty as hell. I'll bet the Komiteh guards were his own sons, and that they burned the trees so that the land could be called uncultivated. Then it would be confiscated and given to them." I was convinced.

"Lily, the land is still yours. What has happened is not really important. People have lost more than a few trees and they are still smiling. Just try to forget about it. Next spring we will plant new ones."

He was right. So much had already been lost that a few trees did not matter at all. People had changed. The new society hated us, and for as long as this revenge-fever existed, nothing constructive could be done. The lower classes wanted revenge for having been poor, the bazaaries wanted revenge for having been disregarded by the Shah, and one's neighbour simply wanted revenge because he did not like you. What was more, everyone felt justified in their vengeance.

We – the Taghoties – were traitors, whores, thieves, spies and whatever else they wished to call us. Stealing from us and lying to us were sanctified by the revolution, which still needed tangible, short-term results. Making up dossiers for 'Corruptors on Earth' had become a daily practice. Evidence could be fabricated overnight and one could be collected and sent to Evin without reason.

The situation was getting more desperate by the hour and neither Mehdi nor I could come up with any plans for the future. The truth was that we could not make up our minds whether to leave and become refugees in a foreign country or stay, accept the system and hope for better days to come in a country that we deeply loved.

A simple telephone call one Friday decided for us.

It was from Mrs Cheragi, Betsabeh's American teacher.

Our conversation was short and to the point. The US Embassy had ordered its citizens to leave the country within four weeks. To facilitate the exodus, non-citizen spouses and next of kin were to be granted US visas. Betsabeh was American and Mrs Cheragi imagined that, as her parents, we would qualify. The Swiss Consulate was looking after US affairs, and she suggested that we go to see them as quickly as possible as the situation was very serious. At the end of the conversation, she asked me not to tell anyone about her call. I promised, and thanked her for thinking of us.

We were shocked by the news and spent the whole afternoon speculating as to what might be the cause of such a drastic move. Perhaps the Americans were expecting an army coup or, even worse, a civil war. We had to leave. I could not expose the children to war.

But how could we leave Iran without any money, and without valid visas?

Mrs Cheragi's suggestion was well-intentioned, but it seemed to us that it would be highly dangerous to approach the Swiss Consulate now that they were looking after US affairs. The 'students of the Immam's line' might attempt to occupy it too, and, naturally, they would find our applications for US visas on the computer. If this happened we would end up in Evin, accused of co-operation with 'the Great Satan'.

Suddenly, in the midst of our confusion, I remembered that Kaman's representative had fallen in love with my house. What if he could be persuaded to buy the house and deposit the money for me in Europe? I immediately told Mehdi of my idea and we decided to contact the man with the offer.

The prospect of getting some cash out of the country made us courageous enough to decide to apply for US visas, and the next day, we took Betsabeh's US passport and all the required documents, including our university degrees as evidence of our western education, to the Swiss Consulate. Fortunately, the reception area was empty of visitors except for one young man, hiding behind his newspaper. A clerk asked us the reason for our visit and then told us to wait. After a few minutes we were summoned. One look by the consul at the age of the passport-holder disqualified us. Betsabeh could not apply for an immigrant visa for us until she was twenty-one years old; we would have to wait for another twelve years. And there was no way that we could obtain visitors' visas under the present circumstances.

In spite of my disappointment at this rejection, I had the presence of mind to ask the official what could be done about Betsabeh's passport in case we wished to leave the country. If such a document was found on us while going through customs, our safety might well be jeopardized. He agreed that the possession of any US document was dangerous these days, and advised us to bring the passport to him should we decide to leave the country. He would put it in a diplomatic pouch and have it delivered to the embassy which was nearest to our destination. We would be able to collect it from there on our arrival. At least one problem was solved.

Now we had to approach the British Embassy. Though my parents did not know it yet, we hoped to be able to stay with them in London.

At home, I called Mahmoud, and told him of the conversation I had had with Mrs Cheragi. He immediately suggested that we leave the country as soon as possible. Mother, who must have been listening on the extension in her bedroom, came on to the line and pleaded with me to get on the next flight for London. I reminded her that we needed visas these days and that could take a long time. I suggested that she ask Mahmoud to try to find a doctor who would be prepared to certify that I was suffering from some sort of illness requiring urgent surgery. The doctor's certificate might facilitate the acquisition of our visas. She promised to look into it at once.

Soon after talking with my family, I received a telephone call from Tooradj's partner informing me that Tooradj had been taken to jail again. Apparently, his telephone had been bugged since his previous release, and the Komiteh was now in possession of the tapes of all his conversations, including the one call he had made to me inquiring about Kaman's fund transfers.

I asked him what they had charged Tooradj with this time. He did not know and warned me not to call Afsaneh who had arrived in the country the previous night. She and the children had returned to an empty home, where a guard was waiting to hand her the tapes. Fear and pity for my cousin were making me feel nauseous. Hurriedly, I thanked the caller, said goodbye, and ran to the toilet to vomit. Nothing but acid came up. I rinsed my mouth, washed my face and returned to my bedroom, where I dropped onto the bed and began to cry.

Poor Afsaneh! First it was her father, now her husband – and that for the second time.

Suddenly, the doorbell rang. I began to tremble. It must be them, I thought. They have come for me believing, perhaps, that I had received a commission from my dealings with Kaman on behalf of Tooradj.

God, what have I done? Please, please, save me.

I heard footsteps.

They were here. They were coming for me.

The bedroom door opened slightly and in crept Afsaneh. For a moment I could not believe my eyes, and then I jumped up to embrace her.

She had lost a lot of weight. Her athletic body seemed to have shrunk, her beautiful, dark eyes were red from crying, and her short, curly hair was half-grey. She was two years my junior, but looked much older. Once, she had been the envy of the town, with her handsome, successful husband and highly-regarded parents. Now she was a beaten woman – lost, dependent, and alone.

Well, I thought to myself: "Call no man happy till he dies." The great Greek law-giver Solon understood life in relation to political forces. And I was learning it over and over with the experiences of the last few months.

Afsaneh sat on the armchair facing the garden. The climbing roses covered the walls, the annual bulbs were flowering and the garden looked quite beautiful. There are many harmless little sub-political pleasures which all humanity can share. But politics, the grab for public power, can stop the spirit from enjoying such small comforts. We took no joy in the spring.

My cousin was cool and composed, a dignified lady in spite of her great distress. I respected her courage, patience, and prudence. From the way she was talking, I gathered she had already become aware of her husband's infidelities and had heard the tapes of his telephone conversations with his lovers and out of the generosity of her heart had forgiven him. She loved him too much not to. I tried to comfort her by attempting to explain the nature of the times in which we were living, and the extent of the frustrations and the fears which we had all had to face. I reasoned that, more than likely, his affairs had taken place not out of love for the women, but out of desperation – to release tension, a mere physical need. After all, he had been living alone for almost a year. She was inclined to agree with me.

After drinking the tea which Fe had brought for us, we decided to walk to Shahjoon's – a little like children seeking comfort. The old princess was lying on her bed, looked tired and sick. She suffered from high blood pressure, but I suspected that it was really loneliness which was taking its toll on her health. With the exception of Afsaneh and me, all her offspring had left the country. She missed Khalleh Victor most of all, and knew she would never see her again.

In a way, Shahjoon was lucky. At least she still had her household staff, which looked after her with affection and loyalty. After the success of the revolution, the majority of servants had become informers against their employers, in the hope that they would be sent to jail and that they could then become the new occupiers of their masters' homes. Others, who still trusted their own masters more than the guards, had nevertheless turned to blackmail.

Shahjoon's pallor vanished as she saw us entering her empty room. To make her happy, we gossiped about the family members who were living overseas and gave her all the good news we could think of – which, under the circumstances, was very little. When it began to get dark, I left for the bakery to buy bread for dinner.

There was a lot on my mind. Mehdi was going to visit the British Embassy the following day and I had not yet been able to liquidate any of my assets or contact Kaman's man. There was talk that the government was going to stop all property transactions. This meant that I had to sell something before it was too late.

Drowned in thought, I only vaguely heard a car honking behind me. Alarmed, I turned to see Javad Agha behind the wheel of a car, and a young couple in the back seat. My heart missed a beat. Forcing a smile, I waved to him. He pulled over to the kerb, stopped the car and got out. Obviously, he wanted something, so I crossed the road to meet him. We shook hands and he introduced the couple as Mr and Mrs Kaman. I nodded to them and waited to see what Javad Agha wanted from me. He began by telling me that Mr Kaman was looking to buy a property in Shemiran and that he had told him about my beautiful house. He wondered if I might be interested in selling. In fact, he said, he had been going to telephone me that very evening to see if the idea appealed. If so, he would like to make an appointment to inspect it.

Excitement combined with paranoia rendered me speechless for a moment, then I pulled myself together and invited them to join me for a drink at the house. They accepted my invitation and he politely opened the car door for me.

When we arrived home, I gave them the grand tour, surreptitiously watching Kaman's facial expressions, then took them into the formal sitting room where we sat relaxing and drinking Arak. I told Kaman that I would only be interested in selling the house if he was able to send the money overseas before I left Iran. He told me that he would let me know of his decision the next day. Still feeling slightly stunned, I urged him not to contact me by telephone. I told him about Tooradj and the tapes. We arranged that I would call him myself at four the following afternoon.

They were just about to leave when Mehdi arrived home from playing tennis at Veissi, the club we had frequented for seven years. The club owner, a Mr Veissi, was now in jail for owning this "Nest of Corruption", in which whores were used to seduce men with their bare legs. Women were not allowed in anymore.

Mehdi's expression told me that he was very surprised to see my guests. I quickly informed him of the purpose of their visit and a broad smile lit up his face.

We saw our visitors out of the house and returned to the sitting room where, in a celebratory mood, we drank the remaining half-bottle of Arak.

In order to beat the crowd at the British Embassy's visa queue, Mehdi left home at five the next morning, but returned around noon, empty-handed. The purpose of the queue that day had simply been to obtain a number, which would be called the following day. He would have to repeat the ritual tomorrow. The letter from the English doctor had not yet arrived and I was becoming nervous. Finally, at 4 pm, I called Kaman. He wanted the house! I was ecstatic. God willing, everything would be well again. Suddenly the headache that had been hurting me for days vanished.

Just before dinner, we received a call from Bayat. He informed Mehdi that the prosecutor general's office was investigating all the Omran Bank's directors, deputies and managers and suggested that if Mehdi had to take any precautionary measures he should do so immediately.

Fortunately, we did not have to worry about taking any 'precautionary measures', as Bayat had politely put it. But this meant that Mehdi was now on the list of individuals who were prohibited from leaving the country.

Before we sold the house, we had to make sure that he would be able to leave Iran. We spent the whole evening contacting those friends who had been turned back at the airport because they had been on the list. From what they told us, it seemed that the traveller knew nothing until the travel agent submitted his passport to the airport authorities for the usual security check. Then, a couple of nights before his departure, the wanted passenger would receive a call informing him that he had to attend the office of the prime minister for clearance before he was permitted to leave the country.

Then, the choice was his. He could either forget about his passport or take the risk of presenting himself to the authorities. Some people who had shown themselves had been cleared, while others had ended up at Evin.

After much reflection, Mehdi decided to book a seat, submit his passport and wait for the call. If he was on the prohibited list, he would face the so-called Clearance Committee, whose decision would determine his plan of exit from Iran. Should he be cleared, he would fly out. Otherwise, he would take the mountain route.

The wisdom of this plan was that it eliminated any possibility of surprise. It also gave us time to organize ourselves and set a suitable departure date.

The next day, again at five in the morning, Mehdi left for the British Embassy and the travel agency. But at noon, he again returned without the visas. The man in charge of the tickets had cancelled all the previous day's numbers because he had discovered that someone had taken ten numbers to sell on the black market.

We cursed our luck and decided not to pursue the matter until we had received the doctor's letter. However, in the meantime, Mehdi tentatively booked himself on a flight to London on June 5th.

From the first of June until the evening, when the call came, we were glued to the telephone, our spirits rising and falling at every call, all of which were irrelevant to our present purpose. Finally, an officer did call, asked for Dr Monadjemi, and very politely, informed him that if he wished to travel he had to go to the office of the prime minister. Now it was Mehdi's turn to test the justice of the regime.

I knew he was good. I knew he was brave. And I knew that he was innocent. But did any of that matter now? The following day, I gave him my pocket Koran for safekeeping, whispered a prayer and sent him out of the house to present himself at the designated address.

I was so worried about what might happen to my husband that I could not keep still. Fe felt sorry for me and suggested that I go for a walk. I wandered around until I found myself in front of Niavaran Palace. A man sitting by the gate was selling beautiful tulips in colours I had never seen before. The flowers were from the palace garden. I purchased two bunches of black and yellow tulips and walked back home.

The parked Fiat indicated that Mehdi was at home and not at Evin. Joyously, I opened the door and, shouting his name, ran upstairs. My darling was sitting in his usual armchair, smiling at me. I ran to him and hugged and kissed him a thousand times. The official in charge, he said, had treated him with great respect and had simply told him that he had to obtain clearance certificates from all the institutions, except the university, which had employed him within the past ten years. That was all, thank God.

It took two weeks of nerve-wracking, humiliating trials by various committees before he was cleared and given an exit visa. He had four weeks to leave the country before the visa expired; to renew it he would have to undergo the same procedure. God only knew who might be sitting in judgment then!

Mehdi was very lucky. His popularity with his employees, as well as his personal generosity to those who had needed help but had not qualified to receive it from the bank, combined to save his skin. For example, at the beginning of his career there, one of his employees had approached him for help. His wife desperately needed an operation for cancer and he simply did not have the funds to pay for it. Mehdi and I had combined forces with my parents and Masoud to finance the operation in Israel and had, in effect, saved the woman's life. This man, once a humble clerk, was now the president of the Omran Bank's Clearance Committee!

The letter from the English doctor arrived at last, and on its basis, the British Consul granted visas to Mehdi, Parissa and myself. For some unknown reason, Betsabeh was denied, but I did not dare to insist in case he changed his mind about ours.

I reminisced about the days of the Shah's reign, when we had not needed British visas at Heathrow Airport. The customs officials had simply looked at one's passport and asked: "Madam, how much money are you planning to spend in London on this trip?" Then, a glance at the bank cheque or the bank account document ensured a six months' permit to stay. Now, we had to beg.

Once the travel arrangements had been made, we met with Kaman to discuss the details of our transaction. He wanted me to turn the deed of the house over to him and to trust him with the transfer of the funds. I refused. He accused me of not having faith in him. I told him I trusted no one, and that if he wanted the house he had to accept my terms. He hesitated, then called me a 'lion of a woman' and agreed to my conditions. First, we had to go to a notary office where the legal transaction would take place. There, to make sure that no one suspected our deal in foreign currency, he was to give me a cheque for the agreed sum in rials. This I would keep until the money was deposited into Mother's bank account. Then the cheque would be returned to him. This was the safest arrangement I could think of. In case anything went wrong, at least I had the sum in rials.

For a change, matters were sorting themselves out at a dizzying pace. My neighbour, a tenant of Mother's, was Dutch and well aware of Betsabeh's visa problem. The kindly man, of his own accord, offered to help us by personally taking her Iranian passport to the Dutch Embassy and obtaining her a visa. Once in Holland, he said, she would be able to travel to England on her US passport. The idea was brilliant and I accepted it with gratitude.

This gave rise to a new plan. We decided that Mehdi and Betsabeh would travel to Amsterdam together and wait for me and Parissa to join them there. I had to enter England before August 7th which, according to the English doctor's letter, was to be the day of my cornea transplant operation. Kaman had promised that the money would be in my account before July 7th.

The plan was immediately put into action and our Dutch visas were obtained within twenty-four hours. Betsabeh's US passport was submitted to the Swiss Consulate and Mehdi was instructed to collect it from the American embassy in The Hague. For the first time in many months, stamina returned to me. All the neighbours' servants with whom I had established good relations were mobilized to help us pack. Mehdi asked his parents if we could leave our valuables at their house and they agreed.

On a bright June day, I drove Betsabeh and Mehdi to the airport. The departure lounge was so crowded that it was almost impossible to move. The large hall was packed with would-be passengers, surrounded by luggage and relatives who had come to see them off. Distorted lines of people stretched in all directions.

At the luggage check-ins, thorough searches were being conducted by the revolutionary guards. I noticed that some were even ripping open the linings of suitcases in the hope of finding money, jewels or other goods which were not allowed out. I thanked God for my foresight.

Since movement was so difficult, I remained standing in a corner, enjoying the warmth of Betsabeh's hand in mine and watching Mehdi take care of the formalities. I was afraid of being left alone in Iran, but I did not dare to express my apprehension in case Mehdi changed his mind and stayed behind to protect me. He was still in danger and had to leave the country now; these days, one could not leave anything to chance. Even if the worst came to the worst, at least two members of my family were going to be safe.

Time was running out and Mehdi and a rather pensive Betsabeh had to leave the lounge. Our goodbye was long and emotional. I wondered what Betsabeh was thinking. She was just a child. She could not possibly conceive of the risks that were involved. But she was a very observant child. I waited until the loudspeaker announced the departure of their flight and then, very slowly, walked to my car.

I told myself that I had to be strong and careful. Very careful. The future of my family depended on my efficiency. Mehdi had left with only 1,000 pounds sterling. I prayed that Kaman's money would be transferred on time, so that I could leave Iran before Mehdi ran out of cash. They could not enter England without me and the doctor's certificate stipulating my need for an operation. The customs official was bound to ask them the reason for their travel and, if they had none, they would be sent back to Iran.

When I reached home, my spirits were lifted by the electrifying commotion going on in the house. Taghi and his wife, along with Fe, Akbar Agha; the husband of Shahjoon's personal maid, and a couple of the neighbours' servants were all busy packing for me. The only servant who was missing was Nematallah. Recently, he had been bad-mannered, impertinent and hostile. Why was he absent?

My antiques and carpets were to go to my in-laws and the rest of my belongings, including all my electrical appliances and my stock of frozen food, were to be distributed among the people who were helping me. This was saying goodbye to a lot of money, but that did not matter. I wanted these people to remember me well, as I would remember them.

Every day, I called Kaman's office to see if the money had arrived, and every day the answer was: "It will be there tomorrow."

I was beginning to get worried. We were well into the first week of July and I had booked for the 20th. The planes were all full and the next available seats after that were not until September 1. I had to leave Iran on the 20th.

The days passed slowly, in a long, lonely haze. My headaches had become more frequent and, sometimes, I experienced dizzy spells. But most of my suffering was from loneliness and fear.

My in-laws probably wished that I had never existed. Since the day that I had taken my valuables to their house, I had neither seen them nor talked to them on the telephone. Fortunately, Tooradj had been released and he and his family had escaped the country on horseback.

I will never forget those unhappy days when, desolate, I would sit by the pool reflecting on the past and not daring to think of the future. What can be righteous about political action which is based on vengeance, and which intrudes into every corner of people's lives? I firmly believed that the state should be the servant of the people, not the people its whipping boy.

Somehow, I did not regret selling my house. I had owned it, perhaps, for as long as I was meant to. Now it belonged to Mr and Mrs Kaman and, when the time came, it would belong to someone else. We are all joined in our love of creature comforts. I felt consoled that someone else, then someone else again, would live in and love my beautiful house. Perhaps one day, I told myself, when the Immam declares a national amnesty and when the persecution mania subsides and stability returns to the country, I might return and buy it back and be one more dweller in the chain.

On July 11th I was informed that Kaman had been taken to prison in the town of Bandar Abass. I was assured that it was a case of mistaken identity and that he would be freed in no time at all. Apparently his namesake was a SAVAK butcher.

On July 14th, Kaman was executed.

I deposited his cheque. It bounced. I could not go to the authorities – it was too dangerous. Thus, I, too, joined the ranks of the disinherited. What were we going to do in England without a nest egg? I consoled myself with the thought that at least I had my carpets and my jewels. They would see us through for a short while.

I called Mahmoud and told him the story. At first he found it hard to believe, then he urged me to leave Iran at once. I asked to speak to my father. The generous man assured me that he would look after us until we found employment. I called Mehdi and gave him the news. He took it calmly and, as always, tried to comfort me. But we both felt that life had been too cruel to us.

On July 18th, when the last of my furniture was being removed, Nematallah and two guards armed with machine guns forced their way into the house. In loud, harsh tones they began accusing me of various sins – of helping the widow of the executed Khadjenouri; of hiding alcohol in the house; and of attempting to flee the country. Tahgi and his wife, along with four other neighbours and Akbar Agha, a Komiteh guard himself, managed to stop them from getting too close.

I was petrified. Parissa was screaming and Fe was trembling with fear as the other servants argued with the revolutionary guards. I cannot remember what was said. I can only recall that Akbar Agha saw the men out of the house and slapped Nematallah on the face, calling him 'Namak nashnas' – ungrateful. When the armed men had left, I lost consciousness. Some hours later, I found myself in bed, Parissa and Fe sitting on the floor nearby. When she saw me stir, Fe rose and left the room, reappearing a moment later with Akbar Agha. He apologized for entering my bedroom, then went on to urge me to leave the house, the next morning if possible. Nematallah could not be trusted, he said, and might return with an order for my arrest. I thanked him for his help and his loyalty. He said goodbye and walked out of the room.

We were left by ourselves, two women and a child.

Nematallah might come back? I was too scared to stay in the house any longer. We had to leave that night. I got up, took a shower and called my mother-in-law to see if we could spend the remaining two nights at her house. Unfortunately, no one was at home.

I could not go to Shahjoon's house. Her safety could not be jeopardized. I called Ellahe, the only friend I had left in Iran. She greeted me warmly and told me that they would come and pick us up within the hour. Together, Fe, myself and Parissa carried the heavy suitcases down the stairs. My little girl, in anticipation of a reunion with her father and sister, was bubbling with joy. How different is the child's world from that of the adult's.

I instructed Fe to call Taghi to come and supervise the distribution of the goods I had left for all those who had helped me. The bedroom furniture had been sold to Kaman's wife, who Fe was to call after I had left the country. She would, no doubt, make arrangements for their removal. Poor woman, she had become a widow at the age of twenty-five. It was quite likely that all her accounts had been closed and that she would not be able to pay for the furniture, but that did not matter anymore. Only our safety mattered.

We double-checked that everything had been taken downstairs. Then I made a final tour of my once-happy home, remembering the wonderful times I had spent with my family and friends in those sunny rooms. It seemed as though the house had a soul of its own and was crying out for me. My home, I sighed. My beloved home. How easily did I lose you? Once the authorities find out about your new owners, they will come and confiscate you for the Foundation of the Disinherited. Am I not disinherited, too?

Slowly, I descended the curved staircase to the once grand hall and went out into the flourishing garden. Mother's tasteful landscaping had made a lush paradise out of Agha Mamani's barren land. I walked the length of the path to my vegetable garden and picked a stem of mint to tuck between the pages of my pocket Koran. It would be a memento from my home. Will I ever have another one, I wondered?

Fe's voice interrupted my thoughts. My friend was waiting for us at the gate. I stood for a few minutes longer, trying to feel the essence of the garden with every nerve in my body. Then I pushed sadness from my mind and, very quickly, walked to the gate.

Fe had already locked up and had placed the suitcases in the boot of the car. She was going to stay with us at Ellahe's for our last two nights. I could not take her with me as the British Embassy had refused her a visa. She had had the choice of returning to the Phillipines, or remaining in Iran. She had chosen to stay.

In the car, I asked my friend to stop by Shahjoon's house so that I could see her one more time. I took Parissa in with me. I wanted her to remember her great-grandmother. My beloved Shahjoon was lying on her bed watching television. I could not tell her that this was a farewell. As I had done when I was a child, I sat on her bed, massaging her thin limbs. Then I kissed her, from the tips of her toes to the top of her head, wishing as I did so that I could turn the clock back. I was crying inside, knowing that this was the last time I would be able to touch this woman I loved so much.

She took my face in both hands, kissed it and invited us to stay for dinner. I made up an excuse and refused. Parissa jumped up onto the bed and gave her a big hug. Tears were in my eyes, but I could not let them loose. I had to leave quickly; otherwise my emotions would overcome my composure. After a final, tight hug, I left the only real treasure I had in Iran. I never saw her again. Shahjoon died in 1983, in the arms of Azar joon; the lady who was and is still there for every one of us.

We drove down Avenue Ehteshamieh for the last time. Agha Mamani's trees had matured and the avenue looked absolutely beautiful. I wondered what the municipality would call it, now that they were renaming the streets in honour of the martyrs of the revolution. Ellahe was very kind and tried to cheer me up as we drove. I appreciated her efforts, but I was in no mood for conversation. I had an excruciatingly painful headache and I had no taste in my mouth. My body was rigid with tension, prepared for flight.

Our last day in Iran passed without event. I stayed in bed most of the time. My health seemed to be deteriorating and I was worried that I would not make it to the airport. Painkillers were proving ineffective.

Our British Airways flight was at 11 am and the travel agent had advised us to be at the airport by six in the morning. My kind and generous friend and her wonderful husband drove us to Mehrabad. Our farewell was sad and sentimental.

The man who inspected my luggage was sympathetic. He made only a superficial inspection of my cases, and then closed them neatly. I wanted to cry in gratitude at his unspoken kindness, but I could not weaken now. Once the luggage had been dealt with, it was time for the body search. A mean-looking young woman in black Hejab showed me into a small, partitioned room and began sliding her hands over my body, sides, front and back. Disappointed at not finding anything, she took a pair of surgical gloves from a wooden chair nearby, and put them on. She told me to take off my underpants. I began to shake and begged her not to subject me to such humiliation. She gave me a sarcastic smile and ordered: "Pull your pants down, or I'll do it for you."

I suddenly felt sick and began to breathe deeply in an effort to control myself.

"Hurry up, woman!" she screamed.

Trembling, I obeyed.

"Spread your legs."

I obeyed again.

She knelt down and proceeded to shove her index finger into my vagina, pushing it as high as she could and turning it around and around, deliberately and sadistically causing me pain. Then, satisfied that I had nothing hidden there, she pulled her finger out and stuck it up my rectum. When she had finished, she smirked and left the room. I felt as though I had been raped.

A spasm of nausea hit me and I bent over to let the liquid spew out of my mouth. I began breathing deeply again, then wiped my mouth with a handkerchief, pulled myself together and left the room. I had never been so sure until now of the wisdom of our decision to leave Iran.

Little Parissa was patiently waiting for me. My headache was getting worse and I had difficulty in keeping my eyes open, but I had to make it to the passport section. I simply had to.

We joined the queue to have our tickets checked and waited. At last, tickets checked and our seats allocated, we joined another queue. After about half an hour we reached the official in charge of the passports. He asked me for my name.

I managed to stammer our names.

He turned to the pigeon holes and turned back with the documents. Thank God, the last bridge to safety had been crossed.

I found two empty seats and walked over to them. Parissa was behaving like an angel. She must have sensed that I was ill. She sat next to me, fidgeting with the hem of the green, oversized coat which I had made her wear in preparation for the cold weather in Amsterdam.

After a delay of three hours, the loudspeaker announced that our flight was now boarding. The passengers rose automatically and began to form a long line. At last, I was dragging myself and Parissa up the steps of the aircraft and inside. The plane took off, and I lost consciousness.

Just before landing in London, where we had to change aeroplanes for Amsterdam, I came to. The passenger sitting next to me left her seat and, shortly afterwards, returned with a hostess. They began fussing around me. When I became fully aware of my whereabouts I told the hostess I felt very ill and wished to disembark in London. Both my child and I had valid British visas, I explained. She replied that, because my ticket was for Amsterdam, I was not allowed to disembark in London. However, she said, they would take me to the sick-room at London Airport and I would be able to stay there until I felt fit enough to fly to Holland.

After we had landed at Heathrow, a wheelchair was brought for me and an orderly took me and my daughter to the airport's clinic. I asked the matron who was attending to me to call my brother and inform him of my whereabouts and to let my husband at Amsterdam Airport know of our delay. I gave her Mahmoud's telephone number and Mehdi's full name. She assured me that she would let them all know where I was, and then she gave me an injection.

I woke up at around ten thirty in the evening, feeling better. The matron returned and asked me if I felt well enough to take the last flight to Amsterdam, at 12 midnight. I gazed at Parissa lying next to me on the narrow clinic bed, fast sleep, thanked the matron and told her that I felt able to travel.

Another wheelchair was brought and we were taken to the appropriate aircraft.

When we landed in Amsterdam and the door of the aeroplane opened, an airport official entered, calling my name. I almost had a heart attack, believing that the arm of the revolution had stretched this far to grab me. Fearful, I decided to keep quiet. He called my name again and a hostess led him to where I was sitting. I was trembling again and everything was starting to go round and round. The man asked me how I was. I was surprised. How did he know I was sick?

"I feel better, thank you."

"You have a husband who loves you very much Madam," he said.

How did he know I was married? He took hold of Parissa's hand and told me to get up and follow him. The rest of the passengers were standing up, preparing to leave the aircraft. I had to follow him quickly, otherwise we would be hemmed in. I collected my hand luggage, handed it to him, walked the distance to the door of the aircraft, then sank into the wheelchair which had been brought for me. The official pushed me through to the lounge, where Mehdi and Betsabeh were waiting for us. Betsabeh was the first to see us. Excitedly, she pointed in our direction and they both ran towards us.

Why were they weeping, and why had this man come to fetch us? Nothing made sense anymore. Reunited, we flung our arms around each other, but I was too sick to feel excited.

The mystery of the strange man on the airplane was soon solved as Mehdi revealed what had happened. Many hours ago, he and Betsabeh had been waiting for us in the arrivals lounge at the time that our original flight was due to arrive. He had spotted our suitcases, but waited in vain for us to appear. Worried, he had contacted British Airways staff seeking information about his two missing travellers. They had gone through the passenger list but had been unable to find our names on it; they had then called London Airport, but had not been able to discover anything about our whereabouts. No one seemed to know what had happened to us between Iran and Holland. To assist Mehdi, British Airways had put an international telephone line at his disposal.

After waiting for three hours, and not finding us on any of three other flights from London, Mehdi had called Mahmoud, then Ellahe. She had told him that they had left me at the airport and seen me head towards the passport section. But that was all she could tell him.

For six hours, we had been lost to all! My family had assumed that I had been taken to Evin.

Finally, the London police, who had been contacted by Mahmoud, informed him that they had succeeded in locating us at the Heathrow clinic. This news had instantly been communicated to Mehdi and, eventually, our names had appeared on the passenger list of an incoming airplane. When it landed, the relieved British Airway official who had been helping Mehdi had boarded the aircraft to collect us. It seemed that the matron at Heathrow had called neither Mahmoud, nor Amsterdam Airport.

Happy to be together again, we drove to the hotel where Mehdi and Betsabeh had been staying. I still felt dreadful and Mehdi immediately arranged for a doctor to visit me. His examination revealed that I had suffered a nervous breakdown. I was kept under sedation for two days, after which we were due to leave for London. Our last worry was whether or not the British officials would let us in. What if they refused? We would have to return to Iran. But to where in Iran?

The flight to England was smooth and the children were very excited, but Mehdi and I were grave and silent. No one must guess at the anxiety and fear which burned inside us. That would give rise to suspicion.

Very composed, we joined the queue for passport check. When our turn came, the officer inundated us with questions, then ordered us to follow the man who was standing next to him. Our visas, it seemed, had to be approved by a higher authority. Alarmed, we followed the second man to a corner where he asked us to sit and wait. We obeyed and waited for a long time, not daring to speak. Finally, he reappeared with our passports which bore a three months' permit to stay.

Again I reflected on the days of the Shah, when the polite questions: "How much money are you going to spend on this trip, Madam?" and, "How long do you wish to stay in London?" guaranteed a six month permit.

But it did not matter. Nothing mattered anymore except being together and being safe. Nothing mattered but the nebulous dream of being able to live without fear; of once again being able to tuck one's children into bed at night, knowing the dawn would come without incident; of being able to walk hand in hand with one's husband through the streets; of having a garden again.
The war with Iraq broke out a few weeks later.

Chapter 17

Pushing the heavy trolleys packed with our remaining belongings, we entered the arrival zone. My father, hunch-backed and pale, standing between his sons was waiting for us. The three looked drawn with faces furrowed by anxiety. My father's handsome face lit brightly when he saw us. I released the trolley handle and ran to hug him. We kissed, embraced, kissed again and out of joy cried – all of us – even my brothers. In the car Mahmoud told us of how worried they had been about the fact that we might not be granted an entry visa to England. Therefore, both he and Masoud had brought with them their passports and bank documents in case we needed their assistance. Apparently, recently a number of Iranian families with legitimate visas had been denied entry to the UK!

At home Maman, Mahtab, Amir Khosro, Keyvan and Niloofar greeted us with joyous excitement. Maman had not changed at all. Her energy was intact, her spirit high and her twinkling eyes bright with happiness. All that mattered to her in the world was to be with her children and now she had them all under her roof.

It had been many years since all of us were together. Those wonderful, wonderful years, when we were neighbours at Avenue Ehteshamieh had passed swiftly. Five generations of us had lived there in perfect harmony. What unappreciated privilege! And now, we were mostly dispersed to corners none of us ever imagined.

Gathered in my Mother's elegant cosy lounge Mehdi and I were engulfed in a warm sense of security. Sinking deep in the feathered cushions of the large sofa we provided answers, unfortunately, none pleasing, to the multitude of questions thrown at each of us. Maman wanted to know if her Dutch tenant, who was responsible for our visas for Holland, could remain in Iran; Masoud was anxious to know if the Komiteh had as yet found out that he was an absentee landlord. Instead of selling his house when he left Iran Masoud had rented it – an unfortunate mistake it seemed now. Agha joon was sitting next to me, holding my hand tightly, remaining silent. He did not dare to ask and I did not dare to tell him that both his hotels and his unfinished apartment block were confiscated. Questions went on: about people, places, trials and executions – matters that none of us could have ever dreamed of happening in Iran.

My Mother had made meticulous arrangements for our stay at 10 Rutland Gate. Two of the three bedrooms on the ground floor and a bathroom were allocated to us. The third bedroom, my parents' own, opened onto a paved landscaped courtyard that boasted of a small pool, a gigantic magnolia tree and many smaller trees, shrubs and flowers; none in bloom except the roses. Maman loved gardening. From the entrance hall a winding staircase led to the levels above. The main attraction of the second floor was the lounge with its corniced high ceiling from which a dainty chandelier hung. On one wall, above a neatly designed wooden framed fireplace, stood an ornamental Victorian mirror that reflected an oil portrait of Nasser Al-Din Shah, hung on the opposite wall. The room was airy with light pouring through from the two large French windows that opened onto a balcony facing the garden and the park beyond. The adjoining dining room led into a well-equipped kitchen. Mahmoud's bachelor quarter was on the storey above. When renovating the house my father had turned the rest of the two top floors and the basement into two independent apartments, the rental income of which was now taking care of the household expenses. Agha joon had also had the most efficient elevator installed for my mother. Her arthritic limbs were giving her much pain. My parents were grateful that fate had spared them this one last asset. So they took care of it with much attention.

After lunch, exhausted by the tension at the airport and the excitement of reunion I went to my room to rest. But Mehdi and the children, accompanied by their playful cousins rushed out to breathe the fresh air of freedom and explore the streets without fear.

The next day, rejuvenated by a long rest; happy to be alive, with my family and in London, I rose very early. The sound of my movement woke my husband up. Cheerful, he too climbed out of the bed. We had a light breakfast and then went for a walk around the Serpentine. For a little while we just enjoyed the freshness of the early morning breeze. I felt as though the world was smiling at me. Everything looked lovely, soothing and welcoming. The ducks, the swans, the tiny birds and the few joggers exuded peace, freedom, a desire to live and let live. Exalted I started in my usual monolithic matter-of-fact way to plan aloud. It was already late July and the schools would start in September. We could not enrol the children in a state school therefore we had to search for a private one. This meant high tuition fees. Our two thousand pounds wasn't adequate which meant I had to sell my jewels. Turning to my husband I asked for his opinion. While I had been talking he had remained silent. I had taken his stillness for contemplation. But looking at him I realized he had been crying. Surprised, I stopped walking; gently grabbed his soft hand, looked into his kind eyes that were wet and asked: "Mehdi joon what is wrong?"

He pulled a neatly folded, white handkerchief out of the pocket of his navy tracksuit pants, wiped his eyes, blew his Roman nose and without uttering a word he tightened his grip on my hand and pulled me towards a bench, moist with dew, that faced the lake. We sat there. Suddenly I felt cold. A bird's abrupt chirp broke the sad stillness. The sun caught a hazel gleam in Mehdi's brown eyes and I was puzzled. Then his gaze became intent with deliberation. Many tormented lines appeared on his broad forehead and I heard the most touching words a wife could ever hear: "Lily joon, you know that I have no material possessions in this world to throw at your feet. All I can offer you is myself and my love." He stopped, swallowed the lump in his throat and then in a voice turned husky, continued: "I am afraid it may not be enough for you!"

My chin dropped, anxiety hit again. I felt colder and then I began to laugh hysterically at the absurdity of his utterance. How dared he doubt my devotion to him? Among the many rich and famous who had courted me I had chosen him, a student with a future uncertain, as tomorrow is for each of us, simply because in my heart I had felt he was a good man, a man who would stand by me, as I would by him – through heaven and hell. The heaven had passed and now the challenge of being decent had started.

To show him that I loved him for himself and not anything that he could throw at my feet, I took his handsome, tanned, tormented face between my cold hands and kissed every chiselled feature on it. Then I rested my head on his drooping shoulder, inhaled his delicious familiar odour and whispered: "I am the luckiest woman on earth. Our love means more to me than the entire treasures of Solomon. The future is ours to make." I stopped, took a fresh breath, kissed him again and continued,

"Once I heard someone say 'knock at every door, somewhere a window might open'. Together we will knock at all doors and if none opens, I'll kick one open!"

My last statement sounded so silly that we both started to laugh.

When we rose to return home the sun had already spread its golden wings over the tranquil lake, promising a warm day. The early morning dew had melted and the grass felt moist under our feet. On the lake, the rowing boats, firmly tied to their posts, calmly floated on their spots and I noticed a company of ducks, including a couple of swans gliding towards a passer-by who was throwing crumbs on the water for them. "If God provides his birds with daily nutrition he will also provide for us!" I surmised with hope.

Inside the house we found my parents sitting at the dining table having breakfast and listening to Parissa's chit chat which was frequently interrupted by Betsabeh. It seemed my girls were competing for their grandparents' attention. Father's joviality expressed his pleasure in being with them. Sitting between the two, he took turns in tickling each one in the hollow of their waist and sharing in their giggles. Mother was busy eating her usual Lebanese bread rolled around a piece of feta cheese and a slice of cucumber. As she saw us enter a broad smile lit her aristocratic face that always bore an expression of absolute authority. We sat around the table and began discussing the children's school. Soon we were joined by Mahmoud in his blue towelling robe holding a mug of coffee. Although he had lost the freshness of youth he looked handsome with his teasing eyes, delicate nose and an everlasting grin. Involving himself in our conversation he suggested we should approach Francis Holland and Hampshire schools, both within our walking distance, each apparently with a two-year waiting list. My generous father, aware of our financial situation, offered to pay for the tuition. Only I noticed the rush of blood to my husband's strained countenance. At this late stage writing to these establishments would have been futile. Therefore, Mahmoud suggested we should walk to the schools and see if we could meet with their headmistresses. A face to face contact could act in our favour. To this end Mehdi and I dressed formally and, arm in arm walked to the schools. Reaching the building of the first, we rang the bell and waited patiently until an elderly lady opened the door. I politely asked whether we could see the Headmistress. The old lady enquired about the nature of our business. I told her. The wrinkled face brightened with a shadow of a smile – probably at our ignorance of how the English private school system operated. She asked us to write down our name and telephone number so that she could call us after having discussed the matter with the headmistress, due at work the following week. Mehdi took a card out of his wallet, a pen from his coat pocket and obliged her request. We both thanked her and left for the second school which was off Ennismore Gardens.

No one was at the second school. Since it was lunchtime, we returned home, where, to my delight, we found my cousin, Afsaneh and Tooradj deep in conversation with my parents. We hugged, kissed, laughed and sat down to lunch. Out of curiosity, I scrutinized their every move; their appearance, their postures, their words. I noticed that they wore elegant clothes, joked and moved with the relaxed confidence of the well-off.

Thank God! Hard times for them seemed to be over, I thought.

A year had given Afsaneh time to come to terms with her tragic losses. Yoga, meditation, physical activity and incredible self-discipline had helped to regain her love of life.

I was dying to hear how they had managed to leave Iran without a passport. As soon as we finished eating I asked her if she would like to take a walk with me around Knightsbridge. A sports freak, her large black eyes sparkled with pleasure and her thin lips bloomed into a sweet smile of agreement.

Walking towards Brompton Road she told me how they had escaped Iran on horseback with their two little sons fastened to their backs. Smugglers had guided them through the dangerous mule paths that wiggled through the mountains to the Turkish border. Twice they were almost caught by the revolutionary guards – each time a miracle had saved them.

My cousin finished her incredible tale with a bright smile. Afsaneh always smiled at life, for perhaps somehow, in the depth of her consciousness, she knew that hers was not to be a long one. My brave cousin, full of life and energy left us all heartbroken when she lost her brave battle against cancer fifteen years later – at the age of forty eight.

Now in the year 2008 her son Ali is a successful investment banker and Amir works for his father.

Tooradj remarried.

Khalleh Victor lives between France and England, where

Masoumeh, her younger daughter is one of the most successful investment bankers of the City. Masoumeh, after the execution of her father, worked to put herself through two degrees at two Ivy League universities in the United States and climbed the ladder of success through sheer hard work, prudence and love of life. She is married to a Gajar cousin, Ardavan Farmanfarmaian, and has two gorgeous sons. Time was racing ahead and, fortunately we were able to get Betsabeh into Francis Holland and Parissa to Hampshire School, which was very near Rutland Gate. This delighted my father as he could take her to school and collect her in the afternoons.

Betsabeh was my mother's favourite. Every afternoon Mother, with a plate of pastry, waited for her to come so that together they would take their tea in front of the TV watching my mother's favourite serial, *Dynasty*. Betsabeh was her patient interpreter. After her snack, my daughter usually retired to the solitude of her room to study and then get ready for her lessons in the Persian language. We were determined to teach both girls good Farsi.

The Iranian community in London was on the increase with the men, from different walks of life, searching for work – a futile endeavour on visitors' visas! Those with money and without permanent residency, hoping for indications of weakness in the hold of the Islamic Republic, spent their days paging the newspapers for news on Iran. Then, disappointed, they would study the interest and exchange rates of different currencies for the most lucrative investment of their capital. Many, whose passports had not been renewed by the Iranian Embassy or those who had fled the country, had to apply for refugee statuses. Thus, while the men we knew tried to find an answer to the riddle of their lives, their wives, not yet quite hit by the reality of their unenviable situation, were involved in lunching out, playing cards and a handful of those with education and a bit of brain were trying to find a job. I even applied for a sales assistant at Harrods only to be rejected. On visitors' visas all doors were closed.

One afternoon when I had returned from my walk around the Serpentine, I found Ahmad Ansari, a friend and cousin of the Empress, having tea with Mehdi. I was pleased to see him. In Iran we had shared many pleasant evenings. After the tragic death of the Shah, Farah had chosen Ahmad to take care of her family's finances. Eventually our light conversation turned lamentable when our friend began his tale of the Shah's last days in exile which were inundated with humiliation and betrayals. The family had left Iran for Egypt and then Morocco where, unlike President Sadat, King Hassan II had not been so welcoming. The Shah had made the mistake of lingering too long in Marakesh, letting the political situation force the States to close its doors to him. Upon application, none of the countries of the Shah's choice, even those in which he owned homes' accepted him. Meanwhile, Princess Ashraf, living in New York, appealed to David Rockefeller and Henry Kissinger, both genuine friends of her brother. Eventually these two men found the Shah a temporary haven in the Bahamas. It was in the Bahamas that the Shah began to feel ill. The Empress summoned the Shah's French doctor Flandrin who arrived soon after to treat his patient.

The nature of the Shah's illness was discovered in 1974 by Professor Jean Bernard and Dr George Flandrin. He had leukaemia in its early stages. The French doctors were asked by the Shah's physician, Doctor Ayadi to keep the patient in the dark. So the Shah was told that he was suffering from a blood complaint called Waldenstrom's disease. The Empress was informed only in 1977. Even she kept it a secret from her husband.

In the Bahamas, Flandrin examined the Shah and explained to him that his condition had turned acute, needing a course of intensive chemotherapy. As the Bahamas was a temporary refuge, the royals were sent to Mexico where the Shah's health deteriorated further. The State Department was informed of the seriousness of the Shah's condition: malignant lymphoma compounded by a possible internal blockage which had resulted in severe jaundice. It took the State Department four days to allow the Shah entrance to the US, and not before having discussed the matter with Prime Minister Bazargan and Foreign Minister Yazdi who, for the first time, heard of the Shah's cancer. They warned Washington against public reaction towards the Shah's entrance to the US indicating that Iranians would never believe the cancer story and would think a conspiracy against the revolution was in progress.

On October 23rd the Shah was admitted to New York hospital – Cornell Medical Center under the name of David Newsome. Further tests revealed a more serious cancer than had originally been treated. A medical press release stressed the serious condition of the Shah's health, emphasizing his need for expert medical care. Outside the hospital demonstrators were shouting "Death to the Shah". Among the Iranians the rumour had it that the Americans wanted the Shah dead.

A vicious circle of mishaps orchestrated against the Shah's recovery and his condition worsened daily. The best facilities for an effective treatment were across the street in the Memorial Sloan-Kettering Cancer Center where the Shah should have been taken from the start. Dr Kean, assigned to the care of the Shah, having discussed the treatment with the doctors at the centre found that some of the surgeons were hostile towards the Shah and didn't want to treat him. Security was also a major concern. The patient had to be wheeled through the underground connecting tunnel at night for treatment. Although this embarrassing routine was exhausting, the Shah's condition responded favourably to the new treatment and he grew stronger until on November 4th, the students invaded the US Embassy in Teheran and took the hostages. In the States, public shock over the seizure of the embassy gave way to anger and the Shah's presence in the country was blamed for the tragedy. The Shah himself understood the gravity of the situation but he couldn't be moved while suffering from pneumonia and waiting to have the last essential operation.

In Iran the "students of the Immam's line", the occupiers of the Embassy, were demanding the Shah's extradition and Abolhassan Bani-Sadr, the acting Foreign Minister, was threatening to withdraw all Iran's assets from American banks. Carter responded by announcing that he would not extradite the Shah.

By the end of November the Shah, feeling better, was able to return to Mexico. Mexico refused to take him back. Heavily guarded, the Shah was smuggled out of the hospital and flown to the security of Lackland Air Force Base in Texas. As time passed and the hostage crisis lingered on, Carter longed to get rid of his burden. The opportunity presented itself in an invitation by General Omar Torrijos, the dictator of Panama. Once Jimmy Carter was sure that Torrijo's invitation was firm he sent his chief of staff, Hamilton Jordan, to Lackland to break the news to the Shah.

A day after their arrival at Contadora Island, Torrijos paid His Majesty a visit. Upon meeting the Empress the general became smitten by her beauty. The commander of the National Guard, Colonel Manuel Antonio Noriega; head of the army intelligence connected both with CIA and the Cuban intelligence, as well as money launderers and drug smugglers, was charged with the security of the Iranian royal family. As the Shah's new location became known to the world, tension grew even in Panama. In Iran Sadegh Ghotbzadeh, the new Foreign

Minister, began trying to use law to secure the Shah's extradition. Iran had no embassy in Panama, so just before Christmas 1979, Ghotbzadeh sent two odd intermediaries; a left wing French lawyer Christian Bourguet and an Argentinian adventurer, Hector Villalon to meet with Panamanian President Royo and Marcel Salamin, one of Torrijos' political councillors. Their mission was to persuade the Panamanians to extradite the Shah and secure the release of the hostages. Panama had no treaty of extradition with Iran. However, it had its own extradition law which required the Iranians to put down their complaint, enumerate the actual crimes for which the Shah was to be extradited, present the witnesses and the evidence with written indictments and have all these filed with the Panamanian foreign ministry.

As 1979 turned to 1980, the hostage crisis remained unresolved, the Soviet Union invaded Afghanistan and a Panamanian emissary flew to Teheran to help Ghotbzadeh to prepare the extradition papers, tailor-made to the Panamanian requirements. Hamilton Jordan in Washington was contacted and warned not to inform the Kissinger/Rockefeller controlled State Department of the progress being made in regard to the fate of the hostages. Jordan, believing that a solution was in hand, remained secretive. Communications and meetings between the representatives of Ghotbzadeh, Panama and Carter continued until after a fresh trip from Teheran, Bourguet and Villalon met Jordan and confirmed the only solution to the hostage problem was the Shah's extradition or his death.

The rumours of the extradition conspiracy had already reached His Majesty. Naturally he was most concerned. On January 23rd, 1980 the Foreign Ministry in Teheran announced that the Shah had been arrested in Panama pending extradition. This news was released to the media by Ghotbzadeh who, in order to buy himself votes in his campaign for the Iranian presidency, during a telephone conversation had persuaded President Royo to acknowledge that the Shah was "under the surveillance" of the Panamanian authorities, a case already in existence. At the White House, immediately upon hearing the news, an astonished Hamilton Jordan called Panama. Torrijos issued a statement to the contrary.

At the beginning of February, the Shah's condition was aggravated by a respiratory infection making surgery imminent. Meanwhile, an exasperated Empress was on the phone to her friend, Jahan Sadat, voicing her fear for her husband's condition and their safety. Mrs Sadat invited them to return to Egypt where the Shah could have his operation.

On March 20th, Bourguet arrived with all the necessary documents needed to file Iran's extradition request with the Panamanian Foreign Ministry. Under Panamanian law the papers had to be filed within sixty days of the original extradition request, making Monday March 24th the deadline. However, the papers had to be presented by an Iranian and Bourguet was not Iranian. The Iranian agent was to arrive on the 24th. Hamilton Jordan, fully aware of the meeting, informed Carter. Washington was against the Shah's trip to Egypt – the royals were determined to go. On March 22nd a Saturday, Jimmy Carter called Sadat to tell him of his vexation over the Shah's possible arrival in Egypt. Sadat ignored the American President's concern and reassured him that he was capable of taking care of his friend. On the 23rd the Shah's party flew out of Panama, while Hector Villalon in Iran was on the phone to the Panamanians, asking them to hold on to the Shah until the hostages were taken from the Embassy to the custody of the Iranian government. Jordan called the Defence Secretary, Harold Brown, in Washington informing him of the Shah's flight, and requesting that their plane be held in the Azores until the Iranian problem was resolved. The plane landed in the Azores for refuelling. While the Shah was fighting a very high fever, the take-off was delayed for two hours. To the conspirator's mortification the militant "students of the Immam's line" did not relinquish the hostages. Receiving the news, an infuriated Torrijos called Jordan and told him the charade was over. Only then did Jordan order the Shah's plane to be released from the Azores.

The royals were received warmly by the Sadats. On 26th March the American medical team arrived to perform the long overdue operation. Ten days after the surgery the Shah left the hospital for the Kobbeh Palace where the couple lived in pleasantly tranquil, blissfully cordial surroundings. On July 26th, as a result of a new infection the Shah's temperature soared. He began to haemorrhage badly and went into shock. While in hospital, his children, princess Ashraf, Zahedi and a few family members who had remained loyal, visited him. Finally, just before 10 in the morning on July 27th, 1980, he died to be buried in a land not his own. A simple tomb in el-Rifa'i Mosque is all that stands in remembrance of Mohammad Reza Shah Pahlavi.

Both Mehdi and I were crying at the time, when our friend finished his tale. Only thinking of the good times – when we all had loved and respected the Shah.

> Farewell, King!
> Cover your heads, and mock not flesh and blood
> With solemn reverence; throw away respect,
> Tradition, form, and ceremonious duty;
> For you have but mistook me all this while.
> I live with bread like you, feel want,
> Taste grief, need friends; subjected thus,
> How can you say to me I am a king?
> Shakespeares' Richard ll.

Was the last Shah of Iran a true patriot or a coward? Only God would know.

Chapter 18

The sun had retired beyond the greying horizon. The crescent of a pale moon was waving on the calm waters of the Serpentine and a cool breeze teased my long hair away. Hand in hand, we were strolling by the lake each deep in thought. An Iranian academic at the University of Kent had helped Mehdi to get a visiting scholar's position without pay until he was able to acquire a work permit. At the same time another friend, an executive director of an American bank in the United States, had offered him a position in their foreign exchange department. Here similarly, payment of salary depended on acquisition of a work permit. After careful consideration Mehdi had accepted both offers hoping that our lawyer could succeed in procuring for us a work permit and if not, doing something useful would be better than promenading up and down Knightsbridge. Both of us knew that we could not live with my parents forever, and we had to do something about our situation – but what?

Back at home, I found my brothers and father in deep discussion over the length of time it would take President Saddam Hussain to rid Iran of the present regime.

The land frontier between Iran and Iraq is a dividing line that erratically wiggles down from the barren mountain ranges of northern Kurdistan to the dusty desert of the oil-rich Khosestan, separating the ancient Mesopotamian plain from the Persian plateau. The war between Iraq and Iran erupted theoretically over rights to the Shatt al-Arab, the 120-mile frontier waterway where the Euphrates, the Tigris both in Iraq and the Karun in Iran, merge flowing into the Persian Gulf. Nearby are located Iraq's main commercial oil terminals around Basra, also Iran's major port and refinery facilities, at Khorramshahr and Abadan. This waterway is Iraq's only outlet to the Gulf sea-lanes. Iran needs the estuary to export oil from its Abadan refinery; one of the largest in the world. Because of the rivers that flow into the Shatt, both Iran and Iraq have claims to the right of its usage.

After the collapse of the Ottoman Empire, when Iraq first became a nation, Baghdad claimed that it had inherited the Ottoman's sovereignty, hence control over the estuary. In 1937, a treaty signed by Reza Shah granted Iraq the control. In 1968, the socialist Baath Party seized power. The new regime tried to charge Iranian ships for its use. The Shah Mohammad Reza refused to pay and repudiated the 1937 agreement. Sporadic frontier tension broiled until 1975. Prior to this date, the Shah had been assisting the rebellious Iraqi Kurds in their fight for independence. It was to terminate this Iranian aid which perpetuated the Kurdish menace at his border that Saddam Hussain, then the deputy chairman of Iraq's Revolutionary Council, signed the agreement of 1975. This treaty corrected the previous one-sided Iraqi arrangement by recognizing the thalweg, or median line of the deepest channel, as the frontier between the two countries. In exchange, the Shah agreed to make some land frontier changes in Iraq's favour, plus dropping his assistance to Iraq's Kurdish rebellion. Saddam, perceiving this treaty as a strategic setback, aimed one day to correct it. The chance presented itself when the Shah left Iran. On September 17th, after weeks of clashes between Iranian and Iraqi forces along the border Saddam with the permission of the United States abrogated the treaty. On 22nd September, from the air, Iraq struck at Iranian oilfields and bombed targets allocated by US satellites, deep inside Iran. On the land Iraqi guns shelled Iranian cities and their troops invaded Iran at several points in the southern end of the vast border. Saddam used chemical weapons purchased from Europe and the United States to use on Iranians and his own Kurds. Among Baghdad's conditions for peace were demands for an Iranian recognition of Iraqi claims to the entire Shatt al-Arab waterway, and the return of the three small Gulf islands occupied by Iran in 1971.

It was the knowledge of this invasion which had impelled the US Embassy in Iran to advise its citizens to evacuate the country. Listening to the war talk of my family, I became confused about America's foreign policy in the Middle East. Why help one dictator and not the other? If they wanted to crush Khomeini why initially did they not help the Shah to defeat him? Or was their support of Iraq to avenge the Islamic militants' hostage taking? Or had the resurgence of Shi'ism become a threat to the West and its allies in the Middle East? In this spirit Saddam Hussain was justified in feeling threatened by the Iranian Revolution, considering it as a destabilizing force in the region and in

Iraq itself which has a large Shi'a population. These people were thrilled by the success of Khomeini. Many had been acquainted with his thesis. As early as the 1930s the focus of Khomeini's sermons was the nature of society. He believed no new society could be created in a vacuum without a true understanding and appreciation of its past. He stressed that in Iran neither the influences of a 25-century-old culture nor of Islam, the dominant religion for thirteen centuries could simply be wiped out by modern reforms. Therefore to succeed, reforms had to take into consideration all social, cultural and religious values of the community they were to serve.

Khomeini perceived faith to be a form of belief that compels man to action. Furthermore he emphasized that it was the religious duty of the individual to seek the rectifications of contemporary political and social problems at any cost. His obsession, throughout his life, was the survival of Islam not merely as a religion but as an all encompassing way of life – a way of life that existed thirteen centuries ago. In his eyes man's evil acts were the bitter fruits of estrangement from Islamic values – values interpreted from the Koran by the Ayatollahs. Khomeini fully understood and utilized the qualities unique to Shi'ism that provided means to counterattack social injustice. Notable among these idiosyncrasies were first the mobilizing power of the mullahs, and second, Shi'ism, an idiom of social protest, standing for fight against injustice. He consistently argued that whatever the cost, the clergy should stand up and fight against injustice represented by the Pahlavi dynasty and their modernizing reforms. Moreover he believed that religion should direct the life of the individual, the community and the state, not only in Iran but in the entire Islamic world. For him the individual had no choice but to follow blindly dogmas interpreted by the clergy. The freedom to choose is one of the bases of human dignity. Somehow in his one-dimensional view of Islam he had forgotten that the essence of the message of our Messenger, Mohammad, was to guide the non-believers to the path of pure monotheism that leads to the acquisition of human dignity by having a one-to-one relationship with the Creator out of an intellectual choice – a choice based on understanding and love. Therefore, it is not surprising that Saddam Hussain, aided by the men in Washington, who probably had by now wised up to their gross mistake in supporting Khomeini to power, hoped to crush this all-expanding ambition – indeed a serious international threat.

"Enshallah, Saddam will defeat the mullahs and open the door for us to return home," Mother proclaimed loudly. She hated politics.

I didn't agree with her wishful thinking of a Saddam victory. During the course of history Iranians had proved their strong sense of patriotism. I thought, regardless of Iran's impaired defensive power the Iranians would unite against the aggressor and offer his forces a prohibitive challenge. Unfortunately, I thought this war would strengthen the hold of the revolutionaries on Iran because it would divert attention from the executions and purges that were plaguing the people. In the end Iran would survive – I surmised and joined my mother in leaving the room to the men.

Uneventful days crawled away during which my mind hunted for something to do which would keep me constructively occupied, as well as provide me with an income that would minimize our dependency on my parents. I had no work permit so whatever venture I delved into had to be cash orientated. My acquaintances continued with their parties. One service they all missed was that of a cook, since none of them as yet had acquired the skill. So catering was much in demand. But I was no caterer myself. However, I was a keen learner, especially in times of need. I shared my thought with Mehdi, who at first laughed at my joke, then when I told him no honourable work was below my dignity he took me seriously.

The proper course of action was to enrol in a cooking course which was very expensive. Then one day, I thought of my Pakistani friend and neighbour Marzieh, an excellent cook with a lot of spare time. Her children were at boarding school and her husband in Pakistan living with his other wives. Fortunately, she did not need much persuading. She had a large kitchen; we could cook there and have the food delivered by her student sister who owned an old Mini-Minor. To my delight, Marzieh volunteered to teach me both Indian and Persian cooking.

For one month, every morning at nine o'clock I walked to her apartment where we peeled, chopped, fried, burnt, swore, tried again, tasted, hated, loved and eventually became proud of our skills. Our trial dishes were distributed among our families and wealthy friends who resided in the neighbourhood. This sly, marketing ploy proved lucrative.

In the evenings, my family looked forward to the arrival of my clattering cardboard box filled with culinary treasures. None of them minded that my hair smelled of fenugreek, my hands of onion and my outfit of curry. Mother was pleased she didn't have to cook the dinner. Father and the children loved our pastries and Mehdi enjoyed seeing me occupied. Soon our business picked up. But the success was short-lived. Marzieh's husband died and she had to go to Karachi. I became frustrated and realized that we could no longer waste our lives in England.

As the rule of the Ayatollahs became more established, the fragile sense of security our togetherness had created turned into a dreadful fear of the unknown which manifested itself in irritability and irrational behaviour. Maman's frugality intensified. Agha joon, by acknowledging the "temporariness of it all" plunged into what gave him most pleasure – spoiling Parissa, who was being punished by the older children, for every indulgence bestowed upon her. It got to a point that I had to forbid my father from paying so much attention to her. Angry, I told him if he bought anything for her, he had to buy the same for all the other children, otherwise I would collect Parissa from school myself. The threat worked and peace was restored amongst our boisterous children, who were wonderfully happy together.

Mehdi remained himself – patient and smiling. I sometimes felt that I really did not know my husband. How could he be so calm under our dire situation while I was having nightmares and was on the verge of another nervous breakdown?

One cold and gloomy morning, I was walking by the lake – alone and forlorn, and I noticed a company of pigeons actively searching for morsels. Then an old man arrived with a plastic bag full of stale bread. He made himself comfortable on the nearby bench, and began crumbling the bread pieces and throwing them to the pigeons. I did not have to contemplate deep. I, again, saw the hand of God at work. Smiling and hopeful, I fastened my pace and returned home a new person.

Our little garden was white, with snow and shimmering droplets of melted ice were bouncing down the scruffy trunk of our giant magnolia tree. A robin, undisturbed by the commotion around it, hunching on a Camellia tree branch, twittered to the brightness of the day and full of joy our children played with snowballs. Exhilarated by fresh air they shouted, laughed, wrestled, slipped, rose again and threw their snowballs at each other. Watching them from the window of the sitting room I wondered at the kind of adults they would grow to become. They were so different in character. Betsabeh, tall, slender and wise always acted as the leader. She was bright, beautiful and athletic. She was obstinate, headstrong and aloof. Parissa was also beautiful but her beauty was more subtle than Betsabeh's. Unlike her sister, she was extremely sociable and shrewd. Amir Khosrow was a devil. Handsome, hyperactive and kind he could never take no for an answer. He was very bright but to his father's disappointment did not apply himself to any kind of academic learning. However, he was very good with his hands and at that young age he could repair household appliances better than his elders. Keyvan was so adorable that nothing he did was ever wrong. Like Parissa he was also the recipient of Amir's frequent punches and kicks. Nilofar was timid, smiling and happy to be with her cousins at Rutland Gate. Sarah, Masoud's youngest, was still a baby. Mahtab had brought their nanny Mariam to England and Sarah spent most of her time on Mariam's lap watching the others.

Standing by that window looking out I was just praying for our children to find stability in their lives. Behind me on the coach my husband was sitting toying with his tea cup. The usual smile was missing from his tranquil face. Something must be worrying him, I concluded. But I could not ask him what it was. In his own good time he would tell me.

"Lily, I want to talk to you." I heard him say. I turned, and smiled at him.

"Let's go for a walk around the lake."

"I have just returned from my walk and it is bitterly cold outside."

"Okay, then let's go to our room." Something must be worrying him, I thought.

Together, we descended the stairs to our bedroom. I dropped on my bed and he took a chair.

"The lawyer called to say that our application has been rejected. Without a work permit I can't earn and I cannot live in your parents' house anymore. I must return to Iran. You and the children either come with me or stay here – the choice is yours."

"Don't be silly, Mehdi. You cannot return to Iran. They will throw you into jail or kill you. Besides we have not exhausted our options yet."

"What options? We have no other options."

"Yes we do. We can apply for an emigrant visa for Canada or Australia."

"What are we going to do there without knowing anyone or

anything about these countries?"

"Tomorrow we will go to both embassies, and gather information."

Mehdi thought for a while and then nodded his balding head in agreement. Suddenly there was a knock on the opening door and my father stepped in with a letter in hand. He waved the envelope at me and said: "This is for you, Lily. Your mother is serving lunch and wants you down before the rice gets cold." I rose from my bed, took the letter and we went down to the dining room where Maman was filling her plate with rice and Khoresht [137].

Carelessly, I tore the envelope open and took the letter out. It was a bank statement. I put it by my plate and waited until my mother served me. Her cooking was excellent. When finished eating, I took the statement up and began to check the figures. For a while I kept on staring at what danced in my sight. I checked the name on the statement again and again. My name was correctly spelled. I looked at the figures again. Father noticed the rush of blood to my face. Concerned he asked for the cause. I showed him the letter and pointing to the figure I exclaimed: "See this figure! A credit of one hundred and fifty thousand pounds has been made to my account. The bank has made a gross error."

Agha joon adjusted his spectacles, gazed at the statement, did not understand a word, passed the paper to Mehdi who immediately saw what I had seen and whistled his surprise. Father jumped from his seat and, heading for the door ordered: "Let's go and see what Mahmoud thinks!" Bewildered we followed him to my brother's bedroom. Resting in bed Mahmoud was watching Arsenal play against Chelsea.

Mehdi gave him the letter and teased: "Lady Luck has come to your sister!"

Disturbed by our intrusion, anxious to get rid of us, he grabbed the statement, quickly read the content, threw it at me and said: "Run to the bank and have the statement checked by the manager."

I hastely picked up the letter and left the room. Mehdi followed me.

On the way to the bank, one thought preoccupied my mind. It was so far-fetched that I didn't dare verbalize it. So we walked in reflective silence. At the branch I asked to see the manager and was told he was with a client. I handed the statement to the young clerk facing me and told her that because I was not expecting any funds to be deposited

---

[137] Stew.

into my account I wanted to know who had sent the money and from where it had been transferred to my account or if, in fact the bank had made a mistake. She politely took the statement, threw a glance at it, told me to wait and disappeared from our sight for a few minutes after which she returned with an additional document. She handed the paper to me. It was an inter-bank slip. The money had been sent from Kuwait, through the National Bank of Kuwait to my account. It was sent by the order of Mrs Kaman. I hardly heard the clerk say: "Mrs Monadjemi the bank does not make such mistakes." All I did was to smile at her. Words cannot describe my feelings of ecstasy. A lump tightened my throat and tears began to roll down my face. Slowly I turned to my husband. He was staring at me with eyes I never thought could be so wide with surprise.

On the way back, stunned by the incredible incident we were both speechless.

Having crossed Brompton Road I took Mehdi's arm and directed him towards Brompton Oratory and whispered: "We owe Kaman a prayer."

Inside we chose a pew and went on our knees. There, in the privacy of the empty church I let loose my happy tears that washed away the fears, anxieties, doubts and frustrations of the past few months. Yes, the provider had not forgotten his desperate pigeons.

That evening, we invited the family to dinner at our favorite restaurant. There, for the first time since our arrival in London, I ordered to my heart's desire without considering prices. At the table everybody was cheerful. Mahmoud rejoiced the fact that we could buy a flat and move out! My parents, more practical than their son, were full of suggestions about some sort of business investment that could procure for us the much-needed resident's visa. Masoud wished he had also sold his house before leaving Iran. Mehdi enjoyed being the host and I was so high that I just laughed at everything I heard or saw.

The next day, pouring over the map of the world we focused on Australia, so large and so far from all our troubles. The information we gathered hinted that Australia enjoyed a democratic political system and was happily multicultural. That suited us well. Therefore, on another pleasant sunny day, the two of us, went to the Australian High Commission where we completed the necessary emigrant visa forms and submitted them to the officer in charge. The same day we also applied for Canada. Within a month Canada rejected our applications and we forgot about Australia.

The fixed interest earnings on my deposit made such a difference in our lives that at times I thought, "why leave London." Sterling was very high against US. dollars. An adventurer by nature I dared to play the money market with success. Soon I became my father's adviser and made him money, too.

My parents, like most Iranians of their generation were finding it hard to live in a country the language of which they couldn't speak; nor could they relate to its culture. This generation of people depended totally on their children – not for financial support because they were wealthy, nor for the sake of expediency – but for the preservation of their sanity. In their children's proximity and protection, they sought compensation for the absence of the familiar; the loss of valued comradeships and the break-up of their established roots and routines. We, the younger generation of `runaways', were also suffering from similar wounds but adjustment to the change of life was not as traumatic for us, simply because we were gifted with the vitality of youth and knew the language. Of course we had our own burdens to bear. For most of us the major source of concern, besides finding employment, was the upbringing and education of our small children. Mehdi and I constantly thought about the future of our two daughters. In spite of the new financial security, deep down I was terrified of our uncertain future. So at home and in church I kept on praying and praying, until one morning I willed providence to send a postman to the door with a letter from the Australian High Commission bearing the propitious news that our applications for immigration were accepted, pending the results of an interview and a number of medical tests. Indeed, that was one of the happiest days of our lives and one of the saddest of my parents' who obstinately insisted that our decision was unnecessarily dramatic and that we couldn't survive the crudeness of a penal colony.

On the day of our appointment, full of new found confidence, clothed in our best, together with our children we proceeded to oblige destiny. Trying suavely to prove ourselves worthy of acceptance we answered diplomatically the questions asked by a friendly immigration officer; attentively watched a film on Australia and keenly learned about the virtues of our new country-to-be. After four long hours, exhausted yet happy, we left the Australian High Commission to wait for the final approval. It took a fortnight of impatient mail-checking and intensive reading about Australia, before we received a letter granting us a lease to a new life in a country that also understood suffering. From the knowledge I had gathered from my readings, I came to realize that with 40,000 years of Koori hardship and survival on the land, and only 200 years from the agonies of a penal colony, Australians had a resilience, a maverick quality about them and an unfanatical generous attitude to all. Here was real democracy. Australians were united in their sense of the dignity of individual effort, the generosity of second chances and the satirical, wise wariness of government. Deep in my heart I felt in Australia we could integrate within the larger society without being looked upon as second-class citizens. I felt as though God had granted me the salvation I had been praying for. Hopeful, I became my hyperactive self again.

My happiness was interrupted by the news from Shahjoon that the properties of all her children, down to her grandchildren, had been confiscated by the Foundation of the Disinherited, and they were all prohibited from leaving the country until proven innocent of all charges. Khalleh Nayer had been the first victim. A group of Pasdaran, holding a warrant from the Foundation had violated the privacy of her home. Ransacking the house they had confiscated her jewels and gold coins and sealed off the doors of the rooms in which the Gajar antiques her husband, Shahzadeh Farokhdolah, had inherited from his father Kamran Mirza. This meant the old couple were allowed only the use of their bedroom, kitchen and one bathroom. No one knew why the wrath of the revolution had turned to our clan. But the rumour was that someone had reported the family to the office of the Prosecutor General as 'corrupt monarchists'. In Maman's case, her rented villa in Ehteshamieh, lands in Rasht and the beach house by the Caspian were taken. If she wanted to return to Iran to clear herself from whatever crimes she was accused of, she had to be prepared to face much hardship and humiliation. The process of clarification could take years!

Sitting on his bed, Father, who always in times of crisis became philosophical tried to console Mother with finer points of existence. Yet, he, also, was tormented by the vehemence of the irrational vengeance fever which in Iran was destroying so much and so many. I became very scared for my mother. She was a tigress with a mind of her own. I knew her well enough to assume that she had already decided to return to Iran and fight the injustice of the system, if not for her own sake but for ours. We all tried to reason with her – but to no avail. She seemed to believe in the fairness of President Bani-Sader whom she intended to see if necessary – at this possibility we all laughed.

On January 25th, 1980 Abolhassan Bani-Sadr, a tall, lean figure with a neat little moustache, became the first president of the Islamic Republic of Iran. Once the presidential election was over, all political efforts were concentrated on organizing the first parliament, or Majlis. Many politicians, including candidates from the Mojahedin and the communist Tudeh Party, who had previously run for the presidency, tried again for the one-chamber legislature. Added to the contestants for parliamentary power were the members of the Islamic Republic Party (IRP), a political body of reactionaries founded by six members of the Revolutionary Council: Beheshti, Musavi-Ardabili, Hashemi-Rafsanjani, Bahonar, Khamenei and the layman Hassan Ayat. The five clerics were closely associated with Khomeini and enjoyed enormous prestige and power. All of the IRP party members were either mullahs or hardliners faithfully loyal to Khomeini, supportive of the revolutionary organizations and strongly opposed to the liberal political movements. This party had made its first impressive appearance in elections to the Assembly of Experts, a panel of seventy-three wise men representing all religious denom-inations with the exception of the Bahais. Through extensive pre-election lobbying the IRP had acquired two-third majorities in the Assembly and had set to change the content of the constitution from its original democratic secular bias to one, thoroughly Islamic. The new constitution catered for four branches of government: an executive, a legislature, a judiciary and a twelve-theologian-member Council of Guardians which had the responsibility to make certain that all legislation complied with Islamic tenets. The Council also had absolute veto power over Majlis. In the constitution leadership was invested in the person of a Faqih, a Supreme Jurisprudent, or, in the absence of such an individual, a council of between three and five "just ayatollahs". The Faqih was endowed with appointment powers over the judiciary, the military and the Council of Guardians. Enjoying an unlimited term, holding the title of commander-in-chief, his extensive powers allowed him to dismiss the president should it ever become necessary. Khomeini, familiar with Plato's Republic, had borrowed the concept of a philosopher-king, translated it into Faqih and applied it to his system of government:

"Valayat-e Faqih", led by Islamic jurists. Naturally Khomeini became the first Faqih.

Bani-Sadr's vision of a democratic system soon clashed with that of the IRP, who, by pre-polling manipulations had won almost half the seats in the Majlis. While the secular President sought experienced technocrats to manage the various sectors of government the IRP looked for devotees to the ideals of the Islamic Revolution. This internal conflict over the choice of a cabinet continued for eight months, during which the president lost his hold on the reins of power and the Majlis appointed for the office of prime minister the IRP's candidate, Mohammad Ali Raja'i, a former street vendor and school maths teacher, deeply hostile to moderate secularism. The next phase in the life of the government was regular controversy between the President who hoped to introduce law and order through reconciliatory measures, and the prime minister who sought to follow revolutionary measures – and in between the Immam's promise of a better life for the people was forgotten. Bani-Sadr intended to strengthen the military by gradually dissolving the Komitehs and curbing the prohibitive power of the Revolutionary Guards often arbitrarily used to harass and abuse those citizens "perceived" to be corrupt. He considered the State as supreme and in his optimism believed the IRP would eventually become absorbed in a democratic system. The radical mullahs wanted undivided power, and without compassion set to challenge their foe on every front.

Shortly after being appointed by the Immam, the Commander-in-Chief, Bani-Sadr set for the front where he aspired to use the war to improve his national standing. But as the war dragged on to become a stalemate the power struggle spread to military affairs. The Commander-in-Chief wanted the American-trained army to direct the war. The prime minister, apprehensive of a possible army coup against the regime supported the loyal, yet inexperienced and untrained Revolutionary Guards. Swiftly the ferocious controversy between the two men trickled down to create hostile rivalry between the military and the Revolutionary Guards.

Luckily surreptitious negotiations were already in process to release the hostages. The Shah was dead, Ronald Reagan had been elected president and in the eyes of the captors, the hostages had become "a fruit squeezed dry of juice". In fact they had become a liability. Therefore, on January 20th, 1981, the Inauguration Day in the United

States, after 444 days of captivity the fifty-two Americans were flown to a US military hospital in West Germany where they were welcomed by ex-president Carter.

Bani-Sadr's political career began to falter fast. By March 1981, his powers were curtailed by the parliament. The budget for his office was cut and the 'Students Following the Immam's Line' had produced CIA documents, found in the "nest of spies" (the American embassy) revealing that the CIA had contacted him both in Paris and in Iran for the purpose of recruitment as an informer. Khomeini, on many occasions interfered to put an end to this inter-governmental power struggle – but to no avail. Ultimately, when even the Faqih's mediatory efforts failed, Bani-Sadr, by calling a referendum, turned to the nation to decide the issue of government control. This was his kiss of death. In June, his newspaper the *Islamic Revolution*, was ordered to close. Yet refusing to accept defeat he publicly called for resistance to tyranny. Beleaguered from all sides the resilient president bravely continued his struggle for survival, albeit, at the same time pushing the nation to the brink of another revolution. In retaliation the government banned all public demonstrations. The Revolutionary Guards and members of Komitehs were put on alert. An infuriated Khomeini, completely withdrawing his support from his protégé stripped him of his title of Commander-in-Chief. Clashes between the followers of the president and his opponents led to many deaths. Hastily, the parliament convened and declared the president "politically incompetent". Bani-Sadr went underground. His last attempt to rally supporters from his secret base hopelessly failed. Until a new president could be elected, Khomeini invested power in a three-man committee comprising of Prime Minister Raja'i, Parliament Speaker Ali Akbar Hashemi Rafsanjani and Supreme Court Chief Justice Mohammad Beheshti – all members of the Islamic Republic Party.

Thus, cunningly the last of the secular moderates was purged from the political arena and Iran in effect became a theocracy. However, the power struggle was far from being over. A few days later a bomb exploded at the railway depot in Qum, killing eight, injuring many. Another bomb exploded during a Friday prayer service in Teheran seriously wounding Ali Khamenei. One week after Bani-Sadr's fall, on June 28th the IRP called an urgent meeting at its headquarters. Almost one hundred leading party members attended. The gathering was chaired by Bani-Sadr's arch-enemy the IRP secretary and Supreme Court Chief Justice Mohammad Beheshti, one of the most powerful men in Iran. At around 9 pm, while Beheshti was speaking, a massive explosion blew the conference hall to the sky, annihilating seventy-four leading party officials including Beheshti. However, Prime Minister Raja'i was only slightly injured and the Majlis speaker, Rafsanjani, had left the hall just moments prior to the bombing! To further extend the success of their explosive attacks, the dissidents, including the Mojahedin, resurfaced declaring a savage campaign of revenge against the government. The subsequent crackdown by the fundamentalists was so brutal that it quickly became known as the "Reign of Terror". In the meantime, new elections on July 24th for a president and twenty-seven members of parliament to replace those who had embraced martyrdom in the June bomb explosion, saw a huge turnout. The new president-elect Raja'i selected as his Prime Minister, Mohamad Javad Bahonar. The new government accelerated the offensive against the forces of the opposition and sometimes during the crackdowns, Bani-Sadr and the leader of the Mojahedin, Masoud Rajavi managed to secretly fly out of Iran.

This was the situation in Iran when my Mother stepped out of an Iran Air 747 jet to resolve her problems. Slowly dragging her arthritic limbs and holding on to the railing, she descended the steps and set foot on Iranian soil. After two eventful years she was back home. Standing on the tarmac, exalted she looked up at the clear pre-dawn sky and uttered: "Khodaya Shokret" – Thank you, God. With the help of a kind Iran Air personnel she climbed up into the shuttle which drove the passengers to the main terminal. The sight of rifled Revolutionary Guards minding a narrow path to the entrance of the building sent a wave of fear into her stomach. Emotional and ridden with anxiety she took her place in the long queue leading to the check-in area. With one hand she held the two edges of her chador, with the other she held tight to her heavy travelling bag filled with medicine for her geriatric relatives who needed but couldn't find drugs in Teheran. Medicine had become a rare, expensive commodity. Frightened out of her wits, only one question preoccupied her mind: was she or was she not on their wanted list?

Unlike the days of the Shah, the Islamic Republic's terminal was devoid of any foreign visitors, and incredibly hushed. The tense, drooping postures of the patiently waiting passengers exposed their trepidation. On the facing wall a giant portrait of the Immam had replaced that of the Shah. The austere decor together with the sombre atmosphere of the hall revealed the stoic nature of the society to which the visitors were entering. Mother, staring at the portrait, struggled to overcome her detest of the man who had brought so much misery to her life. Bad memories raced in her mind. She felt faint. To maintain her balance, she leaned on one of the poles that held the thick rope which segregated the two queues – one for men the other for women. The long line only crept – so many bridges had to be crossed! An hour passed before her turn came. Deceptively composed, she timidly submitted her travel documents to the bearded immigration officer and stood watching him. The smileless man, in his late twenties, threw a quick suspicious glance at her and began examining one by one, every page of her passport. Then patiently he flipped through a thick folder that lay open in front of him. Maman could hear the throbbing of her weak heart. Finding nothing incriminating, the man stamped the passport and called: "Next."

The officer at the second kiosk was less meticulous. Relieved from tension, forgetting her limp she walked to the final check point. There, she found malice in the hawkish eyes of the young man behind the small table. Suddenly her stomach churned. A sharp pain shot up her left leg. Her mouth felt dry and the quivering of her hand intensified. With pleading eyes and a shaking hand she offered her passport. The man rudely snatched the document from her. Flipping through he found the page he needed, and then referred to a row of boxes holding cards placed in an alphabetical order. He pulled the box bearing the letter A towards himself, lodged it in his line of vision and fingered each card among which one attracted his attention. He pulled it out and focused his narrowed myopic eyes on the small print. Suddenly an ugly grin bloomed on his unshaven, pockmarked face. He darted a dark appraising glance at Monir Aghdas Amir Aslani, put the card down and picked the passport up and began paging it again. Finally, giving a meaningful arch to his bushy eyebrows, he threw the passport on the table and, avoiding the beseeching eyes of the shrivelled woman, nodded to his assistant standing erect behind him. The boy, not much older than sixteen, picked up the passport, gave himself an air of importance and ordered: "Follow me, Sister." Glued to the ground, Maman began to shake, barely conscious of the warm liquid wetting her underpants. "Sister, I am talking to you. Follow me." There was no malice in his cracked voice – only a sort of childish tease.

My mother, trying to steady the trembling of her legs, could only manage to whisper. "Where to, son?"

Pointing with his small hand to the staircase he said: "Down there."

Tears began to trickle down her pallid sunken face. Between sobs she murmured: "What for?" The youngster, obviously enjoying the game, nodded his head: "You shall see." The pain in her limbs intensified. She picked up her heavy bag and endeavoured to drag herself behind the youth, first slowly descending the steep staircase, then crossing a long corridor to an almost stark room, furnished with an aluminum desk, behind which sat another Revolutionary Lieutenant keen to widen the schism between Iranians. Three other individuals, with faces even paler than the newcomer's, nervously fiddling with their cigarettes, sat apart, each deep in thought. Agony oozed out of their rigid entities. They threw a careless glance at the old woman and fell back into their own thoughts – whatever they were.

The air in the chilly room stank of nicotine, odour of nervous perspiration and poignant pain.

The youth ushered her in and conscious of her poor physical condition brought the only other vacant aluminum chair and placed it near the desk. Then proud of his chivalry, with shoulders straight and his narrow chin up, he handed the passport to the interrogator and rushed back to his post. The man carefully examined the passport, referred to a black folder and drew out a decree. Mother's false teeth began to clatter. Her heart raced, her mind flooded with regret for a decision badly made. This was not the Iran she had left behind. These men clearly were not the brethren she had remembered with pride and fondness. To her they were total strangers – in fact enemies.

From across the table, ignoring her pleading, moist eyes the man asked:

"Are you Monir Aghdas Amir Aslani, daughter of Gholam Hussain Amir Aslani and wife of Hassan Izadi Gilani Navad Deux?"

"Yes brother."

"Why did you leave Iran?"

"My husband was sick. We went to England for medical reasons and now, God be praised, he has recovered I have come to prepare our house for his return next week."

The shrewd man, not believing a word he heard, peered deep into her tired frightened eyes and, deciding that at her age she would be no threat to the regime said: "You are free to go."

In awe of her good fortune Mother put what little was left of her energy in her voice and said: "Brother, I hope God will grant you a long, prosperous life." Then she stretched her hand to take her passport. The man was quicker. Picking it up he said: "Your passport is under confiscation. It will be taken to the passport office until you can produce a clearance letter from the Revolutionary Prosecutor-General, upon whose decree I am acting." He stopped talking, picked up a biro from the table, checked the number on the decree that sat in his black folder, wrote it down on a notepaper and handing the paper to Mother said:" This is your file number. You must take it to the headquarters of the Revolutionary Prosecutor-General which is at Evin prison. There a Revolutionary Interrogator will attend to your dossier. If you are innocent of the accusations made against you, you will receive a clearance letter with which you can retrieve your passport." For a while Mother, with her mouth wide open, sat motionless. Then fully realizing the gravity of her situation she swallowed the lump in her throat, took the paper, folded it neatly, and secured it in her coat pocket. Then, gripping the two edges of her crooked chador with one hand and with the other holding to the chair handle for support she slowly rose, whispered her thanks, picked up her heavy bag and in front of the envious stares of the three detainees waiting to be transported to Evin, limped out of the detention centre.

Outside, the chill of the dawn was refreshing for Mother whose wet, itching and fetid body longed for a bath. Grinning brightly, Taghi, moustched and more stocky than ever, ran to greet his Mistress. The sight of the familiar smoothed balm on the stings of the earlier indignities and the sense of belonging overwhelmed all else. She embraced her faithful cook and kissed his hairy forehead.

The revolution had been kind to Taghi: good job, plenty of provision coupons and equality. His vanished subservient attitude was replaced by a politeness born out of loyalty and a devotion that came from the heart. Now it was Mother who needed him – as a friend rather than anything else.

In the cab, to satisfy his Mistress's curiosity Taghi the master-spy embarked on a dramatization of the hectic events that had caused the recent family traumas. What most horrified Mother was his riveting story of the person responsible for the ordeal. According to Taghi's reliable source, (a Revolutionary Guard from the Foundation for the

Disinherited working on our family's case) one of my cousins, to exonerate herself and release her confiscated property, had gone to the Prosecutor General's office where she had been given the choice of either "Reveal the truth" about the rest of the family members and retrieve the house or remain silent and lose it. This selfish girl, out of expediency had alleged much inaccurate and incriminating information on the affairs of the family. Thus, based on her revelations an extensive dossier had been created for each of her aunts, uncles and cousins. A decree signed by the Prosecutor General himself had prohibited four generations of the family from leaving the country and participating in commercial activities. The decree had also put a ban on everyone's bank accounts and any safe deposit safes they might be holding at the Bank Meli. Fortunately, because of the lack of trust in the banking system, everyone in Iran had some cash hidden at home.

Taghi had just finished his narrative when the taxi turned into Avenue Ehteshamieh. Mother's mind immediately became ripped with memories. Time reverted back forty-five years and in the panorama of her mind she saw her father, with his shapely nose in the air, followed by an army of retinue leisurely walking down the newly asphalted main road of his street. At intervals of twenty steps, without halting he graciously dipped the tip of his gold cap cane in the grassy edge of the long pavement that was segregated from the road by a narrow gutter. The small holes were marks for Hussain Agha, the head-gardener who at a respectable distance behind his Master was pushing a large wobbling cart packed with young dusty plane trees. At each hole, Hussain Agha would stop, pull out his shovel from the side of the load, choose a tree and oblige his Master's wish as swiftly as possible. Then he would grab the handle of his cart, and panting and heaving push it forward to the next spot.

Today was sunny with no running water in the gutters. Mother saw two young boys sitting under the shade of one of the trees doing their homework together. Those trees were now tall with branches that arched over the wide avenue.

Suddenly, the car bumped into a surface dent, and Mother's eyes caught the street sign on a corner wall that bore a name different from Ehteshamieh. Shocked, she asked: "Taghi joon, why have they changed the name of our avenue?"

"Khanum joon, a few months after your departure, the Immam ordered all municipalities to immortalize their local martyrs by sanctifying the streets with their names. But since the change has caused so much confusion, particularly for the postmen, people keep using the old names." The so-far silent taxi driver who had been all ears said: "Khanum, please forgive my impertinence, but these people have done nothing for the country but create difficulties. When you are dead what difference does it make whether your name sits on a directory post or not. If they really cared for the people they would stop this ridiculous, expensive war that no one wants. Am I not right, Khanum joon?"

Awed by the audacity of the driver Mother did not know what to say. Questions began to race in her mind: "Who were the 'they' he had referred to?" "Was the guy an informer or just an unhappy citizen?" She could not tell. So to be on the safe side she sighed and replied:

"Brother, I hope one day 'they' will come to their senses."

"Enshallah!" exclaimed Taghi and the driver at the same time.

In her sun-filled bedroom Shahjoon, surrounded by her remaining two faithful servants lay in bed patiently waiting for her daughter. Zari, who had replaced the dear Ashraf Sadat, with her wide sparklingly white linen scarf that spread over her fat shoulders, sat on the edge of her mistress's bed slowly massaging her bony, pain-ridden legs and Nahid, Zari's daughter sat cross-legged on the floor, watching the television.

Shahjoon, the legend of Darous through all the upheavals of her long life still managed to maintain her bright smile and look at her remaining days as a bonus. Two years of separation had diminished her hope of ever seeing her Monir Aghdas. And her return now was a great unexpected gift from the Almighty. As soon as she heard the screech of a car brake she sat up and gazed out of the window next to her bed. Seeing the taxi enter the driveway she ordered Nahid to hurry out and help with the suitcases. The girl rose, fitted her feet into her plastic sandals and rushed outside. Zari followed her and a few minutes later the door opened wide and Monir Aghdas entered followed by Nahid and Taghi, each dragging a piece of heavy luggage. Smiling, she threw her chador on the floor, and bowed before hasting to embrace her mother. The two kissed, cried, laughed, cursed the devils and then settled to enjoy their tea, bread and Feta cheese that was brought for them on a silver tray by Zari. After breakfast, Zari, whose long service allowed her certain familiarity flinched her round nose and politely addressed her guest: "Khanum joon, would you like me to prepare a hot bath for you." Mother suddenly remembering her pungent odour nodded her consent with an appreciative grin.

By lunchtime, one by one, Mother's siblings gathered in Shahjoon's bedroom to welcome their sister and enlighten her with the consequences of the steps they had collectively taken to secure a clearance from the Revolutionary Prosecutor-General.

The next day and every subsequent day with the exception of Fridays Mother rose at six and was out of the house by seven thirty in the morning. In one respect she was very fortunate. She had Taghi to help her. This faithful servant and his wife lived in the servant quarters of her rented house. There they acted as the tenant's gatekeeper with their salary deducted from the rent. Taghi had a full-time job at the Ministry of Transport, but his very religious wife remained in the house. Indeed, this had been a foresighted arrangement made by Mother before her departure in 1979. Nowadays when everybody was an 'enemy', most tenants frequented their local Komitehs with fabricated complaints against their landlords. By blemishing their reputations with dirt, these people tried to justify their own entitlement to the property in their lease. Mother's tenant could do none of the above as punishment for drug use and trafficking was hanging. A good gardener and a marijuana addict she grew Indian hemp in a secluded part of the garden. Taghi knew of this!

To the delight of Shahjoon's household now, Tahgi arrived every morning at 7 am with a bundle of freshly baked, warm Sangak bread, a long-forgotten treat, for breakfast. Then full of zest and gossip, he accompanied his Mistress to wherever she had to go whether it was a Revolutionary Court in Teheran or various Komitehs in the northern provinces where her properties were located.

Regularly for two and a half months, Mother appealed to various investigators and prosecutors stationed at different towns to urge them to expedite the investigation of her case which she found entailed nothing more than an enquiry into the way in which her wealth had been acquired. Finally after many humiliating and nerve-racking interrogations, frequent pleas together with regular recitals in praise of the Immam and presentation of necessary documents it was established that her fortune had been accumulated through legitimate means. To fulfil her religious obligations, and hence bless her worldly possessions, she had been asked to donate to the Foundation for the Disinherited one fifth of the value of her to-be-released assets as Khoms, a canonical tax. She was also requested to give a certain sum of money in lieu of the

Foundations' "endeavours" to guard her assets! Sick at heart and body, but content with the outcome of her tireless efforts, Mother paid to the Foundation the full sum demanded of her. A few days later a letter of clearance bearing the names of all the members of her immediate family was released from the office of the Revolutionary Prosecutor-General to be forwarded to all boarders and all notary offices throughout the country. Since the effective national dispersing of such a document would take eight weeks, a copy was given to her with which she could reclaim her passport. She took four photocopies of this important document and mailed one to each of us in London. Then Mother bought a house for Taghi which he promptly rented.

The hardship she endured during those horrible, crushing interactions gave her angina.

Chapter 19

One last time, before leaving for the airport we went for a walk around the Serpentine. I held tight to the hands of my parents, the two people who had been my pillar of strength throughout my life – always generous – always loving. At that moment, I envied the company of ducks that were sailing on the calm, green water and the group of pigeons that were gliding over them. The eyes of those birds, would every day behold the sight of my beloveds on their slow stroll around the park. I wished I was them. Pressing my convalescing mother's bony fingers I noticed they were unusually cold. I took them to my quivering lips, kissed them many times and pressed them to my cheek. How I loved this physically fragile yet mentally effervescent lady – always loving – always generous and always there for me! As we slowly approached Rutland Gate my heart tightened and I thought I would faint. The time was flying and I wanted it to stop.

Another home lost! Another goodbye! When will it all stop?

Mahmoud and Mehdi fitted the cases into the boot of the Benz. Masoud and his family jammed into his car ready to follow us.

Entrusting to God the safety of the house and its precious occupants, straightening my shoulders, swallowing my grief and putting my chin up, I climbed into the car ready to brave my destiny – however lonely – however far.

At the airport we checked in our luggage and lingered in sorrowful silence until the last call for the British Airways' passengers travelling to Melbourne and Sydney announced that our last few minutes of togetherness had expired. Then, suddenly we let loose the tears we had managed to control. At that moment, in the strength of our blood bond, all ugliness was forgotten and all sins forgiven. Placing my arms around their waists, I pulled my parents to myself and buried my head between their two heaving chests. I could hear their weak hearts race. I held tight to their love, their warmth, their sweet smell, their protection. We sobbed liked children. For how long I do not know. All

I remember is that my mother pulled herself away, took my face between her trembling hands, looked deep into my wet eyes and whispered: "My brave, brave girl! I am so proud of you, for you have more courage than all of us put together." Then she chanted a prayer, blew it above my head, kissed my forehead and let me loose. My father's hand remained tied to mine. I took it to my lips and kissed it again and again. When I let it go it was wet with my tears. Like statues of misery, all of them stood there thinking their own sad thoughts and the four of us, each holding tightly to our travelling bags, walked away.

Twenty hours into our flight the captain's gentle voice cracked the sleepy hush of the dark cabin. The lights blinked on and I opened my eyes. Through the window, I saw the golden dawn sky beneath which lay the equally golden deserts of Western Australia, rusty as that of Iran's. So finally we had arrived and it was the Aussie sky we were flying on, I thought with a sigh of relief. Elated I closed my eyes again and dreamed of our new life in a furnished flat at the Harbourside Apartments, located in a place called McMahon's Point. The flat had been rented for us by Mahmoud's business colleague, Yadi. I had trusted Yadi's choice for he knew Sydney well. I imagined our apartment with its high weekly rent to be huge and luxurious. Smiling to the future, I envisaged for us a glamorous lifestyle the sort of which we used to lead in Teheran – parties, tennis tournaments, skiing trips and friends – many of them. Suddenly a gust of strong hospital smell sent a churning into my stomach, and I opened my eyes to a slowly moving hostess with a can in each hand, spraying the passengers. Curious I slowly dislodged my cramped body, bent over a snoring Parissa and asked the hostess what she was aiming to kill. "Unwanted guests, mate." was her humorous answer. When we disembarked at Sydney airport it was the morning of 1st September 1981, and standing in a taxi queue, I was dazzled by the blueness and clarity of the Australian sky. The nature here felt and smelled different. The heavy air was musky, the sun piercing, the wind gusty, the green of the trees rusty and the people did not seem to care what they wore. In the taxi I started chatting with our driver, a Lebanese, who upon learning we were Iranian relayed the news that a bomb blast in a government office in Teheran had killed many officials including the Iranian President Raja'i and Prime Minister Bahonar. "Thank God, Mother was out of Teheran." I thought. A new life had just dawned for us and it was wrong to let the concerns of the past tarnish its light. So by inundating the driver with questions about Sydney

I stopped him from talking politics. Whilst earnestly listening to him I watched the scenery which I found dull at first, improving as we neared the city and then spectacular. The giant wings of the Opera House casting their huge, grey shadows over the fluffy waves of the Pacific and the metallic dome of the majestic bridge joining the two sides of the city brought a loud wow to our lips.

After checking in at the reception a small lift delivered us to the third floor where a dark, narrow, endless corridor led us to our flat. With the key the receptionist had given him, Mehdi unlocked the door and stood aside. I walked in and was hit by what greeted me. I stood still. A sharp pain stabbed my heart, bile gathered in my stomach and I felt dizzy. The dreamer did not want to wake up in an ugly, two-room, holiday flat. Instead of being realistic I felt terribly cheated. Disappointment faded my rosy illusions. For the first time, I realized we had a very difficult task ahead of us – starting from scratch, on our own, in a place unknown and so far away. Frightened I dropped on the sofa bed in front of me, and to the surprise of the others burst into tears. "Why are you crying, Lily?" a bewildered Mehdi asked. As though he was to blame, banging at the cushions I shouted:

"I hate this place. Look at the dump you have brought me to!"

Cool and in control, my husband made room for himself on the sofa and gently massaging my shaking shoulders tried to console me with soothing words: "This is only a temporary residence, Lily joon. Tomorrow, if you are still unhappy with this accommodation, we will go elsewhere. Just look outside. The view is magnificent." His delicate touch was reassuring. I lifted my head and looked out. The view was indeed panoramic. Still unable to move I rested my head on his shoulder and for a little while let myself be soothed by his loving embrace. My whole entity was exhausted and I was hot and sticky. I needed a shower. So slowly I untangled myself from my husband's grip, kissed his unshaven cheek, rose and went to the bathroom. The shower had power. Its pleasantly warm pressure revived my spirit. My children and Mehdi couldn't wait to go out and besides we needed food.

Outside the modern, glassy high risers blazed under the sun and, the shops were just beginning to open. At a corner I found a butcher and we went in. The meat was excellent and cheap. That night we had a delicious steak for dinner. The next day, when the air was pervaded by the exotic fragrance of climber jasmines and the passive harbour flickered under the rays of a relentless sun the four of us, took the ferry to Circular Quay and from there walked to Martin Place where the Reserve Bank of Australia impressively dominated the promenade. Mehdi in his eagerness to be punctual deposited us on the veranda of the first cafe we saw and dashed to test providence. While in London he had applied for an advertised position for which this interview had been given.

Betsabeh in a smart, navy trouser suit and Parissa dolled up in her still too big green overcoat sat next to me – both pensive and fidgeting with their menus. Jet-lagged but in a slightly improved mood, I was silently praying for what my husband needed most – a job. I had never felt so desperate and cold as I did sitting in that cafe listening to the sad music of a busker and watching a population of pigeons manoeuvring on the stone-paved walkway. Their confidence amazed me. They were not afraid at all. I was terribly afraid. Time dragged on. The square filled with professionals on their lunch break. Some relaxed on street benches munching at their homemade sandwiches, others rushed into nearby take-away delis and some to the cafés. Above, on the sky, the sun played a game of hide and seek with the gliding pearly clouds, causing great variation in temperature here on earth. Walled between Martin Place's high risers the notorious Sydney wind wheezed hard. At times I could hear my teeth chatter. No one had told us Sydney could get so cold! To break their boredom my children visited the toilet at least five times. Finally, unable to bear her tension Betsabeh looked at me with eyes that bore much concern and asked: "Mummy what will happen to us if Daddy can't find a job?"

Instantly Parissa, rocking in her chair, followed her sister:" Will we become poor, Mummy?"

"No darlings – Daddy is an educated man with lots of work experience. He will find a job, if not today, soon. In London he couldn't because he did not have a work permit. That is why we are here." As Betsabeh opened her mouth to say something, our waitress, in her impatience to get rid of us, for the fifth time asked if we needed anything else. Faced with the same curt response, frowning, she left us to our intermittent conversation until a beaming Mehdi returned. He had been offered a two-year contract commencing the following Monday. The dark shadows disappeared and I was warmed by a feeling of pride. The gusty wind turned into a fresh breeze and life became worth living again. The children, filled with joy, jumped to hug their father.

And I heard the voice of my own father say: "One day your inheritance may not be enough to see you through life – but your education will." That was twenty years ago at Charing Cross station, when he was loading me onto the train that was taking me to my first boarding school in Wales. How right he had been!

To celebrate Australia's gift of a second chance we had lunch at Sales, the waterfront fish restaurant near our lodgings.

Back in the flat that looked bigger and better, I called the Hampshires, Mahmoud's friends I had met in London. They invited us to dinner at their house in the eastern suburb of Edgecliff. In the late afternoon, we took the ferry and then the train. Following Jill's directions we crossed Ocean Street to walk through the tree-lined Edgecliff Road. Camellias and azaleas of different colours and breeds abundantly adorned the visible courtyards. Bougainvilleas that grew tiny in Iran had conquered the entirety of a high stone wall and on our path jasmines bushed over many fences. Below the cliff, the blue harbour sparkled with shades of white and silver. Instantly I fell in love with the area and dreamed that one day we would own a home there.

Within a few days we rented an unfurnished flat at Rosemont Garden, a prestigious condominium set in the midst of a large, lush, tropical garden, situated in Sydney's consular belt, close to the amenities of the Edgecliff centre. Upon occupancy with a few tastefully selected pieces of rented furniture and plenty of pretty potted plants I turned our three bedroom duplex into an elegant abode ready for receptions! Then we enrolled the children at Kincoppal Rosebay Convent, an establishment which focused both on academic excellence and human relations. Every morning, uniformed in light blue, Betsabeh taking her little sister's hand walked to the Edgecliff bus station where they caught the school bus. Mehdi travelled by train and I used my legs to explore the city and make friends. The major break in our solitary, yet content existence, came when Yadi arrived in Sydney on business and included us in the guest list of a dinner party given in his honour by an Australian couple, in pursuit of a lucrative project. During that dinner our host and hostess, Mimi and Toby, went out of their way to be obliging. Their hospitality was generous, their attitude polite. Both Mehdi and I were taken by their warmth and I saw a potential friend in Mimi who subsequently gave three luncheons to introduce me to Sydney society. Overwhelmed by the cordiality of this couple I called Mahmoud, and praising their kindness I asked him whether it was possible to favour Toby's firm with the project. Mahmoud promised to do his best. Unfortunately, the business venture went sour and we were abandoned by the couple. However, I had already impressed a number of lovely ladies who eventually became my good friends. Some of these ladies were active members of different charitable organizations which I was promptly invited to join. With my smile and a door that was open to all, I managed to enter the core of Sydney's society. An added bonus to our social life was the arrival of our Iranian friends Dara and Nazy. They, three generations of them, settled near us and Sunday lunches became our Iranian affair. Gradually, to our delight, the number of our Iranian friends increased. Yet we were wise enough to integrate within the larger Sydney society – a society blissfully willing to accept and respect new immigrants.

On the other side of the world, my brother Masoud left England for New York leaving only Mahmoud in charge of our parents. Father, unable to bear the separation became sick. His condition was so serious that Mother dared not let him out of her sight. Worried, I wrote a long letter imploring them to come to Australia where I could take care of them. They arrived on a summer's day when Sydney, echoing with the chirping of its colourful birds and the buzzing of its flies, smelled of a mélange of floral fragrances that lifted my parents' spirit out of its dire state to heaven. Within a short period, the beauty of Sydney bewitched Agha joon, but Maman hated the city more than anything else, because she realized we were there to stay. Together again, for six months we had a fulfilling time. Some of my friends helped to make my parents' visit memorable. Happy and healthy again they returned to London. Their departure was as painful as their arrival was comforting. In the empty house at times I thought I would go mad. One morning, my American neighbour Boby invited me to her flat where an Amway salesman was about to demonstrate the effectiveness of his products.

The super salesman not only sold us a number of his products but also persuaded me to become a representative. Amway provided an opportunity to be in constant contact with people. Gradually, I began to realize I possessed good commercial acumen. Any additional income was a blessing. Purchasing our large townhouse not only had absorbed our capital, but had put us under a heavy mortgage which we hoped to pay off when my in-laws sent me the money they would get from the sale of my gold coin collection I had left in their custody.

Once faced with the reality of life in Australia as new immigrants, my mind relinquished fantasizing. My optimism vanished and gradually my moods became more erratic. In the mornings, I woke up with fear and anxiety. Gripped with remorse I had no energy for socializing. With the passage of time, our novelty wore off and from behind the thin veneer of sociability the few genuine friends we had made revealed themselves. Yet, they too had their own priorities, and I was the one who had to "catch up" with them. After a while, tired of trying, I let my social existence drift into oblivion. The business of mixing had become too laborious.

Happiness is a state of mind – a mind that is clear of fog. Mine was not. Before our lives changed, my clarity of vision was envied by those who knew me. But the traumas of the past few years had brought much confusion to my perception. I could not feel happy, because as yet I had not learnt to focus on myself and my nuclear family and feel secure in my own ability and the unselfish love that existed between the four of us. I still lived in the past and could not adjust to the present – which was so different.

Bad news never stopped coming. Vladimir Kuzichkin, a Soviet diplomat stationed in Teheran, had defected to Britain. During his debriefing, he had divulged the names of Soviet spies in Iran and their Iranian agents, which the British had passed to the Americans who in turn had made the list available to Teheran. The Iranian government had reacted swiftly by purging the Tudeh who in fact had been instrumental in the taking of the hostages. The action was to keep the US Government busy while the Soviets invaded Afghanistan. Many Soviet diplomats charged with espionage were expelled and hundreds of the Tudeh members including my brother-in-law Mehrdad arrested. During the months of crackdown, most Tudeh leaders were put on national television to confess to their crimes, ranging from subversion to espionage for the Soviet Union. As part of a deal, those who had confessed to their crimes and had divulged the names of their associates were given a reduced sentence. Mehrdad was sentenced to six years' imprisonment one year of which was to be spent in a solitary cell. The news was shocking. In spite of the fact that Mehrdad and I had been political adversaries I felt sorry for him and his family.

I began losing weight and at nights I could not sleep a wink. Anxiety was taking charge of me. Mehdi had changed jobs and now he was teaching at the University of New South Wales. The thought of further association with any university was sickening for me. Bad memories occupied my mind more than ever. I was drifting away and Mehdi was not sensitive enough to realize it. My children hated to see me in bed all the time. They suffered too, but I was too far gone to be able to do anything to help.

The mornings were the worst time of the day. I hated light. As soon as the children were prepared to leave for school, I got out of bed, put my ancient long green dressing gown on, but instead of going downstairs to kiss them goodbye, I cuddled myself on the armchair and rocking back and forth sobbed quietly. It was my girls who came to my bedroom. Meekly putting their small heads on my lap, they muttered their prayers, kissed me and quietly left the room. When the house was mine alone, I screamed and screamed: I wanted my mother. I wanted my father. I wanted my old life back. I had lost everything, even the taste in my mouth. I loathed my useless, egoistic, unsupportive husband. I even hated the smell of his eau de toilette. I just wanted to cease to exist. Day by day I shed weight. My hair lost its shine and began to fall out. So did my nails. I didn't want to see anyone at all. I loved the nights when darkness covered the ugly world and the ugly people who occupied it. The telephone hardly ever rang. Twice I contemplated cutting my wrist, but I stopped myself because I didn't want the children to see blood. I loved my daughters; they were my sole purpose for living. One evening, my mother called to tell me Shahjoon had died. I didn't even cry for the lady I had worshipped. My children! Every time they saw their untidy mother in her dirty dressing gown they tried to hide their anguish. But Mehdi cold as ice, remote as a stranger went on living under the same roof without a care in the world. So long as he played his tennis and drank his wine everything else mattered not!

One afternoon, in bed, hidden under my blanket, I heard voices. I listened hard. It was Mehdi and Dr Walker our family physician. I heard footsteps. The bedroom door creaked open. They entered.

"Is she sleeping?" asked the good doctor.

"No, this is her new habit. She doesn't like light."

Gently shaking my leg, Mehdi softly said: "Lily joon, Dr Walker has come to see you." I trusted my doctor so I uncovered my head and peered at him. My pallor, sunken cheeks and untidy hair shocked him. He sat on the edge of the bed and asked me to sit up. Slowly I crawled up. He enquired about the cause of my anxiety. Wordless I fixed my gaze at my tanned husband. Breathing became difficult, I began to heave.

"Would you like to come to my surgery when you feel a bit better?"

I managed a faint "Yes".

"How about tomorrow at twelve?" I nodded my agreement. "Do you still have any of your tranquillizers?"

"Yes."

"Make sure you take one after breakfast and one before bed," he ordered. I nodded again. He rose, patted me on the shoulder and with much concern in his voice said: "Don't forget tomorrow." Then murmuring together, the two men left the room. I sharpened my ears and heard Mehdi say:

"Doctor I am very worried about my wife."

"Liar." I said and delved deep under my blanket.

The next day, after my screams, I forced myself to dress, wrapped my greasy hair in a creased scarf and walked out of the house. The bright light blinded me. The fresh breeze that used to fill me with joy made me shiver. The smell of jasmine that used to tease my nostrils made me nauseated. I walked like a zombie. My eyes saw nothing, not even the car that almost hit me. I only heard the screech of its brake and the swear words of its angry driver. At the surgery, in the presence of a caring professional I poured out my heart. I could see sympathy in my doctor's large blue eyes and concern in his refined features.

"Why do you continue with your life in Australia?" I had no answer. "Will you see a psychiatrist?"

"Yes."

I don't know for how long I wandered from one street to another. When I reached home, the sun had already set and Mehdi was behind his computer. As soon as he saw me, he stopped work and asked what the doctor said. I told him Dr Walker had referred me to a psychiatrist. My husband stared at me with wide frightened eyes.

"A psychiatrist? Why? You are not mad."

"No. Not quite yet." I whispered and headed for the solitude of my bedroom. Lying in bed with the light off I could hear the children talk in Parissa's bedroom.

"Betsabeh, what will happen to us if Mummy dies?"

"Shut up and don't ask such silly questions."

"Why doesn't Daddy try to cheer Mummy up?"

"Because he doesn't know how to and if you don't be quiet I

shall stop helping you with your homework." Then there was no sound except the racing of my heart and Mehdi's footsteps climbing the stairs. Not to see his face, specially his Roman nose with nostrils that quivered when he looked at me, I covered my head under the sheet. I hated it when he disturbed my peace. Munching at his apple which he ate every night instead of a laxative, he entered the room making as much noise as he could. He knew I resented being woken up. I heard him change into his pyjamas, walk with strident steps to the bathroom and bang the door. There I knew he would be meticulously flossing his teeth; another habit of his that I detested. The particles he flossed out mostly sat on the mirror, waiting to be wiped off by me. I heard him turn the bathroom light off, open the door, walk a few steps. No sound. Then he climbed into bed, rolled into a comfortable position – facing me. The heat of his body made me claustrophobic. His hand caressed my back and then began to crawl under my nightdress. His intention horrified me. Sexual intimacy without love repulsed me. Trembling I glued my thighs together and lay as rigid as a cold tombstone. He gently kissed my hair. I shivered. Offended by my stiffness he grumbled:

"Perhaps the solution to your problems is separation from me." I lost a breath, heaved and remained motionless. In the icy stillness of the room, he turned his back and went to sleep. My heart laboured hard. Suddenly in my heart erupted an explosion of hate, anxiety, fear, remorse – all feelings I could no longer bear. Every fibre in my sweaty body was aching. Touching on the threshold of madness I crept out of bed and tiptoed to Parissa's bedroom. Calmly, I stood by her bedside watching her pretty face. I loved her well-shaped lips that remained half open when she slept. Her eyebrows were arched like mine; her eyes were almond shaped like mine, but her rosy complexion was that of her father's. When she smiled two little dimples formed on her cheek. But she had not been smiling lately. I bent over, inhaled her sweet breath and kissed her narrow forehead. She moved and mumbled:

"Mummy, I love you."

"I love you too, my angel." By her side I lingered a little longer then ghost-like tip-toed out of the room, descended the steps and entered Betsabeh's domain. She too was sleep. Staring at her I wondered at fate's meanness, for out of a street full of relatives only these two children were left for me! A moment or so longer I studied my daughter's fragile, sculptured features which were just like mine a thousand years ago. Hungrily I inhaled her sweet breath too, and as I was about to steal a quick kiss from the tip of her straight nose she moved her head but did not wake up. I waited for a second more, kissed her straight, shiny hair that smelt of orange blossoms, and then walked away. In the kitchen I pulled out the cutlery drawer and selected the sharpest knife, the one with which I used to bisect my chickens. Holding it upright I brushed its cutting edge against my lips. It felt cold. Carrying it with reverence I walked to the drawing room, closed the door and turned the light on. The usually spotless room was peppery with dust and littered with the children's homework. There were many creased discarded papers on the carpeted floor. The silver frames holding the images of those I loved were tarnished and pocked with verdigris. The colourful horse-cover of Nasser Al-Din Shah, which I had smuggled out of Iran hung crookedly on the wall facing me. Suddenly I remembered my ancestry.

"I am an aristocrat?"

"My foot!" mocked the demon inside me.

"What then?" asked the tormented soul.

"An unloved, rejected failure!" retorted the demon.

"Yes a lonely, unloved, rejected failure!" I heard myself uttering in a low voice.

Something shimmered on the floor. I bent down. It was a heart drawn with gold ink. I picked the crumbled paper up, sat on the sofa and cautiously placed the knife on my lap. Then I put the creased paper on my knee and began very slowly and methodically ironing out the folds with the palm of my trembling hand. I noticed it was a letter from Parissa addressed to me. Suddenly the writing began to swim in front of my eyes. I wiped the tears off with my sleeve. Now I could read:

"My darling Mummy,

Every night I dream of you – the way you were, the way our life was. At school I always wait for the afternoons so that I can show you off to my friends. My lovely Mummy, when will you get well, dress smartly like you always did and come to pick us up again? When will you smile at us again? I promise I will never be naughty again. Never! Every night after my prayer I ask God if he wants to take you to him could he also take me too? I can never live without you, Mummy joon.

I love you so very very much."

The writing and the golden heart drawn for me began to swim again. I was trembling so hard that both the paper and the knife slid from my lap to the floor. Something snapped in my mind and I could see deeper than I had ever been able to. I wiped my eyes and nose with the end of my gown, kissed Parissa's letter, folded it and put it in my pocket. Then I rose, returned the knife to its drawer and went to bed and slept.

Chapter 20

In Teheran, the second of each month for Doctor Monadjemi and Ezat Khanum was the shopping day; the day of eating a good meal. A scanty income and astronomical prices had limited their purchasing power to what government food coupons allowed which was so inadequate that most people went to bed with rumbling stomachs. To keep their spirits alive, the Monadjemis had permitted themselves one single indulgence – a good meal per month. And the provision for this feast they bought with much delight as soon as they had collected their pensions. Today was a pension day, and the two in anticipation of a good meal had risen earlier than usual. Dr Monadjemi was an elegant man. He was tall, handsome with a head full of grey hair. Always neatly dressed, and shaven he bore himself tall until the deeds of the Revolutionaries took from him the joy of living. Nevertheless, today he had bothered to shave and Ezat Khanum had ironed her usually creased black Ropoush (Islamic cover). Looking respectable and in a splendid mood they strolled down the road to the bank and patiently waited in the usual long queue only to hear their accounts were closed and pension payments stopped. At first Dr Monadjemi with his impaired hearing thought he had heard wrong. Then hoping for a mistake he asked to see the Bank Manager. The clerk who had delivered the news, a bad-tempered woman, grumbling loud enough to be heard, reluctantly left the counter to fetch her superior. After what had seemed to the Monadjemis like eternity the sloppy, frowning manager, grudgingly dragging his plastic slippers, fashionable among fundamentalists, presented himself at the counter. His curt answer to Dr. Monadjemi's enquiry was:

"You better ask the Prosecutor General. We act on his decree." The pair baffled, stood in the middle of the busy bank, gazing at each other – not knowing what to do, or who to turn to.

In his youth Dr Monadjemi, a brilliant student, on a government grant had gone to France to study physics under Madame Marie Curie the famous physicist. Six years later, holding a Docteur d'Etat he had returned home to lecture Physics at Teheran University. A matchmaker had introduced him to Ezat Khanum, the youngest daughter of a respected lawyer, Mr Azimi. The petite lady had stolen his heart and within a month they had married without much ceremony. While most of his peers had served their ambitions by being at the service of the Peacock throne, my father-in-law, like his oldest son, uninterested in accumulation of wealth or acquisition of power had devoted his time to lecturing and research. Now in the autumn of his life his only worldly possessions were his home and his car. Most of his earnings had gone towards the overseas' tertiary education of his two sons. Ezat Khanum, unlike her own friends who had married millionaires and led a lazy life had had to earn a living. This she had done by teaching home-economics at a high school. To her name she had a small house given to her by her mother, Ghamar-Zaman Khanum Amir Aslani. The two were honest, hardworking citizens who had never done anything they could be ashamed of. Why then were they considered criminals in the eyes of the regime? What was their crime?

Panicked that the decree could have also erased their other liberties like participating in financial transactions and travelling abroad, Dr Monadjemi took his wife's shaking hand and pulling her behind him walked as fast as his weak limbs could manage, to a friend's nearby Notary Public Office where all prohibiting decrees had to end up. His bespectacled, old friend, now wearing a thick grey beard, already aware of the decree, with much sympathy in his deep voice confirmed the old man's fears and gave him his file number. In a state of devastation, holding tightly to the piece of paper bearing the crucial number the pair walked home, took their dented old Fiat and drove to the headquarters of the Revolutionary Prosecutor General at Evin where they hoped to unearth the nature of the accusations made against them. Having parked the car on the dirt road that separates the confines of the haunted fortress from the rest of the village they stepped out of their vehicle and facing the sinister, dry, sandy hills stood transfixed to the dusty ground. Yonder on the barren foothills, in a solitary cell their son was being wasted.

"My poor son!" the sobbing Ezat Khanum whispered to herself. Lately her mind had taken to wandering. The problems of her life had become too grotesque to face and too difficult to cope with – besides coping needs will. A will needs energy and energy a nucleus.

That nucleus is hope. Traumas are notorious for their ability to kill hope, especially in people with fragile, mental constitutions such as Ezat Khanum's.

Swallowing the lump in his throat Dr Monadjemi gently took her arm and led her to the small make-shift reception building on the opposite side of the prison gate. There, like two statues of misery they stood in another long queue until their turn came to submit their file number, based on which they could obtain an entry permit. Because in the Iran of the Ayatollahs, people under investigation are considered guilty until proven innocent they were treated by the guards with contempt, malevolence and rudeness. To humiliate the old couple, having registered their number the bearded sombre official – pretending to be a devout Moslem yet acting contrary to the dictates of Islam made the two trembling applicants wait standing in the depressing hall for one hour before telephoning the guard at the check-point for the required permit. The pain in the wrinkled features of the old couple gave him great pleasure – for he bore a deep hatred for those who once had lived comfortably while he laid bricks for their magnificent houses.

In the morbid compound that always smelt of death, after hours of being referred from one bureau to another, they finally found a thick dossier filed under their name. Perplexed, the two begged the secretary of the Revolutionary Prosecutor General in charge of their case to allow them to see the powerful Ayatollah at whose mercy laid their freedom and their right to the ownership of their lifetime's savings! The man secretly laughing at their naivety ushered them out of his office and showed them the long line of gloomy faces waiting in the stuffy smoke-filled corridor for an audience with the same cleric. However, in response to the plaintive pleas of the couple, the secretary, unusually compassionate for his rank, returned to his desk; whizzed through his diary and found the earliest date on which he could squeeze them in.

"Be here at seven thirty in the morning of Azar the fifth. That is the earliest I can fit you in." Azar was in three months time!

"Thank you, Brother. Enshallah God will grant you a long life. Thank you." Dr. Monadjemi uttered rising to leave the room. With him rose his wife, tears rolling down her long, drooping face. Outside in the sunny courtyard, close to the checkout point, Dr Monadjemi bumped into Faraji, an old student whose polite greetings brightened the day for him.

"Agha Faraji, what are you doing here?" asked Dr Monadjemi in a paternal tone. Faraji quickly nodded to Ezat Khanum whom he knew was Dr Monadjemi's wife, then swiftly took the arm of his professor and pulled him away to a secluded corner, shaded by a tall weeping willow. Ezat Khanum, speechless stood still trying hard to hear what was being said.

"Jenab [138] Professor, I am a deputy to the deputy of His Excellency the Prosecutor General. Only yesterday I was reading your file. Sir it is providence that has brought us together. All last night I was thinking how I could contact you without seeming disloyal to the Revolution. Jenab Monadjemi I have never forgotten your generosity with my scholarship. If it had not been for you I could have never afforded to finish university. Sire, serious charges have been laid against you, your wife and your son who lives in Australia, by Ali Agha and his wife, the servants of your wife's late mother. You must find a powerful 'contact' otherwise your problems will be endless."

Dr Monadjemi's jaw dropped, the shivering of his hand intensified, he felt cold sweat soaking his vest and Faraji could hear the clattering of his dentures.

Noticing the pallor in the old man's face, he panicked and, not wishing to have murder on his conscience, grabbed his professor's quivering lanky arm and in a soothing tone promised him assistance if within his power.

The Monadjemis up to then had been under the impression that their headaches with these two employees were over. The God-damned people, shortly after the death of Mrs Azimi, had rushed to the Central Komiteh and charged the family with corruption and anti-revolutionary sentiments. To substantiate their claims the man and wife had created a distorted picture of the family by providing exaggerated and falsified details of the personal and professional life of every member including the deceased's grandchildren. Justified in their crooked minds that as good Moslems they had fulfilled their duty to the Revolution they had taken possession of the dead lady's residence – demanding a huge sum of money to vacate it! Ezat Khanum was the only beneficiary of the deceased's Will present in Iran. Holding powers of attorney from those absent she had refused to oblige this request, simply because she didn't have the money. Nor could she liquidate any

---

[138] Your Excellency often used for University Professors.

assets. Not wasting any time, in case the revolutionary fever subsided, one evening, the two persistent servants accompanied by an armed revolutionary guard had knocked at the Monadjemi door prepared to negotiate new terms! Right at the commencement of their conversation, the armed guard had threatened to kill Mehrdad at Evin if his comrades left the house unsatisfied. Anxious for the safety of her son Ezat Khanum had volunteered to give them a smaller property belonging to the deceased if: they left Mehrdad alone, vacated the residence immediately after the transaction and withdrew their accusations. Impressed by the offer the swindlers had agreed to the terms. Two months later they had moved into their new home – legally owned! Mehrdad remained alive but now it seemed they had failed to execute their third obligation – probably out of malice.

Faraji's promise of support calmed the old man's anxiety and he relayed the whole story to him.

"Jenab Doctor you should not have given the rats anything. It is people like these who bring shame to the Revolution." Not knowing what to say Dr Monadjemi nodded his agreement and then promptly asked:

"Faraji joon, is there anything you can do to help us now?"

"Have they granted you an appointment to see the Prosecutor General?"

"Yes they have, in the month of Azar."

"That is quite close! I cannot do any better for you. With your permission, Jenab Doctor, I must leave now."

Faraji left his professor more bewildered than when he had found him. His offer of help was a phantom for Faraji was himself the investigator of their case.

Thus Dr Monadjemi and Ezat Khanum became prisoners in their own country deprived of all their civic rights: no more travel overseas, no more community respect and no income whatsoever. However it was fortunate that to sell and send the money to Sydney, Dr Monadjemi had recently withdrawn my coin-collection from the bank safe. Now the coins could save them from facing starvation. Cursing the ungrateful nature of all servants, regretting their hasty generosity they drove back in absolute silence – each drowned in their own dark thoughts.

At home Dr Monadjemi, worn to a frazzle, retired to the lounge and stretched on the sofa. Ezat Khanumn, without bothering to change into more comfortable clothes, headed for the kitchen in order to fry some eggs for her hungry diabetic husband before he fell into a coma.

The two miserable occupants of this small, sad house, each in their own corner, were pondering on the ignobility of human greed and its destructive repercussions when the excruciating sound of the door-bell made them jump out of their skins. Ezat Khanum annoyed by the disturbance yelled from her kitchen:

"Agha go and see who the hell has come at this time of the day." Reluctant to exert himself the old man let a few minutes pass before rising slowly from his sofa. Under his breath grumbling about the bossiness of women he dragged himself along the dark corridor to the entrance door. Parkinson's had badly affected his hands; it took him a long time before he could unbolt the lock and open the door to three erect thugs holding firm to their machine guns. As they saw the silver-haired man the oldest of the three stepped forward and asked:

"Is this Dr Mohammad Monadjemi's residence?"

"Who wants to know?" The man quickly and with authority took out a letter from his shirt pocket and impertinently dangling it under Dr Monadjemi's nose said:

"We have a warrant from the Prosecutor General's office to search this house for anti-revolutionary literature belonging to traitor Mehrdad Monadjemi." Whatever colour that was left on the old man's face vanished, his knees began to shake and his heart palpitate. In order not to fall he held tightly to the handle of the entrance door. In mortal fear, without bothering to check the stamp on the warrant he stepped aside to let the guards in. Quickly the louts entered and commenced their aggressive search.

Hearing voices of strangers Ezat Khanum crept out of her kitchen and certain that the guards had come to take them away stood in a dark corner of the hall, moaning to herself. Dr Monadjemi went to her and trying to console her said: "Khanum, don't be too alarmed. They have come to look for alcohol."

"We don't drink."

"Yah but how are they to know! Go back to the kitchen and don't let them see you like this. They might become suspicious."

Ezat Khanum did not obey her husband and for the first time in forty-five years he didn't care. He stood next to her watching the men – then he remembered the coins in his room. Cautiously he gravitated towards his bedroom. The door was open. He slid in and leaned against his closet. Terrified of being left alone with the intruders Ezat Khanum ran to her own bedroom. Cuddling herself she sat motionless on the edge of her bed. Then she began rocking back and forth saying to herself:

"What have we done to deserve this? Immam promised justice. Where is it? Did he lie? Did he? Liars! Executioners! Murderers! Thieves! God damn you all." As long minutes ticked away the men became more impatient with their fruitless search and rougher with their handling of items on their way. Frustrated one of them barged into Dr Monadjemi's bedroom and angrily pushed him aside. Attacking the closet he first went through the suit pockets and then kneeling on the floor he crawled into the depth of the large enclosure. Only a small portion of his big bottom stuck out. After a minute or two during which only the sound of his slithering could be heard he let out a loud whistle that attracted all attention to his location. Slowly he protruded outwards. Once completely out he put his hands on his sides and stretched his back. Then bending again he dragged a heavy object out, waited a few seconds, rose from the floor, stretched his back again, bent down, lifted the container and with a mocking smirk lurking on his ugly unshaven face set the box on the bed and sarcastically called out:

"Look at what I have found in a supposedly poor professor's house!" His declaration was so loud that it even brought the demented woman to the room where she saw the thugs standing side by side staring at the collection with eyes wide enough to burst out of their sockets. The richness of their find was mesmerizing – gold coins of different ages and size – at least two hundred of them. At a short distance from the container the trembling old man unconscious of the droplets of cold sweat running down the side of his bony temples was humming to himself:

"Cursed be those who have brought such misery to this nation."

Stupefied Ezat Khanum stepped close to her husband and gently took hold of his shaking arm.

Having overcome the astonishment of the discovery the man in charge raised an eyebrow and said: "We have to take this box to our headquarters. Tomorrow morning you must present yourselves with your birth certificates to our Komiteh. Questions have to be asked about how with your income you could own this many precious coins."

Timidly Dr Monadjemi asked: "Brother, will you yourself be at the Komiteh tomorrow?" Instead of answering, the man took a biro and the original warrant out of his shirt pocket and placing the paper on the nearby table he quickly wrote something on it, folded it and waving it at Dr Monadjemi emphasized:

"This is your receipt for the coins. Don't forget to bring it with you." Confronting no objection to their confiscation, without bothering to search Ezat Khanum's bedroom the man in charge picked up his gun and the box, closed its lid and together with the others rushed out of the house – leaving the shaken victims in a state of total devastation. For a while nothing moved except a large whizzing fly.

Suddenly Ezat Khanum ran back to her bedroom and began to shout:" Khodaya shokret! Khodaya shokret! (God be thanked!) They did not find Mehdi's share of the coins. At least we have something to live on!" Awestricken the old man followed her to the room.

"What do you mean, Khanum?"

"I mean they did not take the whole lot. I had taken my son's coins out of the box so that his wife couldn't claim them as hers." She smiled triumphantly and then continued; "These coins now will pay for our bread and cheese. We need them. Don't we?" Without letting her husband utter a word she asked more of herself than him:" I was wise, wasn't I?" Uninterested in any replies, deliriously laughing she pushed her hand under her eiderdown and pulled out the pillow she had hidden right at the edge of the bed where she had sat earlier on. Holding the pillow upside down she kept shaking it until a heavy cotton pouch fell out of the dirty white case. Still laughing she grabbed the bag, jingling the contents and began dancing to its music. The old man became emotionally confused. He didn't know whether to laugh or cry. The unusual sparkle in his wife's eyes vexed him. It was not the first time she was behaving strangely. Only the other day, she had wandered out of the house in her dressing gown. If it had not been for a neighbour's thoughtfulness only God knows where she would have ended up. Perhaps he should take her to a psychiatrist – he thought. Although unaccustomed to showing affection, he forced himself to go and embrace her. The two wrapped in each others arms stood in the middle of the dark lounge, lost in their misery – so desperately despondent.

Outside the sun went on shining.

Early the next morning Ezat Khanum showed no desire to abandon her bed. Dr Monadjemi by himself took the letter to the Central Komiteh where the thug had told him he could claim back his coins, after offering justification for their possession.

No one at that komiteh had issued the search warrant. A scrutiny of the letter's stamp by the head Guard revealed the document a forgery. The three had not been revolutionary guards but thieves. From Komiteh the old man drove to the police headquarters at Shemiran. There straight away he was taken to Colonel Namadi, the Chief Constable.

A clean shaven young man in his early thirties the colonel patiently listened to Dr Monadjemi's entire story and when it ended before making any comments he asked:" Agha is Dr Mehdi Monadjemi any relation of yours?" At first the old man didn't know whether it was prudent to claim his son or not. But something in the attitude of the young man induced him to tell the truth.

"Your Excellency, he is my son." Instantly a broad smile appeared on the pleasant face of the young man and his large hands began to clap.

"Well, well! Agha I was your son's student. He was my favourite professor at the National University. Since the coins belong to our Dr Monadjemi, I will do my utmost to help you find them." Then he lowered his voice and said: "These days it is very difficult to know who is a thief and who is not." Then he called the janitor standing by his door and ordered tea. Finding someone from the past – some one who knew who you were was such a happy coincidence that Dr Monadjemi couldn't but smile at his luck.

"Your Excellency, I don't know how to thank you!"

"No need for thanks, Agha. It is my responsibility to help any way but for Dr Monadjemi I will go to the end of the earth. He is such a kind gentleman. Please give me my professor's telephone number. I will call him as soon as I have any news for him."

"My son lives in Australia now, Colonel."

"Australia, I have heard is a beautiful country."

"Yes it is a paradise with excellent meat." Dr Monadjemi replied while extracting his wallet from his shirt pocket. The quivering of his hand was better today. Without dropping anything he pulled out a card and handing it to his son's ex-student said:

"Colonel Enshallah, you can call me with the good news."

"Enshallah, Agha."

Having nothing further to discuss, Namadi rose, left his desk, politely approached the old man who was already on his feet and the two embraced. Dr Monadjemi kissed the face of Colonel Namadi and addressed him as his son. To reciprocate the honour the Colonel paid the old man full respect by walking him to the gate of the station.

Exalted by the serendipitous incident Dr Monadjemi drove home looking forward to his lunch. At home he found Ezat Khanum still in bed. Disappointed he went to the kitchen. There he found only a piece of stale bread and some mouldy feta cheese.

Four days later, Dr Monadjemi was summoned to the police station where from the window of the waiting room, he saw the three louts who had violated the sanctity of his home, handcuffed, standing at a corner. Without their machine guns they looked terribly vulnerable. When brought into the office of the Colonel for questioning the thieves came face to face with Dr Monadjemi. With heads down they timidly confessed to their robbery. To reduce their collective guilt their leader furthered they had been encouraged by their friend Ali Agha, the ex-employee of the family to rob this particular house for it belonged to an unpunished "corruptor on earth". It was Ali Agha who had forged the warrant aware of Mehrdad's imprisonment. In response to the Colonel's enquiry as to what they had done with the spoils, the leader disclosed he had sold them to a jeweller in the bazaar. Instantly Namadi jumped from his seat and with his shapely head gesticulating towards the door said:

"Let us go to the shop of your jeweller." Obediently those present rose and left the room. Almost running, they followed the fast long echoing strides of the Colonel down two flights of steps into the courtyard where the five of them jammed into a police jeep and headed for the bazaar. An hour later, having driven deep into the south of the city where Teheran's dense air-pollution is most suffocating they reached their destination. The driver turned off the siren and parked the jeep right opposite the narrow opening which wiggles through to the heart of the ancient bazaar. The five rushed out of the jeep. "Direct us to the shop." The Colonel ordered commandingly. The leader of the louts, head down with embarrassment for being handcuffed commenced walking.

In the narrow passages that curved and sloped, the sound of purposeful stamps brought the inquisitive shopkeepers to the threshold of the busy shops and frightened passersby moved aside to make way for the police-led group and the curious mob that followed them.

At the small shop threatened by the presence of a Chief Constable, and ill at ease by the attention of the excited spectators, the jeweller confessed to having purchased the sovereigns which he had already sold to a foreigner. Regretting his stupidity and apprehensive of reprisal for dealing in stolen goods, the shrewd bazaari immediately offered to hand over two hundred Khomeini coins in compensation. It was obvious that in the existing economic climate the man could not have unloaded that many rare coins this quickly and to a foreigner. Nor in fact were two hundred Khomeini sovereigns equivalent to what was stolen. Yet, under the circumstances something was better than nothing. Therefore Dr Monadjemi, for the first time in his life abstained from bargaining and accepted the offer.

Back at the station the Colonel ordered the thieves to be loaded into a police van and be taken to Evin where a clergy acting as a jurist would pass a sentence on their crime. The Koranic punishment for theft is amputation of a hand. Dr Monadjemi, in his exalted mood interfered and managed to persuade the Colonel to release the thieves.

Alone in the privacy of Namadi's office, Dr Monadjemi removed the top of the box – guessed ten coins would make a handsome gratuity, but instead of picking them up smiling he *Taarofed* (a ceremonious offer which is expected to be rejected):

"Colonel please take as many as you like."

The Colonel raised his thick black eyebrows and condescendingly said: "Professor, I have only carried out my duty!"

"My son, if it had not been for your efficiency we would have never found the thieves." replied Dr Monadjmei in a tone that expressed his heartfelt gratitude, and then without waiting for the Colonel's reaction he picked up ten coins and dropped them one by one into Namadi's clean ashtray. In silence the Colonel quickly calculated the worth of ten Khomeini coins. It was equivalent to his two months' salary!

"No wonder Mehdi Khan is such a gentleman. He takes after his father." Both men laughed.

From the station Dr Monadjemi drove downtown to Bank Meli where he returned the coins to the security of his safe. Relieved of the burden he hurried home to celebrate with his wife the astonishing retrieval of the coins. However, in the aftermath of a revolution security is a mirage. Two weeks later, by a genuine decree from the Prosecutor General's office the entire contents of the Monadjemi safe was confiscated. For twenty years they stayed at the Foundation of the Martyrs. Dr Monadjemi did not live to witness their retrieval. But what reached my hands out of the 190 were only fifty Khomeini coins!

One late evening, Sydney time, when I had just fallen asleep the telephone rang. It was my father-in-law. He informed me of the incident. Disappointed yet calm I told him not to worry, this was just one more loss added to my repertoire of bereavements. I loved my father-in-law and understood him well. For him, the trauma of having lost face in front of me was much greater than the actual loss of the wealth left in his custody. One week after our telephone conversation he suffered a massive heart attack. But as his time to confront his maker had not yet arrived he defied death.

In Sydney I was doing something which I had not done for a long time and that was examining my face in the vanity mirror. What I saw shocked me. I was only thirty-eight yet the frowning face staring at me was of an old woman with tight muscles, dull eyes, yellowish skin and a mouth that was sealed. I looked deeper into the eyes and beyond their inertness I detected something that remotely resembled a flicker. I concentrated hard. The flicker was of a desire – desire to climb out of the abyss – desire to live again. As though by a miracle the ugly thoughts that had invaded my mind had vanished and I felt a ray of hope touch my heart. So there was still a chance, and a choice to take the chance. I could rot in the darkness of my unreal expectations or change my attitude towards life – a life that involved three wonderful individuals with hearts of gold, who belonged to me and I to them – something that in my selfishness I had forgotten.

I increased my visits to Doctor Whetton and during one of the visits he told me to write my memoirs. He said putting them down on paper would cleanse my mind from the anger that has poisoned it. Then he added that those who hide their grief often become victims of cancer.

According to my good psychiatrist, my fears and anxieties were not fabrications of a sick mind but consequences of experiencing the realities of a life trauma. Separation from loved ones, loss of one's country and drastic changes in life style were devastating dramas requiring much adjustment and positive disposition. Somehow, I had lost that positive disposition and had to regain it if I did not want to be forever hooked on antidepressants. Dr Whetton was right. It was now up to me to want to recover. That day from his office I went home, smartened myself up and then drove to pick up my children from school. Their happy surprise melted my heart. At home I found a letter from

Masoud, informing me that mother was in Iran and my father in New York intending to come to Sydney the following week. Amir Khosro would accompany him. Overjoyed I began to count the days and on the day of their arrival I was at the airport an hour too early. When I spotted my father come out of the custom's area I ran to him, hugged and kissed him a thousand times. Then I held him and looked at him with moist eyes. He was very pale. His remaining hair had turned completely white and his beautiful grey eyes had lost their usual insolence. I thought the long flight had exhausted him. He couldn't walk without leaning on Amir's arm. My nephew had grown very tall, his curly black hair touched the creased collar of his white shirt and he carried himself with a confidence unusual for his age.

Their presence in the house brought much joy to our lives. For four weeks we had a fabulous time. I took them to the zoo to see koalas and kangaroos; to Leura in the Blue Mountains and many dinner parties and luncheons. Sometimes Amir cooked for us. The boy was responsible, almost totally self-sufficient. He attended to his grandfather's needs with unbelievable diligence – bathing him, shaving him, dressing him and tucking him in bed. Agha joon delighted by all the attention given him did not stop smiling. Then Amir returned home.

The academic year started too soon and the children returned to school. Left alone, Agha joon and I became inseparable companions. An observant man it did not take him long to notice my melancholia. One day, when the two of us, in our small courtyard, were relaxing under the mild August sun, he casually asked: "Child why are you so sad?"

As though waiting for such a question I burst out: "Because I am homesick

-because I miss you, I miss Maman, I miss Iran – because I am so desperately lonely."

My outburst took my father by surprise. He looked at me with eyes that bore much love and concern. Then he said: "Let's go and look for a house?"

I could not believe my ears.

"What do you mean Agha joon?"

"If it makes you happy I will sell 10 Rutland Gate and buy a house here."

"Please don't joke. Can you see Maman ever living in Australia?"

"If I buy a house she will."

"But Agha joon, she won't let you buy a house here."

To hide my tears I fixed my eyes on the ground. There I noticed we had a companion. An Indian Minor was peacefully standing under my lemon tree and listening to our conversation. Suddenly, a lizard appeared from under the bark and wiggling its long tail disturbed the bird's peace. Frightened it spread its small wings, flew over my head and relieved its droppings on my coffee cup. Father smiled: "This is going to bring you lots of luck." Angry with the bird I exploded:

"How Father? What on earth could possibly change my miserable life?" My father was astonished by the intensity of my fury.

"Daughter, do you mean you have lost hope?"

"Oh yes, Agha joon. What is there for me to hope for? What on earth could possibly change my life? And who is going to bring about that change?" I asked with much bitterness in my husky voice.

"Daughter, every day is another day. We don't know what destiny has in store for us. Do we?" He stopped and with his index finger lifted my soaking chin up and for a few silent moments searched for his answer in my swollen eyes. When he saw nothing but despair he let go of my chin, nodded towards the sky and said: "Allah only helps those who help themselves. Child, get out of this dire mood and concentrate on the bright side of life. Compare yourself with those who have less than you, and then you will become grateful for your blessings. Besides, remember, I am still alive. As long as I live you can have whatever you wish for. Everything I have is to make my children happy – everything!" He took my cold hand and squeezed it hard. "Child, you must live with hope." His wise words fell on deaf ears but his concern warmed my heart. He released my hand, gently patted me on the shoulder and ordered:" Now get up and call a real estate agent."

"Father I am sorry for raising my voice. Sometimes I lose control."

"Girl, you know I have the patience of Job. Now get going."

In the kitchen, instead of making a call I picked up our copy of the latest *Wentworth Courier*, the Eastern Suburb's real estate bible and took it to the courtyard.

While I was going through the paper, Father kept complaining about his dizzy spells which he said had lately increased in frequency. To set his mind at ease the same day I made an appointment with Dr Walker who in turn referred him to a neurologist. The subsequent results of many tests and a brain scan showed that Father's problems were not cardiovascular but neurological. Apparently in the past he had suffered many minor strokes. In fact each one of his falls had been a small stroke. Somehow, the knowledge that nothing was wrong with his heart improved his spirit. Hence our house-hunting intensified, and on one fine spring day we found the property matching our requirements. Situated in the consular belt of Woollahra it was big enough to accommodate both my brothers and their families should they come to visit our parents in Sydney. Number 46 Wallaroy Road was for auction and we were determined to out-bid the other contestants. That day to celebrate the beginning of a happy era for us in Australia, I booked a table at my father's favourite restaurant Eliza.

I had not even begun getting ready when I saw Agha joon, clean shaven, smartly dressed heading down the stairs. Laughing at his punctuality I told him it was too early to leave. Smiling back at me he said he was going out to post a letter to Amir. Outside it was pouring with rain. I told him to put on his rain coat before venturing out. Half an hour later to get a drink of water from the fridge I ran down the stairs. To my surprise Agha joon was sitting on the last stair, letter in hand.

"What are you sitting on the step for?" I asked in a disapproving tone. He slowly put his hand on his forehead and whispered:

"My head aches, I feel very weak, I cannot go out." Handing me the letter he added: "You post this." I took the envelope and helped him to his feet. Holding his arm tightly I walked him slowly to the lounge. He looked pale. A thin line of saliva streamed down the corner of his mouth. From his rigid facial expression I guessed he was not aware of the flow. I took a tissue and wiped it off. He did not feel my touch.

"Father, I am going to call an ambulance," I said and ran to the kitchen. One by one the rest of the household gathered in the lounge. Leaving my father in their care I dashed to my room to change. Soon the ambulance arrived and the medics began their work. I accompanied my father in the ambulance. The others followed in our car. At St Vincent hospital we were taken to the emergency room where they kept us waiting for hours. Anxious and frightened I was going mad with anxiety. My father, gentle and patient lay there waiting. The throbbing pain in his head was excruciating but he did not groan only flinched. In my desperation to relieve his pain I grabbed a towel hanging near a basin, wet it in cold water, twisted the towel dry and laid it on his forehead. Minutes dragged on in agony. I kept hunting the corridor for assistance. No one seemed to care. Eventually a nurse materialized with a monitor and began to connect it to my father. All I could see was the berserk movement of the handles. Frantic I asked her why they moved so fast. She told me it was a faulty machine and hurried away. I sat on a chair next to the bed and took my father's hand. It was warm. I lifted it to my lips and kept kissing it. The nurse returned with a young male doctor. He ordered me to translate for my father.

"Ask him what his name is." I did. Agha joon gave the correct answer. "Ask him what the date is." I obeyed. Instead of responding Agha joon looked at me with eyes that saw death. For an instant our gaze intertwined and our souls embraced. Then his panicked eyes focused on eternity and his head dropped on the pillow. The doctor pushed me aside and together with the nurse, who swiftly lifted the monitor, propelled the bed forward into another cubicle. Once inside she put the instrument on the bed and drew the curtain hiding my father from my sight. I could hear much commotion in progress. After a long time, another doctor, much older than the first one, emerged from behind the curtain and told me to follow him. He led me to a little private room where he asked me to sit down. Then he closed the door behind him, sat on the chair facing me and calmly whispered that my father had suffered a massive brain stroke. They had managed to revive his heart but as he was very ill he had been sent to the intensive care unit and if I wished I could stay with him. In a state of shock I mumbled a "thank you", rose and walked out of the room. Somewhere in another corridor I found my family. I told them what had happened and asked Mehdi to take the children home as I was going to remain in the hospital.

Mute, I sat by my father's bedside holding his hand. At times I squeezed his fingers for a sign of life. If there was one I became excited and called the nurse. Every time she tried there was no movement. What I had observed had been just a reflex and not a conscious reaction to pressure. I continued my solitary vigil for thirty hours. Unable to feel any exhaustion, stubbornly I held to his hand. At times, resting my head on his stomach, I tried to feel him with every fibre in my body so that I could connect with his spirit and engulf it in mine. Otherwise, how else was I going to survive without him in this miserable world with a thousand faces? Immersed in sorrow, one sentence kept coming to my mind: "Hope, child. Hope". Obeying I continued hoping, praying and trying to bribe God – but nothing improved.

On the second morning another team of doctors arrived. Cold and insensitive, the senior neurologist told me that they had to disconnect the defibrillator because the patient was already brain dead. Bursting into tears I told him he could do no such thing and that they must give my father more time to come out of the coma. "No we cannot. It costs the hospital too much."

Devastated I told the doctor I would not give the hospital my consent until I consulted with my brother in New York. To pacify me the matron in attendance guided me to a telephone. I dialled Masoud's number. He took the call. Having heard my incomprehensible mumbles he asked to be put on to the neurologist. After a few minutes the receiver was returned to me. My brother, trying to control his own pain confirmed that our father was with God and that no machine could bring him back. Therefore I had to let the hospital do what was necessary. Resigned, I put the receiver down and asked the doctor to give us enough time to find a mullah who could come to my father before they actually disconnected the machines. He obliged my request. Mehdi who was by my side immediately went to find a telephone directory. Within an hour a kind and polite Sunni cleric arrived. A thoughtful nurse drew around us the curtain that was hanging from a round pole. Standing by my father's bed the mullah started his prayer and I, holding tight to my beloved's soft hand, resting my head on his leg, inhaling his familiar odour felt the warmth of life slowly leave his body.

At home I went straight to his room, packed his belongings in a large suitcase and turned the room to its original state. I could not have borne it otherwise. Besides that was better for the children. They were staying with my friend Nazy. They did not know that their grandfather had passed away. I had forbidden Mehdi to bring them to the hospital. I didn't want them to see my father in that state. He had to be remembered as the fun-loving, handsome man he had been.

Once in bed I cried myself to sleep. Sometimes before dawn I saw my father enter my bedroom as he had done every morning before – except now he was wrapped in a white shroud. Looking at me he asked: "Child, why are you so upset?"

"Because you have died."

Smiling he said: "Daughter, death is but a welcome redemption from suffering. It is not the end; just a change in life's dimension." Then pointing to his chest he continued: "Look at me and be happy for I am free from my cage. Pull yourself together, Lily joon, and begin to enjoy what is left of your time." To prove to myself that I was not dreaming I rose from my bed to go and hug him. I felt his presence very close yet when I tried to touch him I could not penetrate into his "dimension". The experience was so gripping that when I woke up standing in the middle of the room I found myself rid of the sadness that had so deeply wounded my heart. I desperately missed my father but no longer did I mourn him. I did not tell anyone of my dream for no one would have believed me.

Early in the morning, Mehdi and I dressed in black, went to the Islamic mortuary where they wash the corpse in rose-water and dress it in a white shroud – the only material possession we take to our graves. There, in a small waiting room we remained until a man came to tell us that my father was ready for his last reception. Inside, finding it difficult to believe only two people had come to pay their last respects the mullah asked: "Is this all, Sister?" I released a deep sigh and answered:

"Yes Brother. This is all – from a street full of family!" The man thought I was mad.

Dressed in white, smelling of roses my father's peaceful face looked as handsome as the day my mother had first fallen in love with him fifty years back in Rasht. The poor woman! What must she be going through, unable to attend to her husband's funeral – she was again prohibited from leaving Iran?

From Ashfield we followed the hearse to the Mosque in Lakemba where our handful of Iranian friends had congregated to participate in the Prayer of the Dead. Once the religious ceremony terminated, we drove my father to his final resting place at Roockwood a public cemetery.

The private mausoleum Agha joon had purchased years ago in Teheran's Behesht-e-Zahra was not meant for him. Such is the way of our world!

Chapter 21

It was four months after Father's death that my mother was allowed out of Iran. She arrived in Sydney a hunchback in black. Totally burnt out, nothing could bring a smile to her tight lips. Without her Hassan life was going to be empty and meaningless. Her world was so disturbed that she hated sleep for it meant nightmares. At nights she used to scream and wake up in tears. I understood her fears and kept urging her to live with us in Australia; then neither of us would feel lonely. "No" was her constant answer. True to her word, she stayed for only two weeks and then together we flew to London where my brothers were waiting for us for the reading of my father's will, a formality which we wanted to respect. My father, the thoughtful man that he had been, contrary to Islamic Inheritance Law had willed his estate to be divided equally between the four of us.

We sold 10 Rutland Gate to an Arab prince. With the proceeds my mother and Mahmoud each bought a flat in Rutland Gate. Masoud bought a house in Long Island and I in memory of my father bought 46 Wallaroy Road a dazzlingly white house with its arched windows and sunny rooms overlooking Cooper Park.

Once again I became the owner of a house with a garden. I went to the near by church and prayed in thanksgiving for the dream come true.

The shock of my father's death brought me out of my dark daze and opened my eyes to the things that really mattered in life. Gradually I realized that our trials and tribulations are a learning process to strengthen our will to survive and teach us to appreciate life for the gift it is. As my father had said to morrow is another day.

I learnt to look at my daughters and thank god for them. I learnt to love my husband again and I began to make use of all the talents God had given me. Thus during a luncheon with Edwina Baillieue, my best Australian friend, I told her I was looking for a job. She immediately asked me if I knew anything about advertising. That was one field I knew nothing about and told her so. With her large, beautiful, blue eyes that twinkled with tease she threw me a glance and said: "Lily, is there really anything that you don't know?"

I smiled at her and said: "Yes, I do not know how to sell blank pages of a magazine."

A day later I received a telephone call from Mr Robert Henty, the managing director of the Australian Consolidated Press, the largest magazine publishing house in Australia belonging to Mr Kerry Packer, Edwina's cousin, asking me what he could do for me! Overjoyed I replied: "Sir it is more what I can do for you."

We laughed and an interview was arranged for me to meet a Mr Graham Lawrence who at the time was in charge of the advertising department. The interview was irrelevant because a position was already selected for me on one of their homemaker magazines. However, since I was foreign to the field of advertising I expressed a wish to be trained before commencing full responsibility. The administration accepted my request and provided me with a broad range of learning experiences that proved fundamental to the subsequent success of my career. Within four months not only I had learned what there was to know about magazine publishing but I had proved myself worthy of being promoted to the position of the New South Wales advertising manager of the *Belle* Magazine. From then on my career picked up. From Australian Consolidated Press, I went to Federal Publishing Company to become the head of their women's magazines department. The busier I became the better I felt. The better I felt the more I did for everybody. My children became happy again and a smile returned to Mehdi's handsome face.

Betsabeh frightfully beautiful and very capable had already passed her High School Certificate examinations with high enough aggregates to gain her admission to the Department of Commerce at the University of New South Wales and Parissa as effervescent as ever was labouring hard at high school.

Happy and on top of the world I planned our first family overseas' excursion after six years.

Our reunion with my mother, and brother was wonderful. Together again in London we shopped, dined and had a fantastic time until we flew to Paris to visit my cousins from Avenue Ehteshamieh. There I began feeling nauseated and dizzy. But thrilled by being with my family, I did not take much notice of my failing health.

In Sydney a visit to Dr Walker proved me seriously ill, and in need of an immediate operation. My good friend, Doctor Malcam Coppelsson, operated on me. He told me that I had been a very lucky individual to have found the ailment so soon.

At home I was convalescing in bed when the excruciating sound of the phone pierced my ears. I grabbed the receiver. It was Mehdi's oldest cousin calling from Teheran. In the study next to our bedroom Mehdi had already picked up the receiver and I heard him greet his cousin. I placed the receiver down and waited for my husband to finish his conversation and enlighten me with news from his family.

Unfortunately, it was bad. Dr Monadjemi was very sick and Ezat Khanum had lost her mind. However, investigations of their dossier had proved the accusations groundless and after four years they were free to leave the country.

My in-laws arrived in Sydney three weeks later, on the first day of July 1988, looking so grieved that both Mehdi and I felt guilty for being alive. Ezat Khanum had turned into an old woman with a pair of dead eyes that expressed nothing but despair. Her grey dull hair, once luxuriant, was covered under a huge crinkled black scarf; her diminutive stature was sunk in a long, dirty, black raincoat that acted as her Islamic coat. Hanging on the arm of her equally dishevelled husband she looked completely lost. They seemed as though they had just been released from a Nazi concentration camp – if not worse. A quick glance at my husband's awestricken countenance told me of his inner torment.

Ezat Khanum, unable to believe that they were actually allowed to leave Iran, had gone to the airport with just a handbag. All she had brought with her was what she wore! Fortunately we were of the same size. Her distrust was such that she would not let me take her raincoat to a dry cleaner fearing it would be stolen. I had to creep into her bedroom, take it from her wardrobe while she was asleep and hang it back dry cleaned when she was out of her room. She never noticed the difference. Her deep emotional disturbance needed urgent psychiatric treatment. We gave her a few more days to repose before Mehdi took her to a psychiatrist whose diagnosis was deep depression and paranoia. She needed extensive psychotherapy. Unfortunately, the treatment did not last long. After a few sessions she got fed up with having to unravel the secrets of her soul in front of her interpreter son and refused to go and refused to take the anti-depressant thinking that I wanted to kill her. All we could do now was try to make her feel secure both physically and mentally.

Meanwhile, Dr Monadjemi relieved that his wife was in good hands regained his vitality and let himself revel in the luxury of leading a life untangled by the suffocating tentacles of government control. At first he took great joy in lingering by the shop windows of butchers. Veal was his favourite. I bought for him whatever food he desired. Gregarious, he loved to frequent Double Bay's coffee shops for a *café au lait*, eat French food and drink whisky at home. His capacity for simple pleasures was so inspiring that we obliged his every whim. Eventually even Ezat Khanum began to smile.

My father-in-law and I shared a relationship of mutual love and respect. He was full of praise for my "extraordinary efficiency" and I for his buoyant spirit, forthrightness and independence. Often during the weekends we sat together on our sunny balcony. Enjoying the hilly view of Cooper Park we chatted about the happy times which were turned into nightmares by the satanic actions of ambitious men trying to play God. Our recollections brought smiles to our faces, sighs of regrets to our lips, mists into our eyes and always at the end a feeling of solace – for being together again.

There was such energy in this old man that just by himself within four weeks he saw more of Sydney then we had seen in seven years. His drive for merriment was infectious. Mehdi and I tried to lure our folks to make our home theirs – alas to no avail. Regardless of the miseries they had endured they were set to return to Iran. Mehdi and I thought perhaps if they had their own place here they would remain in Sydney. Therefore, we planned to purchase a small investment property and let them make it their home. To this end on a cold August day, I took my lunch hour from the office, went home to meet with my real estate agent who was to take me for a number of inspections. It was about two thirty in the afternoon when the agent dropped me back to pick up my own car from home. When I opened the gate I found my daughters, their eyes red, cuddled together, sitting on the garden steps next to the blooming orchids waiting for me. The moment they set eyes on me they burst into tears. Astonished I asked what the matter was. Betsabeh managed to mutter: "It is Agha Doctor."

"What has happened to Agha Doctor?"

"He died," Betsabeh said wiping her tears with a crumbled tissue she was holding.

"Mummy, he died on the street!" Parissa added hurriedly.

I wanted the ground to open up and swallow me. I dropped on the step next to my daughters and pleaded: "Betsabeh joon, tell me what happened." She took a deep breath, wiped her eyes and nose with the hem of her skirt and said:

"Mummy, after you left for work Agha Doctor asked if any of us wanted anything from Woolworth. I told him we had everything in the house and that he shouldn't waste his money on food. Laughing he said while in Australia he wanted to do as he pleased and nothing gave him more pleasure than spoiling us." Betsabeh stopped, darted a blaming look at her sister, pointed to her with her elbow and said: "This stupid, spoiled brat ordered lots of chocolates and nibbles. Poor Agha Doctor wrote down her ladyship's orders, then he told us he was going to take his walk around Cooper Park, down Manning road to Woolworth and back. I told him when crossing the roads to remember cars here drive on the wrong side. He kissed me and said I should not worry about him because now that he is with us nothing bad could happen to him. Mummy, those were his last words. When Daddy came for lunch and noticed Agha Doctor had not returned yet he became worried. So he went to search for him in the car. We stayed by the garage door waiting. Daddy returned without Agha Doctor. He went straight to the telephone and called the Paddington police station. The officer on the line suggested he should call St Vincent hospital. He did and was told to get himself there as soon as possible. Daddy and Ezat joon drove to St Vincent's where they were told that Agha Doctor had collapsed in front of the surgery of a doctor in Manning Road. A passerby seeing him fall had instantly sought help from the doctor who had examined Agha Doctor, and called for an ambulance. Since Agha Doctor had reached the hospital dead his body was sent to the morgue." Betsabeh stopped again, swallowed her grief, sighed and then continued: "That is what Daddy told me on the telephone. He asked me to tell you they were about to go to the mortuary. What are we going to do now Mummy joon?"

"Now we have no grandfathers at all!" cried out Parissa, her small nose red and running. For a second I felt giddy, and then I jumped up, ordered the children to go inside, ran out of the house, leaped into my car and drove to my office.

Once I had parked my car in the parking lot, I hurried to the seclusion of my room, sat on my chair, hunched over my desk and gave vent to my sorrow. When my tears dried out I called the chief of Federal's security. I asked him if he could drive me to the morgue. Within minutes he arrived and taking my arm led me to his car. In silence he drove me to my morbid destination where in a cold corridor I found my mother-in-law, lost in thought nestling against her son. Upon seeing me Mehdi rose, took my hand and led me to the stretcher on which his father lay. He gently lifted the white cloth away and I saw a face frozen in the expression of fear, pain or whatever dreadful sensation he had been experiencing when death claimed him. I did not cry for him because I was sure he had found in death what he had so much missed in life – freedom and peace.

My father-in-law was buried a few yards away from my father at Rookwood cemetery – the garden in which our family roots were flourishing.

The blow of her husband's sudden death was the catharsis needed to improve Ezat Khanum's mental health. Gradually, she recovered enough to be able to fly to Paris and spend some time with her daughter Mariam, who was studying to become a pharmacist. It was there that she received news of her son's release from jail. He had served his six year sentence and actually had come out of the monstrous Evin alive! This indeed was an occasion for the whole family to celebrate. Ezat Khanum immediately returned to Iran.

In Sydney our life returned to normal, enabling me to apply myself more diligently to my new expanded responsibilities. Proudly successful, I was counting my blessings when a telephone call from Mahmoud ended my contentment. He told me our mother inflicted with angina might require a heart bypass. From the grave tone of his voice, I guessed the situation was more serious then he wished to communicate. It seemed providence had again become envious of my short liaison with happiness. This time the angel of death was knocking at my mother's door, and I did not want to let him take her before I saw her once more. Therefore, without hesitation, I placed two calls: one to my travel agent; the other to my boss. The following day I flew to London.

At Mahmoud's flat I found my mother shrunken in stature, devoid of any colour, all bone and skin, standing in the hall, waiting for me. Nothing was left of her exuberance. Hiding my shock at her ghastly appearance I hugged and covered her face with kisses. Embracing me tight, she rested her small head on my chest. In her mind she had given up hope of ever seeing me again. Now that I was in her arms she did not want to let go of me.

When Masoud heard the hustle and bustle of my arrival he joined us in the lounge. My heart bled every time I looked at my mother's pale sunken face. Resigned she sat at the dining table playing with her special diabetic's breakfast. Occasionally she released a deep sigh. Watching her I thought she had not seen one day of happiness since her husband died five years earlier. I dreaded losing my mother. I loved her deeply and needed her so much that without her I thought I would perish. Even in her frailty, even living a hemisphere apart she was my pillar of strength. Mentally I was still attached to her by the umbilical cord that neither maturity nor distance had been able to break.

At nine in the morning of the thirtieth January 1989, we submitted our mother to the care of the best heart surgeon at Harley Street clinic and anxiously sat in the corridor watching the minutes turn into hours on the wall clock. Finally sometime in late afternoon, a stout jolly Australian nurse emerged out of the theatre and approaching us declared the operation had been a success and our mother was being taken to the intensive care unit where she would remain until she regained consciousness. We thanked her and left the hospital to celebrate the gift of life. That night I slept well.

Early the next morning the three of us hurried to the clinic where we found Mother in her private room hooked to all sorts of drips and wires linked to different monitors. It was a frightful sight yet we were grateful that nothing had gone amiss during the operation. There had been a chance of a stroke, or falling into a deep coma; neither of which had luckily happened. To keep our mother's company we took turns in staying with her. My two inseparable brothers' shift was from morning to noon when I took over, freeing them to play tennis, and take a sauna at the Queens Club.

It was during the fourth night after the operation when I was woken by the shrill ring of the telephone. I picked up the receiver, wrong phone; it had been Mahmoud's private line. I cursed the caller and went back to sleep. Early in the morning, Masoud entered my room and asked what time I intended to be at the Clinic.

"About the same time as usual, why?"

"Nothing, just don't be too late." Then hastily he left the room. Although it seemed strange that he should be concerned about my time of arrival I thought nothing of the incident.

Outside the weather was glorious; instead of hurrying to the hospital I walked from Rutland Gate through the park to Harley Street. Invigorated by the fresh air I entered the Clinic and saw Masoud sitting in the waiting room calmly smoking his pipe. He looked very distinguished. When he saw me he rose from his chair and waited until I reached him – a respect he never paid me before.

Without beating around the bush, in the manner of doctors, he said: "Lily, unfortunately, last night Maman suffered a stroke. She is paralyzed with her speech disturbed. Don't be too alarmed when you see her. Her condition might improve. It is too soon to know the severity of the stroke." I did not hear what else he reported. To stop myself from falling I sat on the chair next to which I had been standing. My whole body trembled.

I hugged my shoulders and began to hum: "Maman joonam, Maman joonam, what has become of you?"

Masoud stood there for a while, then his patience ran out. "Lily if the stroke has been minor she will recover with physiotherapy and speech therapy. Come on, pull yourself together, and don't let her see you like this. We must give her hope and courage. Go wash your face before entering her room." I had no energy to get up. Gently he took my hand and lifted me up. Hunchbacked, leaning on my unusually kind brother I limped to the toilets. Inside the ladies I washed my face with cold water, waited for a couple of minutes to calm my nerves then slowly walked to my mother's room where I found a deranged child gibbering ridiculous sentences referring to unrelated past incidents. She called me Mahmoud and Masoud was Lily. I kissed her hand, her face, her foot and kept sobbing and laughing at the same time. My head ached, my heart bled and I wanted to disappear from the face of the earth. Suddenly the opening of the door interrupted my delirium. A fat matron accompanied by the head neurologist entered the room. Unconsciously I leaped to my feet, straightened my dishevelled clothes and stood by my brothers. Expecting a miracle all our attention was focused on the entrants.

Exuding vanity the balding neurologist approached Mother, briefly looked at her, turned to Masoud whom he knew was also a doctor and said: "Only time will tell the extent of the stroke's damage. We have to start physiotherapy immediately."

That evening after having witnessed the agony my mother had

endured during her session of physiotherapy I returned home feverish; took two tranquilizers instead of my usual one and went straight to bed. In the middle of the night I felt as though an elephant had stepped on my head. There was so much pressure inside my head that I thought it would burst out. Slowly the pressure moved downward, until it exploded into a loud buzzing sound in my ears. Frightened by the excruciating ring I sat up, held my head with both hands and tried to control my screams from spewing out. I had to do something to ease the pain and stop the noise. With a huge effort I rose, tiptoed to the kitchen, filled my hot water bottle from the tap and returned to bed. Alternately I put the bottle next to each ear leaving it longer on the left one in which the buzz was more profound. As soon as the bottle cooled I refilled it again. This went on until I heard Masoud cough which meant he was awake.

For three days I was in and out of different surgeries only to find that eventually the battering of my life had caught up with me – now physically; I had suffered a brain haemorrhage which had 'fortunately' only impaired the hearing in my left ear leaving behind the aggravating buzz of tinnitus. I was never again to experience the serenity of silence. The doctors were all of the same opinion: the haemorrhage had been caused by excessive stress.

One week after her stroke, we drove our Mother home where a live-in nurse was awaiting her. Thanks to her incredible willpower together with daily physiotherapy, Mother's ability to move slowly began to mend. Since we could not find a speech therapist fluent in Farsi we undertook the task ourselves. We tried patiently to understand her jabbering, and make her reiterate the corrections. Gradually that faculty, too, started to improve. Keeping constant watch over her I was amazed at her alertness. Stretched out in bed immobile, she was quite conscious of the happenings around her particularly the fact that soon Masoud and I were to leave her. Even with a full-time nurse hovering over her she was scared to be left alone.

Every time my mother looked at me her eyes pleaded. I believe she knew that only I, the cat who always landed on her paws, could give her the dedicated supervision essential for her recovery. She also knew I could not remain in London indefinitely.

One day when she heard my departure was close she called me:" Mahmoud joon."

Pointing to my chest I said: "Maman joon, I am Lily"

"Yes Lily joon pl-e-a-s-e don't l-e-m-e a-l-on-ne h-e-ere." As she implored her eyes moistened and her thin lips quivered. I knelt by her bed, took her cold bony ineffective hand, pressed it to my heart and reasoned:

"Maman joon, you know that I cannot stay here. But I can take you with me to Sydney. There we will take care of you. Please come with me."

Stroking my hair with her good hand she whispered: "I n-o die th-e l-o-o-ng airplane?"

"No Maman joon, you will not die during the long flight, but to make sure I will check with your doctor. If he sanctions our plan we will travel first class. You can just sleep the whole way. I will ask Mahmoud to accompany us so that he can help me lift you up when you need to use the toilet. What do you say to that?" Her approving nod together with the sparkle of hope in her kind eyes made my day a brilliant one. Immediately I rose and dashed to the sitting room where my brothers were in conversation. I told them of our decision. Both welcomed the idea,

Two weeks later at the Sydney airport Mehdi, my children plus a wheel chair were waiting for us. In the house Elizabeth, a jolly, plump, live-in nurse began to perform her duties. Since my bedrooms were on the second floor we had difficulty moving Mother up the stairs but as it turned out the steps were instrumental in returning to her the walking skills she had lost. The day after our arrival Dr Walker made a home visit, examined his new patient and satisfied with her condition gave me the name of a physiotherapist who could come everyday to work with her. He also taught me how to test her blood sugar level.

Once I had organized my mother's care I returned to work. I was still suffering from the aftermath of my own affliction yet I had no time to think of myself. All that mattered was my mother's recovery. Between the physiotherapist, and ourselves we made her walk slowly up and down the corridor, talk more coherently and use the pen first to form the alphabet then to sign her name. She never regained the ability to write properly. Mahmoud left Australia certain that his mother was in good hands.

Gradually the permanent effects of the stroke unravelled themselves. Severe depression was to haunt her for the rest of her life. Much of the strength in the left side of her body was lost permanently making unsupervised walking hazardous. Her memory remained erratic;

sometimes she remembered vividly incidents that had occurred decades ago; other times she couldn't remember my name. The stroke had turned her into an anxiety-ridden emotional invalid who needed constant supervision undertaken with love and patient care.

Her depression was too deep for her to be able to appreciate anything. Sometimes I saw flickers of pain in her pleading eyes; other times a tense, limping hand trying to rub a spot on her withered body; yet because she could not communicate coherently I could not understand what ailed her or where the pain actually was. A frown never left her sad face. Hoping for a cure I took her from one specialist to another. "Nothing can be done for your mother" was the regular salt thrown on my wound. Unwilling to accept finality I delved into reading literature on natural healing. Then I remembered my own depression and the craving I had for loving attention. So we each in our own way tried to make a miracle happen. At first it worked then our collective endeavours proved not enough. One thought, and that thought alone preoccupied her mind – seeing her sons again. To make her happy I promised to take her to New York when she regained her strength. This was an incentive for her to try to overcome her defeatism and reduce her fear of death in Australia which was costing a fortune in long distance calls – every time the thought occurred to her she wanted to bid farewell to her sons – one in London, the other in New York! To give her something to look forward to I even set a date for our flight. Thrilled by the thought she made me hang a calendar on the wall next to her bed. She wanted to have the pleasure of ticking the days off. Every tick that brought her closer to her goal – deepened the pain in my heart. In spite of all we were doing for her she still wanted to fly away – to her sons. For the first time in my life I felt pangs of jealousy.

One morning when Mehdi landed the Sydney Morning Herald on my lap I saw a picture of Ayatollah Khomeini. He was dead. The date was June 3rd 1989.

At Wallaroy Road the painful moments dragged, the happy hours raced and the months of our lives flew. Betsabeh graduated from the University of New South Wales with a Bachelor of Commerce degree that gained her a marketing position at an international pharmaceutical company. Parissa no longer cute but charmingly gregarious and extremely elegant became one of the brightest students of her class; Mehdi, now a senior lecturer zealously pursued his academic career and I finished the new apartment I had bought to renovate. Thus we found ourselves on one September day when on her calendar Maman had no more dates to tick off. That early morning the air was sweet with the aroma of jasmine soothing to both humans and a population of chirping Indian Minors that played hide and seek around my huge pots of orchids which with their erect colourful heads majestically guarded the steps that connected the gate to the arched entrance of our Moorish-style building. There, ready to depart, Mother sat on my monk chair by the French window that exposed the breath-taking view of Cooper Park. Gazing out at the misty green lawn that lay yonder she was pondering how she could bear the long flight to New York. The expression of impatience on her drawn sunken face told me these were her last ever moments with me in Australia; that she was never going to return here again. A sense of failure gripped my heart for I had failed to make our home hers. I refused to believe that it was us she was rejecting. Perhaps, at heart she had become a gipsy – now that her children were scattered all over the world! Dignified, sitting on that elaborately carved chair she looked forlorn. To capture her image for the days I was going to miss her I bent down, took out my movie camera from my hand luggage, pulled it out of its case and began filming her. She grumbled: "Khanum p.t tha away an le.s go." Ignoring her request I went on filming.

At Kennedy Airport my brothers received us with joy and Masoud drove us to his lovely house on Long Island. There I found Mahtab, forever jolly, had not aged an iota and in spite of so much change her laughter had retained its crescendo. Amir and Keyvan had grown to graceful youths with a thick American accent that gave their easy attitude a particular charm. Sarah, a stranger to us was thin and cute. She had inherited her mother's teasing Turcoman eyes. The house exuded happiness and my mother was on top of the world. In the company of her sons she became more of her old self – positive, optimistic and fun-loving. Colour returned to her face and the hollows under her eyes disappeared. It made me happy to see her well again. During a family conference, my brothers decided to share the care of our mother until she was well enough to live at her own flat in Rutland Gate.

Back in Sydney I decided to go to Teheran. I wanted to prove to myself that I was not an exile for life. Hashemi Rafsanjani was the new President and he was ready to be benevolent.

Dr. Mahmoud Jahromi, a friend, lived between Sydney and Teheran. He was well connected in the Islamic Republic. Dr Jahromi had once operated on Immam Khomeini, and the success of the operation had won him the respect of the authorities. I planned my trip to coincide with his return home, a security measure in case unpleasantness awaited me at the airport in Teheran in spite of the fact that most of those returning from Iran were full of praise for the President's recent edict that ordered government officials to exercise speed and efficiency in solving people's problems. This was encouraging. The war with Iraq seemed to be ending. Most enemies of the regime were annihilated or forced underground and the intergovernmental rivalries had subsided. Iran had embarked on a reconstruction phase. Consequently now more than ever it needed its talents, technicians and entrepreneurs. The government was sending "talent attracting" emissaries across the world. Their mission was to entice the "educated" to return home. They were making special allowances for medical doctors and university professors. Mehdi had already received his invitation but he was too sceptical. I was more adventurous than my husband. In our lives now everything material was in order yet neither Mehdi nor I could call ourselves happy, for we missed our country and our roots. In 1980 we had taken our lives and run to a "perceived" haven. Now things had changed in Iran and our safety was no longer a question. Therefore should we return to our own country where we belonged? Or was our sense of "belonging" an illusion? Was the life we longed for dead? Or were we burying ourselves under the weight of unreasonable fears? Was our existence in Australia by choice or by force of circumstance? If by choice, then we had to try harder to cultivate in ourselves the senses of "belonging" and "relating" that are fundamental to mental health. And if we were in Australia by force of circumstance, we had to make new decisions. I had to find answers to these mind-boggling questions before I could find true peace of mind. Therefore, for me a return to Iran was an unavoidable imperative. Providence also introduced an extra push. Aunt Azar who was in charge of my mother's financial affairs in Iran had informed Mahmoud, with whom my mother was now staying that the Foundation of Martyrs had sent a letter demanding Mother's presence at their headquarters by a certain date otherwise they would confiscate her properties without her ever again being able to retrieve them. This meant my ailing mother had either to relinquish her right of ownership or brave flying to Teheran by herself. Mahmoud could not accompany her, as his name had appeared on a recently published book of "traitors". During their occupation of the US embassy the "students following the Immam's line" had found and meticulously reassembled all the pieces of files that had hastily been shredded by the embassy personnel before their surrender. The compiled information was now turned into an encyclopedia of treason – bearing the names of people who supposedly were CIA, MOSSAD, MI5 and KGB agents. The book detailed the activities of these so-called traitors. The proof of Mahmoud's treason had been his trip to Jerusalem in September 1975. He had gone there as a tourist on his way to Iran!

In a way it was good that Mother was impelled to return to Teheran too. The cherished family ambience would lift her mood. The two of us were going to stay at my Khalleh Nayer's house in Ehteshamieh. I was both excited and apprehensive. To return to Iran was like entering a jungle full of traps. Apparently the Islamic Republic's spy network was far more sophisticated, thorough and merciless than SAVAK had ever been. It knew all that was to know about ordinary citizens let alone a person with a dossier. Since, in Iran the presentation of a birth certificate or its photocopy has always been required for every single official activity or transaction, it is easy for the security force to compile thorough information on the citizens' affairs. The two most important details by which people are identified are the name of their father and the number on their birth certificate, which has to appear on all legal documents from opening a bank account to purchasing a house, to becoming employed, to occupying a coffin. Copies of legal documents are filed under the individual's maiden name in the headquarters of the country's Prosecutor General. The clergy's security service replacing the SAVAK referred to by the people as SAVAMA, together with the foundations have unlimited access to these records. Often the contents of the files are interpreted in a manner that suits the interpreting agent's intentions! For example an "undesirable" element who had previously worked at the Pahlavi Foundation as a harmless janitor can be declared an "anti-revolutionary". As such, his meagre possessions become subject to confiscation and he, himself, if not jailed, is barred from further employment at government institutions.

So far, many such instances had ruined innocent lives.

Regardless of the contradictory stories we kept hearing, set to go, I began to organize my Islamic outfits. I was so determined to look proper that I put on my head cover in Sydney instead of Kuala Lumpur where we had a five-hour wait for our Iran Air connection in which Islamic Hejab had to be observed.

During our stop over I spent my time browsing through duty-free shops while Dr Jahromi flirted with his last glasses of beer. As the time of departure approached, Iranian passengers began to accumulate by the Iran-Air departure gate. Nostalgic, I began to watch them. It was strange to find them chatting with ease, laughing with delight, frowning in jest and impatiently glancing at their watches. The women seemed quite comfortable in their Hejab. Their relaxed demeanour defied my notion of a nation in distress. Looking at them I felt a tinge of envy. Besides their vitality, what captured my attention most was the number of boxes of electrical appliances each carried. I asked my friend if he knew the reason. Dr Jahromi smiling said: "Look how they are clustered together. Most of these groups are families hired by merchants to travel abroad. You see, Lily, recently the government has allowed each traveller to bring in goods valued up to US $5000. The merchants use this privilege to enhance their business. They commission trustworthy families particularly with children whose allowance is the same as an adult but whose airfare is cheaper, to travel to destinations for which a visa is not required like Malaysia, Indonesia etc. Their mission is to purchase commodities rare in Iran due to international sanctions. It is a clever idea!"

Amazed at the practicality of this commercial connivance I exclaimed:

"Iranians know how to survive, don't they?"

"Sure they do" replied my companion, gloating in pride.

When the call to embark came, the crowd hastily gathered itself into a disorderly queue and began to wiggle towards the gate. Inside the aircraft a song of Koranic verses ushered us into the Ayatollah's puritanical realm. It took a long time for the boisterous passengers to fit their heavy, large loads in the overhead compartments and under their seats. In a corner even a row broke out which was eventually settled by the interference of a hostess. Some even exchanged cross words with the air hostess who was forbidding them to hold the leftover items on their laps. Eventually calm was restored and the plane took off. Too excited to sleep I kept daydreaming until the captain announced our penetration into the Iranian air zone. I looked through my window and saw the desert and the mountains that I loved so much. I felt fully alive. The plane landed smoothly and as I stepped on my country's soil the anxiety that had made my life so miserable vanished – I once again felt light, secure and my old, happy self.

In the terminal, standing in a long queue I was too keyed up to think of any clever answers to possible "whys" that could be thrown at me by the officers checking the passports. In my mind I could hear them ask: "Why did you LEAVE Iran?" "Why are you COMING back?" "Why this?" "Why that?"

Suddenly I wanted to cry out: "Why what, brother! I am an Iranian like you, returning to my country. Surely I cannot be punished for my choice?" But the cold chill, the hushed silence and the austerity of the hall warned that I had to hold my temper and tongue. Clearly here was Khomeini's domain, a society that thrived on punishment and frowned on all the innocent trivialities that gave flavour to life. But I pondered; "Whatever "here" is, it is mine like nowhere else has yet proved to be."

When my turn came I walked the line and greeted the young bearded Pasdar with a polite smile. He stole a quick cheeky glance at my composed face and returned my greeting with a friendly Salam before examining the pages of my passport. If he had listened hard he could have heard the thumping of my heart. But he was busy consulting the books that lay open on his counter. Finally he returned his gaze to my passport, stamped it and then politely handed it back to me with a welcoming smile. The twinkle in his eyes brightened my day. Once I passed the third and the last checkpoint without any hassles, I felt as though I had conquered the entire world. Dr Jahromi joined me at the luggage collection section where his sister, accompanied by their nephew, had come to greet him. This was a forbidden zone. Yet just like the time of the Shah those who had 'connections' could venture in. I noticed my companion was very popular among a number of porters on duty. Inquisitive, I asked him the reason.

Cocky about his popularity the doctor light-heartedly whispered: "They are my patients." When our suitcases appeared on the rotating belt he pointed them to the two porters standing one on each side of him. They swiftly lifted the cases off, placed them on their trolleys and rushed towards a customs inspector. There they momentarily halted, told the inspector that the luggage belonged to the revered doctor and without waiting for his response pushed the trolleys away from under his large nose.

Mehrabad's crowded arrival hall was humming with excitement: tie-less men, women in Hejab and children in their white, long scarves were greeting their travellers. But no one seemed to have come for me. As hard as I looked I could not spot either Ezat Khanum or Mehrdad. Disappointed and embarrassed in front of my friend I did not know what to do. Dr Jahromi, promptly offered to give me a ride in his nephew's car. Gladly, I accepted his kind offer. Outside a pale moon was fighting for recognition against the background of a milky dawn sky as yet not spoilt by the cloud of pollution that would shortly turn it into grey. A pleasant mountain breeze teased the tail of my scarf and the familiar smell of Teheran lifted my spirit out of its long wake. What I saw on the way from Mehrabad airport to Avenue Ehteshamieh elated me. I had expected to find a sad city ruined by bombardments. Instead I found a vibrant capital with magnificent highways, well maintained parks and graceful buildings with exteriors that were predominantly designed in the style of old Persian architecture. At Avenue Ehteshamieh much had changed including its name that I have, to this day, refused to remember. Somehow the cul-de-sac off Ehteshamieh that was named after me had escaped new christening. The luminous white writing on the navy blue tile cemented on the side of Masoud's wall still reads "Kocheh [139] Lily". The wall of my old garden, stretching along the cul-de-sac was hidden under a spread of honeysuckle that Mehdi had planted and now no one had bothered to prune. It hurt to look at my once happy home. As we progressed towards the mountains, I noticed three buildings had been erected in the old garden of my parents' home. Mother had had the good sense to sell this property before it could be confiscated; also the wall to Shahjoon's residence needed repair. Her house was "saheb mordeh" (house of dead). She had died in 1983 and still in 1991 the Foundation of Martyrs would not allow her estate to be divided between her children because their dossiers had not been completely cleared! Zari and her family were still living there. They would not vacate until "financially" satisfied! When eventually the house was sold they were handsomely rewarded for their loyalty.

---

[139] Cul-de-sac

Dr Jahromi unloaded me at my aunt's where I stood ringing the bell. Mariam, one of our old servants, recently re-employed to take care of my mother, opened the door and when she saw me a smile lit her puffy face and she exclaimed: "Oh, Lily Khanum, you were supposed to come tomorrow morning!" So that was why no one had come for me, I thought. With seven and a half hours difference between Sydney and Teheran they had miscalculated my time of arrival. Instead of offering an explanation which she would have not understood anyway I kissed the old maid and entered the house. She shut the door behind her and turned the light on. Instantly my mother and her sister emerged from their respective bedrooms into the hallway. Astonishment glowed from their sleepy, toothless faces – neither had had time to insert their dentures. Once they had overcome their initial shock, excitement filled the room. I cannot describe the intensity of the emotion I experienced at that moment and the following hours. After huge hugs and many kisses, we gathered in my aunt's dining room. Mariam dragged my suitcase to the bedroom I was to share with my aunt then disappeared into the kitchen to prepare breakfast. My aunt at eighty, even though deeply entangled with the office of the prosecutor general, had not changed a bit. At that age and under her perilous circumstances she dared to live by herself. A daily servant cleaned and cooked for her. Both her sons were in France. Yet her zest had remained intact and her mind super alert. My mother, too, was infected by her sister's joie de vivre. She smiled often. I had no appetite for breakfast and was too elated to sit still.

When my aunt realized I was about to venture out she said: "Lily joon, you must never go out of the house without a Roupoosh, I cannot believe no Sister of Zahra objected to your suit at the airport."

"Why, Khalleh joon, my outfit is very Islamic. I don't need a Roupoosh and who are the Sisters of Zahra anyway?" I asked eager to learn. Mariam sitting cross-legged on the carpet, straightened her plump back, cleared her chest, assumed a motherly air and took upon herself the responsibility of "guiding me to the right path".

"Lily Khanum, they are teams of women working for the Ministry of Morality with the task to make certain all women adhere to the Islamic code of conduct paramount to which is Hejab. Khanum joon, your suit is long but it is also expensive. Roupoosh creates equality. Poor or rich we are equal in the eyes of Allah. So we must remain equal in the eyes of man, too. You must always remember that." She emphasized her statement with the wave of her angular index finger which was calloused by endless years of manual labour.

"Mariam Khanum, I wear my Islam in my heart and not on my body," I answered with a broad beam. Nevertheless, not to hurt her, I immediately took off my jacket, put on the black gown my aunt lent me and flew out of the house for a tour of the places that had occupied my dreams for the past ten years. I walked down Ehteshamieh, and passed by the houses that once were ours. The memories returned of those I had loved and had lost to distance, death or execution; of the events that I had shared with my family; of the simple things that had made life worth living. I cried and cried and cried.

I stopped by Khalleh Victor's residence and asked a guard loitering at its gate: "Brother why has this building been burnt?"

"Sister, this used to be a Komiteh. No one knows who set fire to it."

"Probably the wrath of God," I mumbled to myself and continued to walk.

The guard heard me and thought I was mad.

I made a circle around Saltanatabad to Avenue Doulat and back to Ehteshamieh. On my way I noticed some of my relatives' houses which in their absence had been confiscated by the Foundation of Martyrs and turned into schools.

By the time I arrived home it was lunch time. There I found Dai Doctor and Azar joon had come to see me. They seemed very happy for after eight years Dai Doctor had been able to go to New York and see his son Gholam Hussain and his new wife. Soon more relatives arrived. Magically time reverted to when nothing had touched our lives, and the sound of genuine laughter filled the emptiness in the pit of my heart. Happily our bond of kinship had remained undaunted by geographical dispersion. Together again we exchanged many warm feelings and I answered my relatives' questions about Australia. When their curiosity about the "land of kangaroos" was satisfied they began telling me about how hard it had become to maintain a decent standard of living and how interminable were their problems with the office of the Prosecutor General. Their revelations made me acutely conscious of the blows that had bruised the Iranian society during my absence. The most ostensible of the afflictions were the unavailability of basic essentials in the market and the daily rise in inflation. Everything had a US dollar value and with dollar fluctuation the prices changed – always upward. The official exchange rate between rial and dollar was a hundred to one. The black market rate was one thousand, four hundred rial to one dollar. It was this rate that people took into account when pricing their commodities! It seemed the revolution had not eradicated poverty – as promised. It had only changed its face. The new poor were the unemployed, those whose wealth had been confiscated and the wage earners whose salaries were insufficient to tackle the inflation. The revolution had destroyed industry. The war with Iraq had exhausted the government's budget, crippling its domestic reconstruction capacities. International financial agencies such as the World Bank and the International Monetary Fund influenced by the US government's foreign policies refused to lend money to Iran. Yet the city was alive. New buildings were going up everywhere and retail of available merchandize was booming. There were two or three jewellery shops side by side in every corner. It was wise to invest in gold when the currency devalued sometimes by the hour. Teheran traffic was chaotic. The old buses expelled clouds of vapour. To control traffic the town was zoned during office hours. I never faced any difficulties in driving through the city where private cars were forbidden because I hired telephone taxis on an hourly basis. Each locality had its own taxi office. It was expedient to become friendly with the drivers of these vehicles as they made themselves promptly available to their favourite customers. The majority of these drivers were educated men who could not find employment appropriately suited to their professions.

The fruit markets were full of first-class produce but only the wives of the clergy, the rich entrepreneurs, the medical doctors and the middle-men had the purchasing power to visit them. However, no one went hungry. Each person was issued a set number of provision coupons by which food could be purchased from government cooperatives at government prices. Based on their individual needs, families exchanged coupons. People with children usually looked for milk coupons as baby milk powder formula was scarce. Among the wealthy there were those who gave their ration tickets to their domestics or those friends who could not survive otherwise. To fight scarcity recycling was practised. In the early hours of the morning one could hear the drivers of creeping vans singing their requirements through a loud speaker. They each sang a different song: "We'll buy bottles. Bottles, bottles, bottles!"

"Tins, tins, tins. Make money out of tins!"

The population accustomed to suffering from a multitude of shortages, made a conscious effort to help with the recycling. Nothing was thrown away. Even used tea leaves were saved and scattered on flower beds to act as fertilizers. It was amazing how the nation had disciplined itself to rely on its own resources so that it could bear the aftermaths of a revolution, the hardships of a stalemate war together with international ostracism. With solutions to their problems beyond their control people had become streetwise. They had realized their welfare depended on a balance between give and take. Therefore, they delved into an understood system of "if you scratch my back I will scratch yours". Naturally in an economy on the verge of bankruptcy the key to all problems was money exchanged in all forms from bribes to gifts to "tea money". Besides cash the next problem-solver was "connections" particularly with a prominent clergyman. I wised up to the system pretty fast.

On the fourth morning of my stay in Teheran I received a telephone call from Taghi still in my mother's employment. He urged me to immediately get myself to Masoud's house which neighboured my mother's, because the Passdars from the Central Komiteh had broken their own seal and were about to physically occupy the house. Hiding my panic from Maman who just sat and gazed at the tree tops, I quickly finished my breakfast; put my roupoosh on and pretending to take my morning walk, dashed down to Kocheh Lily. Masoud's house was the first in the Kocheh and I found its door wide open.

Three bearded officials with their revolvers and transmitters hanging from their leather belts were busy roaming around. Without being intimidated by their air of authority I stepped inside and politely asked who was in charge. A tall thin man with a trimmed moustache that matched his jet black hair came forward saying: "Who wants to know?"

"I do. I am Mrs Monadjemi, the sister of Dr Izadi. I want to know what you are doing in my brother's property." Taken by surprise by the authenticity of my address, the other two joined their friend and glared at me – an untimely intruder. Mockingly the tall man replied: "We will only talk to Izadi himself."

"He is on the plane at this moment," I lied, and then I softened my tone: "Please tell me brother what you are doing here?"

"We are confiscating this house in the name of the Foundation of the Martyrs. We are going to turn it into a dormitory for the students of the University of Martyrs."

"Why are you doing this? My brother has not committed any

crime to deserve such a penalty."

"If he has not, why has he not shown his face in Iran for the past ten years?"

"Actually he left Iran many years before the Revolution – he is not an escapee. Besides he did not know that he had to come and report his whereabouts to the Foundation!" The man standing next to the tall guy looked meaner than the rest. Aiming to silence me he snapped:

"Now you know. We believe your brother is guilty otherwise he would have responded to the summons we sent him last year. Since we did not hear from him within the period allowed we evicted his tenant, sealed off the house and now that his time is up, we are going to put the house to good use." I was not aware of any summons. This meant Masoud was in serious trouble. Nevertheless ignoring the ugly, broad-shouldered, malevolent guard I addressed the tall handsome one:

"Brother what must Dr Izadi do to retrieve his house?"

"He has four more days to introduce himself to the Foundation of the Martyrs. We will investigate his dossier. If he is innocent he will get his house back, until then we have to proceed with our mission."

My sixth sense told me that I could save the property if I played it right. Fighting with these men would not only solve any problems but it would also get me into trouble.

The tall man emanated a positive aura. He was my only hope. We were in Masoud's huge sitting room that was empty of its elegant furniture but filled with mine that I guess Taghi had taken there while vacating the house for Kaman. I don't know why, but the sight of those red comfortable chairs now purple with dust produced tears in my eyes. The tall man asked why I was crying. "I am crying because we fought a revolution for justice. Look at what has happened to us now. We have become outcasts whose belongings are confiscated for no reason whatsoever. Do you know that there is a store room downstairs with a number of trunks that belong to me and my mother? Also these red arm chairs are mine. What have my sick mother and I done wrong?"

"Khanum we already know that everything which has remained in this house belongs to Izadi's mother and sister. That is why they are still here. We have already removed Izadi's furniture to our safe house."

"God give you a long happy life for being so fair," I whispered loud enough for him to hear.

Curious to see the condition of the house I asked: "Is it at all possible for you to allow me to go through the building, just for old time's sake?"

"Go ahead, Sister."

"Brother, could you please accompany me. It is better if we go through it together." Then I walked straight to my four dusty, discoloured, red armchairs which were placed in an untidy row under the French window through which the once manicured garden lay in waste, and said: "Brother I would like to offer these chairs to the Foundation. I want you to use them for the comfort of the students who would occupy the dormitory should fate turn this house to such an establishment."

"It is very generous of you, sister. But we have no interest in the possessions of good citizens. What belongs to you and your mother will be returned to you."

"Thank you, Brother – I know that the representatives of the Islamic Republic will do what is right by the people. Nevertheless, I insist you keep the chairs for the children of the martyrs of the war.

"Choosing to ignore my offer the tall man asked: "Mrs Monadjemi where do you live?"

"I live with my family in Sydney, Australia."

"Ha! Australia! People say it is paradise over there," he exclaimed with a sparkle of envy in his large black eyes.

"Paradise is the country in which you are born and bred," I sighed heavily.

The way he looked at me was as though I was crazy. "Then why are you still there?"

"The closure of the universities rendered my husband and I unemployed. We used to lecture at the National University. We went to Australia so that we could work and earn a living. At the time we had no other choice."

For a second the man was lost for words. Then nodding his index finger at me he suggested: "You must return to Iran and educate the youths of your own country."

"Yes we must. That is why I am here now. I want to see if people like you will have people like us back." We both laughed at my frank statement which he had perceived as a joke. I sensed a rapport blooming between myself and this great talker of a man. I patiently listened to his speech about the revolution, the eminence of the Immam who had put the Great Satan to shame and the prosperity that awaited the nation.

Touring the house, I led the way to the basement where the

storage room was. Now smiling he took a bundle of keys out of his coat pocket, selected the one he needed, unlocked the door and stepped aside. I entered the airless room where many of our valuables safely packed in cardboard boxes were buried under a thick layer of grey dust. In fact most of the boxes belonged to Mahtab herself but fortunately the men did not know that.

By the time we finished our round it was lunch time. From the minaret of Ghobad mosque the Moaz was calling the faithful to prayer. The guards had to go.

Suddenly it occurred to me that before losing these people, I had to get the address of their Komiteh and the division from which they had been sent. Their name I could never know because for security purposes they functioned under pseudonyms. "Brother, when my brother arrives where can he contact you?"

The man took out a piece of paper and a biro from the pocket of his green parka jacket and wrote down the address of their headquarters. He even offered to give me a lift to my aunt's house. I accepted his offer.

At home, I found my aunt and mother sitting at the dining table waiting for me. From Maman's eyes I realized how worried she had been for me. I quickly explained the situation, and then called Masoud in New York. As I finished talking Mariam appeared with a dish of steaming rice topped with pieces of chicken kebab. The sun's rays were pouring into the cosy room; the smell of kebab was mouth watering and I was extremely happy. I sat next to my mother and let my aunt dish out my portion. Khalleh Nayer, holding my plate lifted her thin, well-plucked eyebrows, looked straight at my Mother and said:

"Monir joon, now that finally your problems with the Foun-dation are over you should sell everything and send the money out." Believing in the wisdom of her suggestion I interfered:

"Khalleh, you are absolutely right. With the way the rial is devaluing if we don't take what we have out now, it will soon amount to nothing." My aunt nodded her head in agreement, handed me my plate and added:

"Azar knows a developer who is interested in properties around here. After my nap I shall call her." This was good news. However, first, we had to give notice to Mother's tenant, a cunning woman who would not leave without some sort of compensation! During the entire course of our lunch Mother, serene and composed said nothing.

The house meant nothing to her anymore. She had already told me if she could get rid of it she would divide the money between the three of us. She could not understand the concept of money anymore. The stroke had destroyed her previously acute commercial acumen.

The next day I was negotiating with Shahin, Mother's tenant, the amount of "remuneration" we had to offer her as the token of our gratitude for her having been a "friend" rather than a tenant, when her maid, looking pale and frightened entered the salon and announced the arrival of a group of men from the Foundation of the Martyrs asking for "Mrs Izadi's daughter who lives in Australia". I panicked. Thinking that I had been foolish in talking with the men at my brother's house I rose, steadied myself on my feet and stepped outside. The same three men were standing by the gate. I was flabbergasted by the ease with which they had located me. My friend, the tall fellow, greeted me warmly and said:

"Could you please make arrangement for someone to come and collect your and your mother's belongings from Izadi's house right now.

"Wonderful," I thought but asked: "Where am I going to store all that furniture now?"

Taghi who had just arrived on his motorbike said: "Khanum, ask Shahin Khanum. She might let you bring them here. We will place them on the veranda until I find a second-hand dealer. There are plenty of them around."

I turned to Shahin who was standing by me and asked her permission. She shrugged her fat, round shoulders and replied. "As long as it won't be for too long." I thanked her and put Taghi in charge of the removal.

Three days later Masoud arrived to exonerate himself from the false accusations that had turned his honest work record into the dossier of a crook. It took him a few months, and much under the table gifts and assistance from his 'connections' to gain the repossession of the house which he promptly sold.

The revolution had changed the regime. It had destroyed the power of the one thousand ruling families and had transformed the appearance of the people in the streets. But it had failed to subdue the vivacious spirit and break the resilience of the people particularly the women. Iran's long history of defeats and conquests has endowed Iranians with an exceptional ability to adjust to the 'requirements of the time'. People who enjoyed moderate drinking had learnt to brew their own wine; gamblers played cards at home, those who loved music brought the musicians to their drawing rooms or purchased black market tapes of Iranian songs recorded in Los Angeles; people who wished to use narcotics grew hemp or poppies in their back yards or gardens; fornicators took Sighehs'; temporary wives; and film-lovers rented from their own special "contact" video's of recent films. So life went on and many preferred living in their own country to becoming émigrés elsewhere. True they did complain at times, but they would not "change their life for all the freedom they could find in the West".

Iran was their country and they loved it.

Chapter 22

It was a calm autumn day; the wild thorny shrubs and the thistles had already dried out. A mild breeze was dispersing the shrivelled leaves and floating them in the air. In a few days the desolate fields would turn into mounds of dead leaves. The singing birds had already migrated; only crows leapt here and there. Today the pollution was not that thick, and the sky over the Alborz range was displaying a rare clarity that was pleasing to the eyes. I was in the back seat of a telephone taxi planning what to do when we reached Galandoak. In my absence, Mashallah, whose sons had set fire to my garden, had taken it upon himself to turn the land into a cherry orchard. Apparently now he was exporting the produce to Israel of all places! While my father-in-law was alive Mashallah had asked him if I would lease him the garden. Dr Monadjemi had immediately rejected the offer. A lease with a man whose sons ran the Komiteh would have meant handing the land to him on a silver platter. However, I had sent a message to Mashallah that if he wanted to sign a lease so that his conscience would be clear in pocketing the benefit from the sale of the cherries he should rest assured that I *Hallal* him the gain. (The concept of *Hallal* is of great importance to a practising Muslim which Mashallah pretended to be. When there is no sin to an act it is deemed *Hallal*. For Mashallah the profit he was making was *Haram* (sinful) unless sanctioned by the owner.) By giving him my blessing I had made him responsible for the safekeeping of my property which otherwise could have been confiscated by the authorities as an asset belonging to an absentee landlord. In that case, the tilling of the land could have been allocated to someone other than Mashallah who knew this and did not want to take the risk of losing his hold on the asset that he counted would ultimately be his. The day of reckoning had arrived and I wanted to strike a mutually satisfactory deal with him. But before taking any steps I had to find out what the village sentiment was towards each of us and whether I had a leg to stand on.

As we finished winding around the rusty hills and touched the periphery of the green village I spotted a real estate agency. I asked the driver to stop. His sudden braking threw me forward colliding with the back of the front seat. My chador slipped from my head. I quickly pulled it up, whispered a complaint, opened the door and got out of the taxi. I went straight in to the shop. An old, bearded agent was sitting behind an aluminum desk above which a huge portrait of the Immam hung skewed. The man calmly directed his curious gaze at me and reluctantly responded to my Salam. "Agha I am looking for land to buy." I asked ignoring his invitation to sit down.

"On the hills or by the river Khanum?"

"By the river, actually I have seen a cherry orchard that runs into the river bed at Saleh Avenue. Do you know if it is for sale?"

"No, Khanum. That property belongs to the niece of Victor, the widow of the late Khadjenouri. No one can buy it because Khadjenouri's gardener has his hold on it. Apparently he has seed right to the land."

"Late Khadjenouri" connoted respect. The sarcasm hidden in his tone while referring to "gardener", a well-known man among the villagers, meant Mashallah and his sons had lost their eminence.

"What is the value of that land, Agha?" I asked.

"One hundred thousand rials per square metre." In possession of the information, I thanked the agent and left. Hiding deep under my chador I directed the driver to the orchard. It looked magnificent. At least two hundred healthy fruit trees stood side by side in uniform rows separated by narrow water canals. A few trees had large, red apples, and the branches of a persimmon tree were bent under the weight of their young green yield. The only familiar aspect of the garden was the wire fence I had made Mashallah install. Sitting in the car I watched it with remorse.

At home I called Taghi and instructed him to contact Mashallah with the message that I wanted to know if he wished to purchase my garden.

Two days later, Mariam had just prepared the afternoon tea when Mashallah and his youngest son Jamshid arrived bringing me a basket of red apples. The gift was symbolic but I chose to ignore its significance. We exchanged the customary pleasantries before I got to the point.

"Mashallah Khan, thanks for taking care of my garden. Please tell me how I can best repay your conscientious efforts?" With his gaze fixed on the carpet Mashallah replied:

"Khanum we have done nothing more than our duty."

"Mashallah Khan, you must have spent money on cultivating those various fruit trees?"

"Yes I have and I have also collected the income. You owe me nothing, Khanum."

"Mashallah Khan, Dr Monadjemi and I have decided to return to Iran. We need to buy an apartment in Teheran for which I need money. Therefore I have to sell the garden and since you have tilled it, I would like to offer it to you first."

Fiddling with his prayer beads Mashallah replied: "We thank you, Khanum, for the chance. Yes, if God wills, I want to purchase your garden for my Jamshid. I am now old, sick and infirm. It would be a blessing for my wife and me to have our son and his family live next door."

"Nothing delights me more than pleasing such a man of God as you." I said trying to catch his down-cast eyes. I noticed Mashallah had very long, black lashes.

Twisting the string of the beads around his index finger and keeping his head down Mashallah cleared his voice and asked: "Khanum, I hope you are going to be generous to us."

"Yes Mashallah Khan, I will be. You know that the price of land in your vicinity is one hundred thousand rials per square metre and as a token of my gratitude I ask you for only seventy thousand." Upon hearing the sum a flicker of a smile passed over Mashallah's black lips. "However there is a condition attached to my offer." I hastily added raising my index finger. "Whatever is your wish, Khanum." The old man replied still keeping his head down.

"In my absence, Jamshid must accept the responsibility for the execution of the necessary legal procedures. My aunt has total power of attorney from me for the final signature. It should not be a difficult task as everyone at the municipality is related to you therefore they won't create any unnecessary delays for us – would they Mashallah Khan?"

Mashallah, stopped playing with the beads and pensive, began to toy with his grey beard and then, for the first time looked me straight in the eyes and said: "Khanum, my son is at your service but you must become more generous to this old man who has dedicated his entire life to the service of your family?"

"My foot" I thought. On Mohsen Khan's trial he had been one

of the accusers and not a supporter. Nevertheless I said: "I cannot, Mashallah Khan, for then I would not be able to buy anything for myself. Do you wish us to remain exiles for the rest of our lives?"

"God forbid! No Khanum. You belong to Iran." Jamshid detecting the finality in my tone and unable to conceal his excitement anymore broke politeness and interrupted his father:

"Khanum, God bless you. Now I can own a home next to my father."

"Enshallah, Jamshid," I said as I picked up a plate of sweets from the table and offered it to my guests: "Mobarak-etan Bashe (congratulations). To celebrate please sweeten your palates," I said smiling and thinking that I had won my bet with Masoud who had refused to believe that I could ever get anything out of Mashallah. In the corner of my eye I saw Mariam, who had hidden behind the curtain, leave to make tea. She was my mother's eyes and ears. Before my guests departed I gave Jamshid a copy of my clearance letter without which he could not conduct my legal affairs.

Two days later Jamshid called from Galandoak's Notary office. I was both prohibited from participating in any commercial transactions and leaving the country. I could not believe my ears. He explained that the letter was a clearance for Lily Izadi and not X Izadi, the religious name that was registered on my birth certificate and legal documents. I instantly realized the cause of the mistake. In Iran most people are given two names, one that belongs to a favorite Immam and one by which the person is addressed. Usually the latter, is excluded from being registered on the birth certificate. Since I had always been called Lily, my cursed cousin who had betrayed us had been unaware of my legal name. This new problem meant I had to report the mistake to the office of the Prosecutor General hoping they would correct the error! I was terrified. With or without selling the land I had to leave Iran on schedule otherwise I would lose my job. Immediately I called for a taxi, covered myself with a heavy, black chador which I had to wear over my scarf and Roupoosh – a must when entering a government office and rushed outside to wait for the car.

At Evin I instructed the driver to wait for me and silently praying entered the small, ominous reception hall from where I had to get permission to enter the compound inside which the actual offices were located. The room was large, austere and chilly. A wooden counter divided the area into two zones. Three different individuals stood under separate wooden signs reading: Official, Sisters and Prisoners. Since my problem was official I joined that queue. When I reached the frowning clerk I politely explained the reason for my appeal and presented to him my birth certificate and the clearance letter. He took the documents, placed them on a pile of papers in front of him, pulled out a numbered ticket from a nozzle, threw it on the counter and mumbled: "Come back in four weeks' time." My stomach churned.

"I cannot Agha. I am leaving Iran in a fortnight."

"If you want to resolve your problem, come back in four weeks."

From his hostile stare I concluded further argument would be useless.

"May I have my papers back please?" He darted an angry glance at me before throwing my documents on the counter. Furious and terrified I returned to the cab.

At home Maman saw the fear in my eyes, and began to stutter something before she lost her ability to form any coherent word at all and began to cry. With difficulty I swallowed the lump in my own throat, hugged and kissed her. Mariam brought tea and I recounted my experience at Evin and sought my shrewd aunt's advice. Patient and focused she sank deep in thought and then calmly patted my knee and said: "Don't worry, child. I will put you in touch with a man well-connected inside the Prosecutor General's office. His fee is only three hundred thousand rials! But he is trustworthy and good." Nervous and scared, I displaced my fury on my poor aunt:

"Khalleh why then this powerful connection of yours has not as yet been able to help you?"

In her deep understanding of human nature she chose to forgive my impertinence, let out a long deep sigh and replied:

"Khanum, my problems are not comparable to yours. They want me to give the Foundation 40% of what I own as Khoms, before they remove my Prohibitions. I will give them forty big farts instead of that much money! You see child, their pockets are bottomless, their greed insatiable! And I am not going to give them the satisfaction of squeezing me dry."

That night I could not sleep. Plans raced in my agitated mind. By dawn I knew I was not going to take no for an answer. At 7 am I returned to the hated office and hoping to receive a softer response I approached the counter for 'Sisters'.

"What brings you here, Sister?": asked a kindly old man.

"An official error, Brother – the wrong name appears on my

Prosecutor General's clearance letter. I am a mother of two. I live with my family in Australia. I have come to visit my dying mother. Now because of this mistake I cannot return to my home and children. Please help me." Frowning he unfolded the letter; looked at its date and reference number, checked my name on my birth certificate, compared it with the name on the letter, pondered a while and then picked up the phone and dialled a three digit number. After a few minutes of whispering he put the receiver down, turned to me and in a fatherly tone said:

"Take a seat, sister. I will call you."

"Thank you and may God grant you a long life." Grateful that I had not been sent away I settled myself on a bench and began to watch the other people who were also waiting! Each one of them – the sacrificial lambs of the revolution – looked sad, beaten and resigned – and I had become a prudent liar!

As minutes turned into hours and my stomach rumbled, I began to lose patience. I went to the counter and asked the man how much longer I had to wait. From the guilt on his face I realized he had forgotten all about me. He quickly picked up the phone again, gave my reference number to whomever he was speaking to, waited a little, then put the receiver down and wrote something on a small piece of paper which he handed to me.

"Sister, present this at the gate and ask for office number 20 where your dossier is."

"Again many thanks, Brother." I said before running to the gate of the fortress.

At the gate two rifled soldiers stood sombrely to attention. The senior of the two guided me inside a kiosk where another soldier asked for either my passport or birth certificate. Since I had not had time to change my birth certificate to that of the Islamic Republic's and my Pahlavi one bore my bare headed photo I handed him my Islamic Republic's passport which at that moment seemed to be useless. He gave me a receipt and a hurried direction.

The sinister compound seemed endless. Many prefabricated interconnecting bungalows, assembled temporarily, were annexes to the main office of the Prosecutor General. Beyond, hidden within Evin hills was located the actual body of the prison and the execution grounds. There was no breeze otherwise I would have breathed the smell of fresh blood that daily pervades the valley. After asking around I found office number 20 in one of the bungalows. It was a small austere room with shelved walls packed with untidy, aged and dusty manila folders arranged in alphabetical order. Two uninviting aluminum chairs faced a bearded, untidy looking Pasdar who was sitting behind a cloud of smoke, puffing nervously at his cigarette. A dirty ashtray placed next to a half-empty tea glass ornamented his otherwise stark, black, plastic, desktop. Somehow as he saw me, the shadow of a smile lit his bored face.

"Sister take a seat and let me know how I can help you." Very politely I explained my problem, then handed him my Clearance letter. He studied the document and then opened the first page of my birth certificate on which was written my father's name, he rose from his chair, straightened his back and walked to the left wall where he stood scanning the shelves. After a few minutes, he pulled out a folder, carried it to his desk and began scrutinizing its content. I felt a sharp spasm in my stomach. It was my spastic colitis playing up again. The long silence was nerve-racking.

Unable to sustain my anxiety I asked: "Brother, what is the problem?" The man looked at me. The muscles of his face had tightened now and his eyes had lost their amicability. Ignoring my question in a cold and impersonal tone he asked: "Do you know Naghi Kashichi?"

"No Agha."

"Do you know Zahra Chopoonzadeh?"

"No Agha." The names were not even familiar. Suddenly I thought perhaps they have mistaken me for a Mojahed, and if so that meant disaster. When my inquisitor finished his questioning he closed the folder with a snap, wrote a number on a piece of paper and gave it to me to take to another office. For two hours I went from one room to another until eventually I reached the office of the Deputy to the Prosecutor General on the second level of the main building – where I should have been sent initially.

This chamber was large. Two composed male secretaries sat behind their desks. Five occupied and one empty chair crowded the room that stank of cigarette and body odour. The two secretaries pretended to be busy with paperwork while the waiting men played, nervously with their prayer beads. The room was very stuffy and I was at my wits' end. Before I had time to sit, the door opened and a short, unshaven, tie-less, limping man entered. Absolute authority oozed out of his small stature and the odour of stale sweat from his brown, one-size-too-small jacket. Suddenly there was a commotion and polite whispers of "Salam alaykom". Everyone rose and stood to attention.

The man momentarily stopped and staring at me with narrowed, condemning eyes said: "We will not serve women in improper Hejab." Flabbergasted I turned my face to the wall, adjusted my chador which must have slipped slightly away from covering my silk scarf, turning my furious face to the unreasonable man said:

"This is entirely your fault. I have been trying to rectify a simple mistake that your office has committed since seven in the morning without success. Room to room I have gone, insult on insult I have received, for what! This is three in the afternoon. I have not had lunch or even a drink of water," I uttered fixing my infuriated glare at the midget.

My outburst confused the man. He turned to one of his secretaries and ordered: "See how this sister can be helped."

Hyped up, I interrupted: "He cannot help me. Only you can."

"In that case wait until I call for you," The deputy replied while pushing open the door to his adjoining office. Dropping on the empty chair I released a sigh of relief.

The oldest of the men rolled his eyes up, lifted a black bushy brow and sent an "Allah Akbar" to the ceiling, meaning "women be damned" then facing the two secretaries said: "How lucky you are to have such a brave man as your superior. Brother Mohamadi lost his leg in the war."

"Yes. It is an honour to be serving Deputy Mohamadi," answered the senior of the two and before he could offer his own praise the phone shut him up. The call was to send me in. I quickly rose, straightened my chador and went inside.

With his hand Mohamadi gestured me to sit. I sat, put the documents before him, and for the twentieth time that day began explaining the reason for the mistake. He patiently listened, then examined my letter, compared the names with that registered on my birth certificate, confessed to the silly error, wrote a little note and handing it to me instructed: "Take this to the file-room and bring me your master file."

In the file-room I offered the note to the young, good-looking official sitting behind a small, empty, metal desk, and who appeared seemingly frustrated with the entire world. Without responding to my

Salam, he grabbed the paper and read it. Then with a pair of hostile, blue eyes that were very beautiful but malicious scrutinized me from top to toe, did not like what he saw and said: "I am not going to release anything to you."

"Why not Agha, this authorization is from the deputy himself."

"Yes I can read. You go ask him to come and collect it himself."

Furious, I returned to the deputy and deliberately delivered the message verbatim. The man embarrassed, left his desk; limping he led me to his secretaries' room and ordered the senior secretary to accompany me. On seeing the secretary, the man in the file-room lost his air of arrogance, promptly took the note from me, left his desk, referred to a wide wall of files; quickly found what he was searching for which indeed was a thick bundle and handing it to the secretary mocked: "Not a thin one hah!" Then he turned to me and nodding to the surrounding walls retorted: "All those files belong to the Amir-Aslani family. How many of you are there?" I smiled and replied:

"You should know. You keep the files!"

While the deputy was writing a new clearance letter I was thinking about Masoud. He had the same problem as me. So I sent a silent prayer for help and said: "Dear Agha, you have seen my documents and my birth certificate. My eldest brother, Masoud on the list suffers from the same problem. His name on his Birth certificate is X. Could you please be kind enough to include his legal name on this letter too?"

The deputy lifted his head, smiled and asked: "Have you his birth certificate with you?"

"No Agha. I only have my honour upon which I swear that I am telling you the truth."

"Your brother is lucky to have a sister with such presence of mind."

"Thank you, Agha. He has been a good brother."

Mr Mohamadi finished the letter and giving it to me instructed: "Take this to the typing-pool on the next level up." I took the letter, ran out of the room and Batman-like flew up the steps that led to a wide grey tiled corridor on the left side of which were two holes covered with black curtains. Between the two curtains a sign read: Hand in your documents for typing. I pushed the curtain aside and shoved my hand in. A woman clad in a black chador snatched the letter and rudely ordered:

"Wait until your name is called out." I did not resent her hostile manner for if I had been in her place working in that dark, windowless, enclosure, clad in heavy fabrics, from seven in the morning until four in the afternoon I would have lost respect for myself let alone for others.

Waiting in the corridor, I thought of my colleagues at the university who had joined the marches against the Shah and began to laugh – albeit silently. Then I became fascinated by the number of officials in plastic flip-flops, rolling their sleeves up while hurrying down the stone stairs, their footsteps echoing in the naked stone corridor. It seemed they were baring their hairy arms for the obligatory ablution before a prayer. Totally lost in my thoughts, I faintly heard my name called before I saw a hand waving a letter protrude out of the opening. I rushed to the hand, took my letter, thanked the faceless typist and hastened back to the deputy.

He immediately signed and stamped the letter, folded it neatly before fitting it inside an official envelope and sealing it off. Waving the white envelope at me he said: "To prove to you that we are here to solve the problems of our citizens I will give you this important document to take yourself to the country's head office of Birth, Death and Property Documentations (Edareh Sabte Ahval va Asnad Kol Keshvari), otherwise it will take several weeks to be delivered. From there, this notification will be distributed nationally to all notary offices and borders. Now Sister, get going, as it is, I am late for the ceremony at the mosque. It is the anniversary of the death of Immam Khomeini's son."

At home we celebrated my great conquest. My aunt could not believe that during one day I could manage to have the mistake rectified. The next day the same taxi driver picked me up. The office of Birth, Death and Property Documentations is at Toop Khaneh, right in the heart of Teheran's south where the pollution is almost lethal and the traffic bumper to bumper. As the taxi crept into the vicinity, the visage of the city changed to one that the Shah had never noticed. If he had, and had the sense to recognize it for what it stood, he would have never lost his throne: the face of a traditional society happy with its heritage, unashamed of its Islamic appearance and accepting of its principles. Here the women in their bellowing black chadors comfortably floated around. The men rugged in appearance went about their business with the air of austerity typical of the Middle Eastern male, and door-to-door vendors slowly pulled behind them their donkey-driven carts, heavily loaded with sacks of fresh herbs and/or fruit. Some of them, to attract customers, melodiously sang the praise of their merchandise – scenes one would visualize when listening to tales of *One Thousand and One Nights*.

My taxi driver dropped me off in front of the huge building and gave me directions as to where he would be parked.

In the Islamic Republic every government building has separate entrances for females and males. On the threshold of the entrance for women there is a small kiosk in which females are checked for Hejab. The inspectors even look at your nails. All makeup – signs of Western decadence, are to be removed before permission to enter is granted. The slight glitter of my nail strengthener brought upon me the wrath of the examiner who viciously barred me from entry until I removed the polish. Irritated, I ran out of the suffocating hole to find a pharmacy where I could purchase a bottle of nail polish remover. After a long search I found an alchemy shop that had acetone but no cotton wool. I used a tissue instead. With the shine removed from my nails, I passed the second inspection and entered the building.

Asking around I found the office where I had to submit the sealed envelope. This chamber was shared by ten young women in black chadors, working under a middle-aged, fat supervisor whose entity exuded nothing but malevolence. It was to her I had to deliver my letter. I presented myself at her desk, took the envelope out of my bag and handed it to her. Puffed up with importance she grabbed the envelope, broke the seal, pulled out the letter and registered its reference number in a thick book that lay open under her round pockmarked nose. Standing by her desk, glowing with happiness I asked: "Sister, am I free to travel now?"

"Not for another four weeks," She curtly replied in an unpleasant voice.

"Why?"

"Because that is the length of time it takes for these documents to be distributed."

"In that case, could you please give me my letter so that I can photocopy it?"

"I cannot. I have already filed it."

"Sister, it is sitting on your desk. Please! I have to leave Iran very soon. According to you the borders will not have this release document before a month. If I have a copy to present to the official at the airport he will allow me to leave. Please, Sister, help me out!"

"Go woman, I have no time for the likes of you," she said diverting her attention to the next applicant.

Insulted, panicked and infuriated I demanded: "Who is your superior?"

"The Managing Director himself."

"Where is his office?"

"On the fourth floor and you are wrong to think that he will break the rule for people like you," She yelled throwing her white fluffy saliva at my face. With the corner of my chador I wiped off the moisture from my cheek, darted her a murderous glance before leaving the room and flying up the four flights of steps. There I saw a floor janitor. Puffing and heaving I asked him for guidance. He pointed to a door which I opened and barged in without knocking. My intrusion broke the conversation of the men in the room. All eyes turned to me, and then they were diverted to the floor with the exception of those belonging to the young clean-shaven man sitting behind a large neat desk. He calmly asked:

"What brings you here, Sister."

"Hostility, lack of compassion and understanding," I burst out.

"Please explain yourself, sister." So I did with tears running down my quivering cheek. When I finished he picked up the phone, dialled a number and amongst the hushed silence of the room, ordered his deputy to go downstairs, get a photocopy of my letter and bring it to him. Within ten minutes during which I was given a cup of hot tea to calm me down, I was in possession of the key to my freedom – recognition of citizenship of the country in which I was born.

Outside, my driver was patiently waiting in his taxi. From the way I walked he guessed at my conquest. He had been driving me around ever since I had come to Teheran. During the hours caught in Teheran traffic we had poured out our grievances against the regime. Thus a rapport was established between the two of us. He was a chemical engineer hoping to go to the States and never return to Iran as long as the Ayatollahs reigned! When I waved my letter at him he smiled and exclaimed: "Mashallah Khanum, you are a lion of a woman. Usually it takes years before people get what you got in such a short time. Khanum joon, to celebrate I want to invite you for an ice cream."

"That would be lovely, Rostam Khan." But since it was haraam for unrelated men and women to socialize we could not enter an ice cream shop together. On our way back Rostam Khan stopped by a confectionary shop, purchased two creamy Persian ice creams, which we enjoyed within the confines of the car.

Early the following day, Mehrdad collected me in his car and we drove to deliver the new clearance letter to Jamshid in Galandoak. Prison and financial need had mellowed Mehrdad and revolution had diluted our political differences. Now instead of fighting we could actually talk and relate. One delicate and intriguing subject that I had not dared to touch on was his imprisonment. Our privacy in the car provided me with the opportunity.

"Mehrdad would it hurt too much if you told me about your time at Evin?"

He gave me one of his quick nervous laughs, coughed and said:
"It does but I'll tell you anyway."
"Thank you!"

He coughed again. Pneumonia in prison had wrecked his respiratory system and left him with a bad cough which often came when he was stressed.

"When the Tudeh persecution started I knew my days were numbered. I could have fled but it wouldn't have been fair on my family. 'They' would not have shown them any mercy. They would have taken my family members hostage until I showed up. I could not allow that to happen."

"Were you not scared?"

"Oh yes and how! It was my fear that gave me spastic colitis. Every time I returned home I expected to find them waiting for me and one evening I did. Three of them, in plain clothes sitting in my lounge playing with my daughter Roky. Their eyes – I'll never forget their cruel eyes. They gave me just enough time to say goodbye to my pregnant wife, and Roky. They knew I would not run away so they did not handcuff me there. They also allowed me to stop by my parents' flat on the ground floor. Fortunately neither was home. The sight of the men would have finished my mother off. In the street, quickly they shoved me inside their special van parked close to our gate. In the vehicle I was handcuffed and blindfolded.

"For one year, without trial, they kept me in a solitary cell with one small window so high up that I couldn't reach even if I stepped on my bed. It was the ray of the sun pouring in through that small window that kept me alive. When there were no rays it was total darkness. It was like living in my grave with nothing but pain, fear, regrets and hate. Every day I shivered when I heard their footsteps approaching to blindfold and take me to the torture room. No one saw the faces of the interrogators or the torturers. We only heard and felt." Mehrdad stopped. I guess the memory was too painful. I noticed a thin stream of sweat running down his narrow temple and regretted my request. "Lily, punishment at Evin prison was tailor-made for maximum effect. They knew of my colitis. Every time they became frustrated by my lack of cooperation, they forced laxatives down my throat and then barred me from using the toilet to relieve myself. The excruciating pain usually went on for hours. A few times I lost control and soiled my pants in which I was made to remain until the stench offended my jailor. They burnt the soles of my feet with cigarette butts, broke my ribs and a couple of my teeth by their punches and kicks. Several times in company of others, I was blindfolded and pushed and kicked to the gallows where I had stood waiting for death. Each time the reverberating sound of machine guns almost shattered my eardrums but nothing hit me. Those anticipating moments are dreadful. Your body tenses so much that the senses freeze. I guess that is the brain's defence against intense fear. Then when you hear others fall and you are still standing you cannot move a single muscle for your entirety remains in that state of paralysis. After every mock execution they had to drag me back to my cell. Day and night you think of nothing but death and the moment that those bullets will eventually be for you. Every footstep is for you and at the end you sit waiting for it. For four years I lived with that fear, until finally I was given a trial without defence and a sentence of six years' imprisonment. Fortunately the years I had already spent in jail were taken into account. My last two years were not that bad. I learnt carpentry which I enjoyed." Mehrdad stopped talking, took a deep breath and said: "Well Lily, I consider myself lucky for I am still alive and can breathe the smell of the cow manure coming from the fields."

We both burst out laughing. Outside the sun was shining brilliantly, the air was pure and the mountains as majestic as ever. Indeed it was good to be alive.

Back at my aunt's house I found Mother in an exceptionally jovial mood. Surprised I asked my aunt if anything had happened while I was at Galandoak. She gave me a happy wink and answered: "Someone wants to buy Monir's house and he, too, will accept responsibility for the legal procedures. But, my dear, more important than that, Mariam has agreed to accompany Monir joon to London. She will take care of her for a period of two years."

Thrilled I rose and passionately kissed the wrinkled smiling face of the old maid. She was sitting cross-legged on the carpeted floor, rubbing my mother's bad leg. "What a splendid blessing." I thought feeling as light as a feather. Now Mother could stop being a nomad and return to live in her own London flat. I believe the Almighty had granted her this last wish because she was such a good human being – always giving without ever expecting.

With everything in good hands I spent the remaining days of my stay in Teheran partying. No longer did I feel rootless. I don't know what the direction of my life would have been had we remained in Iran. But my visit proved to me that I could not regret having made Australia my new home. So I returned to Sydney a different person. At home, I actually found it possible to taste my food, relax peacefully and wake up in the mornings without anxiety. Then it dawned on me that Mehdi had to do the same. He too had to return to Iran and face whatever was waiting for him. Only then could he find peace. Fortunately, it did not take me long to persuade him to take the risk.

We went to Iran together. Mehdi was on both lists. However, as I had predicted many of his students, the flag bearers of the revolution, now held high government positions and through their assistance, Mehdi came out of the list that prohibits travel but his apartment at Omran Techlar remained confiscated. A decree gave him right of ownership from 1991 on. The affair took three months and much nerve-wracking leg work. But it was worth it.

In Sydney, we were happy enough to return to high society.

Two months later, I received a call from Mahmoud that Maman had fallen and broken her hip. She had been taken to hospital where she had been administered a drug that had caused internal bleeding. I was on the phone almost three times a day. Finally Mahmoud called with the news I did not want to hear. Mehdi and I flew to London for her funeral. Maman was buried in London under a beautiful weeping willow with a robin perched on a branch, calmly watching us. Mahmoud came to me and whispered: "Lily, look at the robin. It is mother. She is watching us."

I raised my eyes to the robin. With its wide eyes it returned my gaze – unafraid it remained watching.

In Sydney, Betsabeh was promoted to the International Marketing Director of her company and Parissa had received her acceptance to the

London School of Economics. At work, as the Federal Publishing company expanded their management system changed and I did not like the new faces around me, so I resigned and delved fully in real estate development.

Then one day we discovered that Mehdi had prostate cancer. His first words to me were: "Lily, I have never asked anything of you. This is my first request and I hope you love me enough to respect it. Please don't let my sickness affect our lives." Weeping, I promised, knowing in my heart that I was lying. Every evening I went on my knees begging God for a cure and every morning I played tennis with him and at nights we dined and danced as though life was a piece of cake.

Mehdi had his operation. It was a success.

Parissa finished her studies and returned to Sydney with a good job at Deutsche Bank. Then she realized she could never be happy in Australia and decided to leave. My cousin, Gholam Hussain, a Managing Director at an American Bank, became instrumental in her future career. Parissa flew to New York, passed her interviews and tests and began work. During September 11, she was at a meeting at the World Trade Center and missed death by ten minutes.

From Sydney Betsabeh was posted to Europe as her company's International Marketing Director. The girls gone, it was only Mehdi and I left in a huge empty house. To cheer ourselves up we looked at our situation as our second honeymoon. However, honeymoons never last long.

In Iran Ayatollah Khatami had become the president. People were happy with his liberal reforms and the country's economy was improving. My brothers wanted to sell our coastal inherited house. The only relic of the past we had was that dilapidated, four times confiscated seaside villa and I wanted to preserve it. So I went to Iran, bought my brothers' shares, found and commissioned an architect famous for his design of Old Persian Architecture to build a house for us – all of us – so that once more we could say we have a home in Iran. Meanwhile, during my travels between Iran and Australia my husband became ill again. That was when I decided it was time for us to return to the Northern Hemisphere and spend the few years left to us near our children and the rest of our family. With the help of a friend who knew a European Consul General in Sydney we managed to procure the necessary visas.

Parissa, who was taking an MBA course at HEC (*Hautes Etudes Commerciales*) introduced her sister to her friend Julien, a well-educated, handsome French young gentleman from an old established family. Within one year they married.

Julien is the son I never had.

Settled in Europe, we bought a dilapidated flat, which I renovated – it has become our family home.

Mehdi and I work hard at learning a new language – alas at our age it seems an impossible task! But we are trying.

Parissa moved back from New York to Europe and works for an investment bank.

Betsabeh left her job and is now a successful entrepreneur roaming around the world. She and Julien have been blessed with a gorgeous son, who is the image of Mehdi and a beautiful daughter.

My granddaughter has Betsabeh's Gajar eyes and joint eyebrows, Julien's high forehead, Parissa's vivaciousness and Mehdi's bright smile. Like Khatoon she is half French and half Persian.

I have to wait to see what she has of me. I hope it will be my will to survive.

Enshallah.

> I hold to no religion or creed,
> am neither Eastern nor Western,
> Muslim or infidel,
> Zoroastrian, Christian, Jew or Gentile,
> I come from neither land nor sea,
> Am not related to those above or below,
> Was not born nearby or far away,
> Do not live either in Paradise or on this Earth,
> Claim descent not from Adam and Eve or the Angels above.
> I transcend body and soul.
> My home is beyond place and name.
> It is with the beloved, in a space beyond space.
> I embrace all and am part of all.
> Jelaluddin Rumi

Ali Ghapu Palace, Isfahan

A tribal woman attending to her baby by her yort (tent)

یکزن ایرانی با چادر و چاقچور و روبند
(پیکر از تور دوموند برداشته شده در باره هشتاد سال پیش است)

A city woman in Chador and Roobandeh, 18th Century Iran

A tribal woman in warrior gear, 18th Century Iran

A horse-driven palanquin, 18th Century Iran

The Shah's. Nader Shah Afshar, Agha Mohammed Shah Gajar, Karim Khan Zand, Fath Ali Shah Gajar, Abass Mirza, Mohammed Shah, Nasser Al-Din Shah, Mozzafar Al-Din Shah, Mohammed Ali Shah

The marble throne at the balcony of the Palace of Golestan

The Palace of Golestan

Amir Aslan Khan Majdowleh
(Mehdi and Lily's great great grandfather)

Malek Jahan Khanum, the Mahd Olia when young

Mahboubeh, Mahd Olia's favourite dancer

Malek Jahan Khanum, the Mahd Olia when older

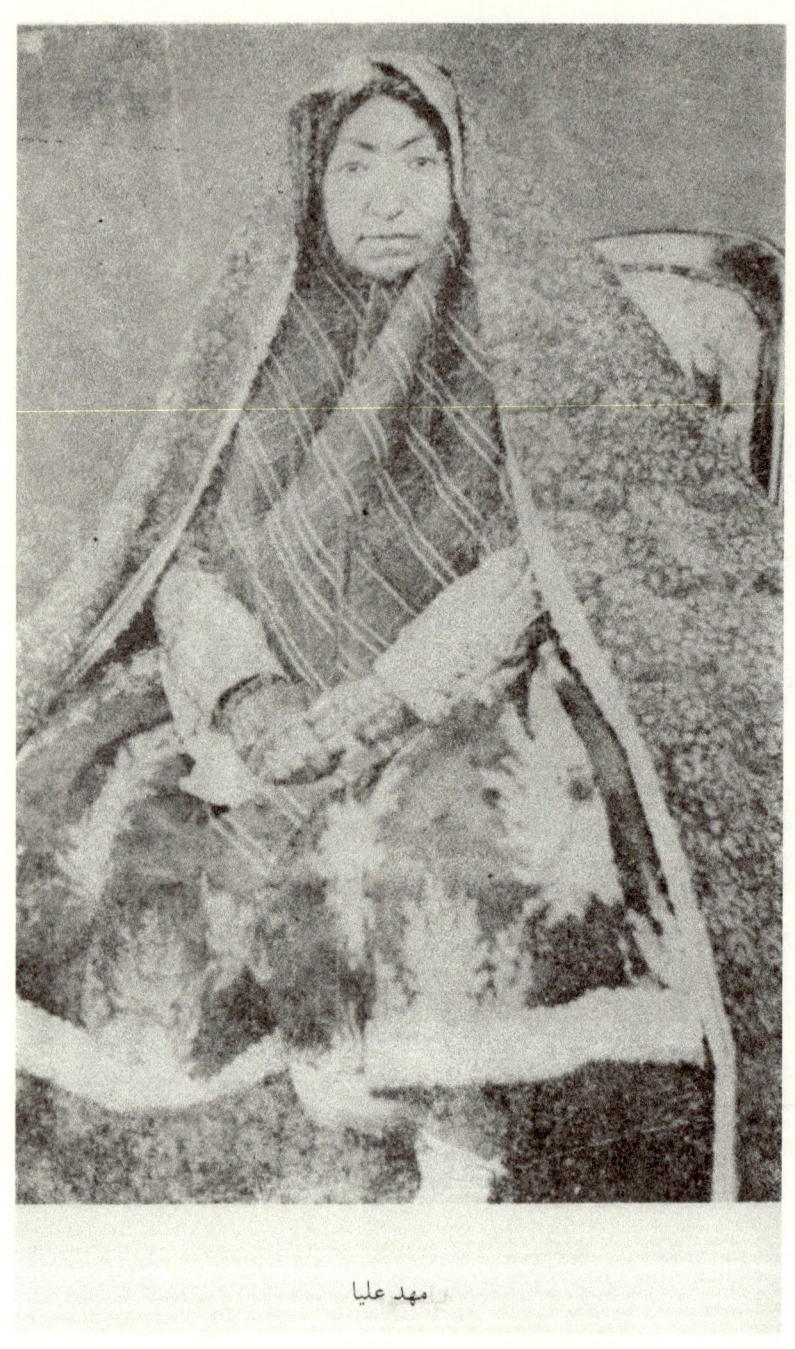

مهد علیا

Malek Jahan Khanum, the Mahd Olia

Nasser Al-Din Shah

Nasser Al-Din Shah and his wives, including Jayran who is sitting by his knees.

Aziz Sultan (the Malijak) and his wife Akhtar Dowleh and their book reader, Ehteram Khanum

Anis Dowleh

Mahboub Saltaneh (Lily's great grandmother)

سه تن از دختران ناصرالدین‌شاه

Three of the Shah's daughters: Sharaf Saltaneh, Ghodrat Saltaneh and Ezza Sultaneh

Princess Ezza Saltaneh (Lily's grandmother)

Ehtesham Al-Molk Amir Aslani (Lily's grandfather)

Seated is Nasser Gholi Khan Amjad Dowleh (Lily's great grandfather) on his right is Ehtesham Al-Molk his eldest son and Dr Hussain Gholi (Amid Al-Molk the second) Amir Aslani and his youngest son Amid Al-Molk the first

Three Andaroon women musicians

Nasser Al-Din Shah's last picture

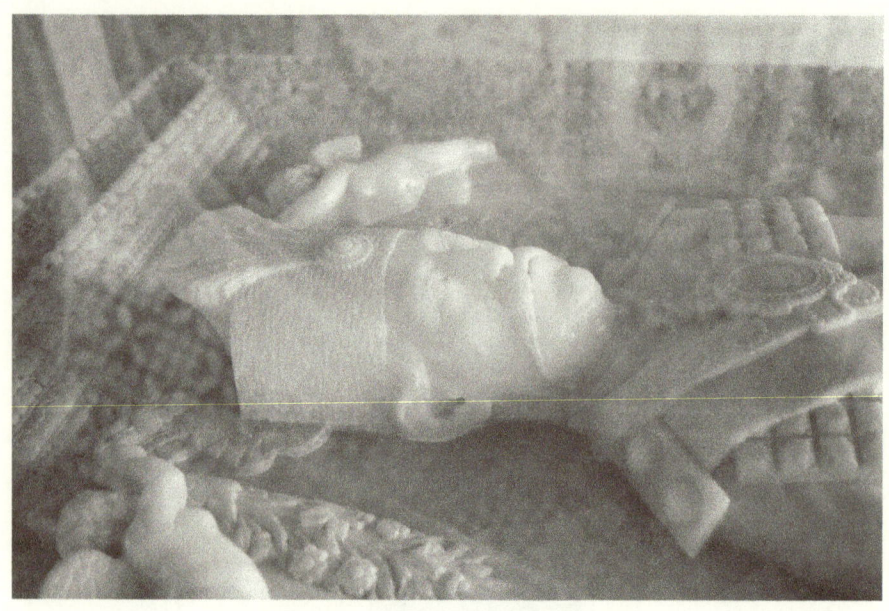

The tomb stone of Nasser Al-Din Shah carved from a single marble slab removed from his grave by the revolutionaries and placed at the palace of Golestan

The nobility at the palace of Golestan, during Nasser Al-Din Shah

The Prime Minister and the nobility standing in front of Nasser Al-Din Shah sitting on the marble throne during the New Year audience

Sarchesmeh Cross Road, Teheran 1835

Baharestan Square where Parliament is, Teheran 1911

The Bab Homayun Avenue, Teheran 1871

Mozzafar Al-Din Shah with Edward VII in London

Ahmed Shah

Reza Shah Pahlavi with the first group of students he was sending to France to study. The last person on the right is Mohammad Monadjemi (Mehdi's father)

The directors of the First National Bank of Iran in Rasht. Mohammad Izadi, Lily's paternal grandfather is the first on the left.

Crown Prince Reza, Empress Farah, Mohammed Reza Shah Pahlavi

Ayatollah Rohollah Khomeini

Hassan Izadi, Lily's father

Monir Aghdas Amir-Aslani-Izadi (Lily's mother)

Princess Ezza Saltaneh in the middle with her children, grandchildren and great grandchildren in the garden at Ehteshamieh

Lily in her mink coat

At Galandouak: Zivar, Lily, Afsaneh, Ziba, Mamal Khan and Bahram

Nilofar, Amir Khosro, Amir Keyvan and Betsabeh

Parissa in Sydney

Lily by her sofreh Aghad

Mohsen Khan Khadjenouri

Hassan Izadi, Victoria Khadjenouri, Monir Aghdas Izadi and Keyvan Izadi

The burnt Khadjenouri residence

The tomb stone of Princess Ezza Saltaneh which reads: The resting place of Khadijeh Nasseri Gajar Amir-Aslani daughter of Nasser Al-Din

Dr Monadjemi, Ezzatzaman, Betsabeh and Parissa

Lily, Teheran 1967

Mehdi Monadjemi, Australia 1999

Ramsar in Islamic Hejab, Lily and Setareh Farhaghi, 2009

A Glossary of Persian Words and Phrases

Aba	Cloak
Agha	Gentleman, sir, mister
Aghd	The ceremony during which the marriage contract is signed
Akhound	Slang for priest
Alam	The universe
Alhamdellah	God be thanked
Allah	God
Allah Akbar	God is great
Ameh	Aunt from the father's side.
Amin	Trustworthy
Amir	Chief
Amir Nezam	Commander-in-chief
Amniat	Security
Amou	Uncle from the father's side
Andaroon limit	The ladies, quarters within the house, off to men not next of kin.
Ashagabash	Turkish for "below the river".
Ashura	The most holy day in the month of Moharam.
Attabak	Teacher
Ayatollah	The highest rank in Shia clerical hierarchy.
Azam	Great
Azan	Time when each daily prayer is announced from the minaret of the Mosque
Aziz	Dear
Azizam	My dear
Babi	Follower of Sayyid Ali Mohammad Shirazi Known as Bab, the chief of the Bahais.
Baygum	Lady in Turkish

Bazaar	Market place – a center of commerce.
Bazaari	Merchant who operates in the Bazaar.
Behaya	Without virtue.
Behesht	Paradise
Bibi	A term of endearment often used to call a mother or grandmother.
Biruni	Exterior. The male quarters within the house.
Chador	A traditional one-piece, long veil worn mostly by Iranian women.
Chopogh	A long traditional pipe
Dadsetan	Prosecutor
Dadsetane Kol	Prosecutor General
Dai	Uncle from the mother side.
Dalak	The person who washes the bathers in public baths.
Darya	Sea
Darya-e-nour	Sea of Light – The name of one of the two large, diamonds Nader brought to Iran from India.
Dasteh	Handle, conglomerate; it also refers to a flagellating group.
Divan	Collection of poems
Doghan	Chief in Turkish.
Dolat	Government
Eftar	Breaking of the fast.
Enghelab	Revolution
Ettelaat	Information
Ezrael	Angel of Death
Faghih	The most knowledgeable in religious dogma.
Falak	A method of punishment by which the sole of feet is lashed.
Farangestan	Land of the foreigners.
Farman	Command
Farsi	Language spoken by the Iranians.
Fath-nameh	Letter bearing the news of a conquest.
Ghanat	Outlet of subterranean water.
Ghebleh	The direction towards which Moslems pray.
Gilaki	Those who come from Gilan. It also refers to their dialect.
Golestan	Flower garden
Haj	Pilgrimage to Mecca
Haji	The person who has taken the pilgrimage.
Halal	Permitted, particularly relating to sex and food.

Haraam	Taboo
Haraamzadeh	Bastard
Haya	Virtue
Hejab	The Islamic wear – cover.
Homafars technicians	The western educated, air force who were non-commissioned officers.
Immam	Pontiff
Immam Jomeh heads	Chief pontiff of the Capital who Friday prayers.
Iran	The land of the Aryans.
Jahad	Holy war
Jahan	World
Jahan-souz	The one who can burn the world
Jahn	Life
Jenab	Excellency
Jahn/ Joon	Dear
Kaabe	The house of God in Mecca
Kabir	Great
Karballa	A Shia holy city in Iraq.
Khalgh	Creatures.
Khan	Chieftain
Khanum	Lady, mistress.
Khasegar	The willing one – suitor
Khasegari	Traditional marriage proposal.
Khazineh	Ponds in public or private baths.
Keshvar	Country
Khoda	God
Khoms	An annual religious due. Fife
Khoresht	Stew
Komiteh	Committee
Kooh	Mountain
Kooh Nour	Mountain of light; one of the largest diamonds in the world.
Koucheh	Cul-de-sac
Madar	Mother
Mah	Moon
Mahboub	Loveable, beloved.
Mah-e-man	My moon, a term of endearment used by lovers
Mahd Olia Shah	A Gajar title given to the mother of the
Maidan	Square
Majles	Gathering, also the House of Parliament
Maman	Mummy

Manbar	Pulpit
Mar Mar	Marble
Mashallah	God be praized.
Meli	National.
Mirza	Contraction of the word Amirzada, meaning off-spring of an Amir or chieftain.
Moez	The one who calls the faithful to prayer.
Moghofeh	The entity of a religious endowment.
Moharam	The mourning month for the Shiat
Mohr	A backed mold of earth on which the forehead is placed during Moslem prayer.
Mojahed	The one who participates in Jahad, holy war.
Mojahedin	The plural form of Mojahed.
Mordeh	Dead
Mullah	Priest
Najest	Unclean, usually referred to religious taboos.
Namak	Salt
Namak-nashnas	Ungrateful
Namahram	The one not intimate enough to enter the ladies' quarters.
Nashnas	The one who does not recognize
Nayeb	Deputy
Nayeb-Al-Saltaneh	Regent
Norooz	New day – referring to the Iranian New Year, a maintained Zoroastrian tradition.
Paloudeh	A traditional sorbet originating from Shiraz
Pasdar	Guard
Pasdaran	Guards
Pasdaran-e-enghelab	Guardians of the Revolution Pishkesh
Pishkesh	Present
Rial	Iranian currency
Roobandeh	Face cover
Rouhollah	The soul of God
Roupoosh	Uniform
Sabzeh	Sprouts
Sadre	Upper part, the place of honour.
Sadre Azam	Prime Minister
Saheb	Owner
Saheb mordeh	A house or an object whose owner is dead
Salam	Salutation
Salam-e-Norooz	The royal ceremony during which the Shah receives the greetings of his subjects.
Samanou	A wheat germ dish

Sangak	A flat bread
Sazeman	Organization
Seyyed	Title given to descendants of the prophet.
Seer	Garlic
Senjed	Fruit of Jujube
Shah	King
Shahanhah	The king of kings
Shahid	Martyr
Shahjoon	An abbreviated term of endearment which royal parents were called during the Gajars.
Shahzadeh	The child of a Shah: prince or princess
Shaikh	A venerable old man, a learned man who can also be a priest.
Sharaf	Honour
Sharbat	Sweet fruit juice drink
Shokr	Thanksgiving
Shokret	(Khodaya shokret) Thanks be to God
Showra	Committee
Sib	Apple
Sigheh	Temporary wife
Sofreh	Table cloth
Sogoli	The favourite wife
Somagh	Sumac
Sonbol	Hyacinths
Sormeh	Kohl
Tazieh	Shia Passion play performed during the month of Moharam
Tooman	Unit of Iranian currency. There are a hundred rials in one tooman.
Tudeh	Masses, also the name of the Iranian Communist Party.
Ulama	Religious scholars, philosophers.
Vali-Ahd	Heir to the throne
Vakil	Representative
Zafaf	Copulation taking place during the first night of marriage.
Ziarat	Pilgrimage
Yort	Mobile hut, tent. A Turkish word
Yukharibash	Turkish for "above the river".

Bibliography

Alam, Assadollah: The Shah and I (I.B. Tauris & Co Ltd, London, New York, 1991)

Amanat Abbas: Pivot of the Universe, London, 1997.

Amirsadeghi, Hossein: Twentieth-Century Iran, Heinemann, 1977

Armstrong Karen: ISLAM A Short History, Phoenix Press 2001 Atkin M: Russia and Iran 1780-1828 Minneapolis, 1980

Avery, Peter, Hambly, Gavin and Melville, Charles: The Cambridge History of Iran, Volume 7, From Nader Shah to the Islamic Republic, Cambridge University Press, 1991.

Bakhash, Shaul: The Reign of the Ayatollahs: Iran and the Islamic Revolution, Basic

Books, New York, 1984

Backhash Shaul: Evolution of Qajar Bureacracy: 1797-1879, Middle East Studies 1971.

Bakhtiary Esfandiar:, Princess Soraya in collaboration with Louis Valentin. Translated from the French by Hubert Gissbs: Palace of Solitude ,Quartet Books Ltd, London 1991.

Bakhtiari-Assl, Fariborz : Zanan Namdar-e Tarikh-e Iran, Mahd Olia, Mother of Nasser Al-Din Shah, Zavar Teheran 1375

Bani-Sadr, Abolhassan: Islamic Government. Translated by M.R.Ghanoonparva, Mazda, Lexington, KY., 1981) Benjamin, S.G.W: Persia and the Persians. London 1887

Brown, Edward G:. Literary History of Persia. 4 vols. Cambridge 1928 Brumberg, Daniel: Reinventing Khomeini: The Struggle for Reform in Iran, University of Chicago Press, 2001

Curzon, G.N: Persia and the Persian Question. 2 Vols London 1892

De Villiers: Gerard with Toucais, Bernard & de Villiers Annick. Translated from the

French by June P. Wilson and Walter B. Michaels: The Imperial Shah – An Informal Biography , Weidenfeld and Nicolson, London, 1976.

Ebadi Shirin: Iran Awakening. Random House, New York 2006 Enayat A. Amin al-Zarb. Encyclopaedia Iranica.

Farman Farmaian: Sattareh, with Munker Dona: Daughter of Persia ,Crown Publishers Inc., New York, 1992.

Etemad Saltaneh Mohammad Hassan Khan: Journal of the Memoirs of Etemad Saltandh. Amir Kabir, Teheran 1345/1966

Follett, Ken: On Wings Of Eagles , Collins, London, 1983.

Forbis, William H: Fall of the Peacock Throne: The Story of Iran, Harper & Row Publishers, New York, 1980.

Ghani Ghasem: Collection of Qajar Documents, Manuscripts and Archives, Sterling Memorial Library: Yale University. Series 1-8

Halliday, Fred: Iran: Dictatorship and Development ,Penguin Books, London, 1979.

Hedayat Mehdi Gholi Mukhber al-Salatanh Guzarishe Iran: Vol. 11 & 111 Teheran 1333/191

Huyser, General Robert E: Mission to Tehran, Andre Deutsch Ltd, London, 1986.

Jahangir Mirza Qajar: Tarikhe Naw. Ed. A. Igbal. Tehran 1327/1948

Kinzer Stephen: All The Shah's Men, John Wiley & Sons, Inc., Hoboken, New Jersey 2003.

Lambton, Ann K.S.: Qajar Persia, I.B. Tauris & Co. Ltd. London, 1987. Lindholm Charles: The Islamic Middle East, An Historical Anthropology, Blackwell 1996

Malcolm, J: The History of Persia, London 1815.

Malkum Khan Mirza: Majmoeh Asare Mirza Malkum Khan Ed. M. Muhit Tabatabi. Teheran 1327/1948.

Mahmoud Mirza Qajar: Akhbare Mohammadi, Melli Library.

Moayer Al Mamalek Doust Ali Khan: The Memoirs of Nasser Al-Din Shah's Private Life. Published by History of Iran 1372

Milani Abbas: The Persian Sphinix, Amir Abbas Hoveyda and the Riddle of the Iranian Revolution. Mage Publishers, Washington, D.C 2000

Motazed Khosro & Dr. Tafasoli Abolghasem: From Forogh Saltaneh to Anis Douleh, Golriz Teheran 1378/1999

Mulk Ara, Abbass Mirza: Shahre Hale Abbas Mirza Mulkara. Navi and Iqbal Tehran l355/1976

Nahavandi Manuchehr: Iran The Clash Of Ambitions, Aquilion Ltd. United Kingdom 2006

Nashat G: Anis al-Dawal Encyclopaedia Iranica.

Nasser Al-Din Shah Qajar: Correspondence of the Imperial Majesty Nasser Al-Din shah of Persia from l848-l896. British Library BL Or. 11665 & Or. 11665. Nasser Al-Din shah Gajar: Safar dovome faranghestan (The diary of his majesty's second visit to Europe 1878) Handwritten account in private possession.

Navab-Bakhash A: Zan Dar Tarikh-e Iran, Gutenberg Teheran 2537 (2537 is the Imperial calendar of Iran, in existence for a few years until the demise of the Pahlavi dynasty).

Niazmand Reza: Reza shah: Birth to Kingship (Foundation for Iranian Studies) Pahlavi Ashraf: Faces In a Mirror, Prentice-Hall, Inc., Englewood Cliffs, N.J. Parsons Anthony: The Pride & the Fall – Iran l974-l979, Jonathan Cape, London, l984.

Perry J.R: Agha Mohammad Khan Qajar Encyclopedea Iranica Richard Yann: Shiíte Islam, Blackwell, l995

Roosevelt, Kermit: Counter Coup: The Struggle for Control in Iran, McGraw-Hill, New York, l979.

Sadigh Essa: The History of Persian Culture, written in Persian and published by Zibba 1354.

Shariáti, Ali: Marxism and Other Western Fallacies Translated by R. Campbell. Mizan Press, Berkeley, Calif. 1989.

Shawcross William: The shah's Last Ride, The Story of the Exile, Misadventures and Death of The Emperor, Chatto & Windus, London, l989.

Shiel Lady: Glimpses of Life and Manners in Persia – London 1856, the Persian translation.

Sick Gary: All Fall Down , Random House, New York, l985.

Sick Gary: October Surprise: America's Hostages in Iran and the Election of Ronald

Reagan: I.B. Tauris, 1991

Sullivan, William H.: Mission to Iran,,W.W. Norton, New York, 1981.

Taj Al-Saltana: Growing Anguish , Mage Publishers Washington, DC 2003 Taj al-Saltana, Khatirate Taj al-Saltana: Edited by. M. Ittehadiya (Nizam-Mafi) and S. Sadvandiyan. Tehran, 1361/1982

Talequani, Mahmood: Islam and Ownership. Translated from the Persian by Ahmad Jabbari & Farhang Rajaee: Mazda, Lexington, KY., 1983.

Templeton, Peter Louis: The Persian Prince, Persian Prince Publications, Printed in Great Britain, 1979.

Timmerman, Kenneth R: The Death Lobby: How the West Armed Iraq, Houghton Mifflin, 1991.

Toluie Mohammad: The Seven Gajar Shahs, volume 1 & 2. In Persian, published by Nashre Elm. 1377

Wright D: The English Amongst the Persians. London 1977.

Wright, Robin: In The Name of God, The Khomeini Decade, Bloomsbury, London, 1990.

Yusuf Ali: The Holy Quarán, Translation and Commentary, Islamic Propagation Centre International 1946

Zelle al-Sultan, Masoud Mirza: Tarikhe Sargosashte Masoudi. Teheran 1325/1907

Milton Keynes UK
Ingram Content Group UK Ltd.
UKHW032358031124
450530UK00003B/24